Practicing Ministry in the Presence of God

Practicing Ministry in the Presence of God

*Theological Reflections on Ministry
and the Christian Life*

John Jefferson Davis

CASCADE *Books* • Eugene, Oregon

PRACTICING MINISTRY IN THE PRESENCE OF GOD
Theological Reflections on Ministry and the Christian Life

Copyright © 2015 John Jefferson Davis. All rights reserved. Except for brief quotations in critical publications or reviews, no part of this book may be reproduced in any manner without prior written permission from the publisher. Write: Permissions. Wipf and Stock Publishers, 199 W. 8th Ave., Suite 3, Eugene, OR 97401.

Cascade Books
An Imprint of Wipf and Stock Publishers
199 W. 8th Ave., Suite 3
Eugene, OR 97401

www.wipfandstock.com

ISBN 13: 978-1-4982-0205-3

Cataloguing-in-Publication Data

Davis, John Jefferson.

    Practicing ministry in the presence of God : theological reflections on ministry and the Christian life / John Jefferson Davis.

    viii + 320 p. ; 23 cm. Includes bibliographical references and indexes.

    ISBN 13: 978-1-4982-0205-3

    1. Theology, Practical. 2. Pastoral theology. 3. Christianity and culture. I. Title.

BV4011 .D39 2015

Manufactured in the U.S.A.   07/07/2015

Contents

Preface | vii

1 The Role of Theology in the Life of the Church | 1
2 American Evangelicalism 3.0: A Proposal for a New-Paradigm Evangelicalism for the Twenty-first Century | 6
3 Practicing Ministry in the Presence of God and in Partnership with God | 40
4 Conversion Isn't What It Used to Be | 70
5 Salvation Reconceptualized: Is Our Western Gospel Big Enough? | 125
6 Where N. T. Wright Isn't Quite Right: Further Brief Perspectives on the "New Perspectives" on Paul | 150
7 "Teaching Them to Observe All that I Have Commanded You": The History of the Interpretation of the "Great Commission" and Implications for Marketplace Ministries | 158
8 Why Most American Christians Don't Pray Very Much | 176
9 Is Scripture Memorization *Still* Relevant? | 198
10 1 Timothy 2:12, the Ordination of Women, and Pauline Use of Creation Narratives | 213
11 Incarnation, Trinity, and the Ordination of Women to the Priesthood | 226
12 How to Get More Out of Committee Meetings in Your Church | 249
13 "Would John Calvin Stay in the Episcopal Church?" | 254
14 Thoughts on Hell and Everlasting Punishment | 263
15 Will There Be *New* Work in the New Creation? | 271

Bibliography | 291

Preface

THE FIFTEEN ESSAYS COLLECTED in this volume around the theme of "Practicing Ministry in the Presence of God," some of which have been previously published, represent the third part of a trilogy of writings that explore the truth of the *real presence* of God with his people—in worship, in the devotional reading of Scripture, and in ministry and the Christian life. The first aspect was developed in *Worship and the Reality of God: An Evangelical Theology of Real Presence* (IVP Academic, 2010), and the second in *Meditation and Communion with God: Contemplating Scripture in an Age of Distraction* (IVP Academic, 2012). The present work explores the theme of God's presence in relation to the ministry of the church, evangelism, discipleship, salvation, ordination, Scripture memorization, prayer, church unity, and the nature of the life to come.

The central idea expressed in this theme is that all Christian ministry—and all of the Christian life—is not exercised independently, but *in the presence of God* and in partnership with God, based on the promise of Christ to be with his people (Matt 28:20), and the reality of our abiding union with Christ (John 15:5). Authentic biblical ministry is not done in merely human energy, but in union with Christ and in partnership with other gifted members of the body of Christ.

I wish to thank the editors of Gordon-Conwell's *Contact* magazine, of the *Evangelical Review of Theology*, and of the *Priscilla Papers*, in whose publications several of these essays have previously appeared. I also wish to thank my students at Gordon-Conwell, and especially those in my Systematic Theology III classes, whose comments, questions, and suggestions have added to my own understandings of these issues in theology and ministry.

—John Jefferson Davis

Gordon-Conwell Theological Seminary
South Hamilton, MA

Summer 2015

1

The Role of Theology in the Life of the Church

"What is role of theology in the life of the church?" Some busy pastors in American churches today might be tempted to answer, "Honestly, not much; I haven't thought much about 'theology' since I left seminary; I'm too busy preparing sermons, attending committee meetings, and dealing with conflicts and problems in my church to give much attention to theology." However, I would like to suggest that for even such busy pastors, a more accurate image of the role of theology in the life of the parish would not be that of a neglected textbook on the pastor's shelf, but rather that of a *backbone* in a healthy body. The backbones in our bodies, like the foundations and electrical and plumbing systems in our homes, are usually taken for granted—until something goes wrong. Like a healthy backbone in a healthy human body, sound biblical theology can provide support, shape, and stability to the body of Christ.

Catechesis, Apologetics, Polemics, and Homiletics

In the early church the development of Christian theology was shaped by four important functions it served in the life of the church: the *catechetical*, the *apologetical*, the *polemical*, and the *homiletical*.[1] All four of these functions of theology in the early church are still vital for the ministry of the church today. In its catechetical function, theological instruction prepared converts for church membership and participation in the Eucharist, instructing them in basic Christian doctrine. This process of catechesis is

---

1. J. J. Davis, *Foundations of Evangelical Theology*, 50–51; see also Garrett Jr., *Systematic Theology*, vol. 1, 12–15, and Braaten and Jenson, eds., *Christian Dogmatics*, vol. 1, 20–23.

often referred to as "discipleship" or "discipling" today. Converts were instructed in the "rule of faith," a summary of Christian doctrine that formed the basis of the later Nicene and Apostles' Creeds. Such early summaries of Christian belief are found in the New Testament itself, e.g., Paul's summary of the *kerygma* in 1 Corinthians 15:3-5: "For what I received I passed on to you as of *first importance* [emphasis added]: that Christ died for our sins according to the scriptures, that he was buried, that he was raised on the third day according to the scriptures, and that he appeared to Peter, and then to the Twelve...."

Augustine's *Enchiridion* or *On Faith, Hope, and Love* (c. 421) was prepared as such a catechetical manual, following the outline of the Apostles' Creed, the Lord's Prayer, and the two great commandments. In the preface to his 1560 French edition of the *Institutes*, John Calvin stated that it was his intention to provide a summary of Christian doctrine that would help Christians in their reading of the Old and New Testaments. Today, new converts and new church members still need to be catechized and instructed in the fundamentals of the faith. Books like John Stott's *Basic Christianity* or R. C. Sproul's *Essential Truths of the Christian Faith* can assist the pastor in this historic task.[2]

The apologetic task of theology in the early church was to defend and explain the faith to outsiders (see 1 Pet 3:15, "Be prepared to give an answer to everyone who asks you to give the reason for the hope that is in you"). Early Christian apologists such as Aristides, Diognetus, and Tertullian responded to misunderstandings and accusations from the pagans, and Justin Martyr responded to criticisms from the Jews of his day. Thomas Aquinas in his *Summa contra Gentiles* defended the Christian faith in the face of Muslim criticisms. In today's religious climate of religious pluralism and the "new atheism," the need for informed Christian apologetics remains as relevant as ever. Several generations of Christians have been helped by classics such as C. S. Lewis's *Mere Christianity* and *Miracles*. Tim Keller's *The Reason for God* provides cogent responses to many of the criticisms of the faith in our own day.

In its *polemical* function, Christian theologians defended and expounded the biblical faith against heretical threats from within the church. Irenaeus, bishop of Lyons, in his massive *Against Heresies* (c. 185), defended the biblical faith against the threat of Gnosticism, teachings which denied the goodness of the physical creation and placed the biblical story into an alien context of Gnostic cosmological speculation. In the face of the Arian

---

2. Excellent resources for the catechetical ministry of the church include the book by my colleagues Gary Parrett and S. Steve Kang, *Teaching the Faith, Forming the Faithful*, and Thomas F. Torrance, *The School of Faith*.

threat, Athanasius vigorously and tenaciously defended the full deity of Christ, and together with the Cappadocian fathers of the fourth century, laid the basic foundations of Christology and trinitarian theology that have guided the church ever since. In the modern period orthodox theologians have labored to preserve the historic Christian faith from the attacks of Enlightenment biblical criticism, deistic denials of miracles, and Unitarian denials of the Trinity, original sin, and substitutionary atonement. More recently, revisionist readings of biblical sexual ethics, Dan Brown's *Da Vinci Code*, feminist criticisms of the "patriarchal" language of the Trinity, and "Open Theism" have questioned or rejected historic orthodox belief. The Pauline admonitions to "watch your life and doctrine closely" (1 Tim 4:16) and for believers not to be "blown about by every wind of teaching" (Eph 4:14) but to grow mature in the faith, are just as relevant as ever.

The fourth function of theology in the life of the early church was the *homiletical* one: assisting preachers and teachers in the exposition and teaching of Scripture (see 1 Tim 4:13: "Until I come, devote yourself to the public reading of scripture, to preaching and teaching"). The church leader is to "hold firmly to the trustworthy message as it has been taught, so that he can encourage others by sound doctrine and refute those who oppose it" (Titus 1:9). Knowledge of sound doctrine aids in preaching and teaching not only by the avoidance of heresy, but also by enabling the preacher to place the particular text in the larger context of redemptive history: creation, Fall, redemption, and new creation. This was precisely what the Gnostics in the early church failed to do, wrenching the biblical texts out of their biblical contexts and placing them in the context of an alien system of thought. Heterodox religious movements today, such as the Jehovah's Witnesses or Mormons, can distort the biblical teachings in the same way. Sound teachers in the early church such as Irenaeus, and effective preachers today such as John Stott, John Piper, John MacArthur, Haddon Robinson, Timothy Keller, Gordon Hugenberger, Mark Dever, and others have robust theologies that enable them to place the biblical text in its wider redemptive-historical context, and so preserve the distinctive *Christian* identity of the message.

Vitality, Vision, and Assessment

In addition to these historically recognized functions of theology in the life of the church, a sound biblical theology can provide *vitality, vision,* and standards for *assessment* in the local congregation. Church history shows that a robust biblical theology can contribute to church growth and vitality. The opposite is also the case: churches and denominations that tolerate doctrinal erosion tend to have tepid worship and declining membership. During the decades between 1965 and 1999, for example, the Presbyterian Church USA, the United Church of Christ, the Episcopal Church, and the United Methodist Church lost, respectively, 40 percent, 29 percent, 26 percent, and 24 percent of their total memberships. Growing churches were generally those committed to an orthodox and biblical theology.

As the leader of the flock, the pastor is responsible for casting a *vision* for the church. The biblical metanarrative of creation, Fall, redemption, and new creation provides the theological framework and context for such a vision. Salvation itself is not only forgiveness of sins and hope of heaven in the future, but an experience beginning now of entering into the life of the triune God.[3] Because of Jesus' incarnation, death, resurrection, ascension to the right hand of the Father, and sending of the Holy Spirit, we—as adopted sons and daughters in Christ—can begin to experience the love of Jesus' Father for his beloved Son, in the communion of the Holy Spirit, looking forward to its culmination and never-ending deepening in the presence of God in a gloriously beautiful new creation (Rev 21–22). Such a theological vision can energize and unify a congregation, just as John F. Kennedy's famous vision-casting of May 25, 1961, to a joint session of Congress—"A man on the moon by the end of this decade"—energized NASA and the nation for the Apollo space mission.

Finally, sound theology provides a standard for congregational *assessment*, a basis for asking and answering the question, "How are we doing as a church?" For example, the biblical doctrine of the church, that specifies worship, discipleship, and mission as the three God-ordained purposes of the church, then provides the basis for asking questions such as "How well are we worshiping God? Are we as a people growing deeper and more mature in our relationships with Christ and one another? How effective are we in reaching out to others—in service and proclamation? Are we growing as a church that is 'deep, thick, and different'—deep in our worship and knowledge of the triune God; 'thickly' committed in love and service to one another, and distinctive from the secular culture in our beliefs, lifestyle, values, and hopes? Are we growing both in our obedience to the 'Great Commandments' and in our fulfillment of the Great Commission?"

And so it is that theology now, as in the New Testament and subsequent centuries of church history, can play a vital role in the life of a healthy church. As pastors, teachers, and lay leaders may we continue to "teach and admonish with all wisdom, so as to present everyone mature in Christ" (Col

---

3. A trinitarian vision of Christian life and salvation has been very helpfully articulated by my colleague Donald Fairbairn in *Life in the Trinity*.

1:28), and so be able to say with the Apostle Paul at the end of our ministries, "I have fought the good fight, I have finished the race, *I have kept the faith*" (2 Tim 4:8, emphasis mine), in the expectation of that crown of righteousness to be awarded by the Lord to his beloved church.

2

American Evangelicalism 3.0

A Proposal for a New-Paradigm Evangelicalism for the Twenty-First Century

He will fall down and worship God, saying, "God is really (ontos) among you!"

1 CORINTHIANS 14:25

IN THIS ESSAY I wish to discuss the "Ontological Project"[1]—a proposal for a "New Paradigm" evangelicalism, an "Evangelicalism 3.0"—a proposal for

---

1. The term *ontology* is a branch of philosophy that is concerned with such questions as "What types of things exist? What is the nature of ultimate or fundamental reality?" The "Ontological Project" is a proposal to make the *doctrine of the Trinity* more integrally and centrally the fundamental starting point of Christian thought and practice. Such a project is also in keeping with the prominence of the concept of a Christian *worldview* or *Weltanschauung* that has been prominent in the evangelical theological tradition since the pioneering work of James Orr and Abraham Kuyper, and subsequently in the work of Carl F. H. Henry, Gordon Clark, Herman Dooyeweerd, Francis Schaeffer, and others: see David K. Naugle, *Worldview*, "Original Worldview Thinkers in Protestant Evangelicalism," 5–32. On biblical worldview, see also my colleague David W. Gill's *The Opening of the Christian Mind*.

On the general subject of ontology, see "Ontology," in "Logic and Ontology," the *Stanford Encyclopedia of Philosophy*; and the very helpful chapter in Keith Ward, "A Range of Philosophical Views about What is Really Real," *More than Matter?*, 21–37, arguing against materialism and for the primacy of mind rather than matter as a fundamental explanatory principle. On the wider issues of metaphysics (including the nature of space, time, causation, and freedom), see Peter Van Inwagen, *Metaphysics*. The Ontological Project being proposed here, with the doctrine of the Trinity as the "Archimedean point" a fresh revisioning and recontextualizing of the American evangelical tradition for a post-Enlightenment, postcolonial, and post-American[2] global context. The term *post-Enlightenment* expresses the view that the American evangelical churches need greater awareness of and greater critical distance from a worldview dominated by the scientific method and modern technology,[3] especially digital technologies. The term *postcolonial* is used to express the view that American Christians should see themselves as partners in mission with the churches of global South, and not as the directors or predominating leaders in the work of the Great Commission.[4] The term *post-American* is used to suggest that American evangelicals should seek to place greater critical distance between themselves and the dominant values of American culture—wealth, power, reliance on technology, comfort, entertainment, personal autonomy, and individualism.[5] The vision here is

---

for a Christian view of reality, is a way of "pushing back" against the predominant materialistic and naturalistic worldviews that have arisen since the Scientific Revolution of the seventeenth century.

2. In using the term *post-American* I am not claiming that the United States will not continue to have a large if not dominant position in the world for the foreseeable future; I am merely invoking this language to suggest that American evangelicals need to place greater theoretical and practical "distance" between themselves, their church life, and the dominant values of American culture in the years ahead.

3. However, it is not the case that this essay is either anti-science or anti-technology in its basic stance; science rightly understood, and biblical truth, rightly understood, are understood to be complementary and not antithetical ways of knowing reality in its various aspects and dimensions. On this "complementarity" stance toward the natural sciences, see my earlier book, *Frontiers of Science and Faith*. Nor is the use of the term *post-Enlightenment* meant to deny positive elements in the Enlightenment tradition such as respect for rigor in argumentation, reason and evidence, and concern for the rights of women and minorities and human rights generally.

4. Such a post-colonial point of view in this sense is expressed by the American missiologist J. Nelson Jennings in his recent book, *God the Real Superpower*. On the growth and spiritual vitality of the church in the global South, see Philip Jenkins, *The Next Christendom* and *The New Faces of Christianity*. Demographic trends in global Christianity have been authoritatively documented by my colleague Todd M. Johnson and his associate Kenneth M. Ross in the *Atlas of Global Christianity*. Johnson is director of the Center for the Study of Global Christianity at Gordon-Conwell Theological Seminary.

5. This "Ontological Project" and proposal for a "New-Paradigm" evangelicalism can also be seen as a continuation and extension of my colleague David Wells's critique of a culturally-accommodated American evangelicalism, as expressed in his *No Place for Truth*, and subsequent volumes: *God in the Wasteland*; *Losing Our Virtue*; *Above All Earthly Powers*; and *The Courage to Be Protestant*. I propose to extend Wells's analysis by taking into account the fundamental metaphysical (ontological) assumptions of a modernity built on the scientific method, and to place in contradistinction to such naturalistic assumptions an ontology or theory of reality in which the doctrines of the Trinity, union with Christ, and realized eschatology are central and constitutive for

for evangelical churches that are "deep, thick, and different"[6]—deep in their worship experiences of God, "thick" in the *koinonia* relationships in the church, and different from the culture in belief and practice.

In proposing a New-Paradigm evangelicalism, an "Old Paradigm" is presupposed. For the purposes of this essay, the old paradigm for evangelical life and mission can be viewed in terms of a historical trajectory beginning with Evangelicalism 1.0 (from Wesley, Whitefield, and Edwards to Finney) and continuing into Evangelicalism 2.0 (from Finney to Ockenga and Graham). Evangelicalism 1.0 represented a recovery of the doctrine of justification by faith alone and the experience of the New Birth. Evangelicalism 2.0 witnessed the rise of "celebrity" evangelists and organized, urban, parachurch evangelism, and subsequently, the emergence of the "New Evangelicalism" under the leadership of Ockenga, Graham, and Henry. Evangelicalism 3.0 calls for a recovery of a more pre-Constantinian, church-based form of discipleship and evangelism as noted below, together with a more robust and trinitarian understanding of the gospel itself and the salvation that it offers, as also noted below.[7]

Five assumptions of the Old Paradigm Evangelicalism (1.0 and 2.0) are here placed in question: 1) that "top-down" political strategies are effective ways of exerting Christian influence on the culture;[8] 2) that parachurch organizations, rather than local churches, can be the predominant agencies for evangelism and discipleship; 3) that church-growth focused, niche marketing strategies are the effective means of drawing the unchurched into the churches; 4) that the central and defining reality in Sunday worship is hearing a message *about* God, rather than the actual, living, active *presence* of God among his gathered people through Word, Spirit, and sacrament;[9]

evangelical theology and practice.

6. I have used this terminology earlier in my *Worship and the Reality of God*, "From Niche-Market Church to Deep, Thick, Different," 180–85.

7. My proposals for a revisioning of the work of evangelism in terms of a more church-centered, catechesis-based view of discipleship and conversion is contained in the essay "Conversion Isn't What It Used to Be," chapter 4 in the present volume. I am fully supportive of the emphasis on catechesis as argued by my colleagues Gary Parrett and S. Steve Kang in *Teaching the Faith, Forming the Faithful*, and also of a new paradigm for evangelism beyond the "truncated gospel" as called for by my colleague Samuel R. Schutz in his article, "The Truncated Gospel in Modern Evangelicalism." In the New Paradigm, the local church, rather than parachurch organizations and revivalism, is seen as the primary and preferred platform for conversion and discipleship.

8. This point has been forcefully argued in James Davison Hunter, *To Change the World*.

9. I have argued for such a paradigm shift in the received understandings of evangelical worship in *Worship and the Reality of God*. The call for a recovery of such an understanding of "real presence" is not intended as a substitute for or diminishing of

and 5) that current formulas and presentations of the "gospel" and "salvation" are adequate expressions of the New Testament kerygma—especially in regard to the centrality of the doctrines of the Trinity, resurrection, and the promise and power of the Spirit.[10]

The assumption of this essay, however, is *not* that there is *only* discontinuity between the older paradigm and the one being proposed here. Rather, the purpose of this proposed New Paradigm is to subsume and retain the strengths[11] and doctrinal fundamentals of the Old Paradigm and to recontextualize the tradition in a form suitable for the changed circumstances of American life and the emerging global context.

The term "ontological" points to such questions as "What is real?" and "What is the nature of ultimate reality?" New Testament texts such as Luke 24:34, "The Lord was really (*ontos*) raised and appeared to Simon" and 1 Corinthians 14:25, "He [the outsider] will fall down and worship God, declaring, God is *really* (*ontos*) among you!" remind us that in the early church there was a vivid sense of the power of the resurrection and of the presence of the living God in the midst of his worshiping people: "When you gather in the Name of the Lord Jesus, and the *power* of the Lord *is present*" (1 Cor 5:4).

The "Ontological Project" is a proposal for a fresh revisioning of the evangelical tradition so as to recover this vivid sense of the real, powerful presence of God among his gathered people in worship, discipleship, ministry, and mission. The proposal for an "ontological" project is believed to be timely, insofar as Christians today live in highly pluralistic environments in which the very notion of *reality* is contested, and competing visions of

---

the historic Reformation emphasis on the cruciality of expository preaching, but rather as an essential enhancement to it.

10. On this point, see the article by Schutz, "The Truncated Gospel," and my article "Conversion Isn't What It Used to Be," especially the section entitled "Recovering the Fullness of the Gospel for a Post-Christendom American Church." The latter article advances the claim that in any evangelistic presentation of the "gospel," the resurrection, and the reception of the Holy Spirit are integral to the message, bound together with the cross and atonement—and not merely incidental or non-essential elements.

11. The commitments of the New Evangelicalism of Ockenga, Henry, and Graham to the scholarly defense of biblical orthodoxy, to engagement with the social needs of society, and to world evangelization can and should be continued in Evangelicalism 3.0. The hoped-for renewal of the mainline denominations has presented a very mixed picture, and strategies for social renewal need to be refocused away from more political, top-down strategies to those of local initiatives and ministries of "faithful presence" (see Hunter, *To Change the World*) and service. On the "New Evangelicalism," see Rosell, ed., *The Surprising Work of God*, especially chapters 7-9, "Reclaiming the Culture"; "Renewing the Mind"; and "Reaching the World," 161-224.

Ultimate Reality are on offer by Christians, Buddhists, Hindus, New Agers, neo-pagans, New Atheists, and a host of others.[12]

At the core of this proposal for a New-Paradigm Evangelicalism are the "Five Pillars of Right Understanding and Practice," as described below. The first four "pillars"—ontology, epistemology, anthropology, and soteriology—are focused on "theory" or doctrine; the fifth pillar, ministry, is focused on practice. The first four pillars propose fresh emphases for the current evangelical understandings of 1) God; 2) the nature of knowledge; 3) the nature of the self or the human; and 4) the nature of salvation.

The first pillar, ontology, will argue for a shift of focus in the evangelical tradition from a "practical Unitarianism of the second person (Jesus)" to a more biblical understanding of God as fundamentally trinitarian, which recognizes the Trinity—holy, loving, divine persons in eternal relationship—as the fundamental paradigm for the Real. The second pillar, epistemology, will argue for a post-Enlightenment "Logopneumatic" epistemology of Word and Spirit that challenges the hegemony of naturalistic theories of knowledge that recognize only reason or sense experience as valid ways of knowing. The third pillar, anthropology, proposes the trinitarian-ecclesial Self, integrating the biblical understandings of the Trinity, the body of Christ, and union with Christ as the Christian alternative to modernity's theories of the autonomous self, and as the basis for true Christian identity and self-understanding.

The fourth pillar, soteriology, proposes a "new" understanding of salvation and the gospel: the "good news" is not merely that our sins are forgiven in Christ, and that we will live forever with him in the life to come, but that beginning now, we can participate in the very inner life of the triune God—enjoying and experiencing the love of the Father for the Son, the joy of the Son in the Father's love, and the peace and the glory of the Holy Spirit who joins in communion the Father and the Son and the people of God.[13] This part of the proposal argues, in effect, that the *forensic* categories of Western soteriology need to be more fully integrated with and completed by the more *participationist* and trinitarian categories of the East.

The fifth pillar, ministry, will argue for a fresh understanding of worship, discipleship, ministry, and mission in which the realities of the *presence* of the living God and *nearness* of God are central.[14] Ministry is here understood as

---

12. For a discussion of the competing ontologies of scientific naturalism and postmodern virtualism, see my *Worship and the Reality of God*, 39–48.

13. I am very supportive of my colleague Donald Fairbairn's recent book, *Life in the Trinity*, and its trinitarian understanding of the nature of salvation: see especially chapter eight, "Redemption: God's Gift of His Son's Relationship to the Father," 157–83.

14. I wish to acknowledge the work of my colleague Jeffrey J. Niehaus relating to

taking place both in the presence of God and in *partnership* with the triune God. It will be suggested that such a model of ministry can help to mitigate the problems of burnout and individualism in the work of ministry.

The core of this proposal for a New-Paradigm Evangelicalism 3.0 is that the doctrines of the Trinity, of union with Christ, and realized eschatology be more fully integrated into the dogmatic and systematic structure of evangelical theology and practice, while at the same time retaining the doctrinal strengths and commitments of Evangelicalism 1.0 and 2.0.

Before presenting the core proposal as described above, a second section of the essay will examine various factors that indicate the need for such a project and its timeliness, and a brief third section will indicate some of the barriers and obstacles to the project, including three "heresies" of modern evangelicalism: Deism, Pelagianism, and individualism.

The Need for an Ontological Project and New-Paradigm Evangelicalism

Seven factors in our current cultural context could be noticed that point to the need for and timeliness of a proposal for a New-Paradigm evangelicalism: 1) stagnation in American church attendance and membership figures; 2) diminished Christian impact on the secular culture and inconsistent patterns in Christian personal transformation; 3) the passing of the generation of the "founding fathers" of the postwar evangelical movement; 4) the growth and vitality of the church in the global South; 5) the growing religious pluralism of American culture, including the emergence of the New Atheism; 6) the dominant influence of science, technology, and entertainment media in American culture; and 7) the eschatological warnings of the New Testament concerning conditions at the end of the age (e.g., 2 Tim 3:1, 5). Each of these factors calls for brief comment and discussion.

During the period between 1910 and 2010 the percentage of self-identified Christians in the total American population declined from 96.6 percent to 81.2 percent.[15] During this same 100-year period the rate of the growth of Christianity was 1.12 percent per year, less than the annual population growth rate of 1.28 percent.[16] Despite reports during the 1970s that

---

the theme of the divine presence of God with his people, in his *Ancient Near Eastern Themes in Biblical Theology*, especially 99–110, "Image: Divine Presence in the Temple."

15. Johnson and Ross, eds., *Atlas of Global Christianity*, 192.

16. Ibid., 193. By way of contrast, Rodney Stark has argued that in the period between 250 and 350 CE, the Christian movement in the Roman empire was growing at a rate of 40 percent per decade, primarily through social networks of friends, family,

"conservative churches are growing,"[17] recent trends leave little room for evangelical complacency. American church membership figures for 2010 showed a decline of .42 percent for the Southern Baptist Convention, a decline for the United Methodist Church of 1.01 percent, and an overall decline in church membership generally of 1.05 percent. Meanwhile, the Jehovah's Witnesses grew by 4.37 percent in 2010, and the Mormon Church grew by 1.42 percent in that same year.[18] Such figures raise questions about the effectiveness of the current evangelical paradigm and evangelistic practices.

A second reason for questioning the effectiveness of the Old Paradigm is the diminished impact of the Christian church on the larger culture—and, perhaps even more ominously, on church members themselves. Since the 1960s the secularization of the key institutions of American culture—law, the courts, elite universities, the media and entertainment industries—has been especially evident, continuing trends that began in the latter decades of the nineteenth century.[19] Christian cultural conservatives have won some limited victories in the "culture wars" in the right-to-life movement, but lost others in areas such as the teaching of "creation science" or "intelligent design" in public schools. In recent years public opinion appears to be swinging in the direction of greater acceptance of same-sex marriage, though opinion remains sharply divided in many areas of the country. Politically oriented strategies of the Christian Right for social change have come to be viewed with increasing skepticism.[20] As income distributions in the United States have become increasingly skewed toward the wealthy, and as the country has remained mired in costly military involvements in the Mideast and Afghanistan, with the social safety net at risk in the face of monumental budget deficits, neither the Christian Right nor the Christian Left appears to be exerting significant impact on the political processes in Washington.

Perhaps even more alarmingly, there are reasons to question the effectiveness of the existing paradigm on transforming the churches' own members. White evangelicals are among the most likely groups to object to neighbors of another race; evangelical youth differ little from their peers in rates of premarital sexual activity; divorce rates are higher in the Southern states, where evangelical Protestants are the predominant religious group;

---

and neighbors: *The Rise of Christianity*, 20. Even if Stark's estimates are considered to be unrealistic, it remains the case that pre-Constantinian growth rates were notable.

17. Kelly, *Why Conservative Churches Are Growing*.

18. Linder, ed., *2011 Yearbook of American and Canadian Churches*, 14.

19. Various aspects of this process of secularization have been examined in Neuhaus, *The Naked Public Square*; Carter, *The Culture of Disbelief*; Himmelfarb, *One Nation, Two Cultures*; and Marsden, *The Soul of the American University*.

20. See, for instance, Hunter, *To Change the World*.

a study by the Christian Reformed Church found that physical and sexual abuse was as common in their churches as in the general population.[21] With the notable exception of right-to-life activities, self-described conservative churches are less likely than liberal or mainline congregations to offer social outreach services or programs to the wider community.[22] The transformative power of a Wilberforcian antislavery crusade or the impact of the early Christian church on Roman society[23] appears to be missing today in the American evangelical community. Is it not time to reconsider the Old Paradigm and to seek a more adequate one?

The passing of the generation of the "founding fathers" of the postwar American[24] evangelical movement—Harold John Ockenga, E. J. Carnell, Carl F. H. Henry, Billy Graham—also points to the timeliness of reconsidering some of the root assumptions of the New Evangelicalism that emerged in the 1940s and 1950s.[25] The United States in the early decades of the twenty-first century is a dramatically different society than the one that gave birth to the New Evangelical movement, and the global context of the movement has altered dramatically as well. The Old Paradigm commitments to the authority of Scripture, to the fundamentals of Christian doctrine, to missions and evangelism, and to the life of the mind and high standards of scholarship need to be retained and affirmed. The vision of the transformation of the culture through evangelical witness and activism—at least in its more political and "top-down" expressions—may need to be revised with a more modest and yet perhaps more realistic "bottom-up" and "localist" strategy of "faithful presence at the margins."[26] Evangelical churches need to first experience a more powerful transformation of their own members by a recovery of the

---

21. Sider, *The Scandal of the Evangelical Conscience*, 13, 19, 27.

22. Robert D. Putnam, *Bowling Alone*, 78. There are notable exceptions, of course, to this general pattern, and Charles Colson's Prison Fellowship could be mentioned as an excellent example of evangelical social outreach.

23. On the social impact of early Christianity, see MacMullen, *Christianizing the Roman Empire*, and Dodds, *Pagan and Christian in an Age of Anxiety*.

24. On the other side of the Atlantic, figures such as John Stott, J. I. Packer, C. S. Lewis, and F. F. Bruce made enormous contributions to the renewal of the postwar evangelical movement; this generation of leaders is likewise passing from the scene.

25. The passing of John Stott in July of 2011 should also be noted. On the rise of the New Evangelicalism, see Rosell, *The Surprising Work of God*. On the history and development of American evangelicalism generally, see Hunter, *American Evangelicalism*; Noll, *American Evangelical Christianity*; Sweeney, *The American Evangelical Story*; and Smith, *American Evangelicalism*.

26. The phraseology of "faithful presence" is taken from Hunter, *To Change the World*.

reality of the living God in their midst before they will be in a position to effectively and lastingly transform the surrounding secular culture.

The remarkable growth of the church in the global South—in Africa, Asia, and Latin America—as documented by Philip Jenkins[27] and others, is further reason to consider a fresh paradigm for ministry and mission. Many of these churches display the avowedly supernaturalistic manifestations of the Spirit such as visions, signs, wonders, and healing that were prominent in the early church, yet are rare or non-existent in the established and more affluent churches of Western Europe and North America.[28] As of 1981, for the first time in about 1,000 years, the numerical center of gravity of the Christian church was *south* of the equator, having moved from its earlier European and North American base.[29] The "typical" Christian in today's world could be represented by a poor woman in Latin America, Africa, or Asia, who worships in a Pentecostal church. Spanish has surpassed English as the language spoken by the most Christians today.[30] These global Southern Christians may have less money, technology, and formal education than American Christians, but have much to teach us about dependence on God, the power of the Spirit,[31] and prayer.

Yet another factor that points to the timeliness of a New Paradigm is the growing religious pluralism in America, a pluralism both without (in the culture) and within (in the individual's mind). The United States has become one of the most religiously diverse nations in the world. Since the 1960s Islam and Asian religions such as Buddhism and Hinduism have become

---

27. Jenkins, *The Next Christendom* and *The New Faces of Christianity*.

28. Mark Noll has observed that Western Christians "who minister in Latin America, China, the Philippines, Africa or the South Seas consistently report that most [global South] Christian experience reflects a much stronger supernatural awareness than is characteristic *of even charismatic and Pentecostal circles in the West*"(emphasis added): *The New Shape of World Christianity*, 34.

29. Johnson and Chung, "Christianity's Center of Gravity, AD 33–2100," 50–51.

30. On the new global realities of the Christian movement, see also Chandler, *God's Global Mosaic*.

31. In the New-Paradigm evangelicalism being proposed here, the power of the Spirit is understood in terms of the "*extraordinary* supernatural" (the miraculous) as well as the "*ordinary* supernatural"—i.e., the quiet, undramatic work of the Holy Spirit in empowering and making spiritually fruitful the expository preaching and teaching of Scripture, and the ongoing ministries of catechesis, discipleship, worship, and evangelism. The "ordinary supernatural" presence of the Spirit (e.g., Acts 1:14, Christ giving the disciples instructions about the kingdom of God *by the Holy Spirit*) should be recognized as a constant presence in the life of the church and in all ministry. It is less subject to the problems of "burnout," emotionalism, and division that sometimes occur when the presence and ministry of the Holy Spirit are understood *only* or primarily in terms of the extraordinary and the miraculous.

a significant presence in American religious life; immigration from Latin America and the Caribbean has increased the "market share" of Roman Catholicism in America's religious mix, and the percentage of Americans identifying themselves as "agnostics" or "atheists" has increased significantly.[32] This religious pluralism is not only a matter sociological diversity; it has increasingly become a frame of mind and way of thinking, especially among the young. Sociologist of religion Robert Wuthnow has observed that for most Americans now, "Pluralism is within us as well as without us."[33] According to Wade Clark Roof, "No generation in American history [like the present one] was ever exposed to or more devoted to pluralism as a social and religious reality."[34] Christian Smith has noted that today's "emerging adults" (eighteen- to twenty-three-year-olds) in America today are "social constructionists" in that they instinctively tend to believe, in the face of the diversity and pluralism within which they have been raised, that all human beliefs, including religious and ethical beliefs, are human constructions that are historically contingent, changeable, and particular.[35] Doing effective evangelism and discipleship today must take into account this new pluralistic environment in which all claims to *the* truth or an exclusive way of salvation tend to be viewed with skepticism.

New-Paradigm ministry practices also call for a renewed awareness among American evangelicals of the pervasive impact of modern science, technology, and electronic media on our assumptions about reality and ways of "doing church." The Scientific Revolution of the seventeenth century inaugurated by Galileo, Descartes, and Newton, with its emphasis on the material, the visible, and the measurable—for the purposes of humankind's power over and control of nature—has tended to push the interests of modern humankind in *naturalistic* and this-worldly directions.[36] The Industrial Revolution of the eighteenth and nineteenth centuries applied the findings of modern science to the production and distribution of an unprecedented

---

32. On these trends toward greater religious pluralism, see Eck, *A New Religious America*; and the Pew Forum on Religion and Public Life, "U.S. Religious Landscape Survey (2010)." Based on surveys of 35,000 Americans eighteen or older, the Pew survey found that religious affiliation in the United States is both "very diverse and extremely fluid." In the survey, 16.1 percent of the respondents identified themselves as "atheist," "agnostic," or "nothing in particular."

33. Wuthnow, *America and the Challenges of Religious Diversity*, 107.

34. Roof, *A Generation of Seekers*, 245.

35. Smith, *Souls in Transition*, 50.

36. For studies of how the Scientific Revolution introduced a new naturalistic view of the universe, see: Westfall, "The Scientific Revolution of the Seventeenth Century"; Burtt, *The Metaphysical Foundations of Modern Science*; and Dijksterhuis, *The Mechanization of the World Picture*.

quantity of consumer goods, making life better for countless multitudes, but at the same time producing levels of material wealth and affluence that sapped the spiritual vitality of individual Christians and churches. The temptation for the church is to depend on the scientific and technological means that have made the United States and Western Europe economically and militarily great—rather than on the spiritual means that God has ordained for the spiritual growth of the church. The late twentieth century ushered in the information revolution of electronic and internet technologies, inundating Americans with a wealth of information, data, images, videos, and entertainment—while at the same time fragmenting and shortening attention spans, and distracting Christian minds from the invisible realities of eternity and heaven.[37]

The eschatological warnings of the New Testament can also alert us to the wisdom of thinking of fresh paradigms for church life and ministry. As he neared the end of his life and ministry, the Apostle Paul warned the church that as the end of history approached, there would be "times of stress . . . . Men will be lovers of pleasure rather than lovers of God . . . having the form of religion but denying its power" (2 Tim 3:1, 4-5). Whether the end in absolute terms is imminent or distant,[38] the church needs theological foundations that will sustain not merely the "form of religion," but that can give it power, depth, and stamina in the face of cultural forces oriented toward pleasure, comfort, entertainment, and material wealth and power.

Obstacles to a New-Paradigm Evangelicalism in the American Context

Before presenting the key elements of the New Paradigm and the central notion of the real presence of God, we will briefly take note of three obstacles to the implementation of such a paradigm: the common-sense bias toward visual perception; the bias of scientific naturalism toward the material and the measurable; and the impact of electronic entertainment media on the "colonization" of the Christian imagination. We will also briefly note three "heresies" of popular evangelicalism that are the unintended results of these influences: Deism ("God is far away"); Pelagianism ("We can 'do church' with our human power and technology"); and individualism ("I can do ministry by myself").

---

37. See J. J. Davis, "Conversion Isn't What It Used to Be," chapter 4 in the present volume; and *Reality in Meditation*, 9–12.

38. For an insightful critique of popular dispensational eschatologies, see Isaac, *Left Behind or Left Befuddled*.

The first obstacle is the common-sense bias toward our visual sense: "seeing is believing." This could also be called the "primate bias." As higher primates—we are not worms or moles or bats—we receive the vast majority of our sense impressions through our eyes and what they can see, and our model of reality is formed on that basis. At the very outset this circumstance of our biological nature as *Homo sapiens* creates a tension with our *Christian* identity, in that *hearing*, not seeing, is privileged as the means of knowing the invisible God, of whom no idols or visual representations are to be made (Exod 20:4, no graven images). It is through hearing the *words* of God (see Deut 6:4, "*Hear* O Israel, the *decrees* and the *laws* [not images] that I am about to teach you")[39] as they are illuminated by the Holy Spirit (John 16:13–14; 1 Cor 2:10–13) that human beings can have a saving knowledge of the one and only true God.[40]

Our unaided human eyesight gives us only a partial and selective view of natural reality, and is inadequate to give us knowledge of unseen, spiritual realities. As *Homo sapiens*, our sight is limited to what we call the "visible" light spectrum; we cannot see into the ultraviolet spectrum like honeybees, or into the infrared spectrum like sidewinder snakes. Without the aid of radio telescopes, we cannot see in the night sky the x-ray or gamma-ray radiation emitted by the stars that are not apparent in the visible spectrum. Neither can our eyes detect the radio waves and microwaves and television transmissions that fill the air around us. *Solid, material objects in the visible light range that are apparent to the senses are only a small part of physical reality.* This latter proposition about "what exists" is even more dramatically underscored by the discovery of so-called "dark matter" and "dark energy" by astronomers in recent decades. It is now generally believed by cosmologists that approximately *94 percent* of the total matter and energy in the physical universe is constituted by so-called dark matter and dark energy that is not visible to the senses and that does not interact in the normal ways with "normal" matter and energy.[41] "Normal" matter and energy thus

---

39. Deuteronomy 6:4, the *Shema*, is the central prayer of Judaism. See Deuteronomy 4:15: "You *saw no form* of any kind the day the Lord *spoke* to you at Horeb out of the fire."

40. As to be noted below, a Christian view of reality requires a *LogoPneumatic* epistemology of Word and Spirit to account for the knowledge of God and spiritual realities.

41. The existence of dark matter and dark energy has been inferred indirectly from the observed rotation of galaxies, and from the observed rate of the expansion of the universe, which appears to be accelerating. See Papantonopoulos, *The Invisible Universe*, and Matarrese et al., eds., *Dark Matter and Dark Energy*; for a more popular account, see Bello, "What are dark matter and dark energy and how are they affecting

constitutes only 6 percent of the known physical universe, and the rest is not apparent to the senses. Even in this 6 percent, most of the energy represented by electromagnetic radiation is not limited to the visible light spectrum that our eyes can detect. The point of the foregoing observations is that the Christian needs to consciously recognize and make efforts to compensate for this natural "primate bias" of "common sense" toward the visual in order to live out the command to avoid "graven images" (Exod 20:4), and to heed the apostolic admonition that "we fix our eyes not on what is *seen*, but on what is *unseen;* for what is seen is temporal, but what is unseen is eternal" (2 Cor 4:18).

The second obstacle to a New Paradigm, "real-presence" evangelicalism is the relentless influence and pervasiveness of the modern scientific worldview that is constantly pressing the Christian mind into its own naturalistic mold. The Scientific Revolution of the seventeenth century gave man unprecedented understanding of and control over the forces of nature, and in the Industrial Revolution that followed in its wake, unprecedented amounts of wealth and material possessions. And as Deuteronomy 8:10–14 predicted, increased wealth and material comfort tends to produce forgetfulness of God, as both the history of Israel and of late modern Europe and North America have confirmed.[42] While not rejecting the scientific method per se, the New Paradigm calls for the coming generation of evangelicals to recognize its "naturalizing" influences and to reject its hegemony over the Christian mind, imagination, and church practices.

As already noted in the previous section, the explosion of electronic entertainment media has inundated the Christian mind and imagination with a ceaseless torrent of images, messages, texts, emails, videos, MP3 music files, and so on. The dangerous result is a "colonizing" of the Christian imagination by an alien power—the rulers of "This Age." The notion of the "colonizing of the imagination" is taken, of course, by way of analogy with the tragic experience of Native Americans and other New World peoples, whose languages, customs, stories, and traditions were often destroyed by the white European and American colonizers.

For many modern Christians, sadly, biblical images of heaven and hell and the world to come are far less real, familiar, and vivid than the images

---

the universe?"

42. It is the case that the United States is something of an exception to the "secularization thesis," in that it is both an affluent nation and at the same time a nation with relatively high levels of religious belief and affiliation: see Berger, *Religious America, Secular Europe?* However, as David Wells and many other critics have pointed out, many American churches are highly accommodated to the surrounding culture and are deficient to varying degrees in theological depth and spiritual vibrancy.

of a Monty Python or *Saturday Night Live* entertainment world. A New Paradigm with a new ontology and epistemology is needed to restore the Christian imagination under the conditions of late modernity, so that it can once again begin to focus attention in a serious and sustained way on the unseen, eternal reality (2 Cor 4:18) above, where Christ is seated at the right hand of God (Col 3:1-2), and to live *out of* that greater reality above and more effectively *into* this visible world below.

These obstacles—the common-sense "primate bias" toward the visual sense, the influence of scientific materialism, and the colonizing of the Christian imagination by electronic entertainment media—have each contributed to the (unintended) and largely unrecognized "heresies" of popular evangelicalism: Deism, Pelagianism, and individualism. Deism is the belief that, in our perception and practice, God is far away (only "in heaven") and not really truly present and *active* on earth in the midst of his people gathered as a church. Pelagianism is the belief that the work of the church can be successfully performed with the human power, knowledge, planning, programs, measurable goals, objectives, and technologies that produce success in the business and entertainment worlds, and that gave the United States and Western European nations predominance over the nations of Africa, Latin America, and Asia during the colonial era.[43] Individualism is the heresy that expresses the attitude, in practice, that "I can do ministry by myself" and that I am an *independent* individual rather than an *interdependent* individual.

These "heresies" need to be corrected in a New-Paradigm evangelicalism that operates with a new trinitarian ontology; a new concept of the here-and-now, real presence ("theomesic") of God among his people; and a new "trinitarian-ecclesial" view of the Self that recognizes the Christian as an interdependent being, living in communion and partnership with Father, Son, and Holy Spirit—and in partnership and communion with the members of the body of Christ.

---

43. Friedrich Schleiermacher believed that the modern churches of Europe in his day no longer needed the supernatural power of miracles: "Even if it cannot be strictly proved that the Church's power of working miracles has died out . . . yet in general it is undeniable that *in view of the great advantage in power and civilization which the Christian peoples possess over the non-Christian* [emphasis added], the preachers of today do not need such signs": quoted in Horton, *The Christian Faith*, vol. 2, 450. The irony here is that many evangelicals, who would disagree with Schleiermacher's liberal theology, in practice would seem to agree that the work of the church does not need the supernatural assistance of God.

Essential Elements of the New Paradigm: The Ontological Project

Ontology: Trinitarian-Resurrectional

The first "pillar" in the New Paradigm is a *trinitarian-resurrectional* ontology as the foundation for a Christian and biblical understanding of ultimate reality. The doctrine of the Trinity is the "foundation of foundations" for Christian theology, and should be the starting point for all further faith and practice. Similarly, the *resurrection of Jesus Christ* was the starting point historically for the existence of the Christian movement; without it, the Jesus movement would have ended on Good Friday, with his dead body remaining in the tomb and his disappointed and disillusioned disciples being consigned to a minor footnote in the history of Second Temple Judaism. The resurrection of Jesus Christ, and the subsequent arrival of the Holy Spirit, moved the Apostle Paul and the early Christian church from a Jewish and (only) monotheistic view of God to a trinitarian view of God and of ultimate reality. The resurrection of Jesus Christ ushered in the promised Age to Come, an *inaugurated* eschatology, in which the powers of the Age to Come were already arriving in the community (Heb 6:5). An inaugurated eschatology ushered in an inaugurated *ontology* in which God could be known and salvation experienced in a new way, as participation in the very life of God as Father, Son, and Holy Spirit.

Old-Paradigm evangelicalism (Evangelicalism 1.0 and 2.0) affirmed, of course, both the doctrines of the Trinity and of the resurrection. What is being proposed here, however, is to make these realities and doctrines more central and constitutive as the dogmatic core of the theology of New-Paradigm Evangelicalism 3.0, and to develop more consistently the implications of this starting point for Evangelicalism 3.0's epistemology or theory of knowledge; for its anthropology, or view of the Self; and for its soteriology, or doctrine of salvation.

In this section[44] I wish to argue that the seeds of this new "inaugurated ontology" and worldview were sown in Paul's encounter with the risen Christ in his Damascus road conversion experience. I believe that the New Testament scholar Seyoon Kim was essentially correct in arguing in his book, *The Origin of Paul's Gospel*, that the origins of the apostle's distinctive message and understanding of the gospel was not to be found in parallels with Hellenistic mystery religions, gnosticism, Hellenistic Judaism, and so

---

44. The following discussion is taken from my book *Reality in Meditation*, 38–39, slightly adapted.

forth—but rather in his encounter with the risen Christ on the Damascus road. According to Kim,

> The characteristics of Paul's doctrine of justification *sola gratia* and *sola fide* are due to his insights into the . . . law, human existence and man's relationship to God which he developed out of his Damascus road experience . . . it was by seeing the risen and exalted Christ as the Son and image of God . . . that Paul developed his soteriological conception of the believers' being adopted as sons of God, their being transformed into the glorious image of Christ and their being made the 'new man' or *kanei ktisis* [new creation] through their incorporation into Christ, the Last Adam . . . [as the] the new humanity . . . . [I]t is clear that Paul's gospel and apostleship are grounded . . . in the Christophany on the Damascus road. The Damascus event is the basis both of his theology and his existence as an apostle.[45]

Other New Testament scholars have contested Kim's thesis in the part or the whole, but I believe that Kim is fundamentally correct in seeing the *resurrection of Jesus Christ,* and Paul's personal encounter with the risen Christ on the Damascus road, as the great "paradigm shifter" both for his theology and more generally, for his view of reality as a whole.[46]

For Paul, it is not too much to say that *the resurrection and arrival of the Spirit changes everything* and that *the resurrection of Jesus Christ makes it necessary to revise all previously existing concepts of reality.* Paul's encounter with the risen Christ changed his views of God, the world, the self, history, and salvation. Paul knew that being "in Christ" meant that a man was a "new creation" (2 Cor 5:17); the old ontology was gone; a new ontology had come.

Paul's understanding of God was transformed from the (monotheistic) God of Abraham, Isaac, and Jacob into a trinitarian understanding of God

---

45. Kim, *The Origin of Paul's Gospel,* 332.

46. Kim has summarized and further developed his thesis, and also responded to his critics, in his subsequent book, *Paul and the New Perspective.* The pivotal place of the resurrection of Jesus Christ, and its implications for an entirely new view of reality has recently been argued in the magisterial work of N. T. Wright, *The Resurrection of the Son of God:* "The early Christians insisted that what had happened to Jesus was precisely something new; was indeed, *the start of a whole new mode of existence, a new creation* [emphasis added]. The fact that Jesus' resurrection was, and remains, without analogy is not an objection to the early Christian claim. It is part of the claim itself . . . . [The resurrection blasts] its way through the sealed tombs and locked doors of modernist epistemology . . . Indeed, the holding apart of the mental and spiritual on the one hand from the social, cultural, and political on the other, one of the most important planks in the Enlightenment platform, is itself challenged by . . . Jesus' resurrection": 712–13.

as Father, Son, and Holy Spirit.[47] The world itself—"cosmology"—had been changed for Paul; the world in its present form was passing away (1 Cor 7:31), to be replaced by a new physics, a new order of creation. Because of the resurrection of Christ and the arrival of the Holy Spirit, he could no longer think of the self or the human being in the old way. The new person in Christ was a new way of being a human being (Eph 2:15, "his purpose was to create in himself one new man"). The new Christian self is not a separate and independent self, but rather, an *interdependent* self, one whose very existence and identity is that of being baptized into the body of Christ (1 Cor 12:13) and connected to Christ (1 Cor 6:17, "he who unites himself to the Lord is one with him in spirit") and to other Christians by the Holy Spirit.

Paul's understanding of time and history was fundamentally altered by his encounter with the risen Lord. The Age to Come was not merely a future reality to be anticipated, but a presently arriving ("already") reality to be experienced now in the Spirit, and by faith in the name of Jesus (see 1 Cor 5:4, "when you are assembled in the name of Jesus, *and the power of the Lord Jesus is present*"; emphasis mine).[48]

Paul's soteriology or view of salvation was fundamentally changed: the paradigm was no longer Moses and the Law, but Jesus and the Spirit. Salvation was not fundamentally a matter of "works of the law," but rather a matter of faith in Jesus as God's messiah vindicated by his resurrection (see Rom 4:25, "delivered over to death for our sins and raised to life for our justification"); fundamentally a matter of a faith like Abraham's, who could believe that God gives life to the dead and "calls things that are not as though they are" (Rom 4:17). In light of the resurrection Paul understood that the covenant with Abraham had been fulfilled in Jesus' death and resurrection, and that the gift of the Spirit and the experience of the supernatural powers of the Age to Come came not by observing the Law but through hearing with faith (Gal 3:5). In sum, then, Paul's encounter with the risen

---

47. See Fee, "Christology and Pneumatology in Romans 8:9-11." Fee argues that Paul had become a "functioning trinitarian," having had his Jewish understanding of God transformed by his saving experience of God as Father, Son, and Holy Spirit. See also the important work of Bauckham, *God Crucified*, arguing that New Testament Christology was "high" from the start, with Jesus "at the right hand of God" (Ps 110:1) being integrated into the very core identity of Yahweh as revealed in the Old Testament. Bauckham argues that from this point of view later patristic trinitarian doctrine was not in tension with Jewish monotheism, but a natural development of it.

48. It is not too much of a stretch to suggest that in early Christianity, every Sunday morning worship service—e.g., 1 Corinthians 5:4—was a "power encounter" with the risen Lord, by virtue of the presence and power of the Spirit, and in a sense, analogous to Paul's Damascus road encounter. See Revelation 3:20, "Behold I stand at the door and knock": the risen Christ comes in the Spirit and Word to be present to the believers in the church of Laodicea.

Christ on the road to Damascus produced an "inaugurated eschatology" which for him was the basis of an "inaugurated ontology" or comprehensive new paradigm of reality.

For the Christian,[49] the triune God is *ultimate reality*, the "bottom line" in our view of the real, the ontologically or metaphysically ultimate category, "that than which none more 'real' can possibly be conceived," to paraphrase Anselm. The doctrine of the Trinity is a bedrock metaphysical distinctive that sets the Christian faith apart from other world religions and competing worldviews. Judaism, Christianity, and Islam are Abrahamic faiths that share a common monotheistic heritage, but only Christianity affirms a one God fully revealed in three coequal and coeternal, distinct persons as Father, Son, and Holy Spirit.

As over against atheism, materialism, and scientific naturalism, Christian trinitarianism affirms that matter is real, and essentially good—but denies that matter is the ultimate metaphysical reality. God, who has existed eternally, and who is invisible spirit (John 4:24), created matter; matter and material forces (e.g., natural selection) did not create God or the idea of God. This is a crucial truth for the Christian to keep in mind, because "common sense" and the consumerism of late industrial capitalism and the advertising and entertainment industries are continually trying to convince us that *material* objects and possessions are the keys to human satisfaction, and that life's fulfillment is to be found in *this* world, not in a new creation from above.

The doctrine of the Trinity also distinguishes the Christian worldview from Hinduism and Buddhism.[50] In these Eastern religions, the metaphysically ultimate category—Brahman, Nirvana, Sunyata[51] ("emptiness")—is considered to be spiritual or non-material in nature, but this metaphysi-

---

49. The following section is taken from my *Reality in Meditation*, 41–43.

50. It is sometimes said that there is a Hindu "trinity" of Brahma ("creator"), Vishnu ("preserver"), and Shiva ("destroyer"), but this is not a true parallel to the Christian Trinity, because these three Hindu deities are not considered to be eternally distinct, but manifestations of one another (see *modalism*, from a Christian and trinitarian point of view); nor are the "incarnations" or "avatars" of Vishnu, e.g. in the form of Krishna, truly historical in character. As Sen has pointed out, "Unlike Christianity which accepts only one unique Divine incarnation in Jesus Christ, Hindus accept many incarnations of God": *Hinduism*, 73. The devotees of Vishnu and Shiva are in fact two distinct "denominations" within the broader Hindu family of religions. See Klostermaier, "Lord Vishnu and His Devotees," and "Shiva: The Grace and Terror of God," in *A Survey of Hinduism*, 239–77.

51. On the variety of Buddhist understandings of the concepts of Nirvana and Sunyata ("emptiness" or the "Void"), see: Rahula, *What the Buddha Taught*, (Theravada Buddhist perspective); Williams, *Mahayana Buddhism*; and Yandell and Netland, *Buddhism*.

cal ultimate is *impersonal* and without real distinctions.[52] This is one of the deepest questions in all of human philosophy and religion: is ultimate reality *personal* or *impersonal* in nature? For the Christian, *persons in loving relationships* are metaphysically ultimate; for Buddhists and many Hindus, the idea of human or divine "personality" must finally be transcended in union with an impersonal absolute.

In relation to the heritage of Greek philosophy which formed an important part of the context in which the early church and Christian theology developed, the Christian doctrine of the Trinity asserts that *person* is the ultimate metaphysical category, not an abstract concept of changeless Being (Parmenides), or an atomistic concept of matter (Democritus)."Being" is *personal* being, being-in-relationship.[53] There is no abstract concept of "Being" as such that is metaphysically or epistemically prior to the reality and being of the triune God, Father, Son, and Holy Spirit—persons eternally in loving, joyous, holy, and glorious relationship.

The Christian doctrine of the Trinity, then, is the foundation of a Christian understanding of ultimate reality, and has consequences for all Christian thought and practice, including prayer, meditation, and ministry. As we shall see, the doctrine of the Trinity, that implies the primacy of *invisible spirit* over *visible matter*, will have important implications for how we understand a Christian epistemology (theory of knowledge) and other aspects of a biblical worldview.

Epistemology: LogoPneumatic[54]

The basic premise of this section is that the inaugurated eschatology of the New Testament—the new reality that the powers of the Age to Come have already arrived in the church, because of the resurrection of Jesus Christ and the outpouring of the Spirit (Heb 6:5)—implies a new "inaugurated epistemology" that is different from the old epistemologies of "this Age," the old age that is already passing away. Because of the resurrection of Jesus and the arrival of the Spirit, fundamental questions such as "What types of

---

52. On the comparative claims of Buddhist and Christian epistemologies and the problem of choosing a "Metaphysical Ultimate," see my article "Buddha, the Apostle Paul, and John Hick."

53. This fundamentally important insight has been argued in the seminal work of Zizioulas, *Being As Communion*.

54. This section on a LogoPneumatic epistemology has been taken from my book *Reality in Meditation*, 56–58.

things exist?" and "How do we know them?" cannot simply be answered in the same old ways. A new *ontology* demands a new *epistemology*.

The proposal here is that we need to recognize an "inaugurated epistemology" in Paul, a *LogoPneumatic* ("Word and Spirit") theory of knowledge that had its origins in the apostle's encounter with the risen Christ on the Damascus road and his own personal reception of the Spirit (Acts 9:17–18). Because of these life-changing experiences, Paul knew that he himself was a new creation (2 Cor 5:17), and that his mind had been transformed to look at the world in a fundamentally new way (see Rom 12:2).

Paul's transformed theory of knowledge that we are calling a "LogoPneumatic" doctrine, because of the central roles played in it by revealed words of God and the Holy Spirit, transcends the limits of theories of knowledge of "this Age" that could be described by the terms "empiricism" and "rationalism." By empiricism, I mean a theory of knowledge that holds that the primary (or exclusive) basis of knowledge of the "real world" external to the human mind is sense experience. By rationalism, I mean a theory of knowledge that holds that the foundations of knowledge (if such foundations exist) are to be found in reason, logic, and clear ideas.[55]

Paul would recognize that the sensible things of this world (e.g., "The sun is shining today") are indeed knowable by sense experience, and that some propositions are established by logical argument (e.g., "If the dead do not rise at all, then Christ has not been raised either," 1 Cor 15:16). But Paul would deny that sense experience and reason *exhaust* the possible sources of knowledge; he knew that God's words of divine revelation and the Spirit of God are sources of knowledge about the invisible realties of God, salvation, heaven, eternal life, and the world to come. If in fact there are realities that truly exist, and that are not detectable by sense experience or unaided human reason alone, then neither empiricism nor rationalism would be adequate to cognize these ontological facts. An enlarged epistemology would be needed.

It is not difficult to demonstrate the apostle's *LogoPneumatic* epistemology from his writings. A good point of departure is the text in 1 Corinthians 2:9–14, where Paul is contrasting the divinely revealed origins of the gospel as the wisdom of God with the worldly wisdom of human philosophy:

> As it is written, "No eye has seen, no ear has heard, no mind has conceived, What God has prepared for those who love him"

---

55. In the history of Western philosophy, generally speaking, Aristotle, Locke, and Hume would be seen as standing in the empirical tradition, and Plato, Descartes, and Hegel in the tradition of rationalism or idealism. Kant attempted to integrate these traditions in his "transcendental" and "critical" theory of knowledge.

[Isa 64:4]—but God has revealed it to us by his Spirit. The Spirit searches all things, even the deep things of God. . . . No one knows the thoughts of God except the Spirit of God. We have not received the spirit of the world but the Spirit who is from God, *that we may understand what God has freely given us* (emphasis added). This is what we speak, not in words taught by human wisdom but in words taught by the Spirit, expressing spiritual truths in spiritual words. The man without the Spirit does not accept the things that come from the Spirit of God, for they are foolishness to him, and he cannot understand them, because they are spiritually discerned.

For Paul, the gospel, the wisdom of God, is beyond the reach of empiricism ("no eye has seen, no ear has heard") and rationalism ("no mind has conceived"). There is a principle at work here that "like is known by like." The things of physical sense are known by the physical senses; the things of logic and mathematics are known by logic and mathematics; but the things that are ontologically *spirit* (the mind of God, words of God, the content of the gospel) must be known by the Spirit ("God has revealed it to us by his Spirit," v. 10).

The Holy Spirit reveals the words from the mind of God, searching the very depths of the divine being (v. 10b), and *illuminates* these words to our human understanding (vv. 12 and 14, "that we may understand what God has freely given to us . . . they are spiritually understood").[56] Human reason in its natural state is fallen, darkened by sin (Eph 4:17–18), and needs to be regenerated and renewed by the Holy Spirit (Col 3:10). There is a natural tendency of the fallen human mind to suppress the truth of God in unrighteousness (Rom 1:18), despite the fact that the existence of God and his power and divine nature are revealed in nature and the human conscience (Rom 1:19–20; 2:14–15).[57] When we become children of God by adoption, the Spirit supervenes directly upon our human spirits to give us a personal, experiential knowledge of God's love and fatherly character (Rom 8:15, "by

---

56. On the long tradition of a doctrine of the *illumination* of divinely revealed words by the Holy Spirit in Christian theology, including, but not limited to Augustine, Bonaventure, Aquinas, and Calvin, see: Warfield, "Calvin's Doctrine of the Knowledge of God," in *Calvin and Augustine*, 29–130, and "Augustine's Doctrine of Knowledge and Authority," ibid., 387–477; Bonaventure, *The Mind's Journey into God*; Richard, "The Epistemological Relevance of the Word and Spirit," in *The Spirituality of John Calvin*, 136–66. On Aquinas and the Thomistic tradition in epistemology, see Jacques Maritain, "Knowledge by Connaturality," in *Distinguish to Unite*, 260–62.

57. On the general revelation of God in nature and conscience, see Demarest, *A General Revelation*; on the "noetic effects of sin," or the darkening of the human mind in matters moral and spiritual, see Moroney, *The Noetic Effects of Sin*.

him [the Spirit] we cry, 'Abba, Father'"; Gal 4:6, "God sent the Spirit of his Son into our hearts, by which we cry, 'Abba, Father'").

We may note the presuppositions regarding *ontology* and *anthropology* that stand behind Paul's LogoPneumatic epistemology. Paul knows that *words* and things *spiritual* in nature are not less "real" than visible, molecular objects. In fact, given the eternal existence of the triune God, Father, Son, and Holy Spirit, and given the eternal and necessary existence of God's invisible spiritual essence, the *invisible* and the *spiritual* actually have ontological and logical primacy over the material and the visible. God has existed eternally and necessarily; visible matter has not existed eternally, but began to be when God spoke it into being; matter exists contingently, not necessarily. God's ways of knowing, not human ways of knowing (dependent on the physical senses) are fundamental and constitutive. God's eternal self-knowledge—by Word and Spirit—is ontologically prior to man's ways of knowing by the physical senses, inasmuch as in the divine eternity, prior to creation, *there were no sensible or material objects to be known.*

Linguisticality—words, communication—are intrinsic to the eternal being of God (John 1:1, in the beginning was the *Logos*); words as means of personal communion preexisted the creation of matter, being eternally present within the Trinity. Consequently, we can recognize that *materiality* is derivative from *linguisticality* and spirit—not the other way around.

As regards anthropology, it is a "normal" and not extraordinary state of affairs for humans to know spiritual things, for man as the image of God, and who has a spirit (1 Thess 5:23, body, soul, and *spirit*),[58] was created for the purpose of knowing God in personal relationship—God who is spirit (John 4:24). A biblical, LogoPneumatic epistemology is necessary for the Christian to "push back" against the unremitting pressures of Reality 1.0 (the molecular world) and Reality 2.0 (the world of digital technology and entertainment), and to know, experience, and enjoy the blessings (Eph 1:3) of Reality 3.0 (the heavenly world to come: Col 3:1–2; 2 Cor 3:18; Eph 2:6; John 17:24; Heb 10:19–22; 12:22–25).

Anthropology: Trinitarian-Ecclesial Selves

The proposal here is that the fundamental concept in anthropology (understanding of the human or the person) for New-Paradigm Evangelicalism (3.0) should be that of the *trinitarian-ecclesial Self.* The biblical and

---

58. On Paul's distinction of spirit from soul and body in man, see Jewett, *Paul's Anthropological Terms.* "Spirit" is that part of man that is sensitive to and open to the transcendent and to the Spirit of God.

theological basis of such a notion has been presented in my earlier writings,[59] so there is no need to repeat that prior discussion. The fundamental concept is that for the Christian believer, one's core identity is established *relationally*—being constituted by relatedness to the triune God, Father, Son, and Holy Spirit, and by relatedness to the other members of the church, the body of Christ.[60] These relationships are *intrinsic* to the core reality and identity of the Christian, and not merely *instrumental* to other purposes and functions in the life of the Christian and of the church.

My relationship, through adoption and being baptized into the body of Christ by the Holy Spirit (1 Cor 12:13) to my holy, loving Abba Father, through union with Christ and the fellowship of the Holy Spirit, and to my brothers and sisters in Christ as my family of God, is *who I really am*.

The bond of the Holy Spirit that connects me to Christ in living union with him (1 Cor 6:17; John 15:5), and through Christ to the Father and to the other members of the body, is a *real relation* and not merely a notional or conceptual one. The Holy Spirit is real, and those relations have been foreseen, intended, and predestined in the eternal mind and purpose of God (Eph 1:4) before creation began; humans were never intended to subsist as independent and autonomous individuals, but as *interdependent* individuals, subsisting, and functioning in communion and partnership with the persons of the Holy Trinity and with the members of the body of Christ. My Christian identity must not be limited by what a naturalistic epistemology can see—my "independent" physical body/self—but must be expanded, with an epistemology of Word and Spirit to recognize the more weighty reality of the Spirit that links me to God and to the family of God.

In terms of the basic dogmatic structures of Christian theology, this proposal for an anthropology of a trinitarian-ecclesial Self is, in effect, a proposal to shift the hermeneutical focus in the doctrine of man from the Old Testament category of the *imago Dei* (Gen 1:26)[61] to the New Testament (and specifically Christian) categories of the Trinity, adoption, union with Christ, the Holy Spirit, and the church (ecclesiology). The Old Testament doctrine of the image of God is not being "left behind," but rather subsumed and integrated into the fuller New Testament revelation.

---

59. See J. J. Davis, "The Ontology of the Self: Trinitarian, ecclesial and doxological" in *Worship and the Reality of God*, 66–75, and "Reading Scripture as Trinitarian-ecclesial Self," in *Reality in Meditation*, 49–52.

60. On the relational nature of the self, see the essays by Grenz, "The Social God and the Relational Self," and my colleague Richard Lints, "Theological Anthropology in Context."

61. On the doctrine of the *imago Dei*, see Berkouwer, *Man: The Image of God*; Hughes, *The True Image*; and Cairns, *The Image of God in Man*.

Systematically, this proposal for a "new" anthropology for Evangelicalism 3.0 is a proposal to bring doctrines that have tended to be at the margins of the Christian doctrine of man—the Trinity, adoption, union with Christ, the church—and make them the *center* and core of that understanding. An almost-exclusive focus on Genesis 1:26–28 and the *imago Dei* can have the unintended effect of leaving the impression that an *individual* relationship to a "Unitarian," Old Testament, "individual" God is adequate to conceptualize *Christian* identity. This traditional focus on the *imago Dei* in isolation does not provide the conceptual resources to adequately challenge and withstand the excessive individualism of late modern Western culture.

Logically and theologically, if the doctrine of the Trinity is the fundamental Christian doctrine, and the reality of the eternal Trinity is the fundamental reality in the universe, then the Christian understanding of man should incorporate these truths from the outset. All thinking about what it really means to be a human person should be grounded in the triune reality of eternal, divine persons subsisting in holy, loving relationship and communion.

Historically, in Western theology, the doctrine of justification has tended to overshadow the doctrines of adoption[62] and union with Christ,[63] reflecting, understandably, the controversies of the Reformation period. This proposal would bring both adoption and union with Christ to a more central and constitutive place dogmatically; who *I really am* is my identity as a beloved son/daughter of my Abba—Father, living now and forever in union with Christ his beloved Son.

Similarly, the doctrine of the church, which has not received as much attention in Protestant theology[64] as has the doctrine of justification, is here proposed as a constitutive element in Christian anthropology. My identity is not that of an autonomous modern or postmodern individual; I am an

---

62. On the doctrine of adoption, see Packer, "Sons of God," in *Knowing God*, 181–208, especially 182 and 186. Older theological studies of adoption that are still worth consulting include Candlish, *The Fatherhood of God*; Webb, *The Reformed Doctrine of Adoption*; and Shaw, *The Christian Gospel of the Fatherhood of God*.

63. On union with Christ, see J. J. Davis, "Union with Christ: Real Presence, All the Time," in *Reality in Meditation*, 23–30, and the literature cited there; note especially Barclay, *Christ in You*, 5–19, for a review of modern scholarly discussions of the Pauline "Christ in you/me" language. See also Wikenhauser, *Pauline Mysticism*, 93. Other studies include: Smedes, *All Things Made New*; Billings, *Calvin, Participation, and the Gift*; and Tannehill, *Dying and Rising with Christ*. In my view, the work of Wikenhauser provides the most incisive discussion and recognition of the clearly *ontological* dimensions of the apostle's thought.

64. On this point, see Pannenberg, "Excursus: The Place of Ecclesiology in the Structure of Dogmatics," in *Systematic Theology*, vol. 3, 21–27.

interdependent individual whose identity is rooted in my true *family*, the people of God and the body of Christ. It is believed that this proposal for a revised anthropology that takes both the doctrine of the Trinity and of the church as *integral* and intrinsic to Christian identity is both theologically sound and practically advantageous, in that it gives the modern (American) Christian a better basis for resisting the excessive individualism of the surrounding culture,[65] and for cooperating with other Christians in the work of ministry.

Soteriology: Trinitarian-Eschatological: Trinity, Salvation, Inaugurated Eschatology

The fourth doctrinal "pillar" for New-Paradigm Evangelicalism 3.0 is a *trinitarian-doxological soteriology* or doctrine of salvation. The heart of this feature of the proposal, in terms of the structure of dogmatic and systematic theology, is to bring the doctrines of the Trinity, union with Christ, and inaugurated eschatology from the margins of popular evangelical faith and practice into the core of an "enhanced" evangelical soteriology—without sacrificing, compromising, or minimizing the historic evangelical commitments to justification by faith alone, penal substitutionary atonement, or imputed righteousness. The proposal, in effect, is an attempt to integrate the foundational *forensic* categories of Western and Latin Christianity with the *participationist* categories of Eastern[66] and Greek traditions.[67] This is an East-West "fusionist" soteriology—built on a Western base.

---

65. The anthropologist Edward C. Stewart in his *American Cultural Patterns* (11, 17) has observed that "In the United States, individual achievement is usually valued above family relationships.... The middle class American usually thinks of himself as an individual, the world as inanimate, success as his goal, impersonal cooperation with others as desirable, and doing as his preferred activity."

66. The trinitarian and participationist understanding of salvation in the Eastern fathers is sympathetically portrayed in Fairbairn, *Life in the Trinity*; in his book *Grace and Christology*, Fairbairn expounds the participationist soteriology of Cyril of Alexandria (chapters 3–4); in his *Eastern Orthodoxy through Western Eyes*, Fairbairn presents a sympathetic but critical appraisal of the Orthodox understanding of salvation: "Salvation: The Path of Theosis," 79–95. On salvation as participation in the life of the Trinity, see also Gruenler, *The Trinity in the Gospel of John*, esp. 128, on John 17:21: "That they also may be in us."

67. This, as I understand it, is the basic stance found in Horton, *Covenant and Salvation*; see especially "Mystical Union in Reformed Theology," 129–52. I concur with Horton's understanding that logically and theologically, the forensic categories of atonement and justification—God's solution to the problem of human sin and guilt— are prior to and necessary for any human participation in or experience of union with Christ and communion in the life of the Holy Trinity. As here understood, the forensic

Inasmuch as the Trinity, ontologically, is ultimate Reality, "that Reality more real than which none can be conceived," it naturally follows that the doctrine of the Trinity should be integral to any proper understanding of salvation. For our purposes here, I propose to refocus the received soteriology of popular evangelicalism (E:1.0 and E:2.0)—"Christ died on the cross for my sins, so that I can go to heaven and be with him when I die"[68]— with the doctrine of the Trinity as the hermeneutical focus. This proposed trinitarian-doxological soteriology is an attempt to provide fresh, biblical answers to four fundamental questions about God in relation to salvation: "Who is God?" "*Where* is God?" "What is God doing now?" and, "How does God feel about us ?"[69]

The Christian answer to the question "Who is God?" is, of course, a trinitarian answer: the one true God exists eternally in three coequal persons, Father, Son, and Holy Spirit. This trinitarian reality challenges and corrects the "practical Unitarianism" or "Jesus-centric" nature of some popular evangelical piety. Salvation is surely a matter of having a saving knowledge of Christ, but it is not only that; salvation is also knowing the one true God who is the *Father* of Jesus Christ (John 17:3). Salvation is not only "having a personal relationship with Jesus Christ," though it is indeed that. Salvation is *having a close and satisfying personal relationship with all three persons of the Trinity*: experiencing the love of God the Father for Christ his Son and for us as his daughters and sons; experiencing the joy that Jesus experienced as a Son deeply loved by the Father; and experiencing the deep peace and sense of well-being of God the Holy Spirit, who brings us into the very inner life and dynamic subjectivity of the triune God. Salvation, then, is an ever-deepening experience—beginning now and extending into eternity and the new creation—of the love, the joy, the peace, the glory, and the very fullness of the triune God (Eph 3:19).[70] A "Jesus-centric" soteriology can leave us in

---

categories of the West are *necessary, foundational,* and *prior* in the *ordo salutis* ("order of salvation"; see Rom 8:30), but they are not *exhaustive* expressions of the fullness of salvation. The forensic categories could be said to be *penultimate* in relation to the *ultimate* purpose of salvation: ever-deepening, never-ending *communion* with God, Father, Son, and Holy Spirit, an ever deepening experience of the joy and the love of the inner life of the Trinity, of being "filled to the measure of *all the fullness of God*" (Eph 3:19).

68. The point of this proposal is not to question the truth or biblical basis of the popular understanding, but rather to argue that it is a limited and partial understanding of a deeper and richer biblical doctrine of salvation.

69. Some aspects of this revised soteriology have already been presented in my earlier writings, e.g., "The Ontology of God: Your God Is Too Light," in *Worship and the Reality of God,* 48–60, and in "Teleology and Soteriology: The Purpose and Fulfillment of Human Life," *Reality in Meditation,* 52–55.

70. The forensic category of justification (Rom 8:30c) is perfected in the

the individualism and privatism of the secular culture; trinitarian salvation brings us out of ourselves into the community of God and of the church, the body of Christ.

A trinitarian-doxological soteriology answers the question, "Where is God?" by affirming that God—all three persons, Father, Son, and Holy Spirit—are *near* to the people of God, and that this *proximity* and *accessibility* of God is a constituent element of a biblical doctrine of salvation. God is not a God who is far away, but a God who has drawn near to his people to enjoy communion with them in worship, personal devotion, and Christian service. God affirmed to Moses that "I will dwell among the Israelites and be their God. They will *know* that I am the Lord their God who brought them out of Egypt [salvation] *so that I might dwell among them*" (Exod 29:45–46). Note carefully: the very purpose for which God saved his people was that he might enjoy being close to them and that they might enjoy being close to him—both spatially close and emotionally close. The divine presence and proximity is, in fact, the prime "identity marker" that distinguishes the people of God from the unredeemed world and that manifests the reality of God's grace and favor: "How will anyone know that you are pleased with me and your people *unless you go with us? What else will distinguish . . . your people* from all the other people on the face of the earth?" (Exod 33:16). This Old Covenant reality is now fulfilled in the New Covenant, when God meets his people in the new tabernacle and new temple—the church, the body of Christ assembled in his name, where the power of the Lord is present (1 Cor 5:4; 14:25).

This nearness or proximity of God to his people needs to be understood in terms of a notion of the "tri-locality" of God, inasmuch as Scripture indicates that God is *simultaneously* present in three locations—heaven, "home" (church, body of Christ), and the "heart" (the inner life of the believer). God's *transcendent* location is heaven, God "above" us, and the believer, because of the finished work of the atonement (Heb 10:19-22), and because of being seated with Christ in the heavenlies (Eph 2:6), is close to God in his heavenly location. God's *internal-immanent* location, God "in" us, is the individual believer's heart, where all three persons of the Trinity have come close to dwell (John 14:15, the Counselor "lives with you and will be in you"; 14:23, "My Father will love him, and *we* will come to him and make our home with him"). The third location is God is the *theomesic* or *external-immanent*[71] ("God *among* us": Matt 18:2; 18:20: *en meso auton*)

---

participationist categories of *glorification* (Rom 8:30d) and "pleromafication" (Eph 3:19). On the renewed interest in participationist soteriologies by some Baptist theologians, see Medley, "Participation in God."

71. In the term *external-immanent*, "immanent" denotes the nearness of God, and "external" indicates that the divine presence is not merely internal, individual, and

presence of God: God really, personally, dynamically present in the midst of his people gathered in his name (1 Cor 5:4; 14:25), by virtue of his extended presence in Word and Spirit, to enjoy fellowship with them. This objective, *theomesic* presence is a crucial counterweight to merely private and subjective experiences of God; God's real presence among the body pulls us out of ourselves into community. Salvation, then, is joyous experience of enjoying the nearness and presence of God in all three locations: "heaven," "house" (church), and "heart."

The answer to the third question, "What is God doing—now?," in relation to salvation, is "Quite a lot—more than you generally suppose." The question itself may seem to be an odd one, in that we generally think of the *finished* work of Christ in salvation, and God's "resting" (see Heb 4:4–5). It is most certainly true that God's work of salvation in one respect was finished at the cross, and that God and Christ "rest" from the work of atonement. Yet in another sense, the triune God is not "resting" but very *active* in the *application* of that salvation, not only working within individuals, but being at work and active[72] in the midst of the gathered, worshiping assembly.

The point here is to see that salvation is the reality of God's presence to his people, his being near them (Exod 29:45–46), but that also, this presence is not a passive and inert presence, but one that is an *active* and *efficacious* personal presence. God has not gone on a furlough or into retirement; God is doing something in the midst of his people. God is speaking through the words of the human preacher (1 Pet 4:11). All three persons of the Trinity are personally present and active in the worship and ministry of the gathered assembly: the Spirit is acting as gifts of healing, teaching, exhortation, and so forth are exercised; the Lord Christ is active as people serve one another in his name; the Father is working through them all (1 Cor 12:4–6).[73] Christ continues to preach the gospel and "proclaim light to the Gentiles"

---

subjective—but external to the individual, an objective presence of God on earth *in the midst* (spatially) of his people.

72. In regard to God as the active Subject in the life and the worship of the church, the massive project of Karl Barth can be seen as one long protest against the man-centered orientation of modern liberal Protestantism. Barth emphatically insisted on the primacy of the "divine God who is something other than man, who sovereignly [and actively] confronts him, who immovably and unchangeably stands over against him as the [active] Lord, Creator, and Redeemer": *The Humanity of God*, 39–40. I wish to thank my colleague Peter Anders for drawing my attention to this reference.

73. There is the danger that in discussions of the "gifts" in 1 Corinthians 12 and 14, attention will be focused on the visible, *functional manifestations* of the Spirit, and on the human agents exercising them, rather than on the Spirit, who is the primary personal Subject who is acting through them, who gives to each one as *he* determines (1 Cor 12:11).

through his servants on earth (Acts 26:23). He intentionally and personally, in the Spirit, comes to the congregation to continue the table fellowship that he enjoyed with his disciples during the days of his earthly ministry (Rev 3:20). Christ, as the High Priest, is now praying for his people (Rom 8:34), and as ascended High Priest, continues to invoke the blessing of God on them (see Luke 24:50-51).

God the Father is even portrayed in Scripture as one who, in the midst of his redeemed people, *sings with joy* over them: "The Lord your God is *with you* [divine presence], he is *mighty to save* [active and efficacious presence] . . . . He will *rejoice over you with singing*" (Zeph 3:17).[74] It is not only the people of God who can sing with joy to God; God himself sings with joy over his people. All three persons of the Trinity, who were involved in the accomplishment of redemption, are active in the present application of that work, and will all three will cooperate to bring it to perfection and completion.[75]

This latter text—Zephaniah 3:17—is a beautiful answer to the fourth soteriological question, "How does God feel about us? What is his fundamental attitude toward his children?" To state what should be obvious, God is fundamentally happy and pleased with his children—*now*. He enjoys being in their presence. A trinitarian soteriology recognizes that salvation is an entry into the love of God for the Son, into the joy that the Son feels in the Father's love, and into the peace and glory conferred by the Holy Spirit. While it is certainly true that as God's redeemed children we still sin and experience God's disfavor and need to confess and repent, this does not change our fundamental position before God as *beloved children*. For the people of God, God's displeasure is an intermittent *state*; the grace and favor of adoption are an enduring and fundamental *status*. The prodigal son has returned home to stay, to be embraced in the arms of a loving Father (Luke 15:20), a beautiful image of the eternal embrace of the Son by the Father (John 1:18), an embrace into which we as the children of God are invited now, and into eternity in ever-deepening measure. Growing awareness of this divine love into which we are invited evokes *doxology*,[76] the heartfelt cry

---

74. I wish to thank the Rev. Mario Bergner for drawing my attention to this text. It is one of the most remarkable images of salvation in all of Scripture.

75. And so it can be said, "We *have* been saved (past), We *are* being saved (present), and We *will* be (future, finally) saved": the section above focused on the "already" aspect of "inaugurated eschatology" and the triune God's activity in the present to make that salvation real in human experience.

76. Hence the term *trinitarian*-doxological *soteriology*: our saving experience of participation in the life of the triune God evokes praise (Eph 1:3, "Praise be to the God and Father of our Lord Jesus Christ, who has blessed us with *every* spiritual blessing in the heavenly places . . ."). In praise and worship we realize the doxological purpose of human existence (see Westminster Shorter Catechism, Q. 1: "What is the chief end

of praise from the heart one who knows that he is deeply loved by the God and Father of our Lord Jesus Christ.

From Theory to Practice: "Practicing the Presence" in Worship, Prayer, and Ministry

In this concluding section of the essay I will briefly indicate some points of application of the proposed New-Paradigm Evangelicalism 3.0 in three critical areas of the Christian life: worship, prayer and Bible reading, and ministry. This section will be brief, since I have addressed these areas of application in other writings or elsewhere in the present volume. In what follows I will attempt to indicate how the three critical doctrines that I have proposed to reposition from the "periphery" of functional evangelical theology to the "core"—the doctrines of the Trinity, of union with Christ, and inaugurated eschatology—can strengthen and correct our current understandings of God, the self, salvation, and service, and consequently improve the quality of our relationship to God in worship, personal devotion, and ministry.

First, the area of *worship*: here, the core concept is the *theomesic* ["God in our midst," Matt 18:2, 20] "near presence" of God among his people gathered in his name (Exod 29:42–46; 1 Cor 5:4; 14:25).[77] God's real presence with us in corporate worship is *near, personal, active,* and *efficacious.* God is not far away, only existing in a distant "heaven" or a distant future, but is near to us *here* and *now.*[78] The living God, the Holy Trinity, Father, Son, and Holy Spirit, is near to us both physically and emotionally. In New Testament worship, God is really as physically close to his people as was Moses at the burning bush—indeed, even closer (Heb 10:19–22). God is as emotionally close to his people as the father of the prodigal son (Luke 15:20); he is "Abba"—not "Allah"—to us as his beloved children. God's presence with us is personal, not impersonal or limited to the form of molecules in a piece

---

of man? The chief end of man is to glorify God and to enjoy him forever"). And this praise can be offered not only for salvation as completed in the past, but for the action of the truly present triune God *in the present moment* continuing, in the midst of the worshiping assembly, to apply his saving work to his people, as he acts to speak, teach, admonish, encourage, commune, heal, and rejoice with them in singing.

77. This new paradigm for the theology and practice of worship has been presented in my book *Worship and the Reality of God.*

78. We are near to God in all three locations of God: near to God in heaven (Eph 2:6, seated with him; Heb 10:19–22; 12:22–25, having immediate access by the Spirit to God in the heavenly Holy Place and the heavenly Jerusalem); near to God on earth in the midst of the church assembly (1 Cor 5:4; 14:25), and near to God in the heart, where God comes home to dwell (John 14:23).

of bread; the risen Christ is with us *at* the table in and by the Spirit, rather than *on* the table, continuing with us the table fellowship that he enjoyed with his disciples during the days of his flesh (see Rev 3:20). God is present and *active* in worship, not only (passively) receiving the praise of his people, but also actively speaking, rejoicing (Zeph 3:17; Luke 15:22–23, "let's have a feast and celebrate"), having table fellowship, and coming to heal and to bless. God's active presence is *efficacious* in that it makes a difference, by conferring insight, instruction, guidance, encouragement, rebuke, healing, forgiveness, and blessing. God, who is the chief and presiding minister and active agent in worship, is acting to actualize and operationalize our experience of salvation, eternal life, and *koinonia* (which is a participation in eternal life and the life of the Trinity, John 17:21, "they in us"; 1 John 1:1–2) in the *here* and *now*. Worship in the New Testament is not only a grateful response to the gift of eternal life, but is also a present, "already" *experience* and *participation* in eternal life—in the here and now.

In order to bring such an enhanced, "theomesic" concept of worship into the life of the congregation, some preparation and teaching is necessary. Christians need to understand that biblical worship is a learned skill and behavior, not something that just "comes naturally" or by instinct; we need to learn new doxological skills and form new habits of worship, and discard some of the old habits and ideas. Learning new habits and skills of worship involves the following fours steps: understanding; belief; redirection (of attention); and persistence (of focused attention on God). First of all, the believer needs to be taught or reminded of the biblical texts that teach the "near, personal, active, efficacious" presence ("theomesic") of God; second, the Christian needs to make the choice to *believe* this biblical teaching by faith, trusting the Scriptures beyond what the physical eyes can see; third, the believer must consciously and intentionally redirect attention away from the human preacher to God himself as the primary focus of attention during Sunday worship. On Sunday morning, we are not so much listening *to* a human speaker as listening *through* the speaker in order to listen *to* God with the "ears of faith." Fourthly, the believer needs to *persist* in giving God full and undivided attention, bringing back that attention to God as our attention frequently wanders."In your presence, Lord; come, Holy Spirit." "Practicing the presence of God"—in church—is indeed a learned skill, and needs study and practice to develop. The rewards can be enormous, however, because experiencing the presence of God is the source of fullness of joy (Ps 16:11), the joy that Christ prayed that his disciples would experience (John 17:13) and that would enhance the credibility of their witness to the truth of the gospel (see John 17:23).

Similarly, in the areas of *prayer* and *meditation* upon Scripture, the New Paradigm seeks to bring the doctrines of the Trinity, of union with Christ, and inaugurated eschatology into the core theological understandings that undergird these spiritual practices, such that the reality of the *near, active, efficacious* presence of God informs and energizes them.[79] Prayer is the experience of communication with and communion with the triune God, bringing us into the presence of the Father and the Son and the Holy Spirit, who are near to us, and personally active and efficacious to bless and to save. As we pray and meditate upon Scripture by faith, in the Spirit, we do so as those who are living in union with Christ, not as independent individuals, but as interdependent individuals in communion with Father, Son, and Holy Spirit and with the members of the body of Christ. Because the Age to Come has already begun to arrive in the death, resurrection, and exaltation of Christ to the right hand of the Father and the sending of the Spirit, we are now in our extended selves connected to Christ (1 Cor 6:17), seated with Christ in the heavenlies (Eph 2:6), close to him in his glorified presence. Beholding him with the eyes of faith as we meditate, we are being transformed by his Spirit from one degree of glory to another (2 Cor 3:18). This transformation is the active agency of the exalted, risen Christ who prayed that his disciples might be with him to see his glory (John 17:24). Christ's prayer is already in the process of being fulfilled by the glorifying action of the Spirit.

Finally, these core doctrines of the Trinity, of union with Christ, and of inaugurated eschatology also form the basis of a New Paradigm theology of ministry as *practicing ministry in the presence of God* and *in partnership with God*. Under this new paradigm when I, for example, preach a sermon, teach a Sunday school lesson, or offer counsel to another person, I do so not alone, only in my human power, but as one who is *in Christ,* whose true identity is that of a trinitarian-ecclesial Self, a renewed individual acting in partnership with all three persons of the Trinity and in partnership with members of the body of Christ. When preaching an expository sermon from the pulpit, I realize that I do so not alone, but in the presence of the risen Christ, who is the one who is "proclaiming light to the Gentiles" (Acts 26:23), and in the presence of the Holy Spirit, who alone can convict of sin (John 16:8) and illuminate the Word for a saving understanding of the truth (1 Cor 2:12,14). As a human preacher, I can cast the seeds of the word on the ground, and water them, but the seeds belong to the Lord of the harvest, and only the Holy Spirit can make them grow fruitfully (1 Cor 3:6) in the lives

---

79. On biblical meditation, see my *Reality in Meditation*, and also the chapter in this volume, "Why Most American Christians Don't Pray Very Much."

of God's people. God is the primary, active agent in ministry, by whose action alone can anything of eternal consequence be accomplished; we are his secondary agents and assistants. In doing ministry with an awareness of the presence of God and in partnership with God, we are doing ministry in the way that Jesus did ministry in the presence of the Father and in partnership with the Father and the Spirit (John 5:19; 8:28–29; Acts 1:2; 10:38).

In such a New Paradigm understanding the crucial, central feature of the Great Commission (Matt 28:16-20) mandate to teach and make disciples is not the "going," which may or may not involve crossing national boundaries, but rather the fact of the personal, active, efficacious *presence of Christ* ("I am *with you* always," v. 20) with us as we preach and teach. He is the Chief Discipler; we are his assistants and representatives. Such a perspective on ministry as centered on the real presence of Christ and of partnership with him and with the people of God takes a great deal of the pressure from the human agent and can help reduce the likelihood of burnout in the ministry. It can be a check to our human pride, for we know that God deserves the credit in every occasion of ministry. We are not doing ministry alone."Surely I am *with you always* . . . . Therefore, go and make disciples" (Matt 28:20, 19).

*He will fall down and worship God, saying,
"God is really (ontos) among you!"*

1 COR 14:25

3

Practicing Ministry in the Presence of God and in Partnership with God

The Ontology of Ministry and Pastoral Identity: a Trinitarian-Ecclesial Model

JOHN JEFFERSON DAVIS

THE PURPOSE OF THIS essay is to argue the following thesis regarding the nature of Christian ministry:

> *Christian ministry is activity by baptized Christians done in the presence of God and in partnership with God, for the purpose of bringing the people of God[1] into deepening communion with God and with one another, and into right relationship with God's creation.[2]*

---

1. The term "people of God" could be broadened to "people" in general, to recognize explicitly the mission of the church to reach out to those who are not yet "people of God," in ministries of proclamation, presence, and service, so as to bring them into communion with God and the people of God. The three generally recognized purposes of the church—worship, edification or discipleship, and mission—could all be seen as fulfilling the ultimate purpose of bringing persons into deeper communion with the triune God, so as to participate in the communion that Father, Son, and Holy Spirit enjoy in their own internal life.

2. The theme of the *new creation* as a basic horizon of a biblical and Christian understanding of redemption has been recently argued by N. T. Wright, *Surprised by Hope*. This theme of creation/new creation, while important for the church's ministry and mission, will not be a major focus of this chapter.

The essay will present a model of ministry that incorporates fundamental categories of biblical theology such as divine presence,[3] divine-human partnership, communion (*koinonia*), and body of Christ, together with fundamental categories from systematic theology, particularly the Trinity and union with Christ,[4] to argue for an *ontological* understanding of the nature of ministry and pastoral identity, in contrast to prevailing *functional* views.

A concept of the "extended Self" and a "coupled system" drawn from recent work in the philosophy of mind[5] will be invoked in order to explicate the biblical notions of "union with Christ" and "divine-human partnership" in the actions of ministry, such that "union with Christ" is seen not just as a biblical "metaphor," but as having ontological and, consequently, functional significance. On the basis of this new conceptualization of union with Christ, it will be argued that the triune God is the *primary* agent in every act of ministry, while the pastor or human agent is the *secondary* agent in a "coupled system," in which the Holy Spirit couples or links the risen Christ in heaven with the human agent on earth.

The "ontological" model seeks to focus attention on the fundamental state of *being* (communion with the triune God; union with Christ) out of which particular acts of pastoral ministry arise, and in which the pastor's identity is grounded, and also seeks to set this ontological understanding within a *teleological* horizon of the fundamental purpose of all ministry and Christian existence: an ever-deepening experience of communion with the triune God[6] and with the people of God. In this proposal for a trinitarian-

---

3. In my book *Worship and the Reality of God*, I have argued for a recovery of the centrality of the biblical theme of the divine presence in Christian worship: the triune God is *really present* among his covenant people, by Word, Spirit, and sacrament—as they gather in his name for worship. In my book on biblical meditation, *Reality in Meditation*, I have likewise argued that God is really present to the believer through the biblical text of Scripture in an act of faithful, prayerful reading, by virtue of the presence of the Spirit and the believer's union with Christ.

4. In his groundbreaking work, *Reconstructing Pastoral Theology*, Purves has argued for a reorientation for the discipline of pastoral theology in which the categories of systematic theology—e.g., Christology, union with Christ, the doctrine of God—are at the core of the discipline, rather than categories drawn from the social sciences. This project is continued in a more popular vein in Purves, *The Crucifixion of Ministry*. The present essay seeks to continue the conversation from the side of systematic theology that Purves has initiated from the side of pastoral theology.

5. Clark and Chalmers, "The Extended Mind." See also my paper "How Personal Agents Are Located in Space," available on request from the author (jdavis@gordon-conwell.edu).

6. I would like to commend the fine work of my colleague Donald Fairbairn, *Life in the Trinity*, which sets the horizons of Christian life and theology within a trinitarian framework.

ecclesial model of ministry, it will be argued that the pastor's fundamental identity is not grounded in what he or she does, but in *being* and *relationship*: in communion with the triune God, through union with Christ; that, in fact, the pastor's fundamental identity is that of a trinitarian-ecclesial Self, linked ontologically by the Spirit to the Father and the Son and to the body of Christ.

The broader purpose of this essay and its "trinitarian-ecclesial" model for ministry and pastoral identity includes these additional, broader concerns: the gulf between the worlds of academic theology and parish ministry; the secularizing influences of the social and behavioral sciences on the practice of pastoral ministry and pastoral counseling in the last half century; the individualism of American culture and much American church life; and the problem of the separation of the clergy and the laity in many of the ministries of the church. It will be suggested that the "trinitarian-ecclesial" model of ministry being proposed here may have the potential of helpfully addressing issues in all four areas.

The argument of this essay will be organized as follows: first, an historical overview of the history of pastoral theology[7] as a discipline; second, a presentation of the biblical themes of divine presence and divine-human partnership, and the doctrines of the Trinity and union with Christ; and third, a discussion of how the new model being proposed can be illustrated and applied in the specific activities of parish ministry such as preaching, worship, counseling, and committee work.

Pastoral Theology and Systematic Theology: Some Historical Perspectives

In his widely influential critique of theological education in America, *Theologia: The Fragmentation and Unity of Theological Education*, Edward Farley pointed to the thirteenth century as a watershed in the way in which ministers were trained for service in the church. With the rediscovery of lost writings of Aristotle and their dissemination in the universities, theology was transformed into a university-based "science" rather than the "holy wisdom" of the church fathers and the monasteries.[8] This introduction of

---

7. For the purposes of this essay, the terms "pastoral theology" and "practical theology" will be considered to be essentially equivalent, referring to the full range of responsibilities of a pastor in the local church, e.g., preaching, teaching, leading worship, visitation, pastoral care and counseling, spiritual direction, and administration. For a discussion of terminology, see Woodward and Pattison, "An Introduction to Pastoral and Practical Theology."

8. Farley, *Theologia*, 38.

Aristotelean logic and dialectics into the medieval universities as the basis for the study of theology by Aquinas and the schoolmen had the unintended effect of widening the gap between the church and the "academy"—a gap which is very much in evidence in the modern period. Jaroslav Pelikan has noted that from 100 to 600, most theologians were bishops; from 600 to 1500 they were monks; and from 1500 to the present they have tended to be university professors![9]

The model of a university-based, rather than church-based, context for the teaching of theology was given further impetus in the Enlightenment period, and especially by the German university system exemplified by the University of Berlin. It was in this context that Friedrich Schleiermacher's celebrated four-fold division of the theological curriculum was launched: ministerial training came to be defined as a course of study progressing through the exegetical, historical, systematic/philosophical, and practical disciplines.[10] "Practical theology" or "pastoral theology" were understood primarily in functional terms, in relation to the tasks of parish ministry. This understandable focus on the *practices* of ministry, however, was to further the distance between the student's study of theology ("theory"; doctrine; specialized knowledge) and pastoral ministry ("practice"; professional skills), especially with the subsequent growth and specialization of university-based knowledge in the later nineteenth and twentieth centuries. The older patristic idea of theology as a *habitus* or way of spiritually forming the soul tended to be lost in the modern university setting.

Another obstacle to the integration of pastoral and systematic theology can be found in the internal history of theology as a discipline, namely, the fact that ecclesiology—the doctrine of the church—did not become a separate *loci* or topic of focused discussion for theologians until the fifteenth century.[11] Ecclesiology—the natural location for discussions of the nature of ministry—became more prominent as a theme in systematic theology as a result of the sixteenth-century Reformation controversies between Catholics and Protestants, but even here, the focus of attention was on such matters as the doctrine of the sacraments and the identity of the true church, and so forth, and not on the nature of ministry as such. Modern systematic theology textbooks tend to follow in well-worn tracks laid down at that time—the nature and government of the church; discussions of baptism and the Lord's Supper—but

9. Pelikan, *The Emergence of the Catholic Tradition*, 5; cited in Purves, *Reconstructing Pastoral Theology*, xxixn27.

10. Schleiermacher, *Brief Outline Of The Study of Theology*. Schleirmacher's own schematization explicitly mentions three divisions, but these emerged as a fourfold division of the curriculum in subsequent theological education in America.

11. This history is helpfully reviewed in Pannenberg, "Excursus."

tend not to address a biblical and systematic understanding of the nature of ministry as such.[12] Consequently, modern books written for pastors in the area of pastoral ministry tend to be "how-to" treatments that are usually not grounded in the fundamental categories of systematic theology.[13]

Since any project such as the present one that seeks fresh integration of the disciplines of pastoral and systematic theology needs to be informed by an awareness of the historical development of both disciplines, a very brief overview of the history of pastoral theology will be noted here.[14] During the patristic period works such as Gregory of Nazianzus, *In Defense of His Flight to Pontus*, John Chrysostom, *Six Books on the Priesthood*, and the widely read *Pastoral Care* by Gregory the Great, set pastoral care and theology in a priestly, church-based, and confessional context.[15] During the Reformation period, both Luther and Calvin addressed pastoral as well as theological questions, but the outstanding work of pastoral theology from this period is Martin Bucer's treatise, *Concerning the True Care of Souls* (1538), in which Bucer sought to place the ministerial tasks of the "care of souls" within a biblical context of the doctrine of the church as the fellowship and body of Christ.[16]

In the post-Reformation period the work of the Puritan pastor Richard Baxter of Kidderminster, England, *The Reformed Pastor* (1659), is justly considered a classic in the field of pastoral theology and practice, and

---

12. See, for example the table of contents of widely used textbooks such as Erickson, *Christian Theology*; Grudem, *Systematic Theology*; and from an earlier generation, L. Berkhof, *Systematic Theology*.

13. Commenting on this "gap" between systematic and practical theology in the training of ministers, Ray Anderson has observed that for the typical seminary graduate, much theology is "thrown out with the 'coffee grounds' when the students return to take up their posts on the frontline of ministry. There, under pressure to be successful leaders of the organized church, they are easily attracted to pragmatic strategies for church growth, conflict management, and pastoral counseling": *The Shape of Practical Theology*, 318. Anderson has long been a notable proponent for the greater integration of theology and pastoral ministry. See also Anderson, ed., *Theological Foundations for Ministry*.

14. Helpful resources in this area are Evans, ed., *A History of Pastoral Care*, and Oden, *Pastoral Theology*, "Introduction: What Is Pastoral Theology?," x-xii.

15. For discussion of these patristic authors, see Purves, *Pastoral Theology in the Classical Tradition*.

16. Bucer defines the church as the "assembly and fellowship of those who are gathered from the world and united in Christ our Lord through his Spirit and word, to be a body and members of one another, each having his office and work for the general good of the whole body and all of its members" (*Concerning the True Care of Souls*, 1). Here Bucer anticipated some modern emphases on the church as "body of Christ" and a "body life" ministry of all gifted members — though his treatment as a whole focuses on the ministry of the clergy through preaching, sacraments, and church discipline.

has been widely read down to the present day.[17] Baxter was noted for his program of home visitation and catechizing of the families in his parish, reflecting his conviction that preaching alone was not sufficient to ensure Christian growth and discipleship.

The nineteenth century witnessed a flowering of substantial works in pastoral theology. Among the many works that could be mentioned, the following are perhaps among the most significant: A. Vinet, *Pastoral Theology: The Theory of the Evangelical Ministry* (1854); James M. Hoppin, *Pastoral Theology* (1884); Patrick Fairbairn, *Pastoral Theology: A Treatise on the Offices and Duties of the Christian Pastor* (1875); William G. T. Shedd, *Homiletics and Pastoral Theology* (1873); and Washington Gladden, *The Christian Pastor and the Working Church* (1898).[18] An examination of the tables of contents of these works reveals that the presentations tend to be structured around the functions of parish ministry, rather than an overall theological framework as such.

This focus on the functional aspects of ministry has continued in the twentieth century works in pastoral theology.[19] In 1958 Seward Hiltner of Princeton University published *Preface to Pastoral Theology*, a landmark work that proved to be widely influential in the subsequent development of the fields of pastoral theology and pastoral counseling in the English-speaking world.[20] Hiltner defined pastoral theology as a branch of theological inquiry "that brings the shepherding perspective to bear on all the operations and functions of the church and minister, and then draws conclusions of a

---

17. J. I. Packer described Baxter as "the most outstanding pastor, evangelist, and writer on practical and devotional themes that Puritanism produced" (*The Reformed Pastor*, back cover).

18. It is of interest to note that William G. T. Shedd, who taught for many years at Union Theological Seminary in New York, taught and published both in the areas of systematic theology and practical theology—an interdisciplinary competence that was to largely disappear in twentieth century theological education with the growth of specialized knowledge and professional disciplines.

19. Such a functional emphasis, with varying degrees of theological grounding and reflection can be seen, for example, in Bromiley, *Christian Ministry*; Thornton, *Pastoral Theology* (Anglican); Richards and Martin, *A Theology of Personal Ministry*; O'Meara, *Theology of Ministry* (Roman Catholic); and D. Hansen, *The Art of Pastoring*. The work of Thurneysen, *A Theology of Pastoral Care*, seeks to ground pastoral care in a (Barthian) theology of the "proclamation of the Word of God." Karl Barth discusses pastoral ministry in *Church Dogmatics* IV, 3, ii, *The Doctrine of Reconciliation*, under the rubric of the "Ministry of the Community," 830–901. Barth sees ministry in general as the "declaration of the gospel," but does not relate the specific tasks of ministry to the broad theological loci discussed elsewhere in the *Dogmatics*, i.e., the doctrines of the Trinity and Christology per se.

20. Hiltner, *Preface to Pastoral Theology*.

theological order from reflection on these observations."[21] This definition, according to Hiltner, implied that pastoral theology was an "operation-centered" or "function-centered" branch of theology rather than a "logic-centered" one.[22] In a somewhat Tillichian vein, Hiltner could view pastoral theology as a "method of correlation" in which reflection on the resources of the Christian tradition and reflection on the "shepherding" situations of ministry were held in mutual relation, with theory and practice informing one another. While retaining the historic Christian and biblical metaphor of "shepherding" as an organizing principle, Hiltner wished to integrate into pastoral practice the new knowledge coming from psychology, psychiatry, anthropology and other sources; these "riches are such that no thoughtful person can set them aside."[23]

Hiltner's paradigm for pastoral theology has been predominant in much Protestant pastoral theology and pastoral counseling for the last sixty years in the United States, but it has not been without its critics. Thomas Oden, for example, argued that approaches such as Hiltner's that borrow heavily from the social sciences are in danger of losing their biblical and theological rootings. An area of pastoral practice such as church administration, for example, that borrows heavily from pragmatic management procedures can become "an orphan discipline wondering about its true parentage,"[24] blurring the lines that distinguish a business enterprise from the church.

Andrew Purves has argued that the modern pastoral theology and pastoral counseling movement promoted by Hiltner has been, in practice, more influenced by psychological and social-science concerns than theological and doctrinal ones, with the result that secular goals and techniques of care have come to predominate in pastoral practice.[25] With the loss of Christol-

21. Ibid., 20.

22. Ibid.

23. Ibid., 25.

24. Oden, *Pastoral Theology*, 4. The plausibility of Oden's concerns could be supported by an examination of the table of contents of some current works in the area of church administration such as Berkley, ed., *Leadership Handbook of Management and Administration*; Shawchuck and Heuser, *Managing the Congregation*; McIntosh, *Church That Works*; and Mead and Allen, *Ministry By Objectives*. These works and others like them provide useful information and helpful techniques, but it is not apparent that these techniques are integrated meaningfully within a Christian theological framework and worldview. Oden's *Pastoral Theology* draws from the rich heritage of the biblical and patristic theological tradition, but still follows the older pattern of organizing pastoral theology around the functions of the minister, rather than a doctrinal structure per se, as advocated by Andrew Purves.

25. Purves, *Reconstructing Pastoral Theology*, xiv.

ogy, soteriology, and the Christian doctrine of God, pastoral theology and practice have tended, according to Purves, to focus on "acceptable functioning rather than discipleship," and on "self-actualization and self-realization rather than salvation."[26] The churchly context of historic pastoral care and the ongoing ministries of Word, sacrament, fellowship, and discipline were in danger of being displaced by the *clinical* settings[27] of the secular disciplines of counseling and psychology. Purves has challenged the pastoral theology and counseling movement not to ignore the social sciences, but to reorient these disciplines in such a way that the biblical and Christian confessional heritage and the doctrines of God and union with Christ are the integrative core of theory and practice.[28]

As indicated in the opening section of this essay, one of the reasons for proposing a trinitarian-ecclesial model for church ministry and pastoral identity is to provide a model for ministry that can address the *individualism* of American culture[29] at a fundamental level. The pervasiveness of individual-

---

26. Ibid., xiv, xix, xx. Purves's concerns are shared by other scholars in the field such as Ian Bunting: "In the early part of the twentieth century the role of the pastor as shepherd began to yield its biblical underpinning, theological foundation and its developed church orientation to the more secular rationale of the psychological sciences .... The pastoral counseling movement in particular has tended to use the Bible as a contributor rather than as the foundation of its practice": "Pastoral Care at the End of the Twentieth Century," in *A History of Pastoral Care*, 383–399 (quotations from 387 and 398). On the secularizing influences during the modern period on American pastoral care, see also Holifield, *A History of Pastoral Care in America*.

27. Awareness of the tensions and ambiguities that obtain in the modern pastoral counseling movement, as it attempts to straddle the worlds of clinical practice and the church are reflected, for example, in the work of Wayne Oates, a leading contributor to the movement: "I have sought to set forth ... a strategy and Christian philosophy of pastoral counseling ... deduced from the clinical practice of pastoral counseling .... The central focus of this book is upon the tensions brought about by the ambiguities inherent in the identity and function of a pastor": Oates, *Pastoral Counseling*, 7.

28. This is likewise the perspective of this chapter: not to ignore or reject valid insights from the social sciences, but to reintegrate them around a Christian doctrinal core. On the other hand, some Christian writers in the field, such as Adams, *Competent to Counsel*, have appeared to argue that secular insights have little or no value whatsoever in Christian counseling.

29. As used here, "individualism" is taken to imply "a focus on rights above duties, a concern for oneself and immediate family, an emphasis on personal autonomy and self-fulfillment, and basing one's identity on one's personal accomplishments," and a view of the self that sees the self as more independent than interdependent in the context of the group or larger collective: Inglehart and Oyserman, "Individualism, Autonomy, Self-Expression," 77. The literature on individualism is very extensive; notable scholarly work in this field, from various historical, sociological, psychological, anthropological, theological, and philosophical perspectives would include: Bellah et al., *Habits of the*

ism in American culture is widely recognized, and can be seen to have both its strengths and weaknesses. On the one hand, individualism can support concerns for human rights, rule of law, personal achievement, and the virtues of innovation, creativity, and entrepreneurship. On the other hand, it is generally recognized that individualism in its more exaggerated forms has contributed to the weakening of social bonds in marriage and other personal relationships, and has also contributed to the erosion of loyalty and commitment to churches, denominations, and other social institutions. In the sections of this essay to follow, it will be argued that the biblical and theological categories of the Trinity, union with Christ, and the church as the body of Christ should be recognized as fundamental and intrinsic to the pastor's self-identity and to the nature of ministry as partnership with God. It will be argued that only such an *ontological* or metaphysical understanding of who the pastor *really is* and how ministry *really is* grounded in a spiritual union with and partnership with the triune God and with other Christians can successfully withstand the pervasive individualistic tendencies of modern culture and help to prevent problems of "pastoral burnout" and isolation in the ministry.

A significant element in the broader historical context of this discussion of pastoral theology and the nature of ministry is that of the growing separation between the clergy and the laity that began to develop from the third century onward, and which was only partially corrected in the Reformation and post-Reformation eras of church history. The development of the idea of the priest as one who was uniquely empowered and ordained by God to offer *sacrifices* for the people, on the analogy of the Old Testament priesthood, increasingly tended to marginalize the role of the laity in Christian worship and ministry. These tendencies were strengthened by the development of the doctrine of transubstantiation, beginning in the

---

Heart; Riesman, *Individualism Reconsidered*; Lasch, *The Culture of Narcissism*; Gergen, *The Saturated Self*; and Taylor, *Sources of the Self*. A helpful survey of historical and cultural influences in the American tradition is provided in Hollinger, "American Individualism" in *Individualism and Social Ethics*, 13–51. For American culture as seen from the perspective of cross-cultural anthropology, see Stewart, *American Cultural Patterns*; for perspectives on the self in biblical and ancient Mediterranean cultures, see Malina, "The First-Century Personality: The Individual and the Group" in *The New Testament World*, 51-70; for understandings of the nature of the self in traditional Japanese and Indian culture, see Nakamura, "Primacy of the Universal Self over the Individual Self" (India) in *Ways of Thinking of Eastern Peoples*, 93–106, and "Social Relationships Take Precedence Over the Individual" (Japan), ibid., 409–434. Further cultural background is provided in Giddens, *Modernity and Self-Identity*; and Cushman, *Constructing the Self*, especially "The Self in America," 34–90, and "The Self in Western Society," 371–382. I wish to thank my colleague David Wells for drawing my attention to these latter references.

ninth century, and culminating in its official promulgation at the Fourth Lateran Council in 1215.[30] The role of the laity in the late medieval period was reduced largely to that of being passive spectators, watching the priest consecrate and elevate the elements, in the words of a liturgy in a language (Latin) not understood by the people. The Protestant Reformers made the liturgy available in the languages of the people, and restored the Bible and the preaching of the gospel to a more central place in the life of the church, but Protestant church life and ministry still tended to be dominated and controlled by the clergy.

In the modern period a variety of developments have emerged that have tended to recover a more vital role for the laity in Christian ministry and worship. The Second Vatican Council (1963–65) introduced sweeping changes into the life of the Roman Catholic Church. Conciliar documents such as the "Dogmatic Constitution on the Church" (*Lumen Gentium*) and the "Decree on the Apostolate of the Laity" (*Apostolicum Actuositatem*) emphasized an understanding of the church as the whole people of God, rather than the more juridical understanding of a hierarchical institution controlled by priests and bishops.[31] The post-World War II period also witnessed the emergence of a "theology of the laity" and "workplace theology" that understood ministry as involving all the people of God, and as not being limited to the confines and activities of the institutional church.[32] The charismatic renewal movements that have impacted both the Roman Catholic and Protestant churches since the 1960s have heightened the awareness of the gifting of all the people of God for ministry, and promoted concepts of more participatory forms of ministry understood in terms of "body life" (see 1 Cor 12, 14; Eph 4).[33]

This modern recognition of the calling of all the people of God to be actively involved in the work of the ministry—both inside and outside the

---

30. On the history of this development, see White, "Understanding the Eucharist" in *Introduction to Christian Worship*, 248–59.

31. W. Abbot, *The Documents of Vatican*, 14–101, 489–521. Vatican II made famous a phrase calling for the "full, conscious and active participation" of the people in worship.

32. For historical perspective on these developments, see Banks, "Appendix A: Lay Theology and Education since 1945," in *Redeeming the Routines*, 153–74, and also Neill and Weber, *The Layman in Christian History*.

33. On the modern charismatic renewal movements, see Hocken, "Charismatic Movement," and Hollenweger, *Pentecostalism*. The concept of a "body life" form of ministry was popularized in Stedman, *Body Life*, reflecting the charismatic renewal at the Peninsula Bible Church pastored by Stedman: "Now it is most apparent from Ephesians 4 that all Christians are 'in the ministry' . . . . Pastors . . . must restore to the people the ministry which was taken from them with the best of intentions," 78–79.

church—is to be welcomed and encouraged. The present essay is calling, in effect, for a further "third moment" in the historical trends in Christian ministry, one in which the more active role of the laity will be preserved, but that in addition, the *divine agency* and divine presence in every act of ministry will be recognized: all the people of God, with their various charisms for ministry, are recognized to be acting both in the presence of God and in partnership with God, Father, Son, and Holy Spirit. The God who is actively and really present in the midst of his people is recognized as the primary agent in all ministry.[34] This "third moment" is seen as corrective to the "turn to the (human) subject" that has characterized modern theology since Schleiermacher and much of modern evangelicalism since Finney. The biblical and theological basis for this "triniatarian-ecclesial" model for ministry will be set forth below.

Divine Presence and Human-Divine Partnership in Ministry[35]: Biblical & Theological Perspectives

The themes of the divine presence and divine-human partnership in ministry are significant themes in both the Old and New Testaments, and can be illustrated in the lives of Moses, Joshua, Jesus, and the Apostle Paul. Moses is called by God to ministry at the burning bush ("I am sending you," Exod 3:10), and at the same time, is promised that God will be with him as he fulfills his calling ("I will be with you," Exod 3:12). God will make the Egyptians favorably disposed (Exod 3:21), and will help Moses to speak (Exod

---

34. In my book *Worship and the Reality of God* I have argued for a recovery of the biblical truth that the God who is truly present among his gathered people is the central reality of Christian worship; in this chapter I am arguing, by extension, that it is the presence and action of God truly present that is the central reality of all authentic and fruitful ministry. Jerald C. Brauer, in his seminal essay, "Conversion," has argued that in the historical trajectory from Puritanism to Finney and modern revivalism, with its focus on conversion, there was an (unintended) shift of focus away from God as objectively present and acting toward the human subject and private religious experience.

35. The notion of "practicing ministry in the presence of God" is found in the book by Bruce G. and Katherine Epperly, *Tending to the Holy*, but their theological basis is quite different from the biblical and systematic theology of this essay: "Our own ministerial vision of reality has been influenced greatly by process theology, ancient and contemporary Christian mystical traditions, insights from contemporary physics and cosmology, Jungian psychology, and the practical wisdom of family and congregational systems theory": 11. The current chapter echoes and recalls, of course, the seventeenth-century devotional classic of Brother Lawrence, *The Practice of the Presence of God*, who saw all Christian life and service as being done with an awareness of the presence of God. This chapter is an attempt to generalize Brother Lawrence's insight for church ministry and to give it a more comprehensive biblical and systematic basis.

4:12). Aaron will be Moses's partner in speaking, and God promises to help both Moses and Aaron to speak and to teach them what to do (Exod 4:15). Moses will see what God himself will do to the Egyptians in the plagues and confrontation with Pharaoh (Exod 6:1); it is God, not Moses, who is the primary agent in the deliverance of the Israelites. God will pass through Egypt (Exod 12:12), will lead the Israelites toward the Red Sea (Exod 13:18), going ahead of them and guiding them (Exod 13:21), and it will be God himself, not merely Moses as the human servant, who will be actively fighting for them (Exod 14:14). The Lord himself is present in the pillar of cloud as the "commander-in-chief" of the people of God, and looks down as witness to the mighty deliverance at the Red Sea (Exod 14:24).

After the crossing of the Red Sea and during the wilderness sojourning the Israelites engage in battle with the Amalekites, with Joshua leading the battle, and Moses directing the battle from the top of a hill with the staff of God and Aaron and Hur holding up his hands (Exod 17:8-16). The incident provides a memorable image of "ministry in the presence of God and in partnership with God," since Joshua fights in the presence of God and with the empowerment of God, and Aaron and Hur partner with Moses as Moses intercedes for Joshua in the posture of prayer. Joshua, Moses, Aaron, and Hur are all "partners with God" in the victory over the Amalekites.

In Exodus 18 Jethro, the father-in-law of Moses, gives Moses the wise counsel that his ministry of leading the people and judging all their disputes will inevitably lead to "ministerial burnout," and that he needs to delegate and practice ministry in partnership with other gifted people in the community (Exod 18:21-24).

As the ark of the covenant, the tabernacle, and the consecration of the priests are being prepared, the promise of God's continuing presence as the central reality in the life of the community is again emphasized: "I will dwell among the Israelites and be their God. They will know that I am the Lord their God who brought them out of Egypt *so that I might dwell among them*" (Exod 29:45-46; emphasis added). As Moses and the people anticipate the continuing journey and the entrance into the promised land, God again promises, "My presence will go with you" (Exod 33:14). It is in fact the divine presence that distinguishes the people of Israel from all the other peoples on the face of the earth (Exod 33:16). Moses's ministry to the people is energized by the forty days and nights that he spends in the presence of God on top of Mount Sinai (Exod 34:28); he descends from the mountain with his face shining with the glory of God, a glory that foreshadows the transformative glory that is to be shared by all the future ministers of the New Covenant (2 Cor 3:18). The narrative suggests that all truly transformative ministry, done to the glory of God, first begins with a minister who spends time contemplatively in the presence of God and himself is being transformed by the divine glory.

The themes of the divine presence and partnership in ministry that are central in the Moses narrative are continued in the life of Joshua, Moses's successor. Joshua, who must have sensed a great sense of personal inadequacy to fill the shoes of his enormously gifted predecessor, is promised by God, "As I was with Moses, so I will be with you; I will never leave you or forsake you" (Josh 1:5). The promise and the reality of the continuing "real presence" of the Almighty is far more weighty than the human presence of Moses. God says to Joshua, "Do not be terrified; do not be discouraged, for the Lord your God will be with you wherever you go" (Josh 1:9). As the people are led across the Jordan River—recalling the action of God at the crossing of the Red Sea—the people are to recognize that "the living God is among you" (Josh 3:10), for it is God, the commander of the Israelite armies, enthroned on the ark of the covenant, who is causing the water to cease from flowing (Josh 3:15). In the conquest of Jericho, with the priests carrying the ark of God around the walls, it was in fact God himself present with the people (Josh 6:27) who caused the walls to tumble down and gave Joshua and the people victory. The fallen walls of Jericho were a vivid image of a divine-human partnership in achieving victory, with God as the primary agent, and the people as the secondary agents in partnership with the Lord.

In the New Testament Jesus can be seen as a "second Moses" and "second Joshua" who also exemplifies ministry in the presence of God and in partnership with God. Jesus never acts independently; he constantly and consistently acts in partnership with God his heavenly Father. "The Son can do nothing by himself; he can only do what he sees the Father doing, because whatever the Father does the Son also does" (John 5:19). Jesus does not seek to be "original" or "creative," but rather takes his cues from the Father's actions and presence in the world. "By myself I can do nothing; I judge only as I hear . . . I seek not to please myself but him who sent me" (John 5:30). Jesus tells his disciples that apart from him they can do nothing (John 15:5b) that will produce lasting fruit in the ministry; he himself practices what he preaches by listening to the Father before speaking to others. Jesus is consciously aware of the Father's presence in his own ministry and seeks to follow the Father's initiative: "I do nothing on my own but speak just what the Father has taught me. The one who sent me *is with me and has not left me alone* " (John 8:28-29; emphasis added).

The Gospel narratives, especially those of Luke and John, also make it clear that Jesus' ministry is done with an awareness of the presence and empowerment of the Holy Spirit.[36] As he is praying during the baptismal scene in the Jordan River (Luke 3:21)—prayer being an act of communion with the Father—the Spirit descends upon him, signifying the reality of the Father's love and the peace that characterizes the relationship between the Father and the Son. Jesus, full of the Holy Spirit (Luke 4:1), is led by the Spirit to be tested in the desert, and then returns to Galilee in the power of the Spirit (Luke 4:14) to begin his ministry. As he reads from the scroll of Isaiah (Isa 61:1–2) in the synagogue at Nazareth, his reading of Scripture is anointed by the Holy Spirit (Luke 4:18). When his disciples return from a preaching and healing mission, Jesus exults in praise to the Father, full of joy in the Holy Spirit (Luke 10:21). All of Jesus' ministry in fact flows from the reality that the Father has anointed the Son with power and the Holy Spirit (Acts 10:38).

Jesus goes to the cross in obedience to the Father, offering himself by the strength of the eternal Spirit (Heb 9:14), and is raised from the dead through the Holy Spirit, "the glory of the Father" (Rom 6:4). Exalted to the right hand of God, Jesus receives a fresh effusion of the Holy Spirit from the Father, and then shares this anointing with his disciples on earth, that they might be empowered to continue the ministry that Jesus began on earth (Acts 2:33). The implication of these texts is clear: the ministry of Jesus is trinitarian in nature, in that he, as the eternal Son of God, does ministry in partnership with and in the presence of God the Father and God the Holy Spirit. The ministry of Jesus is the action of the triune God in human history, and provides the paradigm for all ministry in the New Covenant.

Jesus, in commissioning his disciples for ministry, commands them to continue ministry in his own way of communion with God and in partnership with God. They are to abide in communion with him (John 15:5), for apart from this communion with him, mediated by the Holy Spirit, their ministry cannot bear lasting fruit. As Father sent Jesus into ministry by anointing him with the Spirit (Luke 3:21; 4:1, 14), so Jesus imparts the Holy Spirit to the disciples (John 20:21–22; Acts 2:4: "they were *all* filled with the Holy Spirit") before sending them out into the world to be his witnesses and to proclaim the message of forgiveness of sins. As the Father was present with Jesus his Son in ministry (John 8:28–29), Jesus promises that he will be with them as they seek to make disciples and to fulfill the Great Commission (Matt 28:20: "Surely I am *with you* always, to the very end of the age").

The ministry of the Apostle Paul, as it is reflected in his epistles and the book of Acts, gives clear evidence of a style of ministry that could be characterized as "ministry in the presence of God and in partnership with

---

36. An insightful study of the Holy Spirit in Luke-Acts is found in Stronstad, *The Charismatic Theology of St. Luke*, especially chapter 3, "The Holy Spirit in the Gospel of Luke: The Charismatic Christ," 33–48. See also Dunn, *Jesus and the Spirit*.

God"—and in partnership with other members of the body of Christ. Paul's sense of self-identity and his life and ministry are grounded foundationally in his union with Christ: "I have been crucified with Christ and I no longer live, but Christ lives in me. The life I live in the body, I live by faith in the Son of God, who loved me, and gave himself for me" (Gal 2:20). The old self, the old Saul of Tarsus is dead; the new Paul the apostle lives and ministers in union with and in partnership with Christ, who supplies the new life and energy and direction for ministry. Paul's sense of apostolic authority, his awareness that Christ is speaking through him (2 Cor 13:3), is grounded in this awareness of union with Christ. The word of the gospel that the Thessalonians received was not just Paul's human word, but indeed the Word of God spoken by God himself through Paul (1 Thess 2:13). He is conscious that the words that he is writing to the Corinthians are not merely his words; these words are the instruments of the risen Christ who gives his commands to the church through Paul (1 Cor 14:37, "what I am writing to you is the Lord's command").

The gifts of the Holy Spirit that are being manifested in the Corinthian congregation are in fact the actions of the triune God—Father, Son, and Holy Spirit—that are acting through the various members of the body for the good of the whole: "There are different kinds of gifts, but the same Spirit. There are different kinds of service [*diakonioon*, "ministries"], but the same Lord [Christ]. There are different kinds of working [*energeimatoon*, "operations"], but the same God [Father] works all of them in all men" (1 Cor 12:4–6).[37] The individual Christian in Corinth who is exercising a particular charism should be aware of the fact that he or she is actually acting *in partnership* with the Holy Spirit and is *participating* in the action and ministry of the three persons of the Trinity as *they* act in partnership for the purpose of building up the whole body.[38]

The reality of Paul's ministry as one done in the presence of God and in partnership with God is attested in the book of Acts. Paul and Barnabas are in the presence of God, worshiping with the community in Antioch, when the Holy Spirit, present to the assembly, says, "Set apart for *me* Barnabas

---

37. According to Thiselton, the "trinitarian ground plan constitutes an outstanding feature of 12:4–6": *The First Epistle to the Corinthians*, 934. Further: "On the basis of this passage (12:4–6) Athanasius draws out the profound truth that all persons of the Holy Trinity participate in a unified activity which may be thought of as the action of the whole Godhead as Trinity [*Epistle to Serapion*, 1:3]": 934–35.

38. To state the same point in a slightly different way, the one who is exercising a particular charism should see the triune God as the primary active agent in the manifestation and exercise of the gift, and himself or herself as the secondary agent or instrument. See the sentiments of John the Baptist: "He must increase, and I must decrease" (John 3:30).

and Saul for the work to which *I* have called them" (Acts 13:2). The Holy Spirit, a coequal person of the Trinity, is the primary agent in the calling and commissioning of those who are to be the agents of the Spirit in the mission to the Gentiles. Barnabas and his companions are "sent on their way by the Holy Spirit" (Act 13:4), as Jesus had been sent by the Spirit into the desert (Luke 4:1) and empowered by the Spirit for ministry in Galilee (Luke 4:14). When Paul and Barnabas return to Jerusalem, the church meeting in council is aware that its deliberations are done in the presence of the Spirit ("it seemed good to the Holy Spirit and to us," Acts 15:28).

In the second missionary journey, the Holy Spirit deflects Paul and Silas from preaching in the provinces of Asia and Bithynia (Acts 16:6–7), calling them, through a vision, to preach the gospel in Macedonia (Acts 16:8–10). Upon arriving in Philippi, the risen Christ, and the Holy Spirit who is accompanying Paul and his companions, open Lydia's heart to respond to the message ("The Lord opened her heart to respond to Paul's message," Acts 16:14). Lydia's conversion is a result of the divine agency of Christ and the Spirit working through the human agency of Paul. When Paul arrives in Corinth, the risen Christ speaks to Paul in a vision, and encourages him to continue speaking, because "*I am with you* and *I* have many people in this city*,*" Acts 18:9–10). Christ is present with Paul as he preaches and teaches in Corinth.

After his arrest and during his defense before King Agrippa (Acts 26) Paul, in recounting his conversion experience and the essentials of the gospel kerygma, states that in fulfillment of the Scriptures the Messiah would suffer, and "as the first to rise from the dead, *would proclaim light to his own people and to the Gentiles*" (Acts 26:23). Paul is saying here that the risen Christ continues to act in redemptive history as the gospel is proclaimed; Christ's priestly work of atonement is finished, but his kerygmatic ministry continues as he continues to preach through his chosen apostles, empowered by the Holy Spirit. Paul is a "junior partner" in the Gentile mission; the risen Christ and the Holy Spirit are the "senior partners," so to speak.

Not only is it the case that the Apostle Paul works in partnership with Christ and the Spirit; his ministry is notably one of partnership with various members of the body of Christ. A striking example is provided by the term *synergos*, "fellow-worker," characteristic of Paul.[39] This appellation

---

39. Of the thirteen instances of *synergos* in the New Testament, twelve are found in Paul (Rom 16:3, of Priscilla and Aquila; Rom 16:9, of Urbanus; Rom 16:21, of Timothy; 1 Cor 3:9, of Apollos; 2 Cor 1:24, of the Corinthians; 2 Cor 8:23, of Titus; Phil 2:25, of Epaphroditus; Phil 4:3, of Clement and others; Col 4:11, of Aristarchus, Mark, and Jesus Justus; 1 Thess 3:2, of Timothy; Philemon 1, of Philemon; Philemon 24, of Mark, Aristarchus, Demas, and Luke).

is applied to Priscilla and Aquila, Urbanus, Timothy, Titus, Epaphroditus, Clement, Aristarchus, Mark, Jesus Justus, Demas, Luke, and others not explicitly named.[40] Terms such as "fellow-partner" (Phil 1:7, of the Philippians), "fellow-slaves" (Col 1:7; 4:7, of Epaphroditus and Tychicus), "fellow-soldier" (Phil 2:25; Philemon 2, of Epaphroditus and Archippus), and "fellow-prisoner" (Col 4:10, Aristarchus, and Philemon 23, Epaphras) also express Paul's sense of solidarity with his fellow Christians in the ministry of the gospel. Paul's sense of working in partnership with Christ and the Spirit and with his fellow believers arises naturally out of his sense of the reality of his union with Christ and solidarity with the body of Christ; his actions in ministry were a manifestation of his deepest dogmatic and doctrinal convictions.

Systematic Foundations for Ministry in Partnership: Trinity, Union with Christ, Body of Christ

Having in the previous section surveyed the biblical themes of divine presence and divine-human partnership in ministry, we will now turn to reflection on three fundamental topics in systematic theology—the doctrine of the Trinity, union with Christ (Christology), and the body of Christ (ecclesiology)—with a view toward showing how they are foundational for the theology and practices of ministry. Every set of practices, whether in art, music, politics, scientific research, professional sports, or church ministry—presupposes some theory, some general account of reality, of "how the world is and how the world operates" as its background and basis. Any set of practices not in alignment with what is "fundamentally real" will not in the long run be fruitful or successful. Here it is being proposed that the doctrines of the Trinity, union with Christ, and the ecclesiological notion of the church as the body of Christ should be at the core of a biblical theology of ministry.

At the outset we can notice the fundamental nature of the doctrines of the Trinity and of Christology (of which union with Christ is an implication) in the fabric of the Christian faith.[41] The doctrine of the Trinity is the

---

40. For additional discussion of the *syn-* terminology in Paul, see Glover, *Paul of Tarsus*, 178–80; Bruce, *The Pauline Circle*, 81–90; and Banks, "Paul's Co-Workers" in *Paul's Idea of Community*, 152–60. Banks observes that Paul's practice of ministry was notable for including both Jews and Gentiles, and for the prominent place of women as his co-workers (160). See also Ellis, "Paul and His Co-Workers," in *Prophecy and Hermeneutic in Early Christianity*, 3–22. Ellis observes that "Paul is scarcely ever found without companions": ibid., 5.

41. It is sometimes said that the doctrines of the Trinity and of Christology are the two great "mysteries" and defining distinctives of the Christian faith: the Trinity being

basis of the distinctively *Christian* answer to the question, "Who is God?," and the doctrine of Christology gives the distinctively Christian answer to the questions, "Who is Jesus Christ?" and "How does God save?" A foundationally *Christian* understanding of the nature and practices of church ministry would, consequently, be explicitly and self-consciously formulated with these foundational truths in view.

We turn first to reflection on the doctrine of the Trinity and its implications for pastoral theology and practice. In the last several generations there has been a remarkable renaissance of interest in trinitarian theology, reflecting the influence of Karl Barth in Protestant theological circles and of Karl Rahner in the Roman Catholic world.[42] This growing recognition of the centrality of trinitarian theology for all Christian faith and life has yet to be adequately integrated into pastoral theologies and practices of ministry.

The proposition being argued in this section of the essay in regard to the doctrine of the Trinity is as follows:

> *Christian ministry is done in the presence of the triune God and in partnership with the triune God, Father, Son, and Holy Spirit— with the triune God being recognized as the primary, active agent in every ministerial act.*

This proposition further implies that the doctrine of the Trinity provides the irreducible and essential foundation for a proper New Testament understanding of ministry at three basic levels of theory and practice: the ontological, the methodological, and the teleological (purposive). That is to say, the doctrine of the Trinity is recognized as the ultimate Christian reality (divine persons in communion) and hence, the ultimate grounding of the Christian faith, the Christian church, and Christian ministry. Methodologically, the trinitarian pattern of Father, Son, and Holy Spirit acting in concert and collaboration provides the methodological paradigm and model for all Christian ministry. Teleologically, bringing persons into ever-deepening communion with God the Father, through Jesus Christ the Son,

---

the "necessary" mystery of faith (God is necessarily and eternally and coequally one God in three persons, Father, Son, and Holy Spirit), and Christology (the incarnation, death, and resurrection of Jesus Christ; union with Christ) being the "free" mystery (the incarnation not being a necessary act but a free, gracious act of God for the salvation of God's people).

42. For a review of recent scholarship in trinitarian theology, see F. Sanders, "The Trinity." Significant recent contributions in this area include LaCugna, *God For Us*; Moltmann, *The Trinity and the Kingdom*; Boff, *Trinity and Society*; T. Torrance, *The Christian Doctrine of God*; and Zizioulas, *Being as Communion* and *Communion and Otherness*.

in the communion of the Holy Spirit, is recognized as the ultimate purpose and goal of all church ministry (worship, discipleship, mission).

In the previous section reviewing biblical theology the reality of doing ministry in the presence of God has already been noted. The disciples sent out by Jesus the risen Son to disciple the nations are to do so with a consciousness that they do so in the accompanying presence of Christ (Matt 28:20); Christ is truly present wherever two or three of his disciples gather in conscious intent to invoke his name (Matt 18:20). Repentance and forgiveness of sins in the name of Jesus is to be proclaimed in the power and in the presence of the Holy Spirit (John 20:21-22). Since Jesus is in the Father and the Father in Jesus (John 17:21; see John 14:9, "He who has seen me has seen the Father"),[43] where Jesus is, by virtue of the Spirit, his name, and his word, so there the Father is also. All three persons of the Trinity—the Spirit (John 14:16) and the Father and the Son abide with the church forever (John 14:23) and are present with the church in its worship and ministry.

New Testament ministry is performed in partnership with God as the Father's will is done on earth (Matt 6:10). The Apostle Paul is conscious of the fact that he "partners" with the risen Christ in ministry who proclaims light to the Gentiles through his missionary preaching (Acts 26:23), and that the life he now lives he lives in union with the Christ who lives in him (Gal 2:20). The Pauline Gentile mission is characterized by partnership with the Holy Spirit who calls (Acts 13:2), sends (Acts 13:4), counsels (Acts 15:28), directs (Acts 16:6-7), and illuminates the gospel message to effect conversion (Acts 16:14).

This human partnership *with* the triune God, Father, Son, and Holy Spirit is a reflection of the partnership in ministry *of* the triune God and a participation in it. We have previously noted a text such as 1 Cor 12:4-6, where the cooperative, coactive ministry of Father, Son, and Spirit (different gifts, but the same Spirit; different service, but the same Lord; different operations, but the same God) is seen. Likewise, we have noted texts such as John 5:19 and John 8:28-29 that witness to Jesus' cooperation and partnership with the Father in ministry.

These texts and others like them are examples of the trinitarian principles articulated in various ways by the church fathers: *Opera Trinitatis ad extra sunt indivisa*—that is, "The works of the Trinity in the world are indivisible." Father, Son, and Holy Spirit work not independently of one another, but always work in partnership and collaboration. As St. Athanasius stated,

---

43. The mutual indwelling and interpenetration of the persons of the Father, Son, and Holy Spirit is known as *perichoresis* in the theological tradition: see Boff, *Trinity and Society*, 140 and 146, and T. Torrance, *The Christian Doctrine of God*, 179-202, for discussion of this important concept in trinitarian theology.

"The Father does all things through the Word in the Holy Spirit; and thus the unity of the Holy Trinity is preserved."[44] This model of the partnership and collaboration of Father, Son, and Holy Spirit in ministry provides the foundational model for effective ministry in and by the church.

The category of *union with Christ* is another central concept for the trinitarian-ecclesial model of ministry being argued in this essay, and as a fundamental basis for the pastor's self identity. Union with Christ, referring to the intimate, personal bond between the believer and the risen Christ,[45] mediated by the Holy Spirit, is prominent in New Testament theology, especially in the Pauline and Johannine writings. Jesus tells his disciples that he is the vine and they are the branches, drawing their life fruitfulness from him (John 15:5). As Jesus is in the Father, so is Jesus in the disciples and they in him (John 14:20); the Father and the Son will come to the believers and make their home with them (John 14:23). Jesus will continue to make the Father's love known to the disciples in order that the Father's love might be deepened in them and that Jesus himself may dwell more deeply within them (John 17:26).

Union with Christ is a central category in Pauline theology, frequently signified by the terminology of "with" or "in" Christ.[46] For Paul, Christian baptism is baptism into the death of Christ (Rom 6:3); the old self or identity was crucified with him (Rom 6:6). We died with Christ and were buried with him (Rom 6:4, 8). Paul has been crucified with Christ, and the life he now lives he lives by faith in the Son of God and in living union with him (Gal 2:20). Anyone who is in Christ is a new creature (2 Cor 5:17). We were all baptized by the Spirit into one body of which the risen Christ is the living head (1 Cor

---

44. Athanasius, *Ad Serapion*, I, 28; see Augustine, *On the Trinity*, IV, 21: "the Father, Son, and Holy Spirit, of one and the same substance, God the Creator, the Omnipotent Trinity, work indivisibly"; see Basil the Great, *On the Holy Spirit*, 16, 38 ("the cause of existing things is One, creating through the Son and perfecting through the Holy Spirit"); Gregory of Nyssa, *To Ablabius: There Are Not Three Gods* ("Every divine operation touching on creation . . . has its origin from the Father, proceeds through the Son, and is perfected in the Holy Spirit"). The latter citation is found in Jurgens, *The Faith of the Early Fathers*, vol. 1, 50.

45. The Christian concept of union with Christ or mystical union does not involve the destruction of human individuality, but its transformation and renewal in the context of a new relationship lived in interdependence with Christ; union with Christ is not the end of *individuality* per se, but rather the end of an atomistic and autonomous individuality. By way of contrast, in the Advaitavedanta (non-dual) tradition of Hinduism, in which "Atman ('soul, self') = Brahman," the self, upon achieving *moksha*, or liberation, is dissolved in the ultimate reality, the impersonal Brahman, as a drop of ink would be dissolved in the ocean. See Klostermaier, *A Survey of Hinduism*, 204-11.

46. For a helpful survey of the history of modern New Testament scholarship on the Pauline notions of "in Christ" and union with Christ, see Barclay, *Christ in You*, 5-19.

12:13). Christian marriage is a spiritual image of the intimate union between Christ and his bride, the church (Eph 5:25–32). God has raised us up with Christ and seated us with him in the heavenly realms (Eph 2:6).

Just as a man who unites himself to a prostitute is one with her in body (*hen soma estin*), so the one who unites himself with Christ the Lord is one with him in spirit (*hen pneuma estin*) (1 Cor 6:17).[47] Just as union with a prostitute involves body-to-body contact between a man and the prostitute, so union with Christ involves a real spirit-to-spirit contact between Christ and the believer.[48] As the New Testament scholar Alfred Wikenhauser has rightly insisted, this Pauline and Johannine language of union with Christ is not to be taken as only "metaphorical" or as only a figure of speech, but with its real ontological force, as a "real, objective state" that is "true of all [Christians] without exception."[49]

Despite the prominence of union with Christ in the New Testament and in the histories of both Catholic and Protestant theology,[50] this key concept has, for the most part, not been sufficiently integrated into modern theologies of ministry.[51] Part of the problem may be that modern New Testament scholars and theologians, influenced by the materialistic and naturalistic categories of the Enlightenment and modern science, find it difficult to relate the "mystical" dimensions of union with Christ to the categories of modern life. A case in point is provided by E. P. Sanders, who recognizes the centrality of union with Christ in Paul, yet has difficulty in conceptualizing it:

---

47. Montague, commenting on this text (1 Cor 6:17), has observed that "Christian life is a union with the Lord so real that Paul can use the very same verb (*kollomenos*) for union with the prostitute and union with the Lord": McDonnell and Montague, *Christian Initiation and Baptism in the Holy Spirit*, 45.

48. A very rough analogy of this union indicated in 1 Corinthians 6:17 may be provided by the illustration of a light bulb screwed into the socket of a table lamp: there is real (physical) contact between the light bulb and the lamp and the socket, as a result of which electricity (see the Spirit) can flow from the lamp (see the Father) through the socket (see the Son) into the light bulb (see the believer, the church) into the surrounding room (the world).

49. Wikenhauser, *Pauline Mysticism*, 93. Other studies of this topic that could be mentioned include: Smedes, *All Things Made New*; Billings, *Calvin, Participation, and the Gift*; and Tannehill, *Dying and Rising with Christ*. In modern scholarship on this topic, the work of Wikenhauser provides the most incisive discussion and recognition of the clearly *ontological* dimensions of the apostle's thought.

50. For a survey of union with Christ and mystical union in church history, see Dupre, "The Christian Experience of Mystical Union"; for union with Christ in the Reformed tradition, see Horton, "Mystical Union in Reformed Soteriology," in *Covenant and Salvation*, 129–52.

51. Purves, *Reconstructing Pastoral Theology*, is a notable exception in this regard.

It seems to me best to understand Paul as saying what he meant and meaning what he said: Christians really are one body and Spirit with Christ, the form of the present really is passing away, Christians really are being changed from one stage of glory to another, the end really will come and those who are in Christ will really be transformed.

But then Sanders goes on to ask:

But what does this mean? How are we to understand it? We seem to lack a concept of "reality"—a real participation in Christ, real possession of the Spirit—which lies between naïve cosmological speculation and belief in magical transference on the one hand [e.g., Gnosticism or Hellenistic mystery religions: JD] and a revised self-understanding [e.g., Bultmann: JD] on the other. *I confess that I do not have a new category of perception to propose here.*[52]

In order to meet this difficulty in relating the biblical concept of union with Christ to the categories of post-Enlightenment modern thought, we introduce at this point the concepts of the *extended Self* and of a *coupled system*, adapting these concepts from ideas articulated in the article by Clark and Chalmers previously cited, "The Extended Mind."

The notion of an "extended Self" is based on the observation that a personal agent can extend himself or herself into the surrounding environment, beyond the bounds of the agent's physical body (the "empirical Self") through the use of an instrument or tool under the agent's control. The instrument in question can be either physical or electronic in nature. For example, a blind person can extend his sense of touch into the environment through the use of a cane held in his hand; the cane becomes an extension of his body. The blind person and the cane under his control form a "coupled system."

A coupled system and an extended Self may also be formed through an electronic instrument such as Skype software and an Internet connection. If I am communicating with my daughter in California with a Skype connection, my daughter and her Skype icon that appears on my laptop screen form a coupled system; her empirical/molecular self is extended into my physical location, and my physical presence is extended electronically into her physical space by the Skype software and Internet connection. Our Skype icons are instruments of our extended Selves. My icon is "in" her laptop screen and her icon is "in" mine. The connection is a real one because the

---

52. Sanders, *Paul and Palestinian Judaism*, 520, 522–23, cited by Ashton, *The Religion of Paul the Apostle*, 150.

Internet connection is real and the Skype icon and software are real.[53] The "mutual indwelling" ("perichoresis") of Skype icons in a coupled Internet system reminds us that a *molecular* form of presence can be distinguished from a *digital* or *informational* form of presence. Two molecular objects—such as two bowling balls—cannot be "in" the same space, but various forms of digital information can be "in" the same computer hard drive, or in the same wireless Internet broadcast space at the same time:[54] a Google home page, the data available in Facebook or YouTube or Twitter or Wikipedia can all be in the "cloud" in the room around me, simultaneously, available to me if I have the proper receiving device.

To complete this implied analogy between the digital and the spiritual worlds, we can say that in union with Christ, Christ and the believer are a "coupled system"; the Holy Spirit is the real, continuous, "high-speed, broadband 'Internet' connection" between heaven and earth, between Christ and the believer.[55] "If anyone is joined to the Lord, he is one spirit with him" (1 Cor 6:17). We are more deeply and really connected to Christ by the Holy Spirit than we are connected electronically on Facebook to our Facebook "friends." Indeed, what a "friend" we really have in Jesus!

The Holy Spirit extends my empirical/molecular self into the presence of the risen Christ; we are seated with him (by extension) in the heavenly places (Eph 2:6). The Spirit extends the presence of the risen Christ into my space/soul: we are truly connected in a "digital"/spiritual connection and embrace. The risen Christ uses a variety of instruments—his word in the Scriptures, his name[56] (see 1 Cor 5:4: "when you come together in the name

---

53. Material objects are only one form of the "real"; reality also includes entities that are virtual/electronic/digital in nature, and ones that are *spiritual* in nature as well (e.g., God, angels, demons).

54. Here a distinction can be drawn between the *circumscriptive* location of a molecular object and the *repletive* locations of digital or informational entities that subsist in electronic form. My cat George is circumscribed by his carrying cage when I take him to the veterinarian; if he is in the box, he cannot be outside the box at the same time. On the other hand, the home page of Google can be located on my laptop, but is not thereby limited to that location: the Google home page and the information that it represents can be simultaneously widely distributed (repletively) in multiple locations in cyberspace.

55. It should be clearly kept in mind that this Internet analogy is *only* an analogy, not a complete exposition of the doctrine of the Holy Spirit. All analogies of the Trinity or the Holy Spirit are by their very nature partial and limited. Presupposed in this article is the historic, orthodox understanding of the Holy Spirit as a coeternal and coequal member of the Trinity, fully God and fully personal.

56. On the biblical theology of the name of God as an extension of God's self and means of his presence, see Bietenhard, "Name," 648–646; "The fullness of Christ's saving work is contained in his name (as Yahweh's saving work was in his) and is *present in*

of Jesus and the power of the Lord is present"), the sacraments, and his called and gifted disciples to extend himself from heaven to earth; by these instruments, and by the energizing connectivity of the Holy Spirit, the risen Christ is in us (John 14:20) and among us (Matt 18:20) and with us (Matt 28:20). Because I am in union with Christ the Son, I am also in living communion with God the Father and God the Holy Spirit, for the three persons of the Trinity indwell one another, and indwell in us.

Union with Christ is also the basis of the category of the *body of Christ* that is so significant for biblical ecclesiology.[57] Because we are really united to Christ as the head, we are also really united to one another as the living members of his body."By one Spirit we have all been baptized into one Body" (1 Cor 12:13). Union with Christ, then, is the core of our new trinitarian-ecclesial identity as Christians and pastors: I *really am* in communion with God the Father, Son, and Holy Spirit; and I *really am* in communion with my brothers and sisters in the Body of Christ: this is who I *really am,* and I need to constantly recognize this "new creation" identity, and act accordingly.

The old autonomous, independent Self is gone; the new *interdependent*, trinitarian-ecclesial Self has arrived. Our ministry is to flow from the presence of God and to be done in partnership with God and the people of God, because this is the true account of the ways things really are and of who we really are. My self-concept and actions need to be in alignment with the fundamental being of God, Christ, the Spirit, the church, and my deep, continuing bonds with these interconnected and interdependent persons, human and divine.

Presence and Partnership: Some Practical Suggestions and Concluding Remarks

This essay began by stating the following general proposition: *Christian ministry is activity by baptized Christians done in the presence of God and in*

---

the church" (emphasis added), 655.

57. Significant biblical-theological studies of this theme are found in Best, *One Body in Christ*; Robinson, *The Body*; Schnackenburg, *The Church in the New Testament*; Minear, *Images of the Church in the New Testament*; Cerfaux, *The Church in the Theology of St. Paul*; and Mascall, *Christ, the Christian and the Church*. Mascall emphasizes the ontological reality of the body of Christ: "if we are each of us really and not merely by imputation united to Christ, we are by that very fact united to one another. If our adoption into Christ's sonship is ontological [JD: by virtue of the indwelling Spirit: Rom 8:16; Gal 4:6] and not merely legal, so is our brotherhood with one another": ibid., 109–10.

partnership with God, for the purpose of bringing the people of God into deepening communion with God and with one another, and into right relationship with God's creation. It was argued that this awareness of doing ministry in the presence of God and in partnership with God had its fundamental grounding in the doctrines of the Trinity and of union with Christ.

To conclude this essay, I will offer a number of practical observations and suggestions as to how these theological insights could be translated into the specific tasks of ministry: 1) a suggestion regarding the "reframing" of the "Great Commission" (Matt 28:19-20); 2) two anecdotes and illustrations on partnership and divine presence from church history; 3) three "linking" concepts from the first chapter of the book of Acts; and 4) four benefits that can accrue to pastors who implement these suggestions and theological insights.

The first suggestion regards a "reframing" of the way in which the "Great Commission" (Matt 28:18-20) is generally read in the evangelical community. Since the publication in 1792 of William Carey's seminal essay, *An Enquiry into the Obligation of Christians to Use Means for the Conversion of the Heathen*, the "Great Commission" has generally been read through the lens of *foreign missions*.[58] The command in v. 19 to "go and make disciples of all nations" has been understood in terms of crossing national boundaries for the purpose of evangelizing and planting new churches. This is indeed a proper implication from the text, but as various commentators have pointed out, the main verb in the text is *make disciples* (*matheteusate*), and "going . . . baptizing . . . teaching" are all dependent participles.[59]

The proposal here is to read the "Great Commission" in a new way: while not ignoring the missiological and "boundary-crossing" implications of the text, the Great Commission should be seen as a mandate for how *ministry*—especially discipleship, viewed as a lifelong task—should be done in the context of the *local church*. The focus should be on *making disciples*—not on making "converts" or on "going"—and the *risen Christ present in the church* ("I am *with you* always to the end of the age," v. 20) should be recognized as the primary, active agent in the ministry of discipleship, in

---

58. On the history of the interpretation of the Great Commission, see J. J. Davis, "Teaching Them to Observe All That I Have Commanded You." From the fourth century until the time of William Carey the missiological implications of the text were largely forgotten, it being widely believed that the commission had essentially been fulfilled by the apostles in bringing the gospel to the Roman empire; commentators during the "Christendom" period generally focused on issues of baptism and the trinitarian formula for baptism.

59. For an excellent exegetical study of the Great Commission, and the command to "make disciples," see Bosch, "The Structure of Mission," especially 230-33, "Making Disciples."

partnership with whom pastors and laity in the local church are working as a team in partnership with Christ and with one another. The primary agency of Christ is emphatically asserted in the declarative statement, "All authority in heaven and earth has been given to *me*" (v. 18)—not to human agents; the authority and efficacy of the ministry of human agents is derived from the risen Christ who is the primary agent and who is really present with and partnering with the church in its ministries, both locally and globally. The paradigm shift that is needed is a shift from a primary focus on "going" and *foreign* mission to a recognition of the real presence of Christ the Almighty Lord in the midst of the community as it ministers to make disciples.[60] Every particular act of ministry—whether preaching a sermon, leading worship, teaching a Bible or membership class, leading a youth group, doing pastoral counseling, or leading a church committee meeting[61]—should be done with the consciousness that *Christ is present with us* as the primary agent of ministry, and that he is the one who really "makes it happen."

Second, by way of illustration of the principles of ministry done in the presence of God and in partnership with God, I mention two examples from church history, one from the ministry of Calvin, and the other from the ministry of Spurgeon. When Charles Haddon Spurgeon ascended the stairs of the pulpit to preach in the Metropolitan Tabernacle in London, he would say to himself, repeatedly, "I believe in the Holy Spirit . . . I believe in the Holy Spirit . . . I believe in the Holy Spirit."[62] Spurgeon was not doing this to allay any doubts in his mind concerning the doctrines of the Holy Spirit or the Trinity; he was rather, in his personal confession and prayer prior to preaching, recognizing that the Holy Spirit was indeed the primary agent in making the sermon fruitful and effective in the lives of his hearers, and that he, Spurgeon, was merely the secondary human agent and messenger. Spurgeon was partnering with the Holy Spirit and invoking the presence of the Spirit for his preaching.[63]

---

60. This "reframing" of the Great Commission is consistent with the modern recognition in missiological circles that the foundation of the church's mission is the *missio Dei*, the "mission of God"—God the Father sending the Son into the world in the power of the Spirit—the church being called and empowered to participate in God's continuing mission to the world: see Bosch, *Transforming Mission*: "The recognition that mission is God's mission represents a crucial breakthrough in respect of the preceding centuries. . . . It is inconceivable that we could again revert to a narrow, ecclesiocentric view of mission," 393.

61. Chapter 12 in this volume, "How To Get More Out of Committee Meetings in Your Church," applies some of the principles of practicing ministry in the presence of God and in partnership with God and God's people.

62. Cited in Wilson, "The Sacred Script in the Theater of God."

63. In a similar spirit, today's preacher could use a simple prayer of intention such

John Calvin urged the ministers in Geneva to work in partnership, meeting weekly to study and discuss the Scriptures. In his *Draft Ecclesiastical Ordinances* of 1551 he stated, "First it will be expedient that all ministers, for conserving purity and concord of doctrine among themselves, meet together one certain day each week, for discussion of the scriptures; and none are to be exempt from this without legitimate excuse."[64] Calvin did not want his fellow pastors in Geneva to operate as "Lone Rangers." Today, in a multiple-staff church setting, the pastoral staff would do well to discuss the weekly sermon text and topic among themselves, sharing exegetical insights and points of practical application.

Third, I mention three "bridging concepts" from the first chapter of the book of Acts that can help to link the principles of divine presence and divine-human partnership to the specific functions of ministry. These three bridging concepts are 1) the principle of the "ordinary supernatural" (Acts 1:2; 2); the principle of "doing church in the second-person plural" (Acts 1:4–5,8); and 3) the principle of "spiritual alignment" (Acts 1:14). Luke states that during the forty-day period between the resurrection and the ascension, Jesus spoke to the disciples about the kingdom of God (1:3) and gave instructions "through the Holy Spirit" (1:2). Jesus' teaching ministry was "through the Holy Spirit": even before Pentecost, the Spirit that had anointed him and empowered him throughout his ministry (Acts 10:38, "God anointed Jesus of Nazareth with the Holy Spirit and with power") continued to be present with him.

The presence of the Spirit in this teaching by Jesus (Acts 1:2) was not accompanied by any extraordinary manifestations (e.g., tongues, prophecies, miracles), but the Holy Spirit made the teaching effective and fruitful. Ministry involves both the "natural" (e.g., turning on the lights when entering the pastor's study), and at times, can involve the "extraordinary supernatural"

---

as "In your presence, Lord; come, Holy Spirit," during the preparation of the sermon, prior to its delivery, and even after the sermon is preached—asking the Spirit to "water" the seed of the Word (see Isa 55:10–11), that in due time, it might germinate and be fruitful. See also Butin, "Preaching as a Trinitarian Event," where he cites the statement of Calvin [*Institutes* 4.1.5] that in the act of preaching, "*God himself appears in our midst* [emphasis added]. . . . He deigns to consecrate to himself the mouths and tongues of men in order that his voice may resound in them": 205. Butin documents the widely received understanding in the Reformed tradition that biblical preaching is the action of God. In my book *Worship and the Reality of God,* I have argued, consistent with this Reformed perspective, that God is really present not only during the act of preaching, but also during the *entire* worship service as the principal agent of ministry. The preacher, in the act of preaching, is *in union with Christ* and *in communion with the Spirit*, and both Christ the Word and the Spirit who illuminates are themselves acting through the preacher as their human agent.

64. In J. K. Reid, *Calvin,* 60. See also Small, "A Company of Pastors."

(e.g., praying for the healing of end-stage cancer—and the person being dramatically healed), but most ministry is done in the "natural" and in the "ordinary supernatural"[65]—and it is this latter category that is likely to be missed. The point is that the Holy Spirit is present even when there are no visible signs (tongues of fire; a heavenly dove; miracles) or dramatic manifestations; by the "ordinary supernatural" ministry can always be done with a consciousness of the presence and partnership of the Holy Spirit.

Luke's account of the period leading up to Pentecost also embodies the principle of "doing church in the second-person plural." Jesus gave *them* this command: "Do not leave (2p.pl) Jerusalem, but you (2p.pl) wait for the gift... you (2p.pl) will be baptized with the Holy Spirit... you (2p.pl) will receive power... you (2p.pl) will be my witnesses" (Acts 1:4,5,8). All too often, the words of Acts 1 are read as promises and commands to *me*, as though Jesus was primarily concerned about giving me gifts as an individual; the point is that the text is directed to "all of you"; it is about "we," not "me," because the purpose of Jesus is to build a church, a body, and a team."Doing church in the second-person plural" is consistent with the theme of doing ministry in partnership with God and with the people of God.

In Acts 1:14 we find the crucial ministry principle of *spiritual alignment*: "They all joined together constantly in prayer." Luke uses the relatively rare word *homothumadon* (see also Acts 2:46 and 4:24), "of one mind," to describe the mind-set of the disciples, achieved through persistent, united prayer, that prepared these disciples to receive the Spirit and be empowered for ministry—in a way that *united* the community rather than dividing it. The term *homothumadon*, "of one mind," signifies a "togetherness" that means not merely being in the same place physically or geographically, but, as we would say, "being on the same page," having a common focus of attention and shared purpose. The connection between Acts 1:14 ("they were all together... praying") and Acts 2:4 ("they *all* were filled") and Acts 2:41 ("about 3000 were added") is not accidental. The sequence for effective

---

65. In regard to what is here termed the "ordinary supernatural" ministry of the Holy Spirit, Wynne notes that in both Luke and Paul, the action of the Holy Spirit is seen not only in the more dramatic manifestations such as tongues, prophecy, miracles, and exorcism, but also in the "non-ecstatic" manifestations of ethical growth, maturity of character, administration, and practical service: *Holy Spirit and Religious Experience in Christian Literature ca. AD 90-200*, 14–15. In the Gospel and epistles of John there is a "quieter and gentler" ministry of the Holy Spirit, associated with knowledge of the truth (John 16:13), the forgiveness of sins (John 20:22–23) and the conviction of the world of sin (John 16:8), and the discernment of true and false teaching (1 John 2:20). And as McDonnell and Montague have noted, in John's gospel there are no exorcisms, and the word *pneuma* is not associated with any of Jesus' miracles: *Christian Initiation and Baptism in the Holy Spirit*, 57.

ministry indicated in these seminal texts is clear: first, *alignment* (listening for God's voice in united prayer; aligning our wills to God's will; agreeing together to obey God's will); second, receiving *empowerment* for ministry through the presence of the Holy Spirit to the community (Acts 2:4); third, *active ministry* and witness in partnership with God and the church (Peter stood up *with the eleven* [Acts 2:14] . . . and 3000 were added [Acts 2:41]).

The principle of spiritual alignment is so powerful because it is, in effect, an answer to Jesus' high priestly prayer (John 17) that his disciples manifest unity, a unity that in itself gives credibility to the claim that Jesus was indeed sent by the Father and that the Father indeed loves the church as he has loved his Son (John 17:23). Jesus himself practiced the principle of spiritual alignment, aligning his will with that of the Father before he spoke or acted (John 5:19; 8:26, 28-29; 14:10, 31). Because Jesus' will as the Son is in alignment with the will of the Father, the Spirit can flow freely through him and from him in ministry to the world. A church "in alignment" (Acts 1:14) is effective in ministry, because this alignment is a reflection of the life of the triune God,[66] acting in unity and partnership.

Fourthly, and finally, I will mention four benefits that can result from a practice of ministry reflecting a consciousness of the presence of God and partnership with God, grounded in the doctrines of the Trinity, union with Christ, and the body of Christ. The first benefit is that such a practice of ministry can lessen the danger of ministerial *burnout* that seems endemic to so much ministry in the modern church. The trinitarian-ecclesial model of ministry being proposed here encourages a slower, more contemplative approach to ministry, one that recognizes that before the outward act, the pastor should be grounded internally, prayerfully and contemplatively, in the experience of the love of God known through union with Christ, and then empowered to execute that ministry outwardly in partnership with other gifted members of the body of Christ.[67]

Avoiding ministerial "burnout" is also, in effect, a matter of rooting out three "heresies" of ministry: Deism, Pelagianism, and individualism.[68]

---

66. Recall again the patristic saying, *Opera Trinitatis ad extra sunt indivisa*: "The works of the Trinity in the world are indivisible."

67. The excellent book by Scazzero, *Emotionally Healthy Spirituality*, skillfully blending biblical theology, insights from psychology, and his own pastoral experience—and struggles with burnout—calls for just such a more contemplative approach to ministry.

68. The notion of these three in-practice "heresies" of ministry is drawn from Torrance, *Worship, Community and The Triune God of Grace*, especially 19-41, "Worship—Unitarian or Trinitarian?" "What is needed today is a better understanding of the person not just as an individual but as someone who finds his or her true being in communion with God and others, the counterpart of a trinitarian doctrine of God":

Deism signifies the working assumption that "God is really far away" when I am preaching and ministering. Pelagianism is the working assumption that "I can do this ministry in my own human power and ability." Individualism is the "heresy" that "I can do this ministry myself." All three heresies are a sure recipe for ministerial burnout, and all three heresies can be rooted out by a theory and practice of ministry done consciously in the presence of God and in partnership with God and God's gifted people.

This essay has been an attempt to continue, from the vantage point of a systematic theologian, a conversation on the nature of ministry initiated from the perspective of pastoral theology by Andrew Purves. It is my hope that some of my fellow systematic theologians might join this attempt to build more bridges between pastoral and systematic theology by critiquing my analysis and by extending it in various ways.

38–39. Such a "trinitarian-ecclesial Self" has been argued for in this chapter.

4

Conversion Isn't What It Used To Be

Retrieving a Pre-Constantinian Model of Evangelism and Discipleship for Post-Christendom, Post-Revivalist American Evangelical Churches

THE PURPOSE OF THIS chapter is to engage in a fresh examination of the questions, "What *is* the gospel?" and what is "conversion?" with a view to *retrieving* some neglected dimensions of the New Testament gospel, *disenculturating* this message from some of its historic American cultural trappings, and *recontextualizing* the message for a post-Christendom, post-revivalist American[1] church. The primary focus will be on the first question, especially in regard to the *content* and historical and current *contexts* of the core Christian message, but some attention will also be given to the methods and practices of evangelism as well. It will be argued that churches today need to recover a *pre-Constantinian* model of evangelism and discipleship.

It may seem as odd and superfluous to pose the question "What is the gospel?" for an evangelical readership as it would be to ask the De Beers Corporation, "What is a diamond?" or to ask Steven Jobs the question, "Are you sure you know what an iPhone is?" But for the reasons to be outlined below, it should be apparent that a fresh look at this central question for the identity of the evangelical movement is both timely and justified. In particular, the high percentage of Americans who consider themselves "born-again Christians," and at the same time, the growing evidence of the relative

---

1. While this chapter focuses on the context of the evangelical churches in the United States, most of the arguments would apply to evangelical churches in other global contexts being impacted by modernization, religious pluralism, and the "information revolution" of new digital media. I want to thank my colleague Samuel R. Schutz for his article, "The Truncated Gospel in Modern Evangelicalism," which helped to alert me to these concerns. The current chapter attempts to build upon and to extend his analysis.

lack of biblically transformed lifestyles and Christian transformation of the surrounding culture—raise the pointed questions, "Is the 'gospel' being preached in American evangelicalism the genuine article?" and "Is this 'gospel' producing genuine conversions?"—or merely nominal Christians?

A clear, unambiguous, and commonly shared answer to the question "What is the gospel?" is crucial for the identity and mission of evangelicalism as a renewal movement within American religion and society. For various reasons this clarity has become muddied in recent decades. Not only is the clarity of the content of the message a matter of concern, but the changing cultural contexts and the mind-sets of the intended audiences for the "gospel" have undergone significant alteration since the 1960s, and these changing contexts that affect the reception and understanding of the core message need to be recognized and addressed.

This essay will be organized as follows: first, a section outlining both the external and internal contexts of change for the American evangelical movement and its message; second, a review of the gospel in the context of "Christendom," surveying the period from the conversion of Constantine to end of the Middle Ages ("the Gospel Obscured"); third, a survey of the period from the Reformation to modern American revivalism (the "Not-Quite-Full Recovery of the Gospel"). A fourth and concluding constructive section will attempt to propose a fresh expression of the gospel and "plan of salvation" for a post-Christendom American church.

Changing Contexts: American Evangelicalism's Past and Present

The *context* and *audience* will critically affect how any message—including the core Christian message, the gospel—is heard and understood. The same word, *Fire!*, can mean very different things when heard in the context of a condemned criminal facing a firing squad, or that of a crowded theater. Both the *external* and the *internal* contexts within which American evangelicals attempt to communicate the gospel have undergone dramatic changes, as well as the mind-sets and presuppositions of our intended audiences, and these changes need to be noticed and taken into account in formulating effective strategies for communicating the message of Christ to the current generations. *External* contextual factors will be noted in items 1a.—f. below, and *internal* factors in items 1g.—o.

External Factors:

a. *Flatlined Growth Rates:* In 1910 Christian churches numbered some 91,429,000 adherents and constituted 96.6 percent of the population. By 2010, the number of Christian had grown to 283,002,000, but the percentage of Christians in the total population had fallen to 81.2 percent.[2] Under the impact of secularization, the ranks of self-professed agnostics in the United States grew from just over 1 million in 1910 to more than 42 million in 2010.[3] During the same 100-year period the rate of Christian growth was 1.12 percent per year, less than the annual population growth rate of 1.28 percent.[4]

Despite reports during the 1970s that "conservative churches are growing,"[5] the bigger picture of Christian growth trends during the last century show that there is little room for evangelical complacency. American church membership figures for the year 2010 showed a decline of .42 percent for the Southern Baptist Convention, the United Methodist Church was down 1.01 percent, and overall church membership was down 1.05 percent; meanwhile, the Jehovah's Witnesses grew by 4.37 percent and the Mormon Church grew by 1.42 percent.[6] Such trends are indications of the need to ask afresh the question of the fundamental effectiveness of current evangelistic practices.

b. *Questionable Cultural Impact?* The early church prior to Constantine had a vibrant spiritual life and a clear message, and remarkably impacted the culture of the Roman empire.[7] By way of contrast, in recent years evangelical leaders such as Ronald Sider have drawn attention to the apparent ineffectiveness of the evangelical presence in America to transform its own constituency, much less the surrounding culture. In his book *The Scandal of the Evangelical Conscience*, Sider documented the following uncomfortable observations: White evan-

---

2. Johnson and Ross, *Atlas of Global Christianity*, 192.

3. Ibid.

4. Ibid., 193. Due to immigration, the number of Muslims in the United States increased from 11,700 in 1910 to 5,740,000 in 2010, and the number of Buddhists during the same period from 47,200 to 3,720,000: ibid., 192.

5. Kelly, *Why Conservative Churches Are Growing*.

6. *2011 Yearbook of American & Canadian Churches*, as cited in Chandler, *God's Global Mosaic*, 3.

7. See, for example, MacMullen, *Christianizing the Roman Empire*, and Dodds, *Pagan and Christian in an Age of Anxiety*, 133–38, noting both the *uncompromising exclusiveness* of the Christian message, and the *inclusiveness* and generosity of the church's social ministry and fellowship.

gelicals are among the most likely groups in the United States to object to neighbors of another race; evangelical youth differ little from their peers in rates of premarital sexual activity; divorce rates are higher in the southern United States, where evangelical Protestants are the predominant religious group; a large study by the Christian Reformed Church found that physical and sexual abuse was as common in their churches as in the general population.[8] If these findings are credible, does not the apparent lack of behavioral impact in these cases by the Christian "gospel" raise questions about the content of such a "gospel," the clarity of its communication, and perhaps even the depth of such "conversions"?

c. *Pluralism Without, Pluralism Within:* The growing awareness of *religious pluralism*—both outside the church and within the minds of churchgoers themselves—is an increasingly important element of the context within which Christian messages are sent and received. Historically, this growing reality of pluralism in America can be seen to have developed in three stages or three "disestablishments."[9] The "first disestablishment" during the founding period, with its free-exercise and non-establishment provisions in the First Amendment, opened the door to a *de jure* pluralism, while *de facto* Protestant Christianity remained the dominant religion in the United States. In a second "disestablishment" following World War I, Protestant Christians, in the face of large-scale Catholic immigration and growing Jewish diversity, were forced to acknowledge the social and religious diversity of a "Protestant-Catholic-Jewish" nation.[10]

It can be argued that America experienced a third "disestablishment" in the 1960s, especially in the wake of the US Congress's actions in 1965 to remove barriers to immigration from non-European countries. As a result of these changes in the immigration laws record numbers of Latinos, Asians, and Middle Easterners began to enter the United States, bringing with them their Roman Catholic, Muslim, Buddhist, and Hindu, and other religious traditions. As Carroll and Roof note, "Unlike earlier waves of European immigration, this later wave involved traditions that were neither Christian nor Jewish, thus breaking the nation's two historic faith traditions."[11] According to a study released by the Pew Forum on Religion and Public Life, the

---

8. Sider, *The Scandal of the Evangelical Conscience*, 13, 19, 27.
9. The analysis here follows Carroll and Roof, *Bridging Divided Worlds*, 40–43.
10. The designation was popularized by Herberg, *Protestant, Catholic, Jew*.
11. Carroll and Roof, *Bridging Divided Worlds*, 43.

Muslim population in the United States is projected to double over the next twenty years—fueled by immigration and higher than average fertility rates—from 2.6 million now to 6.2 million by 2030.[12]

These dramatic changes in religious demographics since 1965 have caused one religious scholar to describe the United States as "the world's most religiously diverse nation."[13] On the shelves of any large bookstore one is likely to find more books by the Dalai Lama than by Billy Graham or Pope Francis, and within an hour's drive from downtown Washington, DC, one can find Buddhist temples and monks from Thailand, Vietnam, Japan, Korea, Sri Lanka, and Tibet. American evangelical Christians can no longer share their faith in a "Christendom" context where Christianity provides the prevailing plausibility structure for public and private life, and where the dominant culture reinforces Christian values and beliefs.[14]

The new pluralism is not only a matter of external religious demographics, but perhaps even more importantly for the communication of the gospel, increasingly the default *state of mind* among those we may attempt to reach."Pluralism is within us as well as without us," according to sociologist of religion Robert Wuthnow.[15] American religion is shaped by a consumer culture to which all Americans are exposed from early childhood, and many "religious shoppers" take it for granted that they can piece together beliefs and practices from a variety of religious traditions in order to craft their own customized "pastiche" spiritualities.[16] Americans of the Baby Boom generation growing up during the 1960s may have never known a strong religious center for American life, and not only take pluralism for granted, but deeply value it as well. What else could religion be but a personal

---

12. Sacirbey, "Pew Study Charts Growth in Muslim Population."

13. Eck, *A New Religious America*. Eck is Professor of Comparative Religion at Harvard and director of the Harvard Pluralism Project. On the influence of Hindu religious ideas and practices in American life, see Goldberg, *American Veda*.

14. As Tennent has noted, "Protestantism . . . was born in the context of Christendom. This profoundly influenced the way the 'gospel' was understood. To be a Christian within a Christendom arrangement is to see Christianity at the center of all public discourse. Evangelism occurs passively because Christianity is the prevailing plausibility structure": "The Gospel in Historical Reception," 86. The concept of a "plausibility structure" and the impact of secularization and pluralism on religious life and consciousness is analyzed in Berger, *The Sacred Canopy*.

15. Wuthnow, *America and the Challenges of Religious Diversity*, 107.

16. Ibid., 107–8. In his earlier 1998 study, Wuthnow had noted that "Now, at the end of the twentieth century, growing numbers of Americans piece together their faith like a patchwork quilt": *After Heaven*, 2.

"preference"? "No generation in American history," states Wade Clark Roof, "was ever exposed to or more devoted to pluralism as a social and religious reality."[17]

According to Christian Smith, most "emerging adults" (eighteen- to twenty-three-year-olds) in America today are "social constructionists," in the sense that they instinctively believe, in the face of the pluralism and diversity within which they have been raised, that all human beliefs, including religious beliefs, are human constructions that are historically contingent, changeable, and particular.[18] This sensibility leads to a mode of speech in which "I feel that" has largely replaced "I think that" or "I would argue that," and to a personal outlook in which claims are not staked, nor are rational arguments developed, differences engaged, or universal truths recognized.[19] Such a mind-set obviously poses a challenge to the communication of an authoritative gospel message; we need at least to be aware of the existence of such a frame of mind.

d. *The Problem of Biblical Illiteracy:* Effective communication between the sender and receiver of a message presupposes that the both the sender and intended receiver share a certain minimum of background information. For example, in American culture, a mother who invites her child's friends to a birthday party can assume that the guests will have certain expectations: a gift and card will brought (unless specified otherwise); a birthday cake (and perhaps ice cream) will be served; the child whose birthday it is will blow out the birthday candles on the cake, have "Happy Birthday" sung to them, and open the presents. Such background knowledge can be assumed in our culture.

Attempts to "send a gospel invitation" in today's American culture take place in a setting when the basic Bible background knowledge (God, sin, salvation, the life of Jesus, his death and resurrection, the story of Israel, etc.) that is needed to understand the "Good News" can *not* be assumed to be present in the mind of many Americans. In speaking to the typical American today, notes Ronald Johnson, a Southern Baptist professor of evangelism, "you can no longer presuppose that he has a religious orientation to life, particularly a

---

17. Roof, *A Generation of Seekers,* 245. For a classic study of individualism in the Boomer generation and American life generally, see Bellah et al., *Habits of the Heart.*

18. Smith, *Souls in Transition,* 50.

19. Ibid., 51.

Judeo-Christian orientation," and "you can no longer presuppose that he will understand when you present the gospel."[20]

A feature story in *Time* magazine in 2007 reported that only about one half of the adults in the United States could name even *one* of the four Gospels, and that fewer than half could identify Genesis as the first book of the Bible.[21] In a 2009 study, researchers at the Barna Research Group found that most Americans, by the time they reach the age of thirteen or fourteen, believe (mistakenly) that they know much of what the Bible has to teach and have little further interest in learning more biblical content.[22] Effective communication of the New Testament gospel in today's America requires that much of the Bible background information that could be assumed in earlier generations be provided by the evangelist together with the basic message itself.[23]

e. *Negative Perceptions of Evangelicals:* Communications theory stipulates that the reception of a message is influenced not only by the receiver's context, but also by the attitudes and perceptions that the receiver has of the sender of the message. It is important for would-be communicators of the Christian gospel to be aware of those attitudes and perceptions that will color the reception of the message. For example, Phil Parshall, a career missionary in the Muslim world, was startled to realize that Christian missionaries from the West, their own self-images notwithstanding, were often perceived in the Muslim community as nothing more than "efficient secular administrators," rather than as "holy" or "spiritual" men of prayer.[24]

In the current American scene, recent studies have uncovered significant evidence of negative perceptions of Christians among outsiders, especially among those in the sixteen- to twenty-nine-year-old age groups. David Kinnamon and Gabe Lyons found that among the unchurched in this age group, 91 percent considered Christians to be "antihomosexual," that 87 percent saw Christians as "judgmental,"

---

20. R. Johnson, *How Will They Hear If We Don't Listen?*, 48.
21. Hansen, "Why Johnny Can't Read the Bible."
22. Barna Research Group, "Year-in-Review Perspective (2009)."

23. It is significant to note that in Acts 17, when Paul presents the gospel in Athens to a non-Jewish, pagan audience, he begins with the topics of *God* and *creation* before moving to Jesus, the resurrection, and the final judgment. This methodology would seem to be more appropriate to current American settings than the "synagogue" strategy, where Paul could assume extensive knowledge of the Old Testament Scriptures among his listeners as the background for the message about Jesus.

24 Parshall, *Bridges to Islam*, 116.

85 percent as "hypocritical," saying one thing, doing another, and 75 percent as "too involved in politics."[25] "When they see Christians not acting like Jesus," note Kinnaman and Lyons, "the quickly conclude that the group deserves an unChristian label."[26]

One may debate the causes or the accuracy of these perceptions, but the fact remains that such perceptions need to be recognized and hopefully overcome as the gospel is shared in our own American context. By way of contrast, it is worthwhile to recall the grudgingly *positive* perceptions of the actions and attitudes of Christians in the early church, as held even by their opponents. In the fourth century the pagan emperor Julian "the Apostate" could admit that the Christians' "benevolence to strangers, their care for the graves of the dead and the pretended holiness of their lives have done most to increase atheism [i.e., the abandonment of the Greco-Roman pagan religions] . . . . It is disgraceful that when . . . the impious Galileans support not only their own poor but ours as well, all men should see how our people lack aid from us."[27] The good deeds and changed lives of these early Christians created favorable impressions among outsiders that facilitated the spread of the gospel.

f. *The Impact of Digital Media:* The new Internet and information revolution and explosion of digital media have created a dramatically new and challenging context within which American Christians must attempt to communicate the gospel. Never before in human history have potential listeners to the message of Christ been inundated with so many other messages that are constantly competing for their limited and increasingly fragmented attention. Recent studies have found that by the year 2008, Americans were consuming three times the amount of information each day as they did in 1960.[28] The amount of data generated by the Internet, computers, smart phones, research labs,

---

25. Kinnaman and Lyons, *UnChristian*, 28.

26. Ibid., 29.

27. Cited in Hvalvik, "In Word and Deed," 285. Hvalvik also cites the statement of the second-century apologist Athenagoras in his *Plea on Behalf of the Christians*, regarding the lives of Christians: "In our ranks, however, you could find common men, artisans, and old women who, if they cannot establish by reasoned discourse the usefulness of their teaching, show by deed the usefulness of the exercise of their will. For they do not rehearse words but show forth good deeds: when struck they do not strike back; when robbed they do not prosecute; they give to those who ask; and they love their neighbors as themselves": *Legatio* 11.4, in "In Word and Deed," 284.

28. Richtel, "Hooked on Gadgets."

sensors, and digital cameras has been growing at a compound rate of 60 percent annually.[29]

In a recent five-year period there has been a dramatic increase in media use among young people, with the average adolescent spending over seven and a half hours each day, seven days a week, consuming various forms of media.[30] When multitasking is taken into account, these young people actually pack ten hours and forty-five minutes of media use into those seven and a half hours. Every type of media use *except* reading has increased in the last decade.[31] In such a media-saturated environment of fragmented attention spans, the Christian gospel needs to be stated with crystalline clarity and in a fresh and existentially compelling manner.

g. *The Shift of Christianity to the Global South:* Since the publication of Philip Jenkins's *The Next Christendom: the Coming of Global Christianity* there has been increasing awareness in many American churches of the historic shift of the numerical center of the Christian movement to the global South.[32] The remarkable growth of the church in Latin America, Africa, and Asia has been manifested in forms of the faith that are theologically conservative and markedly supernatural in their orientation, with strong emphases on healing, prophecy, and other "Pentecostal" elements.[33] As of 1981, for the first time in about 1,000 years, the numerical center of gravity of the Christian faith was *south* of the equator, having moved away from its former European and North American base.[34] The "typical" Christian in today's world could be said to be a poor woman in Latin America, Africa, or Asia who worships in a Pentecostal church. Spanish has surpassed English as the language spoken by the most Christians today.[35]

---

29. "All too much: Monstrous amounts of data," 5.

30. *Kaiser Family Foundation Study,* "Generation M2: Media in the Lives of 8-to-18-Year Olds: Key Findings," 1.

31. Ibid. For the impact of modern digital culture on contemporary worship, see my *Worship and the Reality of God.*

32. Jenkins, *The Next Christendom.*

33. See also Jenkins, *The New Faces of Christianity.*

34. Johnson and Chung, "Christianity's Center of Gravity, AD 33–2100," 50–51.

35. On the new global realities of the Christian movement, see also: Chandler, *God's Global Mosaic;* for historical perspectives, see Walls, *The Missionary Movement in Christian History,* especially 68–78, "Origins of the Old Northern and New Southern Christianity," and 79–142, "Africa's Place in Christian History."

North American Christians are still in the early stages of assimilating the implications of this demographic shift toward the global South for partnership in world mission[36] and for evangelism at home. American churches that are not already doing so will do well to pay more attention to the avowedly supernatural dimensions of the faith, rediscovering, if need be, that the gospel is indeed the "the power *of God*" (Rom 1:16)—not the power of American prosperity, technology, or marketing strategies. A growing awareness of the increasingly *multicultural* diversity of Christianity in a postcolonial world should also motivate North American Christians to be more reflective and self-aware of their own cultural context, and the ways in which modernity and affluence have compromised the spiritual vitality of their own evangelical faith and worship practices.[37]

Internal Factors:

In addition to these factors in the external environment of American evangelicalism, there are factors *internal* to the movement itself that make the issue of the clarification of the core gospel message urgent at this time. These elements involve both the historical situation (1. h) in which the movement finds itself at this juncture in history and theological issues (1. i-o) at both the popular and more scholarly levels that are eroding the clarity of the gospel in various ways.

h. *Changing of the Guard:* The evangelical movement in America, with its roots in the Protestant Reformation, the First and Second Great Awakenings, nineteenth-century revivalism, and the fundamentalist wing of the modernist-fundamentalist controversies of the 1920s and 1930s, emerged in its most recent form during the 1940s as the "New Evangelicalism" as envisioned by key leaders such as Harold John Ockenga, Carl F. H. Henry, Edward John Carnell, and Billy Graham.[38]

36. On partnership in mission, see Escobar, *The New Global Mission*; D. Smith, *Mission After Christendom*; and Jennings, *God the Real Superpower*.

37. American evangelicals can be nervous about the dangers of "syncretism" when Christians in China and India, for example, attempt to develop less Western and more indigenized local theologies—while themselves being unaware of the presence of syncretism in their own North American theologies and worship practices. One such possible example is the "prosperity gospel" that has been exported from America to many parts of the world: see Micklethwait and Wooldridge, *God Is Back*, especially 213–42, "Exporting America's God," and 243–264, "All That Is Holy Is Profaned."

38. This history has been recounted in, for example: Wells and Woodbridge, *The Evangelicals*; Henry, *Evangelicals in Search of Identity*; Marsden, *Evangelicalism and*

These leaders founded or helped to found institutions such as the Evangelical Theological Society, Fuller Theological Seminary, Trinity Evangelical Divinity School, Gordon-Conwell Theological Seminary, and *Christianity Today*. Across the Atlantic, figures such as John Stott and J. I. Packer were prominent leaders in British evangelicalism. Billy Graham was the iconic face and symbol of unity of the movement, and with the election of Jimmy Carter as president in 1976, *Time* magazine could proclaim that the "Year of the Evangelical" had arrived. A generation later, these founders of the "New Evangelicalism" have already passed or will soon be passing from the scene, and there is no one leader with the international stature of a Billy Graham to function actually or symbolically as a "center" for the movement. American evangelicalism shows serious signs of fragmentation, and the pathway ahead is far from clear.

i. *Health and Wealth?* At the level of popular culture and televangelism, the "Good News" is often packaged with promises of health and financial prosperity in the so-called "health-and-wealth" gospel. Popular preachers such as Kenneth Hagin, Kenneth Copeland, Fred Price, Robert Tilton, Oral Roberts, and others from Pentecostal and charismatic backgrounds have spread a message of divine healing and the blessings of wealth through their churches, publications, seminars, schools, and radio and television outlets.[39] From the time of Benjamin Franklin in the colonial era through the nineteenth-century "New Thought" influences and figures such as Andrew Carnegie and Russell Conwell, American religion has been amalgamated with the prominent cultural values of financial prosperity and Horatio Alger "rags-to-riches" narratives. Such a "gospel" can represent a dangerous form of syncretism, mixing the biblical message of repentance and forgiveness of sins with American cultural values of physical health and financial success. During the twentieth century this American gospel of prosperity has been widely exported to Africa, Asia, and Latin America.[40] Rather than accommodating to the cult of wealth, American evangelicals need to challenge the dominant cultural values by living out a gospel that demonstrates

---

Modern America; Shelley, *Evangelicalism in America*; Balmer, *Blessed Assurance*; and Wuthnow, *The Struggle for America's Soul*.

39. For the historical origins, major personalities, and teachings of this movement, see: Perriman, ed., *Faith*; Barron, *The Health and Wealth Gospel*; Bowman Jr., *The Word-Faith Controversy*; McConnell, *A Different Gospel*; and Hollinger, "Enjoying God Forever."

40. See Micklethwait and Wooldridge, *God Is Back*, especially 213–42, "Exporting America's God"; and Coleman, *The Globalisation of Charismatic Christianity*.

a simple and frugal lifestyle and solidarity with the poor—especially poor Christians—both domestically and around the globe.

j. *Our Kind of People: Church Growth and the "Homogeneous Unit Principle"*: In 1955 Donald McGavran, a career missionary to India, published *The Bridges to God: A Study in the Strategy of Missions*, a book that was to have a pervasive impact on evangelical mission strategy and subsequently, on strategies for evangelism and church planting in the United States and other parts of the globe.[41] McGavran's so-called "Homogeneous Unit Principle" and his proposition that "Men and women like to become Christian without crossing [cultural] barriers"[42] have been the basis for many so-called "seeker-sensitive" and "niche-market" churches that, as an evangelistic strategy, seek to "target" a specific demographic group with the gospel. Such niche marketing, "seeker-sensitive" evangelistic strategies have in recent years spawned "cowboy churches," hip-hop churches, rock and roll churches, jazz churches, and so forth, often tailored to particular musical tastes and "playlists."[43]

While in theory a "niche-marketed," "seeker-sensitive" evangelistic strategy based on the Homogeneous Unit Principle would not necessarily erode the clarity, content, and demands of the gospel, *in practice* it seems to have done so. Churches, in their competition for "market share" can be tempted to tone down the rough edges of the gospel, especially in regard to sin, repentance, and divine judgment.[44]

---

41. McGavran, *The Bridges of God, How Churches Grow*; McGavran and Wagner, *Understanding Church Growth*.

42. McGavran, *Understanding Church Growth*, 164.

43. T. Johnson, "Our Collapsing Ecclesiology," 7. Johnson notes that "now there are two kinds of cowboy churches, rural and urban—the regular kind not apparently not being demographically specific enough. This is the *reductio ad absurdum* of the homogeneous church philosophy. We might call it the 'iPodization' of Christian ministry, as the demographic target is narrowed down finally to each individual, headset firmly on his ears, dialing up exactly the music, readings, sermon, and prayers that he needs": ibid.

44. G. A. Pritchard, in his in-depth study of Willow Creek's "seeker services" concluded that "Willow Creek's gospel emphasizes the loving immanence of God and deemphasizes his transcendent holiness": *Willow Creek Seeker Services*, 277. Pritchard also cites Darrel Schultz, a former senior pastor at a Willow Creek-style church: "For the preacher who wants to be seeker sensitive, the list of potential topics goes up and the list of usable Bible passages goes down. It is more likely that many areas a church needs to hear about (for example, . . . sin, repentance and God's judgment) will fall victim to the preacher's inner censorship board which evaluates all seeker-service events on the criterion of sensitivity to non-churched Harry": ibid. Pritchard's study could not, of course, take into account any responses by the Willow Creek leadership to these criticisms since 1996; however, the Willow Creek internal study of 2007, *Reveal: Where Are*

The "Homogeneous Unit Principle" undergirding these "niche-market" churches has been subject to extensive criticism and has been found to be deeply flawed on biblical, theological, and anthropological grounds.[45] A niche-marketed gospel can, unintentionally, promote an ethnocentric enclave that reflects an unredeemed sociology of the surrounding culture, rather than the "truth of the gospel" (Gal 2:14) that breaks down cultural and ethnic barriers in the local church and models the "new humanity" that God intends (Eph 2:15: "his purpose was to create one *new man* out of the two").

k. *Moralistic Therapeutic Deism:* The massive 2003–2005 National Study of Youth and Religion on adolescent spirituality disclosed the pervasive presence among young people in the United States of religious attitudes that Christian Smith and Melinda Denton have termed "Moralistic Therapeutic Deism."[46] This popular "creed" can be summarized as follows: 1) A God exists who created and orders the world and watches over human life on earth; 2) God wants people to be good, nice, and fair to each other, as taught in the Bible and by most world religions; 3) The central goal of life is to be happy and to feel good about oneself; 4) God does not need to be particularly involved in one's life except when he is needed to resolve a problem; 5) Good people go to heaven when they die.[47]

This "creed" reflects not only the beliefs of many teenagers, but in many cases, that of their parents as well, and is a background message that is constantly reinforced by teachers, school counselors, and the popular therapeutic culture[48] generally. While teenagers who attend conservative Protestant or Black Protestant churches tend to have more robust theological beliefs than those attending mainline Protes-

---

You? (by Hawkins and Parkinson), recognized the evidence that the weekend services were not in themselves fully adequate for promoting spiritual growth and discipleship.

45. See, for example, Laing, "Donald McGavran's Missiology"; Padilla, "The Unity of the Church and the Homogeneous Unit Principle" (biblical-theological); McClintock, "Sociological Critique of the Homogeneous Unit Principle"; and Bosch, "The Structure of Mission," especially 230–40 on "Make Disciples" and "All the Nations."

46. Smith and Denton, *Soul Searching*; research findings summarized in C. Smith, "On 'Moralistic Therapeutic Deism' as U.S. Teenagers' Actual, Tacit, De Facto Religious Faith." The findings of this study and their implications are also analyzed in Dean, *Almost Christian*; see Appendix B, "The National Study of Youth and Religion: Summary of Findings," 201–5.

47. C. Smith, "On 'Moralistic Therapeutic Deism,'" 46–47.

48. On the "therapeutic culture" in modern America, see Rieff, *The Triumph of the Therapeutic*; Vitz, *Psychology as Religion*; and Wells, *Losing Our Virtue*.

tant or Roman Catholic churches, it remains the case that "Moralistic Therapeutic Deism" constitutes a pervasive set of background beliefs and attitudes that function as a preunderstanding for many in America when the biblical gospel is communicated. According to Smith, this is not a "religion of repentance from sin, of living as a servant of a sovereign divine, . . . of building character through suffering . . . . Rather, what appears to be the actual dominant religion among U.S. teenagers is centrally about feeling good, happy, secure, at peace."[49] In fact, Smith has concluded, "a significant part of 'Christianity' in the United States is actually only tenuously connected to the historical Christian tradition . . . Christianity is actively being colonized and displaced by a quite different religious faith."[50] Any would-be preacher of the Christian gospel needs to be aware of this pervasive cluster of beliefs, and needs to challenge it head-on with a razor-sharp presentation of the apostolic message.

l. *"Lordship Salvation"*: In the 1980s the so-called "Lordship salvation" controversy surfaced in certain quarters of American evangelicalism. Some writers from dispensational backgrounds, such as Charles C. Ryrie and Zane Hodges, had been arguing that conversion to "Christ as Savior" did not require an explicit confession of Christ as "Lord," and that the latter requirement would amount to a requirement for "human works" that would undermine the principle of salvation by "grace" alone.[51] John MacArthur, in response, forcefully and cogently argued the case for the confession of Jesus as "Lord" as an essential for biblical conversion and salvation in his 1988 book, *The Gospel According to Jesus*.[52] MacArthur clearly has the better argument here, and the confession of Jesus as *Lord* is crucial for maintaining the clarity of the gospel, and for avoiding the problems of nominal Christianity—and

---

49. C. Smith, "On 'Moral Therapeutic Deism,'" 48.

50. Ibid., 56–57. As a possible historical parallel to the situation as described by Smith, one might think of the threat of gnosticism to the orthodox Christian faith in the second through fourth centuries, when an alien message in "Christian" garb penetrated many sectors of the church: see Jonas, *The Gnostic Religion*.

51. Ryrie, "Must Christ Be Lord to Be Savior?" in *Balancing the Christian Life*, 169–81; and Hodges, *The Gospel Under Siege*, 14. MacArthur responds to Hodges; however, Hodges's main concern appears to be the relationship between faith and works, rather than "lordship" per se. In an earlier generation Lewis Sperry Chafer had made the very dubious claim that "to impose a need to surrender the life to God as an added condition of salvation is most unreasonable. God's call to the unsaved is never said to be unto the Lordship of Christ": *Systematic Theology*, 385.

52. MacArthur, *The Gospel According to Jesus*.

nominal Evangelicalism—that have only become more evident, not less so, since the 1980s.

m. *E. P. Sanders, N. T. Wright and the "New Perspectives on Paul":* The 1977 publication of E. P. Sanders's *Paul and Palestinian Judaism*, with its influential reconstruction of the supposed nature of Second Temple Judaism, and the subsequent work of scholars such as N. T. Wright who have accepted Sanders' reconstruction, has led to the current situation in which the Reformation understanding of justification by faith alone as an essentially forensic reality is widely being called into question. Wright and others have argued that justification in Paul is more a matter of *ecclesiology* (who is in the covenant community) than of *soteriology* (who is "saved"). The New Perspectives' revisionist interpretations of such critical terms in Pauline theology such as "works of the law," the "righteousness of God," and justification have made it more difficult for many to give a clear answer to such questions as "What is the central message of the book of Romans?" and "What is the 'gospel' for Paul—or for us?"

The challenge posed by the New Perspectives is currently one of the most, and perhaps *the* most serious challenge to the clarity of the gospel as evangelicals have historically understood it. From the time of Luther to the present, the doctrine of justification by faith in Christ alone by grace alone has been central to the sense of Protestant evangelical identity, and any movement such as the New Perspectives' that appears to drive a wedge between "justification" and "gospel" represents a challenge to the core of evangelical self-identity.

It is not the purpose of this essay to engage in a thorough analysis of or response to the New Perspectives on Paul, but simply to highlight it as a central point of concern for the evangelical movement going forward.[53] In my judgment, Wright is often helpful in what he affirms, but not helpful in what he appears to deny (e.g., the forensic and soteriological nature of justification; imputed righteousness). He has rightly called attention to the context of Paul's teachings in relation

---

53. Sanders, *Paul and Palestinian Judaism*; Wright, *What Saint Paul Really Said*, and *Justification*. The accuracy of Sanders's reconstruction of first-century Judaism has been criticized by subsequent scholars, as not adequately recognizing the presence of merit theologies in the Jewish sources: Carson, O'Brien, and Seifrid, eds., *Justification and Variegated Nomism*; Elliot, *The Survivors of Israel*; Gathercole, *Where Is Boasting?*. The body of literature generated in response to the New Perspectives is already enormous and still growing. Among many that could be mentioned are the following: Husbands and Treier, eds., *Justification*; Piper, *The Future of Justification*; Waters, *Justification and the New Perspectives on Paul*; Vickers, *Jesus' Blood and Righteousness*.

to the Abrahamic covenant (Rom 4) and to the important connections in the apostles' thought between justification, the resurrection of Jesus (e.g. Rom 4:25, "raised to life for our justification"), and the reception of the promised Holy Spirit (Gal 3:2,5,6,11,14). At the same time, I believe that New Perspectives positions are inadequate or incorrect in the following areas: 1) the meaning of "works of the law" as being primarily concerned with ethnic "boundary markers" such as circumcision and dietary laws; 2) the meaning of the "righteousness of God" as being primarily "covenant faithfulness" to the exclusion of penal or retributive justice; 3) the lack of adequate recognition of merit theologies in Judaism; and 4) construing the focus of justification as being ecclesiology (covenant membership) rather than soteriology (salvation).[54] Going forward, American evangelicals can and must retain the Reformational forensic understanding of justification and imputed righteousness, while at the same time recognizing the importance of other Pauline soteriological themes such as adoption, reconciliation, redemption, union with Christ, and the reception of the Spirit. In short, the New Perspectives should be seen as a supplement—at some points—to historic Reformation understandings of justification and the gospel, and not as its replacement.

n. *Emerging Church: Fuzzy Gospel?* The so-called "Emerging Church" movement associated with figures such as Brian McLaren, Tony Jones, Mark Driscoll, John Burke, Dan Kimball, Doug Pagitt, Karen Ward, and others has posed significant challenges to current understandings of the "gospel" and the debates over the identity of the evangelical movement in America.[55] Its proponents tend to see themselves not so much as an academic, theological movement as an ecclesiological and "missional" one, focusing on a renewed church in the American context with emphases on identifying with the life of Jesus, an "incarnational" and "embodied" way of doing theology, concerns for

---

54. See J. J. Davis, "Where N. T. Wright Isn't Quite Right," chapter 6 in the present volume. On the presence of merit theology and works righteousness within various strands of intertestamental and first-century Judaism, see: 1 Macc 2:51–52; Tobit 4:10; Sirach 3:3–4; 44:20–21; 29:12; Jubilees 23:10; Ezra 8:33; 2 Baruch 51:3,7,11; 4Q399:7–8; Josephus, *Contra Apion* 2.217–18.

55. See McLaren, *A New Kind of Christian* and *A Generous Orthodoxy*; T. Jones, *The New Christians*; Webber, ed., *Listening to the Beliefs of Emerging Churches*; see also the "Emergent Village" website at http://www.emergentvillage.com for other representative voices in the movement. For a sympathetic overview of the movement see Gibbs and Bolger, *Emerging Churches*.

social justice, hospitality, the poor, and ministries contextualized for postmodern cultures.

Critics of the movement such as D. A. Carson are concerned that "emergents" have conceded too much ground to postmodern epistemologies and theories of truth, and consequently are endangering the clear boundaries between truth and error and between the church and the world.[56] Robert Webber, who was somewhat sympathetic to the movement, stated that a significant danger facing the movement was to inadvertently perpetuate the theological pragmatism of the megachurch movement to which it was reacting.[57]

In a June, 2005 "Response to Our Critics," representatives of the movement stated that "we believe there is such a thing as truth, and truth matters . . . we are not moral or epistemological relativists . . . we affirm the historic trinitarian faith and ancient creeds . . . we believe that Jesus is the crucified and risen Savior of the cosmos and no one comes to the Father except through Jesus."[58] Such responses may not fully meet the concerns of the critics of the Emerging Church movement, but they need to be taken into account in the continuing debates over the contested identity of American evangelicalism going forward.

o. *The Disappearance of Hell:* In the New Testament and early Christianity the reality of hell and judgment was the "bad news" in contrast to which the "Good News" of the gospel was understood. The Apostle Paul, in one of the earliest New Testament documents, could remind his new converts in Thessalonica that the Jesus in whom they had believed, who was risen from the dead and who one day would return, "rescues us from the wrath to come" (1 Thess 1:10).

The very rigor and uncompromising nature of the Christian message has been identified by scholars as an important element in the success and growth of the early Christian church. The classical scholar E. R. Dodds noted that in comparison with its religious competition, Christianity "wielded both a bigger stick [eternal hell] and a juicier carrot [eternal heavenly bliss]."[59] The threats of hell and judgment

---

56. Carson's *Becoming Conversant with the Emerging Church* is, at the time of this writing, the most extensive critique of the Emerging Church movement. Carson focuses in chapter 6 on the work of Brian McLaren and Steve Chalke.

57. Webber, *Listening to the Beliefs of Emergent Churches*, 200.

58. In T. Jones, *The New Christians*, 227–32, "Appendix B: 'A Response To Our Critics,'" at 229.

59. Dodds, *Pagan and Christian in an Age of Anxiety*, 135. Dodds comments on the demanding character of the Christian message: "its very exclusiveness, its refusal to concede any value to alternative forms of worship, which nowadays is felt to be a

were a significant elements in the early Christian message and were a factor in the conversion of the pagans.[60] In the year 436 the Roman aristocrat Volusian was confronted by his Christian niece and admonished to become a Christian, to free himself from demons, and warned that he would be burned with them in eternal fire if he did not repent. Volusian was "cut deeply to the heart" and did become a Christian.[61]

Since the 1960s the reality of hell and judgment as forming the background of Christian preaching has receded dramatically, both in American culture generally and the evangelical subculture in particular.[62] Alternatives to the historic view of eternal conscious punishment of the wicked such as annihilationism or conditional immortality and even so-called "evangelical universalism" have been gaining ground in the evangelical community.[63] The disappearance of hell in the modern church and its preaching is likely to be reflective of the secularization of the church under the impact of the modern scientific view of the world, modern medicine and increased life expectancies, relatively secure societies under the rule of law, the affluence of consumerist capitalism, the growth of entertainment media and the therapeutic sensibility—all of which tend to turn the attention of modern man toward a comfortable life in *this world* and away from the life to come and eternity.[64] It remains to be seen if such a "kinder and gentler" ver-

weakness, was in the circumstances of the time a source of strength. The religious tolerance which was the normal Greek and Roman practice had resulted . . . in a bewildering mass of alternatives. There were too many cults . . . too many philosophies of life to choose from: you could pile one religious insurance on another, and yet not feel safe. Christianity made a clean sweep. It lifted the burden of freedom from the individual: one choice, one irrevocable choice, and the road to salvation was clear": 133.

60. MacMullen, *Christianizing the Roman Empire*, 19: pagan critic Celsus complained that the Christians "believe in eternal punishments" and "threaten others with these punishments." According to MacMullen, "Christianity presented ideas that demanded a choice, not tolerance": ibid., 17.

61. Gerontius, *Life of Melania*, 52–55, cited by Kreider, *The Change of Conversion and the Origin of Christendom*, 68.

62. See M. Martin, "Hell Disappeared. No One Noticed. A Civic Argument"; Gomes, "Evangelicals and the Annihilation of Hell"; Mohler Jr., "Modern Theology"; Moore, *The Battle for Hell* and *The Nature of Hell*.

63. Mohler, "Modern Theology," 28–36, traces these developments in British and American evangelical circles. Noteworthy are the positions articulated by Stott in Stott and Edwards, *Essentials* (annihilationism); Pinnock and Brow, *Unbounded Love* (annihilationism); and MacDonald, *The Evangelical Universalist* (universalism). And more recently, see Bell, *Love Wins*, questioning traditional understandings of hell and endless conscious punishment.

64. How different is the early medieval Christian view of life reflected in the words of Columba, the sixth-century Irish missionary: "Here is the way the human being's

sion of the gospel will in fact add to its appeal, or will rather, as the history of Unitarian Universalist movement would seem to indicate, lead to static or declining patterns of growth and marginalization in the broader social order.

Having in this first section (1.a-o) surveyed the contemporary American context in which the gospel is currently situated, the plan for the remainder of the essay will be as follows: a second section examining the "Christendom" period of church history from the time of Theodosius to the Reformation, with special attention to the accommodation of the gospel to the structures of political power and to a sacramental, priestly system controlled by the Roman Catholic Church; a third section covering the time of the Reformation to the present ("the 'not-quite-full' recovery of the gospel"), with special attention being given to *revivalism* as another (Protestant) accommodation of the gospel to prevailing cultural values; and as a fourth section a constructive attempt to reexamine current New Testament scholarship on the nature of the basic Christian kerygma, and to propose a fresh formulation of the gospel contextualized for a post-Christendom America, and for a "Next Evangelicalism" beyond the "New Evangelicalism" of the Ockenga/Henry/Graham era.

The Power of the Gospel Obscured: From Theodosius to the Reformation

With the conversion of Constantine and the issuance of the Edict of Milan in 313, Christianity passed from the state of a persecuted religion to one officially recognized and tolerated in the Roman empire.[65] It was during the reign of Theodosius in the latter part of the fourth century, however, that Christianity became a state religion, and that the foundations of "Christendom" were firmly laid. The "Edict of Thessalonica" issued by Theodosius in February of 380 established the Catholic religion and Nicene orthodoxy as the law of the empire:

---

miserable life runs . . . . You have been created from the earth, you tread the earth, you will be laid to rest in the earth, you will rise in the earth, you will be tried in the fire [purgatory], you will wait the judgment, and then either torture or the kingdom of heaven will be yours forever": cited in Russell, *The Germanization of Early Medieval Christianity*, 161.

65. A recent sympathetic portrayal of Constantine and his legacy is found in Leithart, *Defending Constantine*. See also Greenslade, *Church and State from Constantine to Theodosius*.

> It is our will that all people ruled by the administration of Our Clemency shall practise that religion which ... Peter the Apostle transmitted to the Romans .... The religion followed by Bishop Damasus of Rome and by Peter, bishop of Alexandria ... according to the apostolic discipline of the evangelical doctrine, we shall believe in the single deity of the Father, the Son and the Holy Ghost under the concept of equal majesty, and of the Holy Trinity. We command that persons who follow this rule shall embrace the name of Catholic Christians. The rest, however, whom We judge demented and insane shall carry the infamy of heretical dogmas. Their meeting places shall not receive the name of churches, and they shall be smitten first by Divine vengeance, and secondly by the retribution of Our hostility, which We shall assume in accordance with the Divine judgement.[66]

Beginning in the year 381 Theodosius undertook a series of actions that inhibited the practices of pagan religion, beginning with a reiteration of Constantine's earlier ban on pagan sacrifices. In 389 he decreed that pagan feasts that had not already been converted to Christian ones were now to be workdays. In 391 sterner laws followed, with prohibitions of access to pagan temples and additional prohibitions of purely private rituals. Overzealous Christian mobs and monks took such laws as tacit encouragement for smashing pagan temples and idols.[67] The temple of Serapis in Alexandria, one of the most venerated pagan temples in the ancient world, was razed to the ground by Christian mobs, probably in 391.[68]

The actions of Theodosius, perhaps even more than those of Constantine, had decisively altered the incentive structures within which the Christian church would exercise its life and mission for the next thousand years. The accession of Christianity as the state religion of the empire, with the legal privileges of the church and its bishops, and the social prestige of the emperor's personal religion to back it, had created temporal benefits

---

66. Cited by Williams and Friell, *Theodosius,* 53; they consider this edict "one of the most significant documents in European history." Williams and Friell believe that Theodosius's laws "conflated false belief with criminal intent, and obedience to the church with obedience to the state": 57.

67. Ibid., 70. For citations from the Theodosian Code prohibiting all pagan sacrifices (xvi, 10, 12); exemption of clergy from public service (xvi, 2, 2); exemption from most taxes for church lands (xvi, 2,40); immunity of bishops from trial in secular courts (xvi, 2, 12), and prohibition of intermarriage between Christians and Jews (iii, 7, 2), see Hillgarth, ed., *Christianity and Paganism,* 45–52, "The Roman State and the Church."

68. King, *The Emperor Theodosius and the Establishment of Christianity,* 79. For the pagan rhetorician Libanius's (314–93) appeal to Theodosius to respect the legal rights of the pagans and their temples, see Libanius, *Selected Works,* vol. 2, "Oration 30," 91–151.

and incentives for pagans to "convert" to the new faith. The Christian gospel was henceforth to be intimately associated with the coercive powers of the Roman state as it sought to penetrate the pagan territories at the fringes of the empire during the centuries that followed.

When the Apostle Paul first carried the gospel from its Jewish and Hellenistic environment into Europe, he saw his message as the "power *of God* for the salvation of everyone who believes" (Rom 1:16); he could not claim the coercive power of the Roman state to enforce acceptance of his message. In the succeeding centuries, however, as Christian missionaries spread the faith into pagan lands of eastern and northern Europe, it was all too often the power of *the state* and of a culturally more advanced Roman civilization that provided the impetus for expansion. In this second section of the essay, we will consider several issues, including a) the accommodation of the gospel to pagan cultures and the use of coercion in its spread; b) the linguistic barriers to the communication of the gospel caused by the use of Latin as the language of liturgy and Scripture; and c) theological issues such as infant baptism, purgatory, the doctrine of justification, and the disappearance of effective catechesis as factors that contributed to the obscuring of the gospel in the medieval period.

a. Mission to the Pagans: Accommodation, Conformity, and Coercion

As the Christian faith was carried beyond the borders of the Roman empire into the pagan territories of eastern and northern Europe during the medieval period, the gospel was often inextricably linked with political power and, at times, with the use of coercive means. From the sixth through the ninth centuries the faith was brought to the Angles and Saxons and to the Celtic tribes in Britain; during the ninth and tenth centuries, to the Slavs of central Europe and the Balkans; in the eleventh century, to the Danes and Norwegians; in the twelfth century, to the Poles and Swedes; and in the thirteenth century, to Baltic peoples such as the Estonians and to the Prussians.[69]

---

69. Latourette, *A History of the Expansion of Christianity,* vol. 2, 20. General accounts of the history of Christian missions in the medieval period may also be found in: Neill, *A History of Christian Missions,* "The Dark Ages, 500-1000," (61-98); Bosch, *Transforming Mission,* "The Medieval Roman Catholic Missionary Paradigm," 214-38; Rudnick, *Speaking the Gospel Through the Ages,* "Christianization by Conformity and Coercion: The Middle Ages (500-1500)," 43-76; Markus, "From Rome to the Barbarian Kingdoms (330-700)"; and Mayr-Harting, "The West: The Age of Conversion (700-1050)."

The conversions of these peoples was usually a tribal rather than individual affair, with a king or tribal leader accepting Christian baptism, and subsequently his tribal followers—at times, as the result of some form of coercion." To depart from the cult of one's group was to be guilty of disloyalty," observed the noted missions historian Kenneth Scott Latourette." It was with this concept of religion that most of the converts of these thousand years adopted the Christian faith."[70]

A notable case in point is provided by the conversion of Clovis, king of the Franks. Prior to the year 496, Clovis had been resistant to the intercessions and witness of his Christian wife and queen Clotild.[71] But in that year, when his troops were being slaughtered by an enemy tribe, the Alamanni, Clovis is said to have prayed to Christ for aid: "I want to believe in you, but I must first be saved from my enemies." The enemy was defeated, and Clovis believed that the Christian God had answered his prayers.[72] He accepted Christian baptism at the hands of Remigius, bishop of Rheims, still wearing his battle helmet as he entered the baptismal pool. Three thousand of Clovis's troops were baptized on the same occasion, foreshadowing the mass baptisms of other pagan tribes in the centuries to come. Alan Kreider has noted that the conversion of Clovis, of great significance for the later Christian history of Europe, was the religious equivalent of "fast food." Unlike the conversions of the pre-Constantinian era, its elements—repudiation of idol worship and submitting to the clergy for baptism—could be produced quickly and *en masse*. As such it provided a template for the "conversion" of many Europeans who were to follow in the centuries ahead.[73]

In the eighth century Charlemagne set out to forcibly subdue the pagan Saxon tribes within his realm, and compelled them after military defeat to accept Christian baptism. Once baptized, the Saxons faced execution if they reverted to their traditional pagan faith.[74] Other examples of forcible

---

70. Latourette, *The History of the Expansion of Christianity*, vol. 2, 16.

71. The following account is found in Kreider, *The Change of Conversion and the Origin of Christendom*, 86–88, "The Conversion of Clovis." I wish to thank Richard Peace for calling my attention to Kreider's work in his fine essay, "Prayer, Evangelization, and Spiritual Formation." Peace's concerns to root evangelism in the context of the local church and its ministries of discipleship and spiritual formation parallel the point of view argued in this essay.

72. The parallel to the conversion of Constantine is striking.

73. Kreider, *The Change of Conversion and the Origin of Christendom*, 88.

74. Bosch, *Transforming Mission*, 222–26, "Indirect and Direct 'Missionary Wars,'" at 224. Detailed and nuanced accounts of missionary efforts during the Carolingian period, based on extensive primary sources, is provided in Sullivan, "Carolingian Missionary Methods," and by the same author, "Early Medieval Missionary Activity." In the first article he notes that while a minority of Christian writers during the period argued

conversion include King Olav Tryggvanson's violent Christianization of Norway in the late tenth century, and in the twelfth century the forcible subjugation of the Wends who lived east and north of the Elbe River.[75]

Such forced baptisms were the exception rather than the rule, but the pattern of tribal conversion and mass baptisms was not necessarily exceptional."In Kent, Northhumbria, Moravia, Russia, everywhere the same pattern is apparent," observed the historian L. G. D. Baker."Convert the prince, and an enforced or sycophantic general acceptance of Christianity resulted ... Vladimir of Kiev proclaimed that 'if any inhabitant, rich or poor, did not betake himself to the river Dnieper [for baptism], he would risk the Prince's displeasure.'"[76]

These regrettable episodes where the Christian faith was spread through coercive or even violent means should not detract from the genuinely heroic efforts of individual Christian missionaries such as Columba, Aidan, Patrick, and Boniface, but they should be a salutary warning to American evangelicals to be wary of associating the cross of Christ too closely with the American flag, or of coercively enforcing Christian morals in the "culture wars" through the ballot box or other political means.

During the long course of his controversy with the Donatists, Augustine was led to invoke the coercive power of the state to bring the schismatics back into the fold of the Catholic Church. Invoking the saying of Christ in Luke 14:23, "compel them to come in," Augustine intended state action against the schismatics not to be a form of persecution, but rather a means of spiritual discipline."In acting harshly against dissidents the Church, our true and lawful mother, is not repaying evil for evil. She is applying a beneficial discipline by driving out the evil of iniquity."[77] Augustine's view of the coercive power of the state in such cases envisioned the use of fines, confiscation of property, and exile, but not the use of capital punishment or bodily maiming. Nevertheless, Augustine's teachings here—and his influential doctrine of Christian just war—were to have important consequences in the centuries to come, as Christian rulers and popes increasingly came to see secular power as a legitimate means for extending the reach of Christendom.

---

for persuasion as the primary means of evangelization, the majority, "prompted by a strong conviction that the spread of Christianity was divinely ordained and by a hatred of paganism, felt that pagans could rightly be coerced into accepting Christianity, the most efficient form of coercion being some form of political pressure": 273–74.

75. Bosch, *Transforming Mission*, 224.

76. Baker, "The Shadow of the Christian Symbol," 24.

77. Augustine, *Epistle* 93.2, cited in Swift, *The Early Fathers on War and Military Service*, 147.

Pope Gregory I (c. 540–604) was an advocate of the use of high taxation to force stubborn non-Christians into submission, and gave support to the idea of placing military weapons in the service of missionary activity. He praised Gennadius, a north African ruler, for seeking out battle in order that Christianity might be preached to those who were conquered.[78]

During the course of the Middle Ages, especially with the armed reconquest of the Iberian peninsula during the ninth and tenth centuries, Christian notions of defensive wars became more aggressive, and by the time of Gregory VII (Hildebrand) in the eleventh century had evolved into justifications of Christian crusades for the defense and spread of the faith. By the time of the First Crusade (1096) the notion had arisen that forgiveness of sins was assured for those who died on the campaign, and that death in the holy war was a form of martyrdom. A popular crusading song of the time ran as follows: "Whoever proceeds thither, And should die there, He will receive the bounties of heaven, And live with the saints."[79]

These notions of the legitimacy of the use of secular power and military force in the service of the Christian church received canonical justification by the scholastic theologians of the high Middle Ages. In the *Summa Theologica* Thomas Aquinas argued that while Jews and pagans should not be compelled to accept the faith, it was nevertheless legitimate at times for Christians to wage war with unbelievers "in order to prevent them from hindering the faith of Christ." On the other hand, with respect to heretics and apostates, "such should be submitted even to bodily compulsion, that they may fulfill what they have promised, and hold what they, at one time, received."[80] Such teachings were to bear bitter and tragic fruit during the days of the Spanish Inquisition and the Wars of Religion.

b. Linguistic Loss of the Gospel: Bible and Liturgy in Latin

A second major factor in the obscuring of the gospel in Western Christianity in the medieval period was a linguistic one: the restriction to Scripture and liturgy to the Latin language. The missionary practices of the Eastern and Western branches of the church were quite different on this point. When Cyril and Methodius were sent to the Slavs of eastern Europe as Orthodox

---

78. Gregory I, *Registrum*, I, 73: "You [Gennadius] are often eager for wars . . . for the sake of expanding the Empire, where we see that God is reverenced . . . so that, by the preaching of the faith, Christ's name may be heard everywhere among the subjected peoples": cited in Erdmann, *The Origin of the Idea of Crusade*, 10.

79. Erdmann, *The Origin of the Idea of Crusade*, 344–45.

80. Aquinas, *Summa Theologica* Pt. II-II, Q. 10, art. 8, 1219.

missionaries, they were chosen for their intimate knowledge of the Slavic language, and set about to translate the Bible and the liturgy into the language of the peoples they sought to convert. Missions historian Richard Sullivan has noted that the efforts of Cyril and Methodius in the ninth century were intended "as a way of presenting Christianity in all its complexity so that it would be understood by a pagan audience .... There was to be no simplification of Christianity for pagan consumption."[81]

In the West, on the other hand, monastic missionaries for the most part were not fluent in the local languages and did not translate the Bible and liturgy into the vernacular. Augustine of Canterbury, sent to the British Isles by Gregory I to evangelize England, did not know the local languages, and for centuries after there was no Bible or liturgy in Anglo-Saxon.[82] Patrick, the great missionary to Ireland, though he himself was Celtic and spoke the language fluently, made no attempt to translate the Bible into the native language, and Latin was to remain the language of Scripture and liturgy.[83]

This limitation of the language of Scripture and liturgy to the Latin language in the West made for a linguistically unified "Christendom," at least for an educated elite, but for the generality of church members it meant the sequestering of the gospel message within an unintelligible language. As the Catholic scholar Robert McNally has observed, because of the limitation of the Scriptures to the Old Latin and Vulgate translations, "the Bible was for all practical purposes a closed book .... The spiritual life of the faithful was not extinguished, but languished and suffered acutely from undernourishment."[84] By the ninth century, if not earlier, Latin had ceased to be a living language understood by the people, being replaced by the vernacular languages of Europe, and consequently, the language of the church and its gospel could not be clearly understood by the ordinary Christian.

During the Middle Ages the Catholic Church prohibited translation of the Bible into the vernacular and its private reading and possession by the laity. An enactment of the Synod of Toulouse (1229) is representative:

> The laity shall not have books of Scripture with the exception of the psalter and the divine office. And they shall not have these books in the vernacular. Moreover, we forbid the laity the permission to have books of the Old or the New Testament,

---

81. Sullivan, "Early Medieval Missionary Activity," 26–27. In the ancient churches of the East, the Armenians, the Syrians, the Copts, the Nestorians, and the Ethiopians had the benefit of the Scriptures and the liturgy in their native tongues.

82. Baker, "The Shadow of the Christian Symbol," 24.

83. Walls, *The Missionary Movement in Christian History*, 38.

84. McNally, *The Unreformed Church*, 7.

unless for the sake of devotion one should wish to have a psalter or breviary, or the hours of the Blessed Virgin. But we most strictly prohibit their having these books translated into the vernacular.[85]

The stated rationale for such restrictions was to protect the faithful from heresy, but the effect was to give the clergy monopolistic control over the Scriptures, and to prevent deeper understanding and knowledge of the gospel itself.

It was not only the restrictive use of the Latin language, but also developments in the liturgy itself during the Middle Ages that contributed to the inaccessibility of the gospel. One development was the reduction in the amount of Scripture read during the services. Book viii of the fourth-century *Apostolic Constitutions* gives witness to the practice of the reading of two lessons from the Old Testament, one from the Pentateuch, and one from the Prophets—following the synagogue practice.[86] In the following centuries these Old Testament lessons were omitted, and Scripture readings were limited to the Gospels and the Epistles. Even here, however, it was the case that these lessons, being read from the Latin Vulgate, in many cases could not be understood by the priest—not being, in most cases, trained and educated in the universities—much less by the people.[87]

In the medieval period church architecture was also changing, with the altar receding further away from the people and being placed on the back wall, with the priest performing the mass with his back turned to the people.[88] By the ninth century the eucharistic prayers (the "canon") at the heart of the liturgy, witnessing to the core gospel events of Christ's death and resurrection, were being voiced by the priest in a low, inaudible tone that the people could not hear, even apart from not understanding the Latin language in which they were spoken. The central event of the liturgy had become not a clear statement of the Christian gospel, but a visual experience in which the people watched the priest elevate the transubstantiated host, which was believed to convey spiritual benefits apart from the act of actual participation and communion.[89]

85. Ibid., 76.

86. Baumstark, *Comparative Liturgy*, 23.

87. McNally, *The Unreformed Church*, 70, states: "Within the framework of the liturgy—the Mass, the Sacraments and the Office—the Bible was read in Latin, which normally *was not understood either by the clergy or the laity* [emphasis added], while in the homilies and sermons which were preached to the faithful it scarcely ever received an interpretation that was solidly built on salvation history and biblical theology."

88. White, *A Brief History of Christian Worship*, 88.

89. Klauser, *A Short History of the Western Liturgy*, 103; Jungmann, *Pastoral Liturgy*, 71.

c. Theological Issues: Baptism; Catechesis; Purgatory; Justification

In the medieval period developments in four areas—the practice of baptism, catechesis, and the doctrines of purgatory and justification—each, in its own way, tended to obscure the clarity of the essential gospel message. With respect to baptism, two aspects need consideration: first, the doctrine of baptismal regeneration, and second, the growth of the practice of infant baptism. In the Roman Catholic understanding, baptism in the name of the triune God, administered by the church, is a "birth into the new life in Christ ... by which man becomes an adoptive son of the Father, a member of Christ, and a temple of the Holy Spirit."[90] Water baptism administered by the Church "imprints on the soul an indelible spiritual character" and cannot be repeated.[91] Baptism is a sacrament which "cleanses us from original sin, *makes us Christians* [emphasis added], children of God, and heirs of heaven."[92] Being "made a Christian" though baptismal regeneration became, in the Catholic tradition, what "accepting Jesus as your personal Lord and Savior" came to mean in the Protestant evangelical tradition of revivalism.

By the sixth century, adult baptisms were becoming rare in Europe, and infant baptism was becoming the norm.[93] It is likely that the influence of Augustine's doctrine of original sin, and the high rates of infant mortality, gave impetus to the desire by both parents and ecclesiastics alike to have children baptized as soon as possible after birth.[94] Church teachings held no prospects of salvation for those infants who died without baptism. With infant baptism becoming the norm, the ancient practices of catechetical instruction for adult converts fell into disuse, and as a result, many in medieval Europe grew up in the church as "Christians" but with little in-

---

90. *Catechism of the Catholic Church*, 324–25. For the historical development of this understanding of baptism, see J. N. D. Kelly, *Early Christian Doctrines*, "Early Views of the Sacraments," 193–99; Martos, *Doors to the Sacred*, 161–202.

91. *Catechism of the Catholic Church*, 325. David Bosch has observed in this regard that "Since the act of baptism conferred a *character indelibilis* on the person baptized, nobody could ever undo his or her baptism; even when someone had *resisted baptism*, he or she became a *fidelis* (believer)": *Transforming Mission*, 219.

92. Kelley, *Saint Joseph Baltimore Catechism*, "Lesson 14—On Baptism." The Baltimore Catechism was the standard catechism used in Roman Catholic schools in the United States from 1885 to the late 1960s, and is still in print as the *New Saint Joseph Baltimore Catechism*.

93. Jungmann, "Catechumenate," 240; on historical developments regarding infant baptism, see also Finn, *Early Christian Baptism* and Fisher, *Christian Initiation*.

94. J. G. Davies, "The Disintegration of the Christian Initiation Rite," 409. See also Fisher, *Christian Initiation*, "The Shortening of the Interval between Birth and Baptism," 109–19, for developments in this area in the medieval period.

depth instruction in the core doctrines of the Christian faith. Infant baptism could become, in the worst instances, a form of ecclesiastical magic: "The priest poured the water on the infant's head, saying the right words, and the child was saved from hell."[95] Taken together, the teachings of baptismal regeneration, the predominance of infant baptism, and the disappearance of rigorous catechetical instruction all combined to produce a form of nominal Christianity in Europe and elsewhere that has endured to the present day.[96]

A third element that obscured the gospel in the medieval period was the development of the doctrine of purgatory. The current *Catechism of the Catholic Church* states that "All who die in God's grace and friendship, but still imperfectly purified, are indeed assured of their eternal salvation; but after death they undergo purification, so as to achieve the holiness necessary to enter the joy of heaven."[97] The Church "also commends almsgiving, indulgences, and works of penance undertaken on behalf of the dead."[98]

Belief in purgatory, which appears as early as Clement of Alexandria and Origen, and in many of the later fathers, took hold in the Middle Ages and became more theologically defined in the period from 1100 to 1250 with the development of scholastic theology. Around the year 1274 purgatory was identified as a definite place, distinct from heaven and hell.[99]

The doctrine was officially and dogmatically defined by the Catholic Church at the Council of Florence (1439) and at the Council of Trent (1563), the latter in response to criticisms by the Protestant Reformers. The Council of Trent, in its twenty-fifth session, declared that *"there is a purgatory, and that the souls detained therein are aided by the suffrages of the faithful and chiefly by the acceptable sacrifice of the altar."*[100] This latter statement defends the practice of votive masses: a mass devoted to the memory and benefit of a departed loved one, with the sacrifice of the mass offered by the priest being believed to shorten one's time in purgatory.[101]

95. Martos, *Doors to the Sacred*, 94.

96. On the history of catechetical instruction, see Dujarier, *A History of the Catechumenate*; Murphy Center for Liturgical Research, *Made, Not Born*; Harmless, *Augustine and the Catechumenate*.

97. *Catechism of the Catholic Church*, 268.

98. Ibid., 269.

99. Swanson, "The Burdens of Purgatory," 354. For the history of the doctrine of purgatory, see also: "Purgatory," *Catholic Encyclopedia*; and especially the extensive study of Le Goff, *The Birth of Purgatory*.

100. Rahner, ed., *The Teaching of the Catholic Church*, 421.

101. One of the most extravagant instances on record in this regard was King Henry VII of England, "who made provision in his will for 10,000 masses to be said for his soul after death and who built an ornate chapel at Westminster for the sole purpose of housing monks who would pray in perpetuity for the repose of his soul. This was a king

The doctrine of purgatory obscured the gospel in several important ways. In the first place, the faithful in the Middle Ages could not hope for the immediate joys and "Good News" of heaven in the presence of Christ at the time of death, but the fearful "bad news" of the "purifying" fires of purgatory. The pictures painted for the popular imagination were vivid indeed, even gruesome. The following description from Sir Thomas More in the sixteenth century is representative, portraying the torments of those in purgatory:

> If ye pity the blind, there is none so blind as we, which are all here in the dark, saving for sights unpleasant, and loathsome, till some comfort come.... If ye pity any man in pain, never knew pain comparable to ours; whose fire... passeth in heat all the fires that ever burned on earth.... We... souls lie sleepless, restless, burning and broiling in the dark fire one long night of many days, many weeks, and some of many years together.... Our keepers are such as God keeps you from—cruel, damned sprites, odious, envious, and hateful.... Their company [is] more horrible and grievous to us than is the pain itself: and the intolerable torment that they do us, wherewith from top to toe they cease not continually to tear us.[102]

These popular pictures of purgatory and the doctrine itself were rooted in a faulty view of the atonement: a failure to understand the *finished and sufficient work of Christ on the cross*. The cross, while theoretically the basis of salvation, in practice had to be supplemented by penances, good works, and the sacrifice of the mass to make up for the yet-to-be-paid "temporal punishment due to sins."

These teachings on purgatory are logically and theologically connected with the traditional Roman Catholic understanding of justification. From the time of Augustine forward there was not a clear doctrinal distinction between justification and sanctification, and justification was seen not so much as a completed, punctiliar event in which the righteousness of Christ was *imputed* to the believer, but rather as a lifelong process, beginning at baptism, in which righteousness is *infused* into the believer,

---

who was taking no chances": Griffiths, "Purgatory," 442n13.

102. Cited in Dickens, *The English Reformation*, 29. For another vivid medieval picture of the gruesome pains of purgatory, see "The Knight Owein's Journey Through St. Patrick's Purgatory" (1184), in Shinners, *Medieval Popular Religion, 1000-1500*, 517–30: "Fiery snakes encircled other people's necks, arms, or entire bodies and, pressing their heads against the chests of the poor wretches, they sank the burning fangs of their mouths into their hearts.... Those who were thus pinned and tormented never ceased crying and moaning...": 522.

primarily through the sacraments.[103] Believers, by faith cooperating with good works, can increase in the degree of justification experienced. This synergistic understanding of the relationship between grace and works was stated definitively by the Council of Trent (1548), in response to criticisms of Luther and the Protestant Reformers:

> Chpt. X. The Increase of the Justification Received
>
> Having . . . been justified and made friends of God . . . they are renewed . . . through the observance of the commands of God and the Church, faith cooperating with good works, [they] *increase in that justice received through the grace of Christ* [emphasis added] (James 2:22) and are further justified . . .[104]

This conflation of justification (event) and sanctification (process) is still found in the current standard for Roman Catholic doctrine, the *Catechism of the Catholic Church* (1994), which states that "Justification is not only the remission of sins, but also the sanctification and renewal of the interior man."[105]

A synergistic understanding of the role of grace and human works in justification, and the notion of a justification that increases in degree with further infusions of grace, obscures the gospel message of being made righteous by the grace of God alone through faith alone. The believer's assurance of salvation is also undermined, since the process of justification/sanctification is not completed in this life. Justification not being decisively and completely accomplished by the imputation of Christ's righteousness through faith alone, further purification of the believer must be accomplished in purgatory after death. Recent ecumenical conversations between Roman Catholics and evangelicals, between Lutherans and Roman Catholics, and between Anglicans and Roman Catholics, have manifested movement by Rome in the direction of historic Protestant understandings, but significant differences still remain.[106]

---

103. For a comprehensive study of the history of the doctrine of justification, see McGrath, *Iustitia Dei*.

104. Rahner, ed., *The Teaching of the Catholic Church*, 390–91.

105. *Catechism of the Catholic Church*, 482. The mixture of grace and works can still be found in post-Vatican II popular Catholicism, as witnessed in the answer to Q. 67: "What is necessary for entering heaven?" given in Lodders, the *Pocket Catechism*: 1."We must be baptized." 2."We must believe everything that God has revealed and the Church holds before us for our belief." 3."*We must perform good works. We must truly merit heaven* [emphasis added]." 4."We must appear in the state of grace before God after this earthly life": ibid.

106. For discussion of these recent ecumenical discussions on justification, see McGrath, *Iustitia Dei*, 413–18, and Noll and Nystrom, *Is The Reformation Over?*, 151–83.

3. From the Reformation to Revivalism: Changing Understandings of Conversion and the Not-Quite-Full Recovery of the Biblical Gospel

3.1. Luther and the Reformers

The positive, indeed revolutionary, gains of the Protestant Reformation introduced by Martin Luther and the magisterial Reformers are well known and do not need extensive discussion here: the articulation of the fundamental truth of justification by faith alone in Christ alone; the supremacy of the authority of the Bible for Christian faith and life; the believer's immediate access to God by faith apart from the mediation of a human priesthood and sacramental system; the liberation from the medieval doctrines of purgatory, merit, and indulgences; the translation of the Bible and the liturgy into the vernacular languages of the people, and so on.[107] Protestant Christians today may be tempted to take these gains for granted, but they indeed represented a monumental recovery of the clarity of the gospel and of its accessibility to the believer in the Scriptures and in the life and worship of the church.

At the same time, it can be said that the Protestant Reformation, its enormous biblical and theological gains notwithstanding, represented a "not-quite-full" recovery of the biblical gospel, insofar as the break with "Christendom" as the context of the gospel was not complete. Luther, Calvin, and the English Reformers did not fundamentally question the assumption of Christendom, in place since the time of Theodosius, that the power of the state should be used to enforce Christian orthodoxy and to punish heretics.[108] The *spiritual* "power of the gospel for the salvation of everyone who believes" (Rom 1:16) was still too much embedded in the political, economic, and technological power of Western, European, and American civilization as the colonial powers brought the Christian religion to the peoples of Africa, Asia, and Latin America during the post-Reformation period.[109]

---

107. On the life and thought of Luther in historical context, see: Bainton, *Here I Stand*; Dillenberger, ed., *Martin Luther*; Oberman, *Luther*; Kittleson, *Luther the Reformer*. On the Reformation and the Reformers generally, see the essays in Bagchi and Steinmetz, eds., *The Cambridge Companion to Reformation Theology*; Chadwick, *The Reformation*; Dillenberger and Welch, *Protestant Christianity*, especially 1-98.

108. On this point, the Anabaptists—the representatives of the "Radical Reformation" at times persecuted by the magisterial Reformers—were ahead of their times and more in keeping with modern notions of the separation of church and state.

109. For discussion of the various aspects of the connections between Christian missions and Western colonialism, see: Christensen and Hutchinson, eds., *Missionary Ideologies in the Imperialist Era: 1880-1920*; Todorov, *The Conquest of America*;

A striking expression of this amalgamation of the Christian faith and Western civilizational power is found in Friedrich Schleiermacher's *The Christian Faith* (1828) in which the "father of modern liberal Protestant theology" states that with respect to the churches' powers of working miracles, "it is undeniable that, in view of the *great advantage in power and civilization* [emphasis added] which the Christian peoples possess over the non-Christian [JD: non-European], almost without exception, the preachers of today do not need such signs."[110] Such miraculous powers are "superfluous," in Schleiermacher's opinion. While immediately directed against the claims of the Roman Catholic Church with respect to miracles as evidence of its legitimacy and claims, Schleiermacher's comments in their wider significance are telling evidence of the displacement of confidence in the *supernatural* power of the gospel itself by the scientific and technological power of European culture.

Changing Understandings of Conversion: From the Puritans to Modern Revivalism

Puritanism and the "New England Way"

Modern American evangelicalism is deeply indebted to the heritage of Puritanism, in both its English and American expressions. In England, the Puritans attempted (but did not succeed in) the carrying through of a thorough-going reformation of the Church of England according to the principles of the continental Reformers as they understood them, in their search for a more pure and biblically constituted church. The evangelism and articulation of the gospel by English Puritan writers such as Richard Baxter and Joseph Alleine was based on a robust biblical theology and high standards for repentance and discipleship. In his widely read *Alarm to the Unconverted* (1671) Alleine made it clear that a would-be convert must "choose the laws of Christ as the rule of your words, thoughts and actions . . . . You must choose them all, there is no getting to heaven by partial obedience. It is not enough to take the cheap and easy part of religion . . . . You must take all or none."[111] In a similar vein, Richard Baxter's influential

---

Rivera, *A Violent Evangelism*; W. Edwards, *Forging an Ideology for American Missions*. On Western colonialism and Christian missions in China, see Yao, "At the Turn of the Century"; on the suppression (and destruction) of Native American cultures by (some) Christian missionaries, see Beaver, *Church, State, and the American*; and Tinker, *Missionary Conquest*.

110. Vol. 2, 450.

111. Alleine, *Alarm to the Unconverted*, 115. Both George Whitefield and Charles

Call to the Unconverted (1657) set the bar high for authentic conversion and discipleship: "If you will turn and live, do it unreservedly, absolutely, and universally. Think not to capitulate with Christ, and to divide your heart betwixt him and the world, and to part with some sins and to keep the rest . . . . You must in heart and resolution forsake all that you have, or else you cannot be his disciples. If you will not take God and heaven for your portion, and lay all below the feet of Christ . . . it is in vain to dream of salvation in these terms."[112] For Alleine and Baxter and the Puritans generally, it would have been a biblical contradiction in terms to speak of evangelism and conversion in terms of accepting Jesus as "Savior" without fully submitting to Jesus as *Lord*.[113]

The founding fathers of New England congregationalism brought from England their Reformed and Puritan theology, and attempted to apply the detailed descriptions of saving faith and the process of conversion developed by the Reformed theologians William Ames and William Perkins to standards of church membership, in their quest for pure, biblically reformed churches of "visible saints" and truly regenerate believers. During the period 1640–1662, a system that came to be known as the "New England Way" required a detailed personal testimony of Christian conversion that would be convincing to the whole church as a condition of full communicant church membership. Based on the conversion morphologies of Ames and Perkins and others, as many as ten steps might be distinguished, involving a movement from initial indifference, to the beginnings of spiritual stirrings and awakening to personal need, the beginnings of conviction of sin, "legal fear," periods of anxiety and doubt (that could last for months, or even years),

---

Haddon Spurgeon were influenced by their reading of Alleine.

112. Baxter, *Call to the Unconverted*, 57.

113. For a very helpful discussion of Puritan understandings of evangelism generally, and contrasts with modern methods of evangelism since Finney, see Packer, *A Quest for Godliness*, "Puritan Evangelism," 291–308, and "The Puritan View of Preaching the Gospel," 163–176; on 169 Packer notes that the "Puritan view was that preaching 'gospel sermons' means teaching the whole Christian system—the character of God, the Trinity, the plan of salvation, the entire work of grace. To preach Christ, they held, involved preaching all this"—in contrast to our modern idea that "preaching 'gospel sermons' means just harping on a few great truths—guilt, and atonement, and forgiveness—set virtually in a theological vacuum." The Puritan conception could be termed a "maximalist" understanding of the content of the "gospel" as contrasted with "minimalist" views. See also Wells, *Turning to God*, especially 92–95 for the problematic shift from the Reformation and Puritan understanding of conversion to revivalism's emphasis on the individual's subjective experience, often disconnected from the local church and its regular worship. Wells astutely observes that "evangelism moved outside the churches, not . . . because the churches were inhospitable (as in the case of Wesley and Whitefield) but because it really was a new kind of evangelism": ibid., 93.

achievement of a sense of assurance (understood to never be complete and indubitable), and so forth.[114]

By 1662 it became apparent that the system was not working as anticipated, in that many who had grown up in the churches since the 1640s were not making the expected professions of faith and becoming full communicant church members. A compromise that came to be known as the "Half-Way Covenant" was then instituted, that allowed such individuals who, while not meeting the high bar of a detailed personal conversion narrative, still assented to the basic Christian beliefs and whose outward lives were not scandalous, to present their children for (infant) baptism.[115]

In 1667 Solomon Stoddard, the influential and respected pastor of the church in Northampton, Massachusetts took the bold step of instituting the practice of open communion, that is, admitting to full church membership those who made a credible profession of faith and repentance, even though such professions might be judged to fall short of the detailed narratives of religious experience that had been expected under the former "New England Way." This more inclusive and generous understanding of the standards for church membership subsequently spread to many other New England churches.[116]

In 1748 Jonathan Edwards, now pastor in Northampton, as a result of his experiences and observations of the Great Awakening in the New England churches, repudiated the practice of "open communion" of his grandfather Solomon Stoddard, and returned to the earlier "New England Way" that had required a specific personal narrative of conversion and personal religious experience.[117] In his description of the Great Awakening, *A Faithful Narrative,* Edwards developed a three-stage morphology of conversion that involved 1) conviction of sin; 2) a sense of personal despair; and 3) a joyous sense of personal sins forgiven.[118] According to the church historian C. C. Goen, Edward's description of the pattern of conversion became what revivalists "in and after the Great Awakening came to expect of all converts," and remains influential among evangelicals down to the present day.[119]

---

114. The classic study in this area is Morgan, *Visible Saints*; see especially "The New England System," 64–112, and "The Halfway Covenant," 113–38. Additional, more recent scholarship on the Puritan understandings of conversion include: Pettit, *The Heart Prepared*; Caldwell, *The Puritan Conversion Narrative*; and Cohen, *God's Caress*.

115. See also Pope, *The Half-Way Covenant*.

116. Morgan, *Visible Saints*, 146–52.

117. Ibid., 151.

118. A very helpful discussion of "The Morphology of Conversion" in Edwards is provided by Goen, *The Works of Jonathan Edwards*, vol. 4, *The Great Awakening*, 25–32.

119. Ibid., 28–29.

FINNEY AND THE ORIGINS OF MODERN REVIVALISM

The historical trajectory from Finney through Moody and Billy Sunday to Billy Graham and the present represents a powerful tradition of evangelism and a way of understanding conversion that has deeply influenced the identity of American evangelicalism down to the present day. It is not always adequately understood how indeed revolutionary were the "new measures" in evangelism that were introduced by Charles Grandison Finney in the early decades of the nineteenth century: the "protracted meeting," the "anxious bench" for inquirers, and the notion of the believer's ability to make an immediate decision for conversion to Christ.[120] For much of the history of the Christian church there were no special "revival meetings" apart from the normal weekly worship services of the local church and its resident pastors. With Finney, all this began to change, as evangelism became a predominantly *parachurch* activity conducted by itinerant, independent evangelists not accountable to any particular local church.[121]

With Finney, a momentous shift of emphasis began to occur: from divine sovereignty to human agency in revivals of religion and the process of conversion. In what Charles Hambrick-Stowe has called "one of the most controversial sentences in American religious history," Finney declared that "A revival of religion is not a miracle." A revival "is the result of the right use of appropriate means.... A revival is as naturally a result of the use of appropriate means as a crop is of the use of its appropriate means."[122] In a

---

120. One of the finest studies of Finney and his work is found in Hambrick-Stowe, *Charles Finney and the Spirit of American Evangelicalism*; see also Rosell and Dupuis, *The Memoirs of Charles G. Finney* for the definitive scholarly edition of Finney's memoirs, with comprehensive annotations and notes. For some astute observations on Finney's methods and theology, see Packer, *A Quest for Godliness*, 292–94. The seminal article by Brauer, "Conversion," places the entire trajectory of revivalism into its larger historical and theological context.

121. The history of revivalism properly includes, of course, the work of John Wesley in England and of George Whitefield on both sides of the Atlantic during the Great Awakening, and also the story of the frontier revivals in Tennessee and Kentucky and the Methodist camp meetings that preceded Finney; it is not the purpose of this chapter, however, to address these historical roots of revivalism. On Whitefield, see Stout, *The Divine Dramatist*; on Wesley and conversion, see Rack, "John Wesley and Early Methodist Conversion." On the frontier camp meetings, see Johnson, *The Frontier Camp Meeting*. W. Cross, *The Burned-Over District*, provides important historical context for understanding Finney's work.

122. Hambrick-Stowe, *Charles Finney and the Spirit of American Evangelicalism*, 156; Finney, *Lectures on Revivals of Religion*, 4–5: Lecture 1, "What a Revival of Religion Is." Finney's *Lectures on Revivals* were widely read and debated and have continued to influence evangelists down to the present day. Bebbington has pointed out that the increasing confidence in human agency and ability in conversion had been anticipated in

dramatic break with the theological heritage of New England Puritanism and the Augustinian-Calivinistic doctrines of human inability and total depravity, Finney was in effect declaring that revivals could be predictably "engineered" and that sinners could *immediately* decide to be converted to God: "You know that we call sinners to decide on the spot whether they will obey the gospel."[123]

An unintended but highly significant consequence of the new emphasis on *immediate* decisions for *conversion* was to undercut the importance of long-term, sustained teaching and catechesis in lifelong *discipleship.*"Decisions" as countable and observable manifestations of subjective religious experience began to overshadow the ongoing tasks of Christian nurture and discipleship in the context of the local church community.[124]

Together with his introduction of "New Measures" and the increased emphasis on human agency and ability, Finney believed that evangelists and revivalists needed more "exciting" styles of preaching to meet the needs

---

the New Haven theology associated with Nathaniel William Taylor; Taylor applied the Kantian axiom that "Ought [to convert] implies Able [to convert]": "Taylor's theology, first propounded in 1818, was to be the foundation of Finney's practice in revivalism": Bebbington, "Evangelical Conversion, c. 1740–1850," 19.

123. Finney, *Lectures on Revivals*, 16. Bernard Weisberger has noted that "Finney's generation opened the gates to human arrangement in the plan of salvation, and technique came in through the aperture. And technique was immortal, whereas the day that bred the revival was not": *They Gathered at the River*, 269. Finney's demand for an immediate decision was reinforced by a style described by some observers as "hellfire and damnation" preaching. One description of Finney's early preaching from an observer in Utica, New York is as follows: "You raise your voice, lift high your hand, bend forward your trunk, fasten your eyes upon the auditors, declare that they know it to be God's truth that they stand upon the brink of hell's gaping pit of fire and brimstone, and bending your body and bringing your clenched fist half way from the pulpit to the broad aisle, pronounce *instant and eternal damnation* upon them unless they repent forthwith": cited in McLoughlin Jr., *Modern Revivalism*, 28.

124. As Stout has noted, this disconnection of evangelism from the local church and its regular ministries is a trend that began with Whitefield: "In preaching to mass audiences of disconnected individuals, strangers, Whitefield helped to introduce a new concept of religious experience that grew throughout the nineteenth century into a recognizably 'evangelical' movement. In the new religious experience, piety was no longer something inextricably bound up with local community and corporate spirituality [JD: the local church, its weekly worship, liturgy, and sacraments]. The emphasis shifted to a more individualistic and subjective sense of piety that found its quintessential expression in the internal, highly personal experience of the 'New Birth' . . . . The very meaning of 'revival' shifted from a mysterious, local, communal event to one that was predictable and highly subjective": *The Divine Dramatist*, xx–xxi. These trends introduced by Whitefield were reinforced and "mainstreamed" by Finney and his "New Measures."

of the modern age." Without new measures it is impossible that the church should succeed in gaining the attention of the world to religion . . . . The church cannot maintain her ground, cannot command attention, without very exciting preaching, and sufficient novelty in measures, to get the public ear," he stated. "It is evident that we must have more exciting preaching, to meet the character and wants of the age . . . . The character of the age is changed, and these men [JD: e.g. Presbyterian ministers of Finney's day] have not conformed to it, but retain the same stiff, dry, prosing style of preaching that answered half a century ago."[125]

While Finney could not have anticipated the lengths to which his principle of "exciting" preaching would be taken by Billy Sunday and his theatrical methods, or in some contemporary expressions of "entertainment" evangelism, one can ask whether Finney was in effect forgetting the Apostle Paul's emphasis on the *supernatural*—not human—power of the gospel itself (Rom 1:16), preached in the power of the Holy Spirit (1 Cor 2:4, "not with wise and persuasive words, but with a demonstration of the Spirit's power"; see 2 Cor 10:4; 1 Thess 1:5, "our gospel came to you not simply with words, but also with the Holy Spirit and deep conviction").

Dwight L. Moody, one of the great pioneers of modern urban evangelism, is said to have traveled over a million miles during the years of his active ministry between the years 1875-1899, and to have preached the gospel in person to more than one hundred million people.[126] His critics considered his theology to be simplistic,[127] but Moody's popular, heartfelt style and homely illustrations had wide appeal and brought many to a new or renewed faith in Christ. The historian of evangelicalism David Bebbington credited Moody with changing modern revivalism in these important ways: its interdenominational character; the increased involvement of the laity in leadership; concern for social reform; the emphasis on human emotion and the will more than reason; and its stress on organizational strategy.[128]

Effective preacher and evangelist that he undeniably was, it is to Moody's great credit that he did not overrate the preacher's role in bringing

---

125. Finney, *Lectures on Revivals*, 172-73.

126. Rosell, ed., *Commending the Faith*, xiv.

127. Weisberger, *They Gathered at the River*, believed that Moody had "pared the last theological subtleties from it [the gospel] as he popularized its terminology . . . . As theology grew simpler, technique became predominant . . . . Once, the salvation of a soul had been a miracle . . . . Now it was a nightly crowd performance registered on cards," 270-71. Moody's defenders would, of course, consider this judgment too harsh.

128. Bebbington, "How Moody Changed Revivalism," cited by Rosell, ed., *Commending the Faith*, xxii. It could be argued, however, that the linkage of revivalism and social reform originated with Finney rather than Moody.

people to faith."People are not usually converted under the preaching of the minister," he once stated."It is in the inquiry-meeting that they are most likely to be brought to Christ."[129] Like Finney before him, and unlike some later evangelists who followed him, Moody had personal contact with many of those to whom he preached in subsequent follow-up conversations in the inquiry rooms. He trained his workers to not pressure inquirers to make a premature public profession of faith.[130]

It was not Moody's evangelistic practice to make a final plea for converts in his large public meetings, and it is to his great credit that he did not emphasize numbers in the assessment of the success of his ministry. When asked if he would tell inquirers that they were saved, he replied: "No, let God tell them. That record is kept on high. I think it is very wrong to tell inquirers that they are saved. They can be saved by putting their trust in the Lord God of heaven."[131]

It is not easy to assess the long-term impact of Moody's revival meetings on church growth. Many of the people who responded to Moody were already church members and were renewing their commitments rather than making a first-time profession of faith. In Chicago in 1876 at an inquiry meeting of about 150 people, when the inquiry leader asked all Christians present to stand, almost all stood; when asked how many present were "sinners who anxiously desired to be saved," only three stood up.[132] Moody had a sincere concern to reach the unchurched urban poor, but at his meetings it was the middle- and upper-middle-class church members who were most likely to attend and to respond.[133] Two scholarly studies of the impact of Moody's revival meetings concluded, in general, that numbers of new church members tended to rise for a year or so following Moody's campaigns, but then were followed by downswings that eventually offset the gains made shortly after the revival meetings ended.[134]

129. Cited in Bradford, *D. L. Moody*, 268.

130. Dorsett, *A Passion for Souls*, 401. Dorsett notes Moody's concern for the ancient pastoral practice of "soul care": "He ministered personally as a soul physician and guide. He also trained a generation of pastoral men and women in the time-honored ministry of the care of souls": ibid., 400—a quality of personal care that was often lost in the large urban churches during the modern period. Moody Bible Institute was founded, in part, for the purpose of training workers for such "soul care."

131. Cited in Bradford, *D. L. Moody*, 291.

132. Findlay Jr., *Dwight Moody: American Evangelist 1837-1899*, 267. Findlay provides a careful scholarly assessment of Moody's work.

133. Ibid., 174.

134. Ibid., 271. The studies cited by Findlay are Dike, "A Study of New England Revivals," and Loetscher, "Presbyterianism and Revivalism in Philadelphia since 1875." Findlay concluded that "Evidently there is enough substance in the primary data to

Characterized by one historian as a "pugnacious baseball player-turned-preacher" and the "greatest of the tent and tabernacle revivalists," Billy Sunday had preached to over 100 million people in prisons, rescue missions, hospitals, factories, local churches, tents, and wooden tabernacles by the end of his career in 1935. Perhaps as many a million people had responded to his flamboyant, pulpit-pounding, even theatrical preaching of the gospel and come forward to shake his hand and pray to "receive Jesus as their personal Savior."[135] Billy Sunday had become a national celebrity, and by the time of World War I, according to Lyle Dorsett, a "cult of personality" had developed, with people eager to shake Sunday's hand, buy his picture, and secure his autograph; speaking invitations came in by the thousands, and Sunday was inundated with money received through offerings and the mail.[136]

Billy Sunday unashamedly applied the latest business methods and techniques in his urban revivals, using public relations experts and organizational machinery that surpassed anything ever employed by Finney or Moody.[137] According to historian William G. McLoughlin Jr., Sunday "carried modern revivalism to a new peak of mechanical efficiency."[138] In an outline of a "Sermon to Businessmen" he explicitly compared his revival techniques with those used by big business: "I am not only a preacher, but a businessman . . . I endeavor to bring 1. System and organization; 2. Business principles; 3. 'Common sense' into revival work."[139] According to a *New York Times* reporter, Sunday and his staff ". . . made it clear that they were going after souls as a successful commercial corporation goes after sales."[140]

---

support the claims of both Moody's supporters and his detractors, although the critics seem to possess a stronger case . . . . At the most, mass revivals provided only a temporary uplift. The burden of maintaining a vital church membership rested ultimately, as it always had, in the hands of local churches and ministers": ibid., 272. He cites the statement of a New York minister interviewed in 1896 after one of Moody's campaigns: "I have, in my twenty-six years' pastorate here, added to my church 3000 members. I have done it by hard, steady work, not by fireworks and hurrah methods. New York is so big that shelling the woods doesn't do much good. It is the steady work, directed intelligently, that counts": ibid.

135. Dorsett, *Billy Sunday and the Redemption of Urban America*, 93. McLoughlin notes that Sunday's preaching style was "slangy and flamboyant; he leaped around his revival platform like an acrobat, shouting and telling funny stories and waving the American flag as he stood on top of the pulpit": *Modern Revivals, Awakenings, and Reform*, 147.

136. Dorsett, *Billy Sunday and the Redemption of Urban America*, 99.

137. Ibid., 146.

138. McLoughlin Jr., *Modern Revivalism*, 420.

139. Ibid.

140. Ibid. Robert F. Martin, in his study of Sunday, commented that "Sunday, of course, was not a businessman in the usual sense of that term, yet a part of his appeal

The evangelist responded to critics of the high costs of his revivals by claiming that his meetings produced more converts more cheaply than any other revivalists and even more cheaply than the local churches themselves: "What I'm paid for my work makes it only about $2 a soul, and I get less proportionately for the number I convert than any other living evangelist."[141] Delivering converts at the cost of "$2 a soul" would indeed have seemed like a bargain.

Sunday delivered the historic, biblical gospel as he understood it, but his "invitations" tended to be lacking in theological content and biblical clarity at the crucial point of the Lordship of Christ and discipleship: "You know that God has spoken to you.... How many of you will settle the great question without delay... by coming forward to take me by the hand, and by so doing confess and accept Jesus Christ as your personal Savior? Who will come?"[142] Other invitations included, "I want the inspiration of taking the hand of every fellow who says 'I'm with you for Jesus Christ and for truth.' Come on. You've been mighty fine tonight," or, "Come on down and take my hand against booze, for Jesus Christ, for your [American] flag."[143] Making a "decision for Christ" was as simple as coming forward and shaking the famous evangelist's hand.

It is not easy to assess the long-term results of the presumed "conversions" registered by Sunday's methods, but there are some grounds for skepticism. McLoughlin's analysis of the available statistical data concluded that comparisons of church attendance and membership five years before and five years after a Sunday revival showed that immediate increases were usually counterbalanced by declines thereafter. He concluded that Sunday's big city revivals during the period of 1906 to 1918 "did not seriously alter the over-all picture one way or the other."[144] Sunday sincerely wished to

---

stemmed from the fact that there was much about his life and evangelism that was congruent with the materialistic, success-oriented ethos of the day.... His ministry appeared to operate like a well-oiled machine. Every aspect of a campaign—advertising, financing, organization of personnel..., handling of crowds—was highly orchestrated. Published statistics regarding attendance, revenues, and numbers of 'trail hitters' provided detailed... indexes of the economy, efficiency and effectiveness with which a revival was run. The evangelist and his staff were God's experts, winning souls... with the precision of an engineer and skill of a scientific manager": *Hero of the Heartland*, 49, 104.

141. McLoughlin Jr., *Billy Sunday Was His Real Name*, 116.

142. Cited in Brown, *The Real Billy Sunday*, 146.

143. McLoughlin Jr., *Modern Revivalism*, 434.

144. Ibid., 430-432. McLoughlin cites the statement of the field secretary of the New York Church Federation who in 1928, after one of Sunday's New York meetings, observed that "We find that, taking it on a six-months basis, eighty percent of Mr.

reach the unchurched urban masses, including the lower classes, but his audiences were overwhelmingly white, middle-class church attenders who, for the most part, were not making first-time professions of faith, but "coming forward" to renew or rededicate themselves in faith.

This survey of the history and methods of modern revivalism that began with Charles Finney could appropriately end with Billy Graham.[145] Graham's global ministry and visibility have been unprecedented, and to his great credit his ministry has been marked by consistent, lifelong standards of personal integrity and financial accountability that has not always been the case with other prominent revivalists. For decades Billy Graham has been the most iconic, globally recognized face of the modern evangelical movement and a key symbol of its identity.

We are still in all likelihood too close in time to attempt any more general, overall assessment of the lasting impact of Graham's ministry and methods,[146] but, as history moves American evangelicalism inevitably toward a "post-Graham" era, it is perhaps time to consider new paradigms. Such new paradigms, to be suggested in the concluding section below, would: a) place more distance between *evangelism* as such and *revivalism* as a primary expression and method; b) replace a focus on "decisions" for Christ with a focus on lifelong *discipleship* and catechesis; and c) would see the local church, and not the "stadium" or parachurch organization as the primary context for evangelism (and discipleship).[147] Such a new "post-Graham, post-Christendom," and "post-revivalist" paradigm would also more self-consciously attempt to distance the local church and its ministries

---

Sunday's conversions relapse . . .": ibid., 431n64. The attrition rate appeared to be quite substantial.

145. For biographies of Graham, see Pollock, *Billy Graham*, and W. Martin, *A Prophet with Honor*. Graham's autobiography is Billy Graham, *Just As I Am*.

146. The rather critical assessment provided by McLoughlin Jr., *Billy Graham*, is now seriously dated, and does not cover Graham's career since 1960. McLoughlin echoes critics who saw Graham's preaching as theologically "simplistic" and one-sided, with its focus on soul-winning to the neglect of social justice issues: ibid., 211. Based on the data available at the time of his writing (1960), McLoughlin concluded that 65 to 75 percent of the people who made "decisions" at Graham's crusades were already church members, not first-time initiates of faith: ibid., 182; of the 36,000 decisions registered at the 1954 London crusade, only 4000 represented a long-term and "worthwhile gain to the churches": ibid., 189.

147. In its recent literature the Billy Graham Evangelistic Association has explicitly recognized the importance of the local church in evangelism: "We of the Billy Graham Association are well aware that out coming to a community is of little use unless the church is already doing an effective job of evangelizing": Huston, *The Billy Graham Crusade Handbook*, 20; crusade evangelism is only one form of evangelism and must be kept in perspective with the cooperative efforts of local churches: ibid., 19.

of evangelism and discipleship from dominant American cultural values[148] such as business, sales, marketing, entertainment, and the cult of celebrity that at times have characterized American revivalism in the past.

Recovering the Fullness of the Gospel for a Post-Christendom American Church:

In the second and third sections of this essay, surveying the history of the church since the fourth century, it was seen that in the Christendom period, the gospel was obscured by its too-close association with the dominant power of European culture and by the sacramentalism of the Roman Catholic Church, with its doctrines of baptismal regeneration, purgatory, merits, and works. In the third section, tracing the history of modern revivalism in America since Finney, it was concluded the revivalism had its own problems of acculturation, and questionable effectiveness in reaching the unchurched with the gospel and leading them subsequently into deeper, lifelong discipleship.

In this fourth and final section of the essay, three tasks will be addressed: first, a description of what can be called the "Standard Model" of the gospel in American evangelism; second, an examination of this Standard Model in the light of modern New Testament scholarship on the nature of the gospel, with a view to seeing how this presentation may be incomplete or partial; and third, a set of proposals and recommendations for how these deficiencies could be corrected. These latter constructive proposals constitute, in effect, a proposal for the reshaping and renewing of American evangelicalism's self-identity in the context of a post-Christendom, post-revivalist American church.

The Standard Model of the Gospel in American Evangelical Practice:

One of the earliest twentieth-century examples of a simple formula for the "Plan of Salvation"—here termed the "Standard Model"—was Austin Crouch's five-step "Plan of Salvation" that appeared in 1924.[149] Here we will

---

148. Such a call to the "disenculturation" of the American evangelical church has been consistently voiced in the work of David Wells, most recently in his *The Courage to Be Protestant*, 224: "Churches that actually do influence the culture—here is the paradox—distance themselves from it in their internal life. They do not offer what can already be had on secular terms in the culture. They are an alternative to it."

149. Cited in Schutz, "The Truncated Gospel in Modern Evangelicalism," at 292n2.

consider three expressions of the "Standard Model" that are widely used in contemporary American evangelicalism: the "Peace with God" presentation of the Billy Graham organization; the "Four Spiritual Laws" of Campus Crusade for Christ; and "The Bridge to Life" of the Navigators.[150]

The Billy Graham "Steps to Peace with God" is a four-step presentation:[151]

1. *God's Purpose: Peace and Life:* God is the Master Artist: He created the universe and everything in it, and he made us so that we could have fellowship with him. God loves us and wants us to experience his peace and life—abundant and eternal. [Biblical texts: Rom 5:1; John 3:16; John 10:10]

2. *The Problem: Our Separation:* God created us in his own image to have everlasting life. When we chose to disobey God and to go our own way instead of his, this is sin, and results in separation from God. [Biblical texts: Isa 59:2; Rom 3:23; Rom 6:23]

3. *God's Bridge: The Cross:* Jesus Christ died on the cross and rose from the grave. He paid the penalty for our sin and bridged the gap between God and people. [Biblical texts: John 14:6; Rom 5:8; 1 Cor 15:3-4]

4. *Our Response: Receive Christ:* We must trust Jesus Christ as Lord and Savior and invite him into our life. [Biblical texts: Rev 3:20; Rom 10:9; John 1:12]

The widely used "Four Spiritual Laws" of Campus Crusade for Christ is also a four-step presentation:[152]

1. "God loves you and offers a wonderful plan for your life." [Biblical texts: John 3:16; John 10:10]. *Why is it that most people are not experiencing the abundant life? Because . . .*

---

150. Significantly, all three examples of these widely used evangelistic tools are from *parachurch* organizations—the Billy Graham Evangelistic Organization, Campus Crusade for Christ, and the Navigators—and not from a local church or denomination. It will be argued below that a "post-Christendom" and "post-revivalist" evangelicalism should attempt to shift the center of gravity of evangelism and discipleship back to the *local church* and to the context of its ongoing worship, fellowship, teaching, and discipline—to a "pre-Constantinian" context for the processes of conversion and discipleship.

151. Accessed at http://www.billygraham.org/specialsections/steps-to-peace/steps-to-peace.asp.

152. Accessed at http://www.greatcom.org/english/four.htm.

2. "Man is sinful and separated from God. Therefore, he cannot know and experience God's love and plan for his life." [Biblical texts: Rom 3:23; Rom 6:23] *The third law explains the only way to bridge this gulf . . .*

3. "Jesus Christ is God's only provision for man's sin. Through him you can know and experience God's love and plan for your life." [Biblical texts: Rom 5:8; 1 Cor 15:3-6; John 14:6] *It is not enough just to know these three laws . . .*

4. "We must individually receive Jesus Christ as Savior and Lord; then we can know and experience God's love and plan for our lives." [Biblical texts: John 1:12; Eph 2:8,9; John 3: 1-8; Rev 3:20] *The following explains how you can receive Christ:*

"You can receive Christ right now by faith through prayer:

"Lord Jesus, I need you. Thank you for dying on the cross for my sins. I open the door of my life and receive you as my Savior and Lord. Thank you for forgiving my sins and giving me eternal life. Take control of the throne of my life. Make me the kind of person you want me to be."

The four-step "Bridge to Life" used by the Navigators is quite similar:[153]

1. *God's Love:* God created us in His own image to be his friend and to experience a full life assured of His love. But He didn't make us robots— He gave us the freedom of choice. [Biblical texts: John 10:10; Gen 1:27]

2. *Man's Problem:* Mankind has chosen to disobey God and thus become separated from Him. This separation means the penalty of an eternal spiritual death. [Biblical texts: Rom 3:23; Rom 6:23; Heb 9:27]

3. *God's Remedy:* On our own, we cannot attain the perfection needed to bridge the gap between mankind and God. Christ's death alone is adequate for our sin and bridges the gulf between God and man. [Biblical texts: 1 Pet 3:18; Rom 5:8]

4. *Man's Response:* Believing means trust and commitment—acknowledging our sinfulness, trusting Christ's forgiveness, and letting Him control our life. Eternal life is a gift for us to receive."

As a preliminary observation, it can be observed that all three of these "plan of salvation" presentations state essential aspects of the basic gospel

---

153. Accessed at http://www.navigators.org/Tools/Evangelism%20Resources/Tools/The%20Bridge%20to%20Life. For other examples of the use of the "Bridge Illustration" and the "Roman Road" (Rom 3:23; 6:23; 10:13) see Hybels and Mittelberg, *Becoming a Contagious Christian*, 149–64, "Making the Message Clear."

message (man's sin, the love of God in presenting Christ in his death and resurrection as the remedy for man's sin, the need to respond to Christ as Savior and Lord, and so forth), and have been used in countless instances to introduce people into a saving relationship with Christ. In light of modern New Testament scholarship on the nature of the primitive New Testament *kerygma*, it will be argued that these examples of the "Standard Model" are biblically sound in what they affirm, but deficient in what they omit or fail to emphasize with adequate clarity: 1) the larger biblical context of salvation history; 2) aspects of the attributes of God, especially God's *holiness* and *righteousness*; 3) the fuller implications of the resurrection of Christ; 4) the meaning of the Lordship of Christ in relation to *repentance*, discipleship, and the final *judgment*; 5) the gift of the *Holy Spirit* as an integral aspect of genuine conversion; and 6) the worship, fellowship, and discipline of the *local church* as the essential context for Christian life and discipleship. An "Enhanced Standard Model" of the plan of salvation will be proposed to remedy these defects and weaknesses.

4.2. *Insights from New Testament Scholarship:*

Scot McKnight has observed that a danger of reducing the "gospel" to a "plan of salvation" is that we lose connection with the breadth and expansiveness of the gospel itself.[154] The story of Jesus and our salvation must be seen in the larger context of God's history with Israel and God's plan to ultimately redeem the whole of creation. We have previously noted J. I. Packer's reminder that for the Puritans, "preaching the gospel" meant presenting the gospel story in the context of "the whole Christian system—the character of God, the Trinity, the plan of salvation, the entire work of grace."[155] This placing of the gospel or the "Standard Model" in its wider biblical and theological context is even more important today than it was in earlier periods of "Christendom," given the realities of religious pluralism and alarming rates of biblical illiteracy. It can no longer be assumed that listeners have the needed background information—e.g., the nature and character of the God of the Bible—to properly understand the truths of sin and salvation.

Modern New Testament scholars have drawn attention to the *dynamic* nature of the gospel as understood by Paul and the other New Testament writers. According to Joseph Fitzmyer, the Apostle Paul sees the gospel not as an abstract message of salvation or merely as a series of propositions about Christ to which assent should be given, but rather as a "salvific force

---

154. McKnight et al., *Church in the Present Tense*, 138.
155. Packer, *A Quest for Godliness*, 169.

unleashed by God himself" into human history through the ministry, passion, death, and resurrection of Jesus, "bringing with it effects that human beings can appropriate by faith in him."[156] Gerhard Friedrich states that in the New Testament the gospel (*euanggelion*) "is not an empty word; it is *effective power* which brings to pass what it says because *God is its author* [italics added] . . . God himself speaks in preaching . . . , revealing Himself in grace and judgment through the Word."[157] The word of the gospel both announces God's mighty acts done on behalf of his people and "reveals his *actual presence* [emphasis added] and care for them."[158]

These observations help us to take seriously Paul's statement that the gospel is the "*power* of God for the salvation of everyone who believes" (Rom 1:16). Paul's understanding of the dynamic nature of the word preached is rooted in Old Testament statements such as Isaiah 55:11 ("My word . . . will accomplish what I desire and achieve the purpose for which I sent it") and Jeremiah 23:29 ("Is not my word like fire . . . and like a hammer that breaks a rock in pieces?").

In modern parlance, the gospel proclamation is God's own "performative utterance" and divine "speech-act" that not only announces true propositions—but even more so is a creative energy that brings into reality the things proclaimed. A fresh recognition of the gospel as *divine* agency is needed today to counterbalance the shift from divine agency to human agency in the revival tradition that began with Finney and has continued to the present. The risen Christ is the primary evangelist; Paul is indeed a witness to and herald of Christ, but it is in fact the Christ speaking through Paul who is the One proclaiming "light to his own people and the Gentiles" (Acts 26:23). Christ is the primary agent; the human preacher is the instrument.[159]

---

156. Fitzmyer, *To Advance the Gospel*, 153.

157. Friedrich, "Euanggelion," *Theological Dictionary of the New Testament*, vol. 2, 731, 720. The gospel is not just a recital of past events, but "is experienced as a word charged with power in the present so that it cannot be fettered by human chains"; it is "effective speech, a powerful saying, a word that brings its own fulfillment": Becker, "Gospel," *Dictionary of New Testament Theology*, 109, 113.

158. Strachan, "The Gospel in the New Testament," 3. I have argued the case for a recovery of the early Christian awareness that God is *really present* in the midst of the worshiping community in J. J. Davis, *Worship and the Reality of God*.

159. According to Hatch, "the primitive Christian *kerygma* was regarded as the utterance of God or Christ. Like the Hebrew prophets of old, the preachers were merely the instruments or channels through which the divine message was communicated to man": "The Primitive Christian Message," 10. The emphasis in the apostolic preaching was on divine, not human agency: "God, not man, was the prime mover in the great drama of salvation": ibid., 8.

In a series of seminal lectures given in 1935, and subsequently published under the title *The Apostolic Preaching and Its Development*, C. H. Dodd, based on his examination of the speeches in the book of Acts and the Pauline epistles, identified the core of the early Christian *kerygma* in this fashion:[160]

> The Old Testament prophecies are fulfilled, and the Age to Come has been inaugurated by the coming of the Messiah, Jesus;
>
> He was born of the seed of David;
>
> He died according to the Scriptures, to deliver us out of the present evil age;
>
> He was buried.
>
> He rose on the third day according to the Scriptures;
>
> He is exalted at the right hand of God, as Son of God and Lord of the living and the dead;
>
> He will come again as Judge and Savior of men.

Dodd draws attention to the important point that these facts about the death and resurrection of Jesus are placed in an "eschatological" framework that is essential to understanding their true significance. Such an "eschatological" framework concerning the end of history and the "end time" means that the above facts are not merely historical occurrences within the presently existing framework of history ("This Age"), but in fact announce a momentous transition to a new state of affairs, the "Age to Come," in which the kingdom of God[161] and the very powers of God himself are operating in the ministry of Jesus and the subsequent proclamation about him.[162] The powers of the Age to Come are already being experienced in the New Testament churches that have been brought into existence through the proclamation of the gospel (Heb 6:5).

Modern New Testament scholarship has drawn attention to the fact that in the early Christian preaching it was not the cross alone, but the cross and *resurrection* that were the dynamic elements that were bringing the Age to Come into being. Without the fact of the resurrection, there would have

---

160. Dodd, *The Apostolic Preaching and Its Development*, 17.

161. For a comprehensive study of the centrality of the kingdom of God in the preaching and ministry of Jesus, see Beasley-Murray, *Jesus and the Kingdom of God*.

162. For Paul, by virtue of the death and resurrection of Christ, "the boundary between the two ages is crossed, and those who believe belong no more to the present evil age, but to the glorious Age to Come": ibid., 11.

been no early Christian gospel or early Christian church. In today's cultural setting, the "Standard Model" of presenting the plan of salvation, while not diminishing the centrality of the cross, needs to give greater emphasis to the resurrection of Jesus Christ. The resurrection of Christ—demonstrating that God in Jesus Christ is Lord of the laws of physics and chemistry and biology, the Lord over modern science and technology—is the essential truth that must be more forcefully and robustly proclaimed, in order to give more salience and "bite" to the Christian claims that Jesus is "Lord," that he will in fact return again to planet earth, and that he indeed has plenipotentiary authority to call all humankind to final account as the divine, omnipotent Judge[163] of the living and the dead. Such a more robust proclamation of the resurrection as a core element in the plan of salvation is needed to challenge the privatization of the Christian faith that has taken place since the Enlightenment,[164] and that has been reinforced by revivalism's focus on the individual's private personal experience. The Jesus of the New Testament gospel is not merely my *personal* Lord and savior; this Jesus is *Cosmic and Universal* Lord, whose authority and claims cannot be limited to the private sphere.

It is also evident that in the early Christian preaching the gospel about Jesus was integrally tied to the arrival of the *Holy Spirit* and the formation of the *church*, the new community created by the gospel and the Spirit. As Dodd has noted, the Holy Spirit in the church was the "sign of Christ's present power and glory"; Christ, being exalted to the right hand of God, has

---

163. Moroney has forcefully and convincingly called attention to overemphasis on the love of God and the neglect of the New Testament's witness to the reality of the judgment of God in modern theology and preaching in his recent book, *God of Love and God of Judgment*: "Believing the bad news that God judges our sin naturally precedes believing the good news that Jesus has borne God's judgment in the place of sinners. . . . Nearly every book in the Bible (over ninety-five percent of them) reinforces the picture of God as judge," 65, 68; and citing John Stott; "God's judgment is part of the gospel . . . we cheapen the gospel if we represent it as a deliverance only from unhappiness, fear, guilt and other felt needs, instead of a rescue from the coming wrath," ibid., 59.

164. Lesslie Newbigin has raised the question as to how, in the modern world, "does one preach the gospel as truth, truth which is not to be domesticated within the assumptions of modern thought but which challenges these assumptions and calls for their revision?"; *The Gospel in a Pluralist Society*, 5. In his masterful recent work on the resurrection, N. T. Wright has, in effect, responded to Newbigin's question, and has called the resurrection of Jesus Christ a mighty new reality that blasts "its way through the sealed tombs and locked doors of modernist epistemology" and sees that "one of the most important planks in the Enlightenment platform [JD: the "unalterable laws of nature" that prevent God from acting supernaturally in the world of space and time] is itself challenged by the question of Jesus' resurrection": *The Resurrection of the Son of God*, 713.

given the Spirit that the prophets had said would come in the last days.[165] Peter had proclaimed on the day of Pentecost, "repent, be baptized [become a member of the new community] and you will receive the gift of the Holy Spirit" (Acts 2:38). The connection between true conversion and the reception of the Holy Spirit that was integral in the early church became severed in later Christian centuries in the variegated and inconsistent practices of confirmation.[166] In the New Testament, conversion and empowerment by the Spirit were a "package deal."

At the birth of the church in Acts 2, the church, not a "parachurch" entity, is the platform and base for evangelism. As Strachan has noted, in the New Testament it is assumed that "no disciple of Christ can make adequate profession of faith apart from membership in the Christian community, the new Israel . . . There are no solitary Christians in the pages of the New Testament."[167] The integral connection between evangelism, discipleship, and membership in the local church, that has been weakened in the history of modern revivalism,[168] needs to be recovered in our own post-Christendom evangelical churches.[169]

A Proposal for an "Enhanced Standard Model" for the Plan of Salvation

In this section a proposal will be offered for an "enhanced" version of the "Standard Model" for the presentation of the gospel and the plan of salvation, and some concluding recommendation will be made regarding the practice of evangelism in post-Christendom, post-revivalist settings. The "enhanced" model will use the "Four Spiritual Laws" of Campus Crusade for Christ as a basis, with additions and revisions made on the basis of the

---

165. Dodd, *The Apostolic Preaching and Its Development*, 22, 32.

166. For an account of the variegated history and practices of confirmation in the Western church, see Martos, *Doors to the Sacred*, 203–30, and also Fisher, *Christian Initiation*, especially chapter 8, "The Lengthening of the Interval between Baptism and Confirmation," 120–40.

167. Strachan, "The Gospel in the New Testament," 4.

168. As Brauer, "Conversion," 239, has noted, "Prior to Revivalism, conversion in both England and New England was carefully nurtured within the context of the Christian church."

169. Lesslie Newbigin has astutely observed that the plausibility structures of modernity can only be effectively challenged by "people who are fully inhabitants of another" and that such challenges to the plausibility structures of the Enlightenment and modern science and technology must begin with the "local congregation in which the reality of the new creation is present, known, and experienced": *The Gospel in a Pluralist Society*, 228, 232.

foregoing survey of modern New Testament scholarship; additions and revisions will be noted in italics:

1. "God loves you and offers a wonderful plan for your life." [Biblical texts: John 3:16; John 10:10].

   The identity of the true and living God has been revealed in the history of Israel, the Bible, and in the life, death, and resurrection of Jesus Christ. God, who is the all-powerful Creator of the universe, is a personal God who is distinct from the world and from the human soul, and who is infinitely holy, loving, and righteous.

   Why is it that most people are not experiencing the abundant life? Because . . .

2. "Man is sinful and separated from God. Therefore, he cannot know and experience God's love and plan for his life." [Biblical texts: Rom 3:23; Rom 6:23] The third law explains the only way to bridge this gulf: . . .

3. "Jesus Christ is God's only provision for man's sin. Through him you can know and experience God's love and plan for your life." [Biblical texts: Rom 5:8; 1 Cor 15:3-6; John 14:6]

   He died in our place (Rom 5:8) *to pay the penalty for our sins.*

   He rose from the dead (1 Cor 15:3-6).

   The resurrection of Jesus Christ demonstrates that what God is able to do in the world and in our lives is not limited by the laws of nature or the forces of science and technology. Jesus' resurrection is the promise of our own final resurrection from the dead and the basis of our hope of everlasting life. He ascended to the right hand of God the Father in heaven, and now reigns as Lord, with supreme authority over all our life and over the world; he will return to earth, as the final Judge of the living and the dead.

   It is not enough just to know these three laws . . .

4. "We must individually receive Jesus Christ as Savior and Lord; then we can know and experience God's love and plan for our lives. [Biblical texts: John 1:12; Eph 2:8-9; John 3:1-8; Rev 3:20] The following explains how you can receive Christ:

   - We must receive Christ (John 1:12).

- We receive Christ through faith (Eph 2:8,9).
- When we receive Christ, we experience a new birth (John 3:1-8).
- We receive Christ by personal invitation (Rev 3:20).

Receiving Christ involves turning to God from self (repentance) and trusting Christ to come into our lives to forgive our sins and to make us what he wants to be. *To repent means to consciously decide to turn to God as the new center of our lives and to turn away from sin and sinful attitudes and behaviors.* Just to agree intellectually that Jesus Christ is the Son of God and that he died on the cross for our sins is not enough. Nor is it enough to have an emotional experience. We receive Christ by an act of the will, *turning from our trust in ourselves and what we have done to trust in what God has done in Jesus Christ as the only basis and hope of our salvation.*

"You can receive Christ right now by faith through prayer:

"Lord Jesus, I need you. Thank you for dying on the cross for my sins. I open the door of my life and receive you as my Savior and Lord. Thank you for forgiving my sins and giving me eternal life. Take control of the throne of my life. Make me the kind of person you want me to be."

In receiving Christ as your Lord and Savior, God promises the gift of the Holy Spirit—God personally with us and in us—that we might know the love of God and be empowered to live a new life (Rom 5:5; Acts 2:38). *Having received Christ, you need to be baptized, if you have not already done so, and become an active member of a local church, where you can continue to grow as a Christian through its worship, teaching, fellowship, and service.*

Some Concluding Recommendations

Several general observations could be drawn from this essay's survey of the history of the church and the changing understandings and practices of conversion, evangelism, and discipleship. One broad conclusion that could be drawn is that both the "Christendom" model of conversion ("sacramentalism": infant baptism + baptismal regeneration + assent to church teachings) and the "revivalist" model of conversion ("special meetings" + "instantaneous 'decisions for Christ'") are significantly flawed, and all too often have produced nominal Christians rather than deeply committed disciples. Another conclusion that might be drawn is that today's evangelical churches, in a post-Christendom, post-revivalist era, should seek to return to a pre-Constantinian model of evangelism, conversion, and discipleship, in which the church is at the center of the evangelistic enterprise, and making disciples—rather than registering "decisions"—is the top priority. The challenge then, is to in effect abandon the "Christendom" and "revivalist" models in favor of a "pre-Constantinian" model, in which the local church— self-consciously taking a stance of greater distance from the dominant cultural values of consumption, convenience, speed, and entertainment—seeks to embody in its worship and life a holistic and integrated understanding of the gospel, conversion, and discipleship as a lifelong process. The following recommendations are ways of implementing such a pre-Constantinian model and fresh understanding of the gospel and conversion for our own times:

1. *Use the (Revised) "Standard Model" of the Plan of Salvation at the "back end"—not the "front end" of the conversion process:*

   In this model, tools such as the "Four Spiritual Laws" would best be used *after* a long and thorough exposure to the Christian faith and its teachings, and to the worship and life of the local church. The "plan of salvation" would be taught in the larger context of the larger Christian story, as summarized, for instance, in the Apostles' Creed, or a catechism such as the Westminster Shorter Catechism. Only after an extensive time of catechesis—say, at least a twelve-week new members class—would the candidate be ready to "pray the prayer" and to "receive [or reaffirm] Christ" as Lord and Savior.

2. *Shift the center of gravity from parachurch organizations to the local church as the primary base and context for evangelism and discipleship:*

   The point of this recommendation is not to diminish or discountenance the past, present, or future ministries of parachurch organizations such as InterVarsity Christian Fellowship, Campus Crusade for Christ (now "Cru"), the Navigators, and many others, that have long partnered with local churches in evangelism and discipleship. It is, rather, a challenge to local churches to see afresh their primary responsibility for "making new Christians" (evangelism, conversion) and discipling them, and not to rely on "outsourcing" these responsibilities to parachurch organizations. The early, pre-Constantinian church grew, in fact, not through organized evangelistic programs or special "revivals," but by drawing outsiders, through natural social networks of family, friends, and coworkers, into its own compelling, countercultural fellowship and worship.[170]

3. *Give up "revivalism" as a primary means of evangelism and conversion, and shift evangelicalism's focus from "decisions" for Christ to discipleship understood as a lifelong process in the context of the ongoing ministry of the local church:*

This recommendation is based on a recognition of the crucial point that in the "Great Commission" (Matt 28:16–20) Christ commands the church and his disciples not to "make converts" or to seek "decisions"—but to *make disciples*.[171] "Decisions" may be made in an instant, but it takes a lifetime to "teach them to *obey everything* that I have commanded them" (v. 20). Lifelong Christian education and catechesis[172] and involvement in effective small groups is more likely to build disciples that can observe the Great Commission and make significant impact on the culture.

---

170. On the lack of organized evangelistic programs in the early church, see Hvalvik, "In Word and Deed: The Expansion of the Church in the Pre-Constantinian Era," especially 275–80, "The missing appeal to missionary work." The early church historian Robert Louis Wilken observed that the early church, rather than focusing on changing the culture, focused on building its own sense of community: "It built a way of life. The church was not something that spoke to its culture: It was itself a culture and created a new Christian culture." It did not seek to be "user-friendly" and it was difficult, not easy to join the church; according to Wilken, the lesson from the pre-Constantinian church is the best thing we can do for "seekers" is to "create an environment where newcomers feel they are missing something vital"—a sense of the reality of God and Christ that the culture cannot provide. Wilken, "The Link Interview," 44. The importance of social networks in the growth of the early Christian church is highlighted in Stark, *The Rise of Christianity*, 20, 21, 214.

171. For an excellent exegetical study of the Great Commission, and the command to "make disciples," see Bosch, "The Structure of Mission," especially 230–33, "Making Disciples." Schutz, in "The Truncated Gospel," 296, has noted in this regard that the "Great Commission has but one imperative—'Make disciples!' . . . [But] our methodology too often focuses simply upon getting decisions. We then hold a vague hope that somehow in the future the one who has 'been saved' will 'be discipled' to become a follower of Jesus."

172. The growing renewal of interest in *catechesis* is to be welcomed. For catechesis in the early church, see Harmless, *Augustine and the Catechumenate*, and Westerhoff and Edwards Jr., *A Faithful Church*. The pastoral catechesis practiced by Richard Baxter is described in Packer, *A Quest for Godliness*, 304–8. For contemporary resources on catechesis, see especially Parrett and Kang, *Teaching the Faith, Forming the Faithful*, and Packer and Parrett, *Grounded in the Gospel*. On small groups and Wesley's "class meetings," see Henderson, *John Wesley's Class Meeting*.

4. *Recover the cosmic and public dimensions of the confession 'Jesus is Lord', and give renewed emphasis to the return of Christ as Judge of the living and the dead:*

This recommendation attempts to address the "privatization" of Christian faith and understandings of the "lordship" of Christ that have grown up in post-Enlightenment Christianity and revivalism, and to challenge it with a fresh vision of the lordship of Christ over all of human life and culture. The resurrection of Christ and his exaltation to the right hand of the Father—a present and continuing reality—is recognized as the foundation of this lordship. New emphasis on the *return* of Christ as universal *Judge* of the living and the dead is needed in our time, with its focus on this-worldly satisfactions and diminished senses of the holiness and righteousness of God.

5. *Recover a fresh sense that the gospel message itself is the "power of God" and that God is the primary active agent in the preaching of the gospel:*

This recommendation is a call to newly recognize that God the Father, Christ, and the Holy Spirit are the primary "evangelists" and that the human preacher is the secondary instrument (Acts 26:23; 1 Thess 1:5, 2:13; 1 Pet 4:11). It is a call for the evangelical movement in America to reverse the shift in modern revivalism from divine to human agency,[173] and to return to a more biblical focus of the primacy of divine agency and spiritual power in the conversion of sinners. The more the divine power of the gospel itself (Rom 1:16; 2 Cor 10:4) is more self-consciously recognized in distinction from (American) cultural trappings of digital technology, marketing, and entertainment, the less likely it is that this divine energy of the Holy Spirit will be inadvertently quenched as the message goes forth.

6. *Reemphasize the gift of the Holy Spirit as an integral element of the process of conversion and source of empowerment for discipleship and Christian living:*

This recommendation follows directly from the apostolic command and promise in Acts 2:38: "Repent, be baptized, and you will receive the gift of the Holy Spirit." The separation of "becoming a Christian" or

---

173. Bill J. Leonard, a Southern Baptist Church historian, has noted that once the stress falls "on the human side of conversion [it] can and does lead to a 'transactional' view of evangelism, not as process but as single event. Once the prayer is prayed, and the invitation accepted, then the transaction is over—salvation is secured and heaven achieved. Discipleship, growth, process are obscured for a one-time-does-all transaction": "Evangelism and Contemporary American Life," 114.

"receiving Christ" and receiving the Holy Spirit that has characterized much of the later history of the church needs to be ended in the practices of the churches. Receiving Christ and receiving the Holy Spirit is a "package deal"; "what God has put together, let no church put asunder." Prayers for "receiving Christ" should reflect this biblical truth.

Go therefore and make disciples of all nations, teaching them to observe all that I have commanded you.

MATTHEW 28:19-20

5

Salvation Reconceptualized: Is Our Western Gospel Big Enough?

Reflections on Western and Eastern Soteriologies in the Context of Modern Pluralism

OVER A GENERATION AGO J. B. Phillips in his provocatively titled *Your God Is Too Small* argued that popular Christian understandings of God fell far short of the biblical teachings about God. In similar fashion, the title of this paper suggests that "Our 'salvation' is too small"—that is, that popular evangelical presentations of the gospel in the West fall short of the rich and deeply robust content of the Good News in the New Testament—in short, that our concept of the "gospel" needs to be expanded and reconceptualized for its more effective proclamation and application in our cultural contexts today. Or, to state the thesis more provocatively, it will be argued, in effect, that our current concepts of the "Good News" *are not good enough*.

This chapter will attempt to advance the following propositions: 1) that Western forensic categories such as justification need to be supplemented and integrated with the more participationist categories of the East such as adoption and glorification;[1] 2) that the Western focus on the "how" (the atonement) of salvation needs to be supplemented by the Eastern focus on the (for) "what" of salvation, i.e., the nature and purposes *for which* we have been forgiven through the cross of Christ;[2] and 3) that our Western

---

1. Western soteriologies have, of course, recognized categories such as adoption and glorification—in light of their inclusion in classic texts such as Romans 8:15–16, Galatians 4:4–6 (adoption), and Romans 8:30 ("those whom he justified, he also glorified"); however, these themes, for a number of reasons to be discussed below, have not tended to have received the prominence in the West that parallel categories in the Eastern tradition such as "theosis" or "deification" have received in those Eastern contexts.

2. I wish to thank my colleague Donald Fairbairn for his comments to this effect in

emphases on justification and penal substitution need to be more fully integrated with the doctrines of the Trinity, union with Christ, and realized eschatology.[3] These adjustments to our understandings and presentation of the "Good News," in an attempt to integrate the best insights of both East and West, are not meant as a "replacement" of the "gospel," but as an enhancement that recovers aspects of it that stand in need of retrieval.[4]

The outline of this chapter will be as follows: first, a discussion of various reasons why this topic is both timely and important; second, an examination of the "standard" gospel as usually presented in popular evangelical preaching and teaching, with its strengths and weaknesses; to be followed by an exposition of an "enhanced" gospel ("Salvation 3.0") that integrates foundational emphases of both West and East; and third, an outline of how the doctrines of the Trinity, union with Christ, and realized eschatology provide an essential framework for such an "enhanced" soteriology of ever-deepening participation in the life of the Trinity. In the closing section of the paper certain objections to this project will be answered, and suggestions offered for practical implementation in the life of the church and personal spirituality.

Our Gospel Is Too Small: The Timeliness and Strategic Importance of the Topic

A serious reconsideration of the content of the core evangelical salvation message is timely for a variety of reasons, both religious and secular. Since the end of World War II, America has become an increasingly religiously pluralistic society, in which the evangelical Protestant gospel is only one of many salvation messages competing for market share and attention in the American free market of religion. This competitive marketplace is now characterized by a) the prominent visibility of Eastern and New Age religions; b) by the rise of the religious "nones"; c) by the growth of world

---

a personal conversation—that the "West has tended to focus on the 'how' of salvation (the cross; the juridical language of justification) while the East has focused more on the 'what' of salvation": what is the nature of salvation; *for what* and for what *final end* are we saved? Fairbairn has developed these insights in his article "Patristic Soteriology" (see esp. 308–9), and in his book, *Life in the Trinity*.

3. I have previously argued for a more central place of these doctrines in popular evangelical theology and spiritual practices in my book *Reality in Meditation*, especially chapters 3–6.

4. While it is not the focus of this chapter, it is the author's belief that "Eastern" versions of the "gospel" are likewise incomplete—that, indeed, Eastern notions of "deification" and "theosis" need certain correctives and the more robust theological foundations that can be provided by Western emphases on forensic justification, imputed righteousness, and penal substitution.

Pentecostalism and "prosperity gospels"; d) by the growth of the Church of Jesus Christ of Latter-Day Saints (Mormonism) and its attempt to rebrand itself as a mainstream form of Protestant Christianity; e) by the emergence of Eastern Orthodoxy as an alternative form of Christian faith and spirituality in the West; and f) by the flat-lined growth rates of evangelical Protestantism itself in the United States.

From a nation that could once be characterized religiously in terms of "Protestant, Catholic, and Jew," the United States has now become one of the most religiously diverse nations on the planet, with virtually all world religions and faith traditions represented within its borders. There are more American Muslims than there are American Episcopalians, Jews, or Presbyterians, and Hinduism, Buddhism, and New Age religions are prominently visible in religious life and popular culture.[5] In previous generations, the *Christian* God and Christian understandings of "salvation" could be assumed as the default understandings of the general culture, but no more— for there are now many alternative versions of "salvation" competing for Americans' attention and loyalty.[6] At both the popular and scholarly levels, recent years have witnessed the conversions to Hinduism or Buddhism of those of formerly Christian backgrounds.[7] Another manifestation of the religious pluralism of our times is the phenomenon of "multiple belonging," in which persons self-identify with more than one religious tradition at the same time, e.g., Roman Catholic and Jewish, or Christian and Buddhist.[8] Such blurrings of religious boundaries call, from an evangelical Protestant

---

5. On the pluralism of the American religious landscape, see Eck, *A New Religious America*.

6. The important point that in today's religious landscape there are not only multiple religions available, but multiple versions of "salvation" as well, is argued in Heim, *Salvations*.

7. A notable example is the conversion of the prominent philosopher of religion Michael Sudduth, who after twenty-five years as a Protestant Christian in the Reformed theological tradition, in the fall of 2011 converted to the Vaishnava tradition of Hinduism. He stated that he had "a powerful religious experience of Krishna," and spent countless nights "reading the *Gita*, with tears of joy running down my face as I read the words of Lord Krishna and felt the presence of God": see Sudduth's account at Vallicella, "Michael Sudduth Converts to Vaishnava Vedanta!" For discussion of the theological content of Vaishnava Hinduism, and the worship of Krishna, see Klostermaier, *Hinduism*, "Vaishnava Vedanta," 102–7; see also Carman, *The Theology of Ramanuja*.

8. A notable example of such "multiple belonging" is found in Knitter, *Without Buddha I Could not Be a Christian*. Knitter, who is the Paul Tillich Professor of Theology, World Religions and Culture at Union Theological Seminary in New York, is married to a Buddhist, and in 2008 took Buddhist vows. Knitter stated that the "only way I can be religious is by being interreligious. I can be a Christian only by also being a Buddhist . . . I can truly call myself . . . a Buddhist Christian": ibid., 216.

perspective, for even clearer understandings and articulations of the core Christian message.

Another significant emerging trend in the current landscape of religious pluralism is the rise of the "nones," those Americans who do not identify with any religious tradition—now just under 20 percent of all adults.[9] The vast majority of these unaffiliated say that they are *not* looking for a religion that would be right for them, and think that religious organizations are too concerned with money and power.[10] Almost one-third (32 percent) of younger American adults under thirty have no religious affiliation; these young adults are more likely to be unaffiliated than previous generations were at a similar stage in their lives.[11]

It is now widely recognized that Pentecostalism represents the most rapidly growing stream of world Christianity. While Pentecostals generally identify with the historic doctrinal beliefs of Christian faith, the picture is complicated by the pervasive presence of various "prosperity gospels" in Pentecostal churches, both in the United States and globally.[12] The popularity of such messages highlights the need to make the *biblical* gospel of salvation clear and robust in the face of these attractive alternatives.

Another alternative "gospel" is on offer from the Church of Jesus Christ of Latter-Day Saints (Mormonism), now claiming to be the fourth largest "Christian" church in America.[13] According to its founder Joseph Smith, the Heavenly Father "designed the plan of salvation so that we can be exalted.... This plan contemplated not only salvation from sin and the effects of sin ... but exaltation, glory, power, and dominion ... that we may have a fullness of joy ... and inherit glory, dominion, exaltation, and thrones and every power and attribute developed and possessed by our Heavenly Father."[14] This rather grandiose and inflated version of the ultimate results of salvation is, in part, an exaggeration of certain biblical themes (glory, joy,

---

9. The Pew Forum, "'Nones' on the Rise: One-in-Five Adults Have No Religious Affiliation." The percentage of the "Nones" has increased from 15 percent to just under 20 percent in the last five years.

10. Ibid., 2.

11. Ibid.

12. On Pentecostalism and the "Prosperity Gospel" as a global phenomenon, see Coleman, *The Globalisation of Charismatic Christianity*; see also Fee, *The Disease of the Health and Wealth Gospels*, and Jones and Woodbridge, *Health, Wealth, and Happiness*.

13. The Church of Jesus Christ of Latter-Day Saints Newsroom, "A Christ-Centered Faith." Mormonism can claim to be a "world religion," with more than half of its 14 million members living outside the United States.

14. "Teachings of Joseph Smith: Chapter 17: The Great Plan of Life and Salvation."

dominion) that have been somewhat neglected in some mainstream evangelical presentations of the gospel, and stand in need of retrieval.

One of the most important factors that has emerged in the last generation to fuel the current reexaminations of the nature of salvation has been the rising visibility of Eastern Orthodox Christianity in the West, especially since the fall of the Soviet Union in the late 1980s. After the Russian revolution of 1917, a group of Orthodox scholars including Nicholas Berdyaev, Sergei Bulgakov, George Florovsky, and Vladimir Lossky emigrated to Paris, and through their extensive publications began to influence Christian theological scholarship in the West.[15] These scholars and their publications fueled an ongoing scholarly encounter of the forensic categories of the West with the more mystical and participationist categories of Orthodox soteriologies.[16]

And last, but not least, in this brief initial survey of the current religious landscape is the evidence of the flat-lined growth rates for evangelical denominations in recent decades. Roughly 28 percent of the American population affiliates with conservative, evangelical denominations, and this percentage has been essentially flat since the 1990s.[17] According to Mark Chaves, Christians in the United States are now less likely to say that their religion provides the only way to salvation, and seem to be less tolerant of religious intensity of any sort.[18] American evangelicals have no cause to indulge in religious complacency, and would do well to consider the definitional sharpness and theological robustness of its basic salvation message, because if anything, its message in its present form seems to be losing traction with the general population, and with younger Americans in particular.

Not only the current religious environment, but the *secular* landscape as well calls for a reframing of evangelicalism's basic salvation message. Two aspects in particular may be mentioned: the emergence of various secular "gospels," and the pervasive background "noise" of an omnipresent media-saturated world—the world of "InfoGlut."[19] In recent years a veritable cot-

---

15. See Arjakovsky, *The Way*.

16. Important Orthodox concepts such as "deification" or "theosis" will be considered below in relation to biblical categories such as "glorification" that are more familiar to theologians in the West.

17. Chaves, *American Religion*, 87.

18. Ibid., 37.

19. The phenomenon of "InfoGlut" and modern entertainment media have contributed to a trivialization and "thinning" of the modern imagination of heaven: see J. J. Davis, *Reality in Meditation*, 70–79, "How Heaven Disappeared and How to Get It Back"; and Conyers, *The Loss of Transcendence*. The present chapter is a call for a "thicker" and more robust concept of heaven and of the ultimate purposes of Christian salvation.

tage industry of books about near-death experiences and trips to heaven has emerged. The best-selling *Proof of Heaven: A Neurosurgeon's Journey into the Afterlife*, by the impressively credentialed Eben Alexander,[20] is only one of a growing list of such near-death or out-of-body experiences. The basic message that Alexander brought back from his near-death experience was that "You are loved and cherished.... You have nothing to fear.... There is nothing you can do wrong."[21] This message is, in effect, what could be called an alternative "near-death gospel": a message of unconditional love, a human future with no fear of hell or divine judgment—a rosy picture, but in which the biblical Christ is missing. One observer of this resurgence of interest in the afterlife, Brian Bethune, has astutely noted that this cultural trend may not accidentally be correlated with the aging of the baby boomers, who, facing their own mortality and eventual deaths, would look with favor on a "Good News" message that gives them "scientific" reasons to believe both in the existence of and the very congenial nature of such an afterlife.[22]

Yet another secular "gospel" that has emerged on the cultural horizon is the movement of "Transhumanism." This movement, which emerged in the United States during the 1980s, is committed to the proposition that humanity should use all available technologies—computer, biomedical, genetic, pharmacological, artificial intelligence, and so forth—to enhance human intellectual, physical, and psychological capacities, and to overcome the fundamental limitations of disease, aging, and even death itself.[23] In a somewhat similar vein, some physicists such as Princeton University's Freeman Dyson have speculated on the very, very long-term future of the human race, postulating that the record of human experience and human

20. This book spent many weeks high on the list of the *New York Times* best seller list.

21. Alexander, *Proof of Heaven*, 71.

22. Bethune, "The Heaven Boom," 48. Bethune provides a helpful survey of this current literature, and orients it within larger cultural trends: the culture as a whole is shifting away from more organized and institutional forms of religion to "a more personal spirituality, at once vague and autonomous. Ordinary sinners increasingly don't believe that they deserve judgment, let alone hell. Theists and atheists alike dispute any earthly authority's right to judge, and both feel near death experiences give them reason to hope for something beyond the grave." Ibid.

23. For an overview and history of this movement, see the article by the Oxford philosopher Nick Bostrom, "A History of Transhumanist Thought." For proponents of the Transhumanist vision, see Kurzweil, *The Age of Spiritual Machines* and *The Singularity Is Near*; as well as Ramez Naam, *More than Human*. For some appraisals, see Fukuyama, *Our Posthuman Future*. Fukuyama is concerned that biotechnological interventions into human nature may threaten to undermine equality and human rights. For guarded but somewhat open Christian appraisals, see Peters, *Playing God?*, and Cole-Turner, ed., *Transhumanism and Transcendence*.

sentience itself could be uploaded to computer chips, so as to "live" forever and escape the entropic consequences of the Second Law of Thermodynamics and the final heat-death of the universe.[24] Such scientific speculations and secular versions of human immortality may seem far-fetched and highly improbable. The Christian community, however, would do well not to dismiss such visionary speculation out of hand, but rather use it as an occasion to consider afresh *its own* vision of the ultimate human future—of salvation—and the limits, if any, on the modification and enhancement of human nature.

Attempts to communicate the gospel, the message of salvation, in today's world faces an unprecedented challenge of "InfoGlut." Never before in the history of the human race have so many people been bombarded with so many forms of information from so many sources and from so many personal devices for such unrelenting periods of time. According to one recent study, the typical adolescent in America today, when multitasking is taken into account, spends some ten hours and forty-five minutes per day consuming various forms of media. In the last decade every form of media use *except* reading has increased.[25] For many people in the modern world, "screen time" threatens to displace "face time"—and "God time"—as their primary world of imagination and experience.[26] Modern media not only *distract* and fragment the attention of potential listeners to the gospel, but also tend to *displace* attention to the heavenly and spiritual worlds and redirect it to earthly and temporal concerns.

The overwhelming presence of digital media and on-screen entertainment has drastically changed what information and communications theorists call the "signal-to-noise" ratio.[27] In the high Middle Ages in Chris-

---

24. See Dyson, "Time Without End"; see also Barrow and Tipler, *The Anthropic Cosmological Principle*. For a critical appraisal of such proposals, see "Cosmic Endgame," 159–74 in J. J. Davis, *Frontiers of Science and Faith*.

25. *Kaiser Family Foundation Study*, "Generation M2: Media Use in the Lives of 8- to 18-Year Olds: Key Findings," 1.

26. For the impact of digital media and the internet on human experience and relationships, see J. J. Davis, *Reality in Meditation*, "Reading the Bible in an Age of Information Overload," 21–25; Carr, *The Shallows*; Hipps, *Flickering Pixels*; Turkle, *Alone Together*; Zengotita, *Mediated*. Zengotita argues that our modern media-saturated world reinforces narcissism by placing the self "at the center of a universe of flattering representations" (255) and that modernity's essential aim is "replacing God with me." (266)

27. Information theorist Orrin Klapp has noted that "All too often, media and computers speed up the impact of information upon us without adding to its meaning for us. By taking in too much noise, a person becomes cluttered, not integrated. The result for our information society is that we suffer a lag in which the 'slow horse' of meaning is unable to keep up with the 'fast horse' of mere information": *Overload and Boredom*, 3.

tian Europe the church could command a near monopoly on the sources of information projected into the popular imagination; today, the church has to fight for the attention of its listeners in an environment inundated with the images and messages of the entertainment and marketing industries. In such an environment the basic salvation message of the church needs to be reframed in clear, compelling, and fresh ways that can be heard against the unremitting background "noise" of digital media and the Internet.

This proposal for a fresh reconceptualizing of the traditional evangelical understanding of salvation is not only timely, as noted above, but intrinsically important for its own sake, inasmuch as *salvation* is the very core message of the Christian faith. That message needs to be preached, taught, and lived in the clearest, most robust, and compelling way possible. The early church succeeded in the face of a bewildering area of competing religious alternatives in the Roman empire in no small part because of the clarity, freshness,[28] and compelling nature of its message. In the words of the classical historian E. R. Dodds, who pondered the reasons for the early Christian church's success, in its message, "Christianity wielded both a bigger stick and a juicier carrot."[29] The Protestant Reformation was itself largely a project in clarifying the core message—the gospel—with an emphasis on the "how" of salvation (justification). Today, the need is to build on these historic foundations by making clearer and more explicit the ultimate "why" of salvation (adoption; glorification; participation in and enjoyment of the divine life of the Trinity).

It is here being argued that a fresh reconceptualization of the received notions of "salvation" is needed not merely for pragmatic reasons of effective communication—as important as that is—but, more fundamentally, because the very act of *understanding* the gospel message itself is incomplete if that reality is only explained in terms of "how" without also explaining the "why." In other words, the *functional* elements of salvation need to be

28. Communication theorists Chip and Dan Heath have shown that freshness, unexpectedness, and elements of novelty in messages are crucial elements in attracting and holding the attention of a potential listener: *Made to Stick*, especially chapter 2, "Unexpected." See further Hidi, "Interest and Its Contribution as a Mental Resource for Learning," noting that high-interest materials have elements that are "novel or unusual" and have "characters or life themes with which readers can identify": 557. The assumption of this chapter is that the standard formulation and presentation of the evangelical "gospel" stands in need of some "freshening up"—in order to create greater interest in a somewhat jaded and cynical American public, which, rightly or wrongly, has the attitude, "Been there; done that; we've already heard your message and are not buying it."

29. Dodds, *Pagan and Christian in an Age of Anxiety*, 135. Today, a "juicer carrot" would involve, as to be developed below, the enhancement of evangelical soteriology by the integration of the Western forensic categories of justification and penal substitution with the (Eastern) participationist categories of adoption and glorification ("theosis").

conceptually integrated with the *teleological* and purposive elements in order to have a more adequate and complete understanding of the core message itself. A fresh emphasis on the *final purpose* of salvation—which in effect is a statement about the final and highest purposes of human life—is all the more relevant in view of the denial of any final purpose for the universe and human beings by those who advocate the worldviews of scientific materialism and evolutionary naturalism that are so influential among the cultural elites of our time.[30] Renewed attention to the final purposes of salvation and human life is also needed in the context of an American society that is dominated by science and technology and a tendency to elevate means over ends and material progress over lasting relationships and spiritual depth.[31]

It may be helpful to recall at this point the "Four Causes"[32] of Aristotle (material, efficient, formal, final), viewed by the philosopher as providing four levels of explanation for a more complete understanding of a complex event or reality. The material cause answers the question, "What is it made of?"; the efficient cause the question, "How does it work? What process leads to the finished product?"; the formal cause, the question, "Who designed or thought up this?"; and the final cause, "For what purpose? Why are we doing this?" To explain or understand, for example, a birthday cake, one could describe what it's made of (the ingredients); the process (measuring, mixing, baking in the oven); the personal agent (the mother or father in the kitchen); and, the reason or goal ("for my daughter's sixth birthday").

In the New Testament descriptions of the Christian life this teleological element ("final causation") is not missing. For example, when the

---

30. As for scientific materialism, the Nobel Prize-winning physicist Steven Weinberg has famously stated that "The more the universe seems comprehensible, the more it seems pointless": *The First Three Minutes*, 154. The evolutionary biologist George Gaylord Simpson averred that man "was certainly not the goal of evolution, which evidently had no goal . . . . Man is the result of a purposeless and natural process that did not have him in mind": *The Meaning of Evolution*, 293, 345. Similarly, the paleontologist Stephen Jay Gould concluded that *Homo sapiens* "is a 'thing so small' in a vast universe, a wildly improbable evolutionary event well within the realm of contingency . . . . We are a detail, not a purpose or embodiment of the whole": *Wonderful Life*, 291. Richard Dawkins has asserted his emphatic belief that natural selection "is the blind watchmaker, blind because it does not see ahead, does not plan consequences, has no purpose in view": *The Blind Watchmaker*, 21.

31. The predominance of means over ends in modern societies has been argued forcefully in the works of Ellul, *The Technological Society*, and Borgmann, *Technology and the Character of Contemporary Life* and *Crossing the Postmodern Divide*. The materialistic and utilitarian emphases in American culture have been variously documented by Kluckhohn, *Mirror for Man*; Stewart, *American Cultural Patterns*; and Bellah et al., *Habits of the Heart*.

32. Aristotle, *Physics*, 194 b17–20; and *Posterior Analytics*, 71 b9–11; 94 a20.

Apostle Paul reminds Timothy of the endurance needed as a disciple of Jesus, the three illustrations that he chooses (soldier, athlete, farmer: 2 Tim 2:3-7), he presupposes situations in which all three have clear visions of the goal in mind, clear visions that help them persevere: winning a battle (soldier); finishing the race (athlete); reaping the harvest (farmer). In each case, a full understanding of the *task* or activity presupposes a clear vision of the intended *goal*.

If a proper teleological vision is essential for understanding of Christian life and discipleship, it is no less essential for a proper understanding of the nature of Christian salvation itself. The "how" explanations need to be integrated with the "why" explanations.[33] Popular evangelical articulations of the gospel have, however, tended to focus on the "how" of salvation—in Aristotelian terms, on the material and efficient causes of salvation (the blood of Christ, penal substitution, justification)—and less so on the "why" of salvation ("final" causes, the goal)—e.g., adoption and glorification: full participation in the life of the triune God. This chapter is an attempt to help correct this imbalance.

The "Standard" (Western) Gospel and a Proposed Upgrade: Salvation 3.0

If a typical member of a typical evangelical church were asked to articulate the content of the gospel, an answer such as the following might be provided: "Christ died on the cross to pay for my sins, so that when I die, I can go to

---

33. The Dutch Reformed theologian Hendrikus Berkhof has noted that it "is remarkable how rarely [in much of the history of the church] the question concerning God's *purpose* [emphasis added] in the renewal of man has been explicitly discussed in the study of the faith. Its attention has focused on the renewal itself; its results were preferably called 'fruits,' and so the *goal*-problematics [of salvation; emphasis added] was by-passed": *Christian Faith*, 431. He notes, for example, that in the Apostles' Creed, the emphasis is on the saving facts and acts of God in Christ, with lesser emphasis or explanation on the "why" or "for what purpose" aspects ("forgiveness of sins . . . life everlasting": ibid., 4

heaven and live with God forever."[34] In a somewhat more developed form, what is for the purpose of this chapter being called the "Standard (Western) Gospel" ["Salvation 1.0"][35] is stated in the widely used Campus Crusade for Christ[36] "Four Spiritual Laws" evangelistic presentation: "God loves you and offers a wonderful plan for your life (John 3:16; John 10:10); Man is sinful and separated from God . . . (Rom 3:23; Rom 6:23); Jesus Christ is God's only provision for sin . . . (Rom 5:8; 1 Cor 15:3-6; John 14:6); We must individually receive Jesus Christ as Savior and Lord . . . (John 1:12; Rev 3:20)."[37]

Such presentations of the gospel are soundly based on the relevant New Testament texts, focus on the doctrines of the atonement (penal substitution) and forgiveness of sins,[38] and have been the means by which countless individuals have entered into a saving relationship with Jesus Christ. The point here is not to criticize either the biblical basis, the intent, or the positive aspects that such presentations highlight, but rather to call attention to aspects of a more comprehensive biblical understanding of the "gospel" that are not highlighted in such presentations. The "standard" ("Western") presentation of the gospel tends to focus more on the "how" of salvation (the cross) and the "from-what" of salvation (from sin, guilt, judgment, death) than on the ultimate "why" and "for-what" of salvation (participation in the

---

28). Even these latter elements—forgiveness and everlasting life—are not placed in the context of intimate, personal communion with and participation in the life of the triune God.

34. In its crassest forms, such a "minimalist" understanding of salvation can view the "gospel" as merely a "fire insurance policy" that leaves the believer focused on worldly concerns rather than the final and ultimate ends of human life.

35. In the nomenclature being used in this article, "Salvation 1.0" or the "Standard (Western) Gospel," focusing on the "from-what" of redemption, focuses on the *proximate* benefits of salvation, while "Salvation 3.0," focusing on the "*for*-what," brings more clearly into view the *ultimate* benefits and final purposes of salvation. This "Salvation 3.0" could be paraphrased and summarized as follows: The chief end of man and the ultimate fulfillment of human life is found in "Glorifying God and enjoying him forever' (Westminster Shorter Catechism, Q. 1)" by sharing fully and in ever-increasing measure in the joyous life of the Trinity and God's mission to the world.

36. In 2011 Campus Crusade for Christ changed its name to "Cru," to avoid the negative associations of the word "Crusade": see "Our New Name: Cru."

37. Accessed at http://www.greatcom.org/english/four.htm. For similar evangelistic presentations of the gospel as presented by the Billy Graham organization and by the Navigators, see the references in my "Conversion Isn't What It Needs to Be," chapter 4 in the present volume.

38. The doctrine of justification (by grace alone, received through faith alone) is usually at least implicitly presupposed in such "standard" presentations, though not usually explicitly articulated. Explicit connection of the doctrines of penal substitution and justification by faith through grace may be more characteristic of churches identifying with the more conservative Lutheran and Reformed traditions.

life of the triune God). The understanding of the gospel in popular American evangelicalism tends to be too individualistic as well, with an insufficient integration with the doctrines of union with Christ and the Trinity.

It is the thesis of this chapter that the best features of the Western and Eastern understandings of salvation need to be integrated with one another in order to retrieve the richness and breadth of the New Testament teachings.[39] The enhanced understanding of the Christian message of salvation ("Salvation 3.0") being proposed here consists of the following three propositions: 1) that the doctrines of justification and penal substitution need to be more explicitly connected with the doctrines of *adoption* and *glorification*; 2) that the concept of salvation needs to be informed by the biblical teachings on the Trinity, union with Christ, and realized eschatology; and 3) that the concept of salvation needs to be informed by a *dynamic* sense of the *grace of God*—as a never-ending, inexhaustible experience of divine favor ("pleromafication": see Eph 3:19). Each of these three propositions and "upgrades" to the standard gospel will be explained below.

The first proposition, then, is that the forensic and judicial categories of justification and penal substitution need to be more explicitly connected with the more personal and participationist categories of *adoption* and *glorification,* for purposes of presenting the message of salvation in evangelism and discipleship.

A first step, then, toward an enhanced understanding of the gospel ("Salvation 3.0") would be taken by connecting more explicitly the doctrines of justification and adoption.[40] While adoption is an important metaphor of salvation in the New Testament, especially in Paul (see Rom 8:15; 8:23; 9:4; Gal 4:5; Eph 1:4–5), in both the history of theology and popular preaching it has been largely neglected[41] and overshadowed by the doctrine

---

39. One might recall at this point the much-quoted call of Pope John Paul II for the church, in the interests of Christian unity, to "breathe with two lungs"—with the "lungs" of both the Latin West and the Orthodox East, bringing together the best insights of both traditions: *Ut Unum Sint*.

40. Such a connecting of justification and adoption could be designated "Salvation 2.0"—enhancing a forensic metaphor with one that is more familial and personal. For biblical and theological studies of this important New Testament doctrine, see: Burke, *Adopted into God's Family*; Webb, *The Reformed Doctrine of Adoption*; Peterson, "Toward a Systematic Theology of Adoption"; Packer, "Sons of God," 181–208, in *Knowing God*.

41. For a thorough and insightful review of the history of the doctrine of adoption and its relative neglect, see Trumper, "The Theological History of Adoption." Trumper notes that adoption was overshadowed by justification in Calvin and the Westminster standards, conflated with justification in Turretin and Dabney, and later, overshadowed by regeneration in nineteenth-century revivalism with its focus on the "born-again" experience and "decisions for Christ."

of justification. This predominant focus on justification as the entry point to the Christian way of salvation reflected both the controversies of the Reformation period and the long-standing prominence of legal categories in the theologies of the Latin West.[42]

In recent years theologians and biblical scholars have, happily, been calling for a retrieval of this important biblical doctrine. J. I. Packer was so bold as to claim that our "understanding of Christianity cannot be better than our grasp of adoption," and that adoption is "the highest privilege that the gospel offers; higher than justification."[43] As Alister McGrath has noted, the doctrine of adoption connects with the longings of many today to be *wanted* and *connected.*"These are deeply emotive themes which resonate with the cares and concerns of many in our increasingly fractured society," he observes."To be adopted is to be invited into a loving and caring environment."[44] If justification is God's declaration that "You are fully *forgiven*," adoption is God's declaration that "You are fully *beloved*." Adoption answers the purposive or teleological question, "Forgiven—*for what?* For full inclusion and participation in the loving family of God."

The third and final step, then, toward an enhanced "Salvation 3.0" would be to explicitly connect the doctrines of justification and adoption with the doctrine of *glorification*. This important biblical theme, largely neglected in modern Protestant theology[45] and popular preaching, has in recent years been receiving increasing attention, in significant measure as a result of the interaction of Western theologians with the cognate Eastern Orthodox no-

---

42. The definitive history of the doctrine of justification is provided by McGrath, *Iustitia Dei*. McGrath notes that the sixteenth-century Protestant formulations of this crucial doctrine, and the responses to it at the Council of Trent were of "decisive importance in consolidating the conceptual dominance of justification within Western Christianity," and establishing it as a central identity marker for Protestants in distinguishing themselves from their ecclesiological rivals: ibid., 4. This historic emphasis on justification has been continued (and further complicated) by recent controversies concerning the so-called "New Perspectives" on Paul: on which see, from various perspectives, the articles in Husbands and Trier, eds., *Justification*.

43. Packer, *Knowing God*, 182, 186. He further asserts that the "entire Christian life (e.g., discipleship; prayer) has to be understood in terms of it" (190) and that the heart of the New Testament message of salvation can be summarized in these three words: "*adoption through propitiation*" (194). This latter linkage is what in the present article has been designated as "Salvation 2.0": penal substitution/justification + adoption: the forensic + the familial.

44. McGrath, *Christian Theology*, 144–45.

45. Bernard Ramm's *Them He Glorified* is one of the few full-length book treatments of the subject in modern times. At a more popular level, C. S. Lewis in *Mere Christianity* addressed the topic, stating that God would ultimately bring the Christian to be like a "god or goddess, dazzling, radiant, immortal . . . pulsating all through with such energy and joy and wisdom and love as we cannot now imagine . . . ," 174–75.

tions of "deification" or *theosis*. Since the 1980s ecumenical conversations between the Finnish Evangelical Lutheran Church and the Russian Orthodox Church have spawned a new school of "Finnish Interpretation of Luther," with its focus on recovering the roles of union with Christ and "deification" in Luther.[46] Scholars in the Reformed tradition have been retrieving the theme of "deification" in Calvin.[47] Methodist scholars have rediscovered elements of "deification" in Wesley, arguing that it reflected his extensive reading of the Greek church fathers and shaped his understandings of sanctification and Christian perfection.[48] Baptist and other evangelical theologians have been showing interest in the concept as well.[49] This renewed interest in theosis/glorification as an important theme in Christian soteriology is to be welcomed, for it recovers a much-needed focus on the question of the ultimate result and final *purpose* for which human beings are saved.

The notions of theosis and "divinization," which have been significant elements in Orthodox theology and spirituality since the patristic period, have themselves been given fresh attention by Orthodox scholars in the last several generations. Fresh studies of the pivotal figure of Gregory Palamas (1269-1359), a monk of Mount Athos, and his defense of the Hesychasts and their experience of the "uncreated light" of the glory of Christ, has led to something of a renascence of interest in theosis within Orthodox scholarship itself.[50] From the Orthodox point of view, this renewed interest in the historic theme of theosis is seen as a recovery of a more patristic and genuinely Orthodox vision of the Christian life — a vision, which since the Enlightenment, was believed to have been obscured by the categories of scholastic theology borrowed by Orthodox theologians themselves from the West.[51]

46. See Braaten and Jenson, eds., *Union with Christ*; Meyendorff and Tobias, eds., *Salvation in Christ*; Saarinen, "The Presence of God in Luther's Theology"; Bielfeldt, "Deification as a Motif in Luther's *Dictata super psalterium*"; Peura, "Christus Praesentissimus"; and Isaac, "The Finnish School of Luther Interpretation."

47. See especially Billings, "United to God through Christ," and *Calvin, Participation, and the Gift*; and Mosser, "The Greatest Possible Blessing." For a study of deification in Augustine, see Bonner, "Augustine's Conception of Deification."

48. Christensen, "Theosis and Sanctification"; and McCormick, "Theosis in Chrysostom and Wesley."

49. See Medley, "Participation in God"; and Rakestraw, "Becoming Like God."

50. On Palamas and his understanding of theosis, now considered to be "canonical" by contemporary Orthodox theologians, see Mantzaridis, *The Deification of Man*, and by the same author, "Spiritual Life in Palamism." Mantzaridis was professor of theology in the Theological School of the University of Thessaloniki. See also the careful study of Meyendorff, *St. Gregory Palamas and Orthodox Spirituality*.

51. On the influence of Western rationalism and scholastic theology on Greek Orthodox academic theology since the time of the Ottoman empire, see Yannaris, "Orthodoxy and the West."

Since the 1960s this renewed attention to theosis in Orthodox scholarship has been brought to the attention of wider audiences in the West[52] through the English publications of Orthodox scholars such as Timothy Ware, John Meyendorff, and Vladimir Lossky.[53] Evangelical scholars in the West have been showing an increasing yet cautious interest in this work,[54] recognizing its affinity to the more familiar Pauline category of glorification (e.g., Rom 8:30: "those whom he justified he also glorified"; 8:17, 18, 21; 2 Cor 3:18; Phil 3:21; Col 1:27; 3:4; 1 Cor 15:43), and yet expressing misgivings about the seemingly problematic terminology of "divinization," with its pantheistic-sounding overtones, and the rather unconvincing exegetical basis traditionally cited for this concept (e.g., John 10:34/Ps 82:6, "I say you are 'gods,'" and 2 Pet 1:4, "partakers of the divine nature"). Orthodox scholars insist that theosis does not mean an erasure of the Creator-creature distinction or fusion of the human and divine essences, but is rather a participation of the "whole man" in the "whole (trinitarian) God."[55] It is a full participation of the believer in the Son's communion with the Father (see John 17:21, "they *in* us"), "an eternal progress into the inexhaustible riches of the divine life"[56]—an experience believed to be the proper and ultimate goal for every Christian.

It is time, then, to retrieve and to rehabilitate the biblical teaching of glorification and to integrate it into the basic evangelical understanding of the nature and final goal of salvation. In short, the proposal in this paper is for a "Salvation 3.0" or "Gospel 3.0" that could be diagrammatically expressed in the following formula:

Salvation = Justification + Adoption + Glorification: [S 3.0 = JAG].

---

52. See the responses, from a wide range of theological traditions, in Christensen and Wittung, eds., *Partakers of the Divine Nature*.

53. For representative Orthodox expositions of theosis, see T. Ware, *The Orthodox Church*; Meyendorff, *Byzantine Theology*; Lossky, *The Mystical Theology of the Eastern Church*, 196–216, "The Way of Union," and 217–35, "The Divine Light"; George, *The Deification as the Purpose of Man's Life*. An extensive and judicious study of this entire theological tradition by a Western scholar is provided by N. Russell, *The Doctrine of Deification in the Greek Patristic Tradition*, examining the developments from the Alexandrians and Cappadocians through Maximus the Confessor, John of Damascus, Symeon the New Theologian, Gregory Palamas, down to modern Orthodoxy.

54. Recent American evangelical responses to the Orthodox teachings on theosis also include Fairbairn, *Eastern Orthodoxy through Western Eyes*, 79–95, "Salvation: The Path of Theosis," and Clendenin, *Eastern Orthodox Christianity*, 117–37, "The Deification of Humanity"; see also Ezdenci, *Deification and Union with Christ*.

55. Meyendorff, *Byzantine Theology*, 164, citing Maximus the Confessor.

56. Ibid., 225.

The "Good News" of Jesus Christ begins with justification (and penal substitution): "You are *fully* forgiven"; continues with adoption (sonship): "You are *fully* beloved as a son"; and is completed in glorification: "You will be *fully* transformed in union with Christ and the body of Christ." Glorification is the fulfillment of God's highest purpose for his redeemed people, as they are fully transformed into the image of his Son, and filled with all the fullness of God—his love, joy, peace, and glory—in union with the people of God, in the midst of a renewed and glorified creation.[57] The forgiveness of justification is for the purpose of enjoying the full benefits of being a beloved son or daughter of God; the purpose of sonship is to finally enjoy the fullness and blessedness of Jesus' sonship with the Father—to be filled with all the fullness of God (Eph 3:19), as Jesus himself is filled with all the glorious fullness of the Father's love and life. This *summum bonum* of salvation is captured in the biblical images of Jesus on the Mount of Transfiguration—his radiant glory being a picture of the believer's final transfiguration—and of the New Jerusalem, coming down out of heaven like a beautiful bride adorned for her loving husband (a picture of the glorified church) to stand in the midst of a transformed and glorified creation (Rev 21–22). In the eyes of faith, we can see the consummation of glorification, as it were, by seeing Christ of the Mount of Transfiguration moved inside the New Jerusalem with all its splendor, awaiting to welcome his beloved bride for the marriage supper of the Lamb and to the never-ending joy of the marriage's consummation.

In recent Reformed theology one of the most promising attempts to recover the biblical doctrine of glorification and to reintegrate it as a core element into the concept of salvation is found in Michael Horton's systematic theology text, *The Christian Faith*, chapter 21, "The Hope of Glory."[58] Horton's treatment of this topic attempts to bring into conversation important figures in the Reformed tradition—Calvin, Turretin,[59] the Puritans, Bavinck,

---

57. The biblical vision of a glorified and renewed creation (Rom 8:19-21; Rev 21:5—22:5) reaffirms the goodness and intrinsic value of the original creation (Gen 1:31), and provides a further basis for a Christian stewardship of creation—a basis lacking in world-denying religions such as Buddhism. On Buddhist attitudes toward nature and the material world, see Harris, "Attitudes to Nature."

58. Horton, *The Christian Faith*. For other examples in recent Reformed scholarship to recover the more participationist aspect of soteriology such as union with Christ and glorification, see Muller, *Calvin and the Reformed Tradition*, 202–43, "Union with Christ and the Order Salutis," and Gaffin Jr., "Union with Christ." Gaffin believes that a vision of the glorified Christ, in company with his brethren that share his glory (Rom 8:29-30), "ought to be our constant and controlling preoccupation in all matters that concern the *ordo salutis*": 288.

59. For Calvin on the closely related theme of union with Christ, in relation to which glorification is accomplished, see *Institutes* III.2.24: "Christ is not outside us but dwells within us . . . with a wonderful communion, day by day, he grows more and more

Vos, and Murray[60]—with representatives of the Orthodox tradition—Athanasius, Basil, Vladimir Lossky—in an attempt to enrich the Western forensic categories such as justification with the Eastern participationist categories of theosis and deification (= glorification). As Horton states it, "what happens *for us* [justification] is the basis for what happens *to* us and *in* us" [adoption and glorification].[61] Horton is correct that the "East" needs the Western emphasis on justification and atonement to make its doctrine of theosis/glorification "work," for only a person who has been fully forgiven (justified) can fully enjoy the benefits of sonship, and can begin even in this life[62] to experience the glorious effects of life in the Spirit. At the same time, the West can benefit from the East and its vision of theosis [glorification] as the final goal and purpose of man's creation and redemption.

In order to bring the argument of this paper to a close, two further steps need to be taken: 1) to place the "trajectory" of Salvation 3.0 (justification → adoption → glorification) within a biblical-theological framework in which the doctrines of the Trinity, union with Christ, and realized eschatology are given recognition and weight; and 2) to introduce two new technical terms that can help to explicate the concepts of glorification specifically and of salvation more generally: *intra-hypostatic communion* and *dynamic, perichoretic pleromafication*.

---

into one body with us, until he becomes completely one with us." Turretin's classical treatment of glorification is found in his *Institutes of Elenctic Theology* (1679–1685), vol. 3, where he expounds the four characteristics of the Christian's glorified body as incorruptibility, brightness and glory, power (freedom), and spirituality—based on the Pauline text of 1 Corinthians 15:42-44.

60. John Murray devotes a full chapter to the doctrine of glorification in *Redemption*, seeing it as the final stage of redemption accomplished at the resurrection, and experienced by all the people of God, together, at the same time: 218. Thus Murray emphasizes the "not yet" of glorification—in distinction from the understanding presented in this chapter, viz., that glorification is both "already" (2 Cor 3:18) and "not yet" (Phil 3:21; Rom 8:18-21).

61. Horton, *The Christian Faith*, 710.

62. Horton, ibid., sees glorification primarily or exclusively as the "Not Yet" aspect of our salvation (689), and appears to overlook the force of the Pauline text in 2 Corinthians 3:18, where the believer is in the present ("already") beholding the glory of the Lord and being transformed into the image of that glory. For accounts of Eastern Orthodox saints and desert fathers who were said to have experienced in this life the firstfruits of bodily transfiguration by heavenly light (Seraphim of Sarov; Arsenius the Great; Abba Pambo), see T. Ware, *The Orthodox Church*, 238–39 and 238n4; in the West, see also the account by a visitor to Evelyn Underhill in October of 1937, reporting that "light streamed from her face with a radiant smile.... One could not but feel ... that one was in the presence of the extension of the Mystery of our Lord's Transfiguration in one of the members of His Mystical Body": in Williams, ed., *The Letters of Evelyn Underhill*, 37.

In previous publications I have argued that the doctrines of the Trinity, of union with Christ, and of realized eschatology, while acknowledged in evangelical faith and theology, need to be made more central and explicit in our understanding of Christian life and salvation.[63] This fuller discussion of these themes need not to be repeated here. As has already been stated, salvation is, in fact, the fullness of participation in the life of the Trinity.[64] We experience the benefits of justification, adoption, and glorification through our union with Christ, in the communion of the realized presence of the Holy Spirit, who enables us to experience the communion that Jesus enjoys with the Father.

The first of two new technical terms that are here being introduced to explicate the concepts of salvation (3.0) and glorification is that of *intra-hypostatic communion*. This term attempts to capture the reality signified in the Johannine and Pauline understandings of the believer's union with Christ, e.g., John 17:23, "I *in* them"; 17:26, "that I myself may be *in them*"; Eph 3:17, "that Christ may dwell *in your hearts* by faith"; Col 1:27, "Christ *in you*, the hope of glory," and so forth. Glorification, which is the consummation of the entire trajectory of salvation, occurs through union with Christ, as Christ himself, the second person of the Trinity, abides, through the communion of the Holy Spirit, in the very core of the believer's personhood (hypostasis). The believer experiences a "perichoretic" relationship with Christ, in an analogous yet metaphysically real sense proportionate to the Creator-creature distinction. Christ and the believer share completely and fully one another's interior life and are fully "open" to one another.[65]

The divine hypostasis of Christ interpenetrates the human hypostasis of the believer and is truly present *within* the believer's hypostasis,[66] while at

---

63. See J. J. Davis, *Reality in Meditation*, chapter 3, "The Arrival of the Age to Come," and chapter 4, "Inaugurated Ontology: A Biblical Worldview for Biblical Meditation"; and "How Personal Agents Are Located in Space."

64. As argued in Fairbairn, *Life in the Trinity*, 203: "all aspects of salvation revolve around and derive from the believer's participation in Christ through the Holy Spirit. It is in sharing in the Father-Son relationship that we receive the other benefits of salvation such as justification and reconciliation."

65. The technical terms being proposed here are compatible with the technical terminology of "participation" (*oikeiotes*) used by Cyril of Alexandria to describe the believer's sharing in the intimate communion that Jesus enjoys with the Father: see Fairbairn, *Grace and Christology in the Early Church*, 179. The terms here expounded— *intra-hypostatic communion* and *pleromafication*—are an attempt to give Cyril's terminology of intimate communion even greater specificity.

66. The concept being proposed here is different from the Eastern understanding of theosis, based on the sharp Palamite distinction between the *essence* and *energies* of God. In this Eastern understanding, the believer participates in the "energies" of God but not in the unknowable "essence": see Mantzaridis, *The Deification of Man*, 104–15.

the same time the divine and human hypostases remain metaphysically distinct. The human hypostasis is glorified *from within* by the communication of the divine glory, but remains forever a distinct and human hypostasis.[67] This technical terminology of *intra-hypostatic communion* between Christ and the believer is intended to express a concept of salvation "none greater than which can be conceived" (see Eph 3:19-20), a personal relationship between the triune God and the believer more intimate and deeper than which it is impossible to conceive. Glorification and salvation are consummated in the *deepest and most intense possible relationship with the highest and most ultimate reality:* fullness of union with the triune God, in Christ, through the Spirit. The high point of the Old Covenant was epitomized in the language of "God *with* us"; the yet higher reality of the New Covenant is fulfilled in the experience of "God *within* us." By means of such a conceptuality the evangelical tradition of speaking of having a "personal relationship with Christ" is brought to its highest and ultimate fruition, in "personal" categories that include but go beyond the forensic and functional emphases of the mainstream Western soteriological tradition.

The second technical term that is here being proposed to elucidate the ultimate and highest state of salvation to be experienced by the believing

---

On the contrary, it is here being argued that the very *essence* of God—in the person of the Holy Spirit—is really *present* within the person/hypostasis of the believer. While material and molecular entities such as stones cannot be "in" and interpenetrate one another, non-molecular entities such as the persons of the Trinity and the human soul/spirit (understood as the seat of the human hypostasis = self/person) can interpenetrate one another. On this latter distinction, see the article by J. J. Davis, "How Personal Agents Are Located in Space."

The essence of God is present, and also truly knowable—but only in an analogical and proportionate sense that preserves and recognizes the Creator-creature distinction. The Eastern, apophatic insistence on the (complete) unknowability of the divine essence leaves the Christian understanding of God unprotected from Buddhist and Hindu claims that the "real" and "ultimate" God/reality is beyond all distinctions—including the trinitarian distinction of persons. On this latter danger, see J. J. Davis, "Buddha, the Apostle Paul, and John Hick."

67. The concept of *intra-hypostatic communion* being proposed here is similar to a notion found in Maximus the Confessor (d. 662) in which there is a mutual interpenetration (perichoresis) of Christ and the believer, yet retaining the ontological distinctiveness of each: "The whole of the human being is interpenetrated by the whole of God [like an "iron made red-hot" by the fire: the iron is in the fire, and the fire in the iron—yet both remain distinct] and becomes all that God is, excluding identity of essence ... The human being receives to itself the whole of God and ... inherits God himself": cited in Christensen and Wittung, eds., *Partakers of the Divine Nature*, 141. The terminology here being proposed—*intra-hypostatic communion*—makes it explicit that God himself is present at the very innermost core of the believer's being. In contrast to the Eastern traditions, it is here explicitly stated that the very *essence* of the triune God and the three divine hypostases are present within the hypostasis of the believer.

church is *pleromafication* (see Eph 3:19, *pan to pleroma*, "all the fullness"), understood as a state of "dynamic, perichoretic fullness." This latter phrase, which attempts to unpack the concept of "pleromafication," can be explicated as follows: first of all, the final state of salvation is one of fullness—that is, being "filled with all the fullness of God" (Eph 3:19), as a result of being filled with the risen and glorified Christ himself dwelling in the heart, as enabled and empowered by the glorious Holy Spirit of God (Eph 3:17–19), and consequently, being filled with the love, joy, peace, and glory that the persons of the Trinity eternally share with one another, and have graciously purposed to share with the church (see John 14:26, "*my* peace I give you"; John 17:13, "that they may have the full measure of *my* joy within them"; John 17:22, "I have given them the glory that you gave me"; John 17:26, "in order that *the love you have for me may be in them*, and that *I myself may be in them*").[68]

The final salvific state of pleromafication is "perichoretic" in that it involves an analogous and proportionate yet very real participation in Jesus' relationship with the Father, such that the believer is "in" Jesus and Jesus in the believer (Eph 3:17) just as Jesus is in the Father (see John 17:21, "they *in us*"). To have the risen Christ in the heart is to share in Jesus' heart-experience with the Father; that is, just as Jesus and the Father share completely and fully in one another's interior life, so the believing church is graced to share in that same love, joy, peace, and glory that the Father and the Son share with one another and with the Spirit.

Further, and not incidentally, this "perichoretic" participation obtains not only between the believing church and the Trinity, but also among *all the members of the believing church*: "*that all of them* may be one, Father, just as you are in me and I am in you" (John 17:21). This corporate perichoresis within the church is the perfection and consummation of the "communion of the saints" and an answer to the prayer for unity for which Jesus (and Paul) prayed—a perichoretic unity of openness, harmony, trust, transparency, and shared joy that begins in the present life and is perfected in the life to come. The final state of salvation is not just an individual matter; rather, *we* are *all* finally and perfectly saved *together*. Final salvation is about "we," not "me" (see Eph 3:18, "together with *all* the saints").

Finally, this perfected state of salvation—pleromafication—is *dynamic* rather that static in nature.[69] The inexhaustible God will never cease to do

---

68. Paul's prayer for the church to experience the fullness of salvation (Eph 3:17–19) is parallel to Jesus' High Priestly Prayer for the church (John 17:20–26); the objects for which both Jesus and Paul pray are revelations of the nature of God's ultimate purposes in salvation.

69. Gregory of Nyssa articulated a doctrine of "perpetual progress in salvation" (*epectasis*) in *The Life of Moses* and other mystical writings: "no limit can be set to our

good to his people (Jer 32:40).[70] As the ages of ages in the new creation roll on, the boundless generosity of God to us his people will be expressed in a never-ending stream of kindnesses and mercies (Eph 2:7, "in order that in the coming ages he might show the incomparable riches of his grace").[71] The people of God will share in the unceasing delight and happiness that God the Father enjoys in bestowing his love, joy, peace, and glory upon his Son, and in the Son's unceasing giving of praise, thanksgiving, and glory to his Father. By the supernatural power of the Holy Spirit given to the church

---

progress toward God": cited by Danielou in *From Glory to Glory*, 148. "For Gregory," according to Danielou, "this movement becomes a symbol for the soul's ability to make indefinite progress in grace and perfection as it moves toward the infinite": ibid., 292n30. Gregory presumably found such a notion suggested in Pauline texts such as Philippians 3:13-14 ("Forgetting what lies behind, and *stretching forward* [epekteinomenos] to what lies ahead . . . ."). In a somewhat similar vein Meyendorff has noted as central themes in Byzantine theology an understanding of the human being created to be "essentially open, developing, and growing" and a notion of salvation that involves man growing into God "from glory to glory" (2 Cor 3:18) and "an eternal progress into the inexhaustible riches of divine life": *Byzantine Theology*, 225-26. Gregory of Palamas, in *Defence of the Hesychasts*, 2, 2, 11, had spoken of such a dynamic view of salvation and the beatific vision: "since He who gives Himself is infinite and He bestows abundantly and lavishly, how can the sons of the age to come not progress infinitely in this vision, acquiring grace after grace and joyfully ascending the ascent that never wearies": cited in Mantzaridis, *The Deification of Man*, 125.

70. This remarkable text about the nature of the New Covenant salvation (Jer 32:40-42) was brought to my attention by Piper, *The Pleasures of God*, 180-84. Not only is there the astonishing declaration that God will *never cease* to do good to his people (32:40); there is further the profoundly important statement that God *enjoys* and delights with *all his heart and soul* to do his people good (Jer 32:41). As Piper notes, God "does not bless us begrudgingly. There is a kind of eagerness about the beneficence of God. He seeks us out, because it is his pleasure to do us good": ibid., 184. The "Good News" is not only that God saves us but also that he *delights* and *enjoys* the act of saving us, and then delights in us for our own sake—not because of our works or worthiness or accomplishments—he loves us because he loves us, and he enjoys loving us in the very act of loving us. Huey notes that the phrase in Jeremiah 32:41, that God will delight in doing good to his people "with all my heart [*leb*] and soul [*nephesh*]" is the only instance in all of Scripture where this dual expression is used of God: Huey, *Jeremiah, Lamentations*, 296. Robert P. Carroll observes that this New Covenant between God and his people is "characterized by a tenderness, joy, and concern" implemented by Yahweh "with all his mind and being": *Jeremiah*, 630.

71. The Dutch Reformed theologian Hendrikus Berkhof has commented on the inexhaustible nature of God's salvation: "The New Testament does cater to a static conception of eternal life . . . God is inexhaustible; and the closer we live to him, the more life will reveal itself in all its inexhaustibility . . . ."; he also cites in this regard the statement of Irenaeus: "We hope ever to be receiving more and more from God, and to learn from Him, because He is good, and possesses boundless riches, a kingdom without end, and instruction that can never be exhausted [*Adv Haer* II, 28, 3]": *Christian Faith*, 544-45.

(Eph 3:16–17), Christ will dwell ever more deeply and intimately in the hearts of the believing church, as that same Spirit enlarges increasingly the church's capacity to experience and enjoy the love of Christ and to know the Father more deeply (Eph 1:17). This enlargement in the church's capacity to know the Father and to experience the Father's love has no foreseeable limits (see Eph 3:20, "more than all that we can ask *or imagine*"). No matter how much we grow in our knowledge of God and of the Father's love, there is yet an infinite and unlimited reservoir of divine love and glory for the church to continue to experience, as it is filled—and continuously, dynamically, never-endingly filled with all the fullness of God (Eph 3:19).[72]

Some Concluding Thoughts and Suggestions for Preaching and Teaching

This chapter will conclude by 1) responding to a possible objection to this proposal for an "expanded" gospel; by 2) suggesting some possible advantages of such a view; and by 3) briefly sketching a framework for the practical application of this proposal in preaching, discipleship, and evangelism.

In the first place, it might seem to some readers both unnecessary and even presumptuous to argue that the customary understandings of salvation are incomplete. The received understanding of the gospel in popular evangelicalism, based on penal substitutionary atonement and justification by faith, is in fact well grounded in the biblical revelation. The gospel understood as primarily focused on the call to repentance for the forgiveness of sins, proclaimed in the name of Jesus Christ, and the promise of the gift of the Holy Spirit is well attested in the early apostolic tradition (see Luke 24:47; Acts 2:38, 10:41–43; 1 Cor 15:1–8; Rom 3:21–25).

The response that can be made to this objection is that it is legitimate to recognize a degree of development in the doctrine of salvation within the New Testament canon itself, a development in which elements that were only implicit in an earlier "Galilean" gospel become more explicit in a "post-Pentecost" apostolic explication of the gospel. In the earliest, "Galilean" form of the gospel, as witnessed in the preaching of John the Baptist and Jesus—before the cross, resurrection, and Pentecost—the message is focused on Good News for the Jewish nation of Israel. The programmatic

---

72. Arnold has drawn attention to the very unusual adverb—*huperekperissou*—used by Paul in Ephesians 3:20 to describe the magnitude of God's power and the scope of salvation to be experienced: "quite beyond all measure"; "infinitely more than": *Ephesians*, 219. This adverb is indeed appropriate as the apostle stretches the bounds of human language and imagination to envision a "salvation none greater than which can be conceived."

announcement of this Good News for Israel—"The time has come; the Kingdom of God is near"—was an announcement that the God of Israel, who had departed from the temple before the exile (Ezek 10:18–22) and was no longer present with his people, would one day return to Jerusalem (Zech 8:3) to dwell with his people and would fill the temple with his glory (Hag 2:7). God would gather the exiles and bring them back to the land (Ezek 36:24; Zech 8:7–8; 10:8,9; Zeph 3:19–20) and take great delight in them and bless them (Zeph 3:17; Isa 62:1–5). The Holy Spirit and the voice of prophecy, long silent during the intertestamental period, would be renewed when God again poured out his Spirit, not just on the prophets, but on all his people (Joel 2:28–32; Isa 44:3).[73]

Jesus himself had told his disciples that after Pentecost, after the reception of the Holy Spirit, they would have a deeper understanding of his person, his work, and of his message of salvation (see John 14:20, 26; 16:7, 13, 14: "the Spirit . . . will guide you into all truth . . . . He will take what is mine and make it known unto you"). These promises for the understanding of an "expanded gospel" were fulfilled in the writings of Paul and John and the other New Testament writers. Paul is given deeper insight into the "mystery" of the gospel, i.e., a fuller understanding of God's plan to include the Gentiles together with the Jews into one new body of Christ (Eph 3:6; 2:11–22). John, especially in the farewell discourses (John 13:17), makes it evident that the message of salvation and eternal life goes beyond the Old Covenant promise of "God *with* us" to a yet deeper New Covenant reality of "God *in* us" (John 14:23) and "we *in* God" (John 17:21). Just as during the Reformation the gospel truth of justification was recovered (not invented), so now, in this project, it is being proposed that the integral Pauline connections between justification, adoption, and glorification (Rom 8:1, 15, 16, 18–21, 29–30) be recovered in a "Romans 8 'Full Gospel'" of "life in the Spirit." The proposal is not for a "new" or "different" gospel, but for the recovery of a fuller soteriology already announced in the *locus classicus*, Romans 8:30 ("those whom he justified, he also *glorified*").

I would like to suggest that this proposed upgrading of the "Good News" ("Salvation 3.0") offers a number of benefits and advantages in comparison with current popular evangelical understandings of the gospel ("Salvation 1.0"). For the purposes of evangelism, Salvation 3.0 makes explicit the full range of benefits offered to believers as a result of the life, death, and incarnation of Jesus Christ, and so should make the Christian message even more attractive in an increasingly crowded and competitive

---

73. On the foregoing sketch of the "Galilean" form of the "Good News" as it may have been heard in by Jews in its early first-century Palestinian setting, see Wright, *Jesus and the Victory of God*, 615–54.

religious market place. With respect to the world mission of the church, the message of Salvation 3.0 (Justification + Adoption + Glorification) makes it clear that the ultimate purpose and meaning of human life will be realized in a process of completed transformation (glorification) and experience of joy, beauty, and freedom—in a state of perfected existence to be experienced not alone, but in community with others, and in the context of a renewed and glorified creation. With respect to the church's task of discipleship, Salvation 3.0 could provide the benefit of casting a vision of the *ultimate purpose* and final goal of the Christian life. Salvation 3.0 challenges the believer to "see the end from the beginning"—to understand not only the "how" of salvation, but also its "why"; to understand salvation *for* as well as salvation *from*. With respect to ecumenism and Christian unity, Salvation 3.0 invites further conversations between Western and Eastern Christians, and could help them to recognize the common elements in their respective understandings of salvation.

Finally, by way of practical application, let me suggest a simple formula and mnemonic device that could help in preaching and teaching the concept of Salvation 3.0 (Justification + Adoption + Glorification). The "full gospel" is constituted by the "trajectory" from Justification (and penal substitution) to Adoption to Glorification. Each of these three doctrinal elements of salvation could be associated with a simple "bullet point" or key idea: Justification (the cross): "You are *fully forgiven*"; Adoption: "You are *fully beloved*"; Glorification: "You will be *fully transformed*." For greater ease of memory and retention and affective impact, each of these three doctrinal loci can be associated with two biblical images or narratives[74] that would help the listener to answer the question, "What does this look like? What do justification, adoption, and glorification look like for me?"

For justification, the suggested images (and texts) are those of Christ dying on the cross of Calvary (John 3:16) and the courtroom in which the judge pronounces the verdict of "Not guilty!" (see Rom 3:24-25). For adoption, the suggested images are those of Jesus being baptized in the Jordan River, and hearing the Father's words, "This is my beloved son; with him I am well pleased" (Matt 3:17), and that of the prodigal son being welcomed home and embraced by his loving and compassionate father (Luke 15:20). For glorification, the suggested images are those of Christ on the Mount of Transfiguration, together with Moses and Elijah in their glorified states (Luke 9:28-32)—images of the believer's future glorified state—and that of the

---

74. This method of connecting a biblical concept and a biblical image that illustrates it is reflected in the teaching methods of Jesus, and is adapted in what I have called "whole-brain meditation" on Scripture: see J. J. Davis, *Reality in Meditation*, 142-50.

New Jerusalem coming down out of heaven as a glorious bride adorned for her husband (Rev 21:2), an image of the transcendent beauty of a glorified and fully transformed church in the context of a glorified and transformed creation. The eyes of faith can see, as it were, the Christ of the Mount of Transfiguration enthroned *inside* the New Jerusalem/New Creation/Beloved Bride, waiting for the joyous, loving consummation of his marriage to his radiant Bride in the wedding feast of the Lamb. The trajectory of full salvation, Salvation 3.0, then, could be expressed as a glorious movement and journey of faith "From the Cross to the Courtroom; from the Courtroom to the Father's house; from the Father's house to the glorious New Creation and to the Bridal Chamber, to the Marriage Supper of the Lamb."

Christ loved the church, and gave himself for her, that he might present her to himself as a radiant church, without stain or blemish . . . . Ephesians 5:25, 27.

And we all, with unveiled faces, are beholding the glory of the Lord, and are being transformed from one degree of glory to another. 2 Corinthians 3:18.

6

Where N. T. Wright Isn't Quite Right

*Further Brief Perspectives on the
"New Perspectives" on Paul*

IN MY EARLIER PIECE, "Very Brief Perspectives on the New Perspectives," I noted that N. T. Wright and the advocates of the "New Perspectives on Paul" (NPP) had made real contributions to the ongoing debate on Paul's doctrine of justification by rightly calling attention to the context of his teaching within the Abrahamic covenant (Rom 4) and to the important connections in the apostle's thought between justification, the resurrection of Jesus (e.g., Rom 4:25, "raised to life for our justification"), and the reception of the promised Holy Spirit (Gal 3:2, 5, 6, 11, 14).

At the same time, I believe that Wright isn't quite right in four critical areas, and will indicate my reservations about his position below: 1) the meaning of "works of the law"; 2) the meaning of "righteousness" and "righteousness of God"; 3) the presence of merit theology and works righteousness in Judaism; and 4) construing the focus of justification as being ecclesiology (covenant membership) rather than soteriology (salvation). These problems have contributed to confusion and lack of clarity concerning the Pauline doctrine of justification.

1. Restricting "works of the law" to "ethnic boundary markers" such as circumcision and dietary laws:

    In Galatians 3:10 the apostle writes, "All who rely on observing the law are under a curse," and cites Deuteronomy 27:26, "for it is written, 'Cursed is everyone who does not continue to do *everything* (emphasis added) written in the Book of the Law.'" "Everything written in the Book of the Law" certainly includes circumcision (Gen 17) and dietary laws (Lev 11), but is not restricted to those requirements. It also includes the ethical requirements of the Decalogue (Exod 20), the provisions of civil and criminal law, the laws of sacrifice, ritual purity, and the like. Moses had reminded the people, "If we are careful to obey *all* this law [not just the "cultic" provisions] before the Lord our God, as he has commanded us, that will be our righteousness" (Deut 6:25). The Mosaic notion of "righteousness" here clearly has the sense of "obeying all the commandments of the Torah."

Paul states that on the day of God's righteous judgment those who "obey the law will be declared righteous" (Rom 2:13), and that those Gentiles who "do by nature things required by the law" (Rom 2:14) are a "law for themselves." These Gentiles have not been circumcised and do not observe the Jewish dietary provisions, but their righteous acts are consistent with the moral requirements of the Decalogue and Torah. The "things required by the law" that the apostle is concerned with in relation to the day of judgement are the *moral* requirement of the law. The upshot of this first point, then, is that Wright's interpretation of "works of the law" is too restrictive. This faulty and unduly restricted interpretation of "works of the law" contributes, as we shall see, to a diminished meaning for "righteousness" and the "righteousness of God," as to be noted in point 2, following.

2. Interpreting "righteousness" and the "righteousness of God" as "covenant faithfulness":

In a broader sense Wright and the proponents of the NPP are correct in saying that the "righteousness of God" means faithfulness to his covenant promises. God is righteous in the sense of keeping his promises, just as a righteous human can demonstrate righteous character by keeping his or her marriage promises. It is also the case that the "righteousness of God" is a *redemptive* righteousness in that it connotes God's willingness and ability to rescue his people from peril (e.g., Ps 9:4–5, "You have upheld my right and my cause; you have sat on your throne judging righteously; you have rebuked the nations"; Ps 143:1, "O Lord, hear my prayer . . . in your faithfulness and righteousness come to my relief"). The problem with this interpretation, however, is that it tends to obscure the *ethical* content and specificity of "covenant faithfulness," and also the *retributive* aspect of God's righteousness and saving action in history.

The Old Testament prophets do not understand "righteousness" to mean "covenant faithfulness" in the abstract or only in general, but define this covenant faithfulness very specifically and concretely in moral terms. For Ezekiel, a righteous man (Ezek 18:5–9) is one who "does what is just and right," who does not look to the idols, does not defile his neighbor's wife, who does not commit robbery, who gives his food to the hungry, who judges fairly between man and man, and who keeps the laws of God: "that man is righteous" (18:9). In a New Testament setting, Peter recognizes that a Gentile like Cornelius can be a righteous Gentile, because he fears God and does what is right (Acts 10:35; 22).

The interpretation of the righteousness of God as covenant faithfulness is also problematic in that it tends to minimize the *retributive* righteousness of God (in contrast to his redemptive or "rescuing" righteousness). In the book of Romans, it is clear that Paul's understanding of the righteousness of God has an important element of retributive justice, in that the apostle, grounded in the Old Testament as he is, sees the God of Israel as a God who not only rescues and vindicates his faithful people, but also as a God who punishes the wicked. The righteousness of God that is being revealed in the preaching of Paul's gospel involves the wrath of God against all the wickedness of men (Rom 1:18). On the day of God's wrath his righteous judgment will be revealed (Rom 2:5). Our unrighteousness [violations of the law of God; not just circumcision or the lack of it] is the reason why God is just in bringing his wrath upon us when he judges the world (Rom 3:5).

The loss of focus on the ethical content of "covenant faithfulness" and the retributive dimension of God's righteousness and saving actions in history can contribute, unwittingly, to an *antinomian* tendency to diminish the serious of obedience to the moral law—not a tendency that we should want to promote in our permissive, postmodern cultural contexts. Robust understandings of Christian discipleship and character formation require more specificity in ethical teaching, not less. The diminishing of the elements of retributive justice in the New Testament teaching on the atonement and the work of Christ can diminish the sense of the seriousness and consequences of sin, and so contribute to a trivializing of the gospel itself.

3. Overstating the absence of "merit theology" and works righteousness in Judaism:

While earlier Protestant interpretation may have suffered from an unbalanced and inaccurate picture of second Temple Judaism, the NPP seems to have overstated its claims concerning the absence of merit theology and works righteousness in intertestamental and Second Temple Judaism. Various critics of the NPP have pointed to texts such as the following to challenge this view:

Remember the deeds of the fathers.... Was not Abraham found faithful when tested [Gen 22], and it was reckoned to him as righteousness (1 Macc 2:51–52).

Almsgiving delivers from death and keeps you from going into the darkness (Tob 4:10).

Those who honor their father atone for sins, and those who respect their mother are like those who lay up treasure (Sir 3:3–4).

[Abraham] kept the law of the Most High ... and when tested was found faithful.... Therefore the Lord assured him by an oath that the nations would be blessed through his posterity (Sir 44:20–21).

Store up almsgiving in your treasure, and it will rescue you from every disaster (Sir 29:12).

Abraham was perfect in all his actions with the Lord and was pleasing through righteousness all the days of his life (Jubilees 23:10).

But sympathy for her children did not sway the mother of the young men; she was of the same mind as Abraham (4 Macc 14:20: mother of the martyrs; Abraham: Gen 22).

For the righteous, who have many works laid up with thee, shall out of their own deeds receive their reward (4 Ezra 8:33).

For the righteous justly hope for the end, and without fear depart from this habitation, because they have with thee a store of works preserved in treasuries (2 Bar 14:12).

Also the glory of those who have now been justified in my Law ... may be able to acquire and receive the world which does not die (2 Bar 51:3).

But to those who have *been saved by their works*, and to whom the law has now been a hope . . . there shall be spread before them the extents of Paradise (2 Bar 51:7, 11).

And it shall be reckoned to you as righteousness when you do what is upright and good before him, for your good and that of Israel (4 Q399: 7–8).

However, the reward for such as live exactly according to the laws is not silver or gold . . . to those who keep the laws . . . God has granted them a renewed existence and a better life at the transformation . . . . (Josephus, *Contra Apion* 2.217-18).

All is foreseen, but freedom of choice is given; and the world is judged by grace, yet all is according to the majority of works (R. Akiba, m. 'Abot 3.15).

These texts demonstrate that there were indeed notions of works righteousness in the streams of Judaism that were known to Paul, and against which his teachings of righteousness through faith in Christ alone could have been directed.

The existence of notions of works righteousness in first-century popular Judaism is also reflected in the Gospels, e.g., the question of the rich young ruler posed to Jesus, "What must I *do* to inherit eternal life?" (Mark 10:17). Evidently this young man—who no doubt had been circumcised and bore the sign of covenant membership, did not consider this sign of descent from Abraham sufficient to give him assurance concerning his place in the world to come. In the Parable of the Pharisee and the Tax Collector, Jesus directed his teaching against those who were "confident in their own righteousness and looked down on everybody else" (Luke 18:9), based (in their own view) on their scrupulous observance of the law. Jesus, however, says that the publican, who trusted himself to the mercy of God, not his good works, "went home justified before God" (18:14). Jesus' parable would have been pointless had there been in fact no works righteousness in the popular Judaism of his day.

Paul himself, of course, should be recognized as a first-century witness to the Judaism of his day. As a Pharisee, in terms of legalistic righteousness, he viewed himself as "faultless" (Phil 3:6). And yet after his encounter with the Risen Christ, he abandoned reliance on a "righteousness of my own that comes from the law" for a "righteousness that comes from God and is by faith" (Phil 3:10). It would be strange indeed to suppose that Wright and the proponents of the NPP, writing in the twentieth and twenty-first centuries, would have a better knowledge of first-century Judaism than Paul himself—who was a living contemporary, and knew it as an insider!

Given these considerations, and the evidence for the existence of elements of works righteousness in the Judaism known to Paul, then the appearance of a huge disconnect between the teachings of Paul in his first-century context and the readings of Paul by the sixteenth-century reformers collapses: there were, in fact, problems of works righteousness in both contexts. Both contexts had issues of the *synergism* of divine grace and human works, and Paul's teachings of *sola gratia* and *sola fide* were relevant to both.

4. Focusing on justification as a matter of *ecclesiology* ("Who's in") rather than *soteriology* (salvation):

Finally, Wright's argument that justification in Paul is more a matter of ecclesiology—who is or not in the covenant community, and on what basis—rather than a matter of soteriology or eternal salvation, is quite problematic. This way of framing the question makes an "either-or" choice of what should in fact be seen as a "both-and"; it is a needless and faulty dichotomy. While it is true that Paul's doctrine of justification had ecclesiological implications, e.g., table fellowship between Jews and Gentiles based on faith in Jesus Christ alone apart from circumcision (Gal 2:11–16), it is also the case that the circumcision controversy in the early church was an issue of soteriology and salvation, not only table fellowship. Converts from Pharisaic Judaism were saying that the "Gentiles must be circumcised and required to obey the law of Moses" (Acts 15:5), and that in fact, "Unless you are circumcised according to the custom taught by Moses, you cannot be saved" (Acts 15:1).

Paul's teaching on justification in Romans is clearly framed within a horizon with eternal salvation in view, not merely matters of ecclesiology. The gospel he announces is the "power of God for the salvation of everyone who believes" (Rom 1:16); this gospel saves one from the wrath of God against the ungodliness and wickedness of men (Rom 1:18). Belief in the gospel is urgent in view of the "day of God's wrath, when his righteous judgment will be revealed" (Rom 2:5), the day when God "will judge men's secrets through Jesus Christ, as my gospel declares" (Rom 2:16). Paul's hope for his fellow Israelites is not just that they will enjoy table fellowship with the Gentile believers apart from circumcision, but that his fellow Israelites will have faith in Jesus as God's crucified and resurrected messiah, and so be *saved* (Rom 10:1). His gospel of the righteousness that is by faith (Rom 10:6) is personally appropriated in confessing the Lordship of Jesus, with a heartfelt conviction of his resurrection from the dead (Rom 10:9).

This both-and reading of Paul, rather than the "either ecclesiology or soteriology" reading on offer from Wright, is truer to Paul's intent than the construction offered by the NPP. There is no dichotomy between an "ecclesiological" reading of Paul in his first-century context and a (supposedly mistaken) soteriological reading of Paul by the Protestant Reformers; both concerns are relevant to both contexts. It is simply not necessary or warranted to abandon the hermeneutical insights of the Reformers in order to appropriate new insights from the NPP concerning Paul's first-century context.

In conclusion, then, the position being argued in this essay is that the NPP should be seen as a way of supplementing the historic Reformation understandings of Paul's doctrine of justification—not as its replacement. We can incorporate insights from the NPP such as noted above—e.g., the integral connections in Pauline theology between justification, the Abrahamic covenant, the resurrection of Jesus, and the gift of the Spirit—but without abandoning penal substitution (Isa 53:5, 6, 10, 11; Gal 3:13; 2 Cor 5:21) and imputed righteousness (Rom 4:3, 5, 6, 9, 10, 11, 22, 24; 2 Cor 5:21b). This imputed righteousness is grounded in the reality of the believer's union with Christ (Rom 8:1, "no condemnation for those who are *in Christ Jesus*"; 1 Cor 1:30, "you are *in Christ Jesus,* who has become for us . . . our righteousness, holiness, and redemption"; 2 Cor 5:21, "God made him who had no sin to be sin for us [penal substitution; imputation of our sin to Christ], so that *in him* we might become the righteousness of God" [imputation of Christ's righteousness to us, through union with Christ]).

The historic Reformation understanding of Paul continues to be relevant today, because it is well grounded in the New Testament teachings, and because it speaks with unabated relevance to the problem of *works righteousness* that is a perennial feature in the history of the religious life of mankind. Such expressions of works righteousness—the idea that humans must contribute to or earn their own salvation—seem to be endemic in the religious sensibilities of the "natural man," and stills finds expression today in various forms of Christianity, Islam, and in Eastern religions such as Hinduism and Buddhism. Even after the reforms of Vatican II, the *Pocket*

Catechism answered Question Sixty-Seven, "What is necessary for entering heaven?" as follows: "1. We must be baptized. 2. We must believe everything that God has revealed and the Church holds before us for our belief. 3. We must perform good works. We must truly merit heaven. 4. We must appear in a state of grace before God after this earthly life."[1]

In Islam, the Quran states (S. 23:102–3) that "those whose balance of good deeds is heavy, they will attain salvation; but those whose balance is light, will be those who have lost their souls; in Hell they will abide." In Hinduism and Buddhism, the notions of karma and rebirth are the basis for the beliefs that good works create good karma and merit, and contribute to a better birth in the next life, and to one's ultimate liberation or enlightenment. In the *Dhammapada,* "the Sayings of the Buddha," it is stated, "By oneself is evil done and by oneself is one defiled . . . . Purity and impurity depend on oneself. No one can purify another" (*Dhammapada* 165).

The good news of the gospel, however, is that we are put right with God—justified, accepted, forgiven—by grace alone, through faith in Jesus Christ alone, on the basis of his atoning death and saving resurrection alone. This is Paul's gospel—let us hold fast to it!

---

1. Lodders, *Pocket Catechism,* 25.

7

"Teaching Them to Observe All that I Have Commanded You"

The History of the Interpretation of the "Great Commission" and Implications for Marketplace Ministries

IN THEIR COMMENTS ON the Great Commission's command to "make disciples of all nations" (Matt 28:18–20), the editors of the *Promise Keepers Men's Study Bible* note that these words imply "changing your attitude and being a more positive force at work."[1] The editors of the *Christian Growth Study Bible* comment that Jesus' command to teach "all that I have commanded" applies to "every aspect of life—to our education, our finances, our sexuality, our families . . . , our government and every other influential area."[2] Astonishing as it may seem, there seem to be only a few scattered examples in the history of the church's interpretation of the Great Commission where the powerful implications of this text for the *marketplace ministries* of the laity have been developed.

In this chapter it will be argued that the history of interpretation of Matthew 28:18–20 from the time of the early church to the present shows that the full meaning of the text has been obscured by the ecclesiastical controversies of the day, and by the particular concerns of its clerical and academic interpreters. For many centuries—from the fourth century to the time of William Carey—the full *missiological* implications were largely forgotten. The *marketplace* implications of this crucial text are just beginning

---

1. *The Promise Keepers Men's Study Bible*, New International Version, on Matt 28:18–20.

2. *The Christian Growth Study Bible: New International Version*, on Matt 28:18–20.

to receive attention at the present time. Having examined the history of interpretation of this text, it will then be argued exegetically that the Great Commission inescapably commands the *whole church* to extend the kingdom of Christ not only through personal evangelism and foreign missions, but through witness and discipleship in the workplace and daily life as well.

Matthew 28:18-20 in the History of Interpretation[3]

From the Early Church to William Carey

At a very early period in the history of the early church the idea took hold that the apostles of Christ had taken the gospel to the limits of the known world and had, as a result, "fulfilled" the Great Commission in their own lifetime. In the apocryphal Acts of Thomas, for example, a document from the early third century, probably originating in eastern Syria, it is stated that the apostles, gathered in Jerusalem, cast lots and "divided the regions of the world, that each one of us might go to the region which fell to his lot, and to the nation to which the Lord had sent him."[4]

In the fourth century the church historian Eusebius of Caesarea in his *Ecclesiastical History* cites Tertullian to the effect that Emperor Tiberius actually favored the Christian message and helped to spread it throughout the empire. According to Eusebius, with this providential help the whole world "was suddenly lit by the sunshine of the saving word . . . . The voice of its inspired evangelists and apostles went forth into all the earth . . . . In every town and village . . . churches shot up bursting with eager members."[5] One must question the triumphalistic version of first-century Christian history that Eusebius presents, but the text nevertheless gives witness to the belief that the gospel had reached the limits of the known world in the lifetime of the apostles. Consequently, "foreign missions" as we now understand it was not seen as an urgent and unfulfilled task for the church.

---

3. On the history of interpretation of Matthew's gospel generally, see Kealy, *Matthew's Gospel and the History of Biblical Interpretation*. Kealy deals with issues of overall interpretation and not the Great Commission text specifically. For a brief overview of trends in the interpretation of this text see Bosch, "The Structure of Mission," 218-19, and *Transforming Mission*, 56-57.

4. *The Acts of the Holy Apostle Thomas*, 1, 339.

5. Eusebius, *The History of the Church from Christ to Constantine*, 3.2, 39. See also the statement of Origen in his commentary on Matthew 24:9 that the apostolic preaching had reached Ethiopia, China, India, and other lands: cited in Rosenkranz, *Die Christliche Mission*, 40.

During the patristic period, the reading of Matthew 28:18-20 is dominated by concerns relating to the nature and proper forms of baptism and by controversies relating to the doctrine of the Trinity. Writing in the second century, Irenaeus states that Christ gave the apostles the "power of regenerating in God" when he said to them, "Go and teach all nations, and baptize them in the name of the Father, and of the Son, and of the Holy Spirit."[6] In so doing the disciples would be renewing the pagans "from their old ways into the newness of Christ."[7] This appears to be one of the earliest references to the notion of baptismal regeneration.

Tertullian's treatise *On Baptism*, written between the years 200 and 206, is perhaps the earliest Christian writing devoted specifically to this subject. He quotes Matthew 28:19 in order to demonstrate that the proper form of baptism has been commanded by Christ: "The law of washing has been imposed, and the form has been prescribed: 'Go,' He says, 'teach the nations, washing them in the name of the Father and of the Son and of the Holy Spirit.'"[8] For Tertullian, it is in the church's baptism that "the sins of our earlier blindness are washed away."[9]

In his *Commentaries on Romans*, probably written some time after 244, Origen quotes Matthew 28:19 in order to argue that valid baptism must be performed in the name of the triune God: "the Lord himself told his disciples that they should baptize all peoples in the name of the Father and of the Son and of the Holy Spirit . . . for indeed, legitimate baptism is had only in the name of the Trinity."[10]

Athanasius cites the "Great Commission" passages several times in the context of the fourth-century controversies over the doctrine of the Trinity. In his *Four Letters to Serapion of Thmuis*, written in the years 359-360, the great defender of Nicene orthodoxy refers to those who undermine the doctrine of the Trinity by saying that the Holy Spirit in only a creature, differing from the angels only in degree. These heretics should realize that such teaching is inconsistent with the faith of the Catholic Church, which the Lord founded and rooted on the Trinity when he said, "Go out and instruct every

---

6. Irenaeus, *Against Heresies*, 3, 17, 1. The following patristic citations were found, for the most part, through the use of the helpful Scripture index in Jurgens.

7. Ibid.

8. Tertullian, *On Baptism*, 13, 3, in Jurgens, *The Faith of the Early Fathers*, 1:127.

9. Ibid., 1, in Jurgens, *The Faith of the Early Fathers*, 1:126.

10. Origen, *Commentaries on Romans*, 5, 8, in Jurgens, *The Faith of the Early Fathers*, 1:209. Origen also states that the church "received from the Apostles the tradition of giving Baptism even to infants," for the Apostles knew that in everyone is found the "innate stains of [original] sin, which must be washed away through water and the Spirit": ibid.

people, baptizing them in the name of the Father and of the Son and of the Holy Spirit."[11] In *On the Incarnation of the Word of God*, written c. 365 against the Arians, Athanasius quotes the triune formula of Matthew 28:19 in order to prove the full deity of Christ and the equality of Father, Son, and Holy Spirit: "Just as we are baptized in the name of the Father and of the Son, so also in the name of the Holy Spirit; and we are made sons of God, not of gods ... for the Godhead is one and there is one God in three Persons."[12]

Writing during the years 356–359, during his exile in Phrygia, Hilary, bishop of Poitiers, cites Matthew 28:19 in his treatise in defense of the Trinity and the deity of Christ. The Lord commanded his disciples "to baptize in the name of the Father, and of the Son, and of the Holy Spirit: that is, in a confession of the Author, and of the Only-Begotten, and of the Gift." With respect to Christ, "many of us, indeed, are the sons of God, but not in the way that He is the Son. For He is both truly and properly the Son by origin and not by adoption."[13]

The fourth-century Greek father Basil of Caesarea also quotes the Great Commission text in the context of trinitarian considerations. Having insisted that the Son alone is "begotten," and that the Spirit "proceeds" from the Father, Basil also notes that there is a certain order or way of speaking of the three persons in divine revelation."Indeed," says Basil, "we must preserve unaltered and inviolate the order which we have received from the very words of the Lord when he said, 'Going forth, make disciples of all nations, baptizing them in the name of the Father and of the Son and of the Holy Spirit.'"[14] It is clear from the context that Basil's reading of the text is focused not on missiological concerns but rather on those of trinitarian doctrine.

Cyril, bishop of Alexandria, writing in the fifth century, cites our passage on at least two occasions. In his *Commentary on Isaiah* he quotes the words "All power in heaven and on earth is given to me" to prove that Christ had asserted his authority over all the world.[15] In his *Dialogues on the Holy Trinity* Cyril appeals to the baptismal formula to defend the trinitarian faith

---

11. Athanasius, *Four Letters to Serapion of Thmuis*, 1, 28 and 3, 6; in Jurgens, *The Faith of the Early Fathers*, 1:336–37. Serapion was bishop of the church in Thmuis, near Alexandria, Egypt. Canon 19 of the Council of Nicea required the rebaptism of heretics who had not been properly baptized according to the triune formula: Schaff, *The Seven Ecumenical Councils*, 40.

12. *On the Incarnation of the Word of God*, 10, in Jurgens, *The Faith of the Early Fathers*, 1:340.

13. Hilary of Poitiers, *The Trinity*, 2, 1 and 3, 11; in ibid., 1:373, 375.

14. Basil of Caesarea, *Transcript of Faith* 125, 3, in ibid., 2:5.

15. Cyril of Alexandria, *Commentary on Isaias* 3, 5, in ibid., 3:218.

of the church: "Did he not command that Baptism be given 'in the name of the Father and of the Son and of the Holy Spirit?'"[16]

In his great treatise on *The Trinity*, perhaps the most important contribution to trinitarian theology from the Latin fathers, Augustine confesses, "O Lord our God, we believe in You, Father, and Son, and Holy Spirit." This confession is consistent with the Scriptures, for Christ would not say, "Go, baptize all nations in the name of the Father and of the Son, and of the Holy Spirit," unless God were a Trinity.[17] Like his predecessors, Augustine's interest in the text is doctrinal rather that missiological.

While in this latter instance Augustine quotes the text for trinitarian purposes, it is not the case that the great North African church father is without missionary concern. In a letter written c. 419 to his fellow bishop Hesychius, he states that there are "among us, that is, in Africa, innumerable barbarian tribes among whom the Gospel has not yet been preached."[18] Augustine dissents from the opinion current in his day that the gospel had already been preached throughout the whole world by the apostles.

In the Middle Ages the patristic tendency to read the Great Commission text in terms of trinitarian and baptismal concerns continues largely unabated. Thomas Aquinas cites this text some nine times in the *Summa Theologica*.[19] Two of these citations relate to the doctrine of the Trinity, five to baptism, two to other subjects, and none to missions. For example, when exploring the question of whether a person can explicitly believe in the mystery of Christ without having faith in the Trinity, he answers that "once grace has been revealed, all were bound to explicit faith in the mystery of the Trinity.... All who are born again in Christ have this bestowed on them [in baptism] by the invocation of the Trinity, according to Matt 28:19."[20] If the question is whether or not belief in the Trinity is necessary for salvation, he notes the progressive unfolding of divine revelation over the course of redemptive history, and then cites the Matthean text: "Afterwards in the time of grace the mystery of the Trinity was revealed by the Son of God Himself, according to Matt 28:19, "Going ... teach ... baptizing them in the name of the Father, and of the Son, and of the Holy Ghost.""[21]

---

16. Cyril of Alexandria, *Dialogues on the Holy Trinity*, 2, in ibid., 3:214.

17. Augustine, *The Trinity*, 15, 28, 51, in ibid., 3:81.

18. Augustine, *Letters*, vol. 4, 394: Letter 199, chapter 46. I wish to thank my colleague Timothy Tennent for drawing this reference to my attention.

19. The following citations from the *Summa* are from the translation of the Fathers of the English Dominican Province, 3 volumes.

20. Aquinas, *Summa*, Pt. II-II, Q. 2, art. 8.

21. Ibid., Pt. II-II, Q. 174, art. 6.

"Teaching Them to Observe All that I Have Commanded You"   163

In his five citations of Matthew 28:19 in relation to baptism, Aquinas makes the points that Christian baptism is hallowed by the invocation of the triune name;[22] that the text requires a valid baptism to use a specific form of words;[23] that Christ gave his disciples the command to baptize after his death and resurrection;[24] that proper baptism requires the use of the words of the triune formula;[25] and that the words of Christ in this text confer on the priest the spiritual authority to baptize and to absolve sins.[26]

Aquinas cites the text in two other instances, in relation to issues unrelated to baptism or the Trinity. It was fitting that the gospel be preached first to the Jews and then to the Gentiles, because Christ did not wish his doctrine to be preached to the Gentiles before his passion, according to the statement "Going, teach ye all nations," and so forth.[27] Matthew 28:18 is also quoted to demonstrate that Christ has judicial power over all temporal affairs of humanity, not just authority over matters that pertain to eternal salvation.[28]

The scholastic theologians of the Middle Ages discussed Matthew 28:19 in regard to the particular questions raised by the difference between Matthew and the book of Acts as to the proper words of baptism. The first Gospel uses the trinitarian formula; the book of Acts speaks of "baptism in the name of the Lord Jesus" alone (Acts 2:38; 10:48; 19:5). Alexander of Hales, Albertus Magnus, Bonaventure, Aquinas, and Duns Scotus held that the apostles baptized in the name of Jesus alone in view of a special dispensation. In the period following the Council of Trent (1545–63), however, the prevailing Roman Catholic view became that the apostles in fact made use of the triune formula, but the language of the book of Acts was intended to emphasize the distinction between the baptism of John the Baptist and the proper Christian baptism commanded by Christ.[29]

It is of interest to see how, during the Reformation period, Luther, Erasmus, and Calvin understood the Great Commission passage. There are some forty-six citations of the text in the collected works of the great German

22. Ibid., Pt. III, Q. 39, art.8.
23. Ibid., Pt. III, Q. 60, art.7.
24. Ibid., Pt. III, Q. 66, art.2.
25. Ibid., Pt.III, Q. 66, art.5.
26. Ibid., Pt. III, Q. 84, art.3.
27. Ibid., Pt. III, Q. 42, art.1.
28. Ibid., Pt. III, Q. 59, art.4.

29. Cuneo, *The Lord's Command to Baptize*, 20. This doctoral dissertation is a valuable study on the history of the interpretation of Matthew 28:19 in relation to such questions as the necessity of the use of the triune formula in baptism and the validity of baptisms, in the triune name, performed by heretics.

Reformer.³⁰ Three citations relate to the papacy;³¹ three to the nature of priesthood and ordination;³² fourteen to controversies concerning baptism and the Anabaptists;³³ five to the presence of Christ in the Lord's Supper or the Mass;³⁴ one to the doctrine of the Trinity;³⁵ five to the nature of a true apostle;³⁶ thirteen to the nature of the true church and its teaching;³⁷ two to the enduring nature of the Word of God;³⁸ and five to a variety of other topics.³⁹

In the *one* instance that Luther cites the text in a missiological context, he does not see in it a present-day "missionary" obligation! In a letter of October 2, 1539 to the Elector John Frederick, Luther comments on the use of Matthew 28:19 by Martin Bucer to appeal to Luther to send Melancthon to England to help the cause of the Reformation there. Luther writes that this verse does not obligate him to send Melancthon, because he [Luther] is "Going into all the world . . . to preach" through *his writings*—and he also does not wish to leave the present work.⁴⁰

Elsewhere in his writings Luther does recognize the church's task now called "foreign missions." Christians must go to those to whom "Christ has not been proclaimed . . . so that they, too, may be brought to the spiritual kingdom of Christ."⁴¹ In his commentary on Psalm 117 and the words, "Praise the Lord, all you heathen," Luther writes that the heathen will not praise God unless they have first heard his word."If they are to hear His Word, the *preachers must be sent to proclaim* God's Word to them" (emphasis added).⁴²

---

30. These citations were located with the aid of the Scripture index in *Luther's Works*, ed. Pelikan et al. The following citations refer to the volume and page numbers from this edition of Luther's works.

31. Ibid., 2:99; 35:148; 41:330.

32. Ibid., 36:111; 38:196; 38:212.

33. Ibid., 3:104; 8:81ff; 23:78; 35:91; 38:24; 38:27; 38:87; 38:198; 40:245; 40:252; 51:320; 51:376; 54:55; 54:113.

34. Ibid., 30:38; 34:74,75; 36:351; 37:331; 38:161.

35. Ibid., 12:288. Citations of Matthew 28:19 in the context of *trinitarian* controversy, common in the patristic period, are not frequent in Luther.

36. Ibid., 13:272; 25:8; 26:100; 27:156; 38:161.

37. Ibid., 13:19; 13:49; 15:350; 41:196; 41:481; 41:581; 41:107; 41:132; 41:148; 41:155; 41:202; 46:222; 47:117.

38. Ibid., 17:309; 17:374.

39. Ibid., 6:311 (comfort in affliction); 6:128 (nature of true worship); 20:338 (the Day of Judgment); 28:262 (secret will of God); 51:308 (prayer and faith).

40. Ibid., 50:203.

41. WA, 16, 215ff., cited in Montgomery, "Luther and Missions," 197. See the entire article for other citations in Luther on this point. I wish to thank my colleague Garth Rosell for drawing my attention to this article. *WA* refers to the *Weimar Ausgabe*, the standard critical German-Latin edition of Luther's writings.

42. Luther, "Selected Psalms III," 9. I wish to thank Thorkild Jensen for showing me

"Teaching Them to Observe All that I Have Commanded You" 165

In his commentary on Psalm 2:9 Luther states that "Even the Turks, whom today we seek to overcome only by the sword, ought to be conquered by increasing the number of Christians among them."[43]

This missionary task is not based, however, on the "Great Commission" text. Luther's many citations of this text indicate that his understanding of the passage is more influenced by then-current ecclesiastical controversies than by what later generations would consider the obvious "historical-grammatical meaning."[44]

Erasmus of Rotterdam (c. 1466–1536) was perhaps the earliest biblical scholar to unearth the "modern" understanding of the Great Commission text, in terms of its original historical context. This recovered understanding was reflected in his 1522 preface to the New Testament, his paraphrase of the Great Commission, and in his annotations to the New Testament. Erasmus insisted that those who were baptized must be *taught* the "rudiments and first beginnings of the gospel. For if a man will not believe these rudiments and principles, his baptism will avail him nothing."[45] Erasmus's exegesis greatly influenced the Anabaptist's critique of infant baptism, and also spurred the Anabaptist reading of Matthew 28:18–20 as obligatory in a missionary sense on the church of their own day. Anabaptists such as Hans Hut and Balthasar Hubmaier and their followers frequently quoted the Great Commission in their sermons and writings and understood it to apply to all believers at all times.[46] The Anabaptists, with their passion for the "restitution" and rediscovery of the early, apostolic church, anticipated the recovery of the fuller meaning of the Matthean text that was to be crystallized and popularized by William Carey at the end of the eighteenth century.

The Swiss Reformer Ulrich Zwingli (1484–1531) quotes the Great Commission text on several occasions, but his concerns are baptismal rather than missiological. He cites Matthew 28 in order to defend the practice of

---

this and the following reference in Luther.

43. Ibid., 334.

44. Tennent and others have noted that the Reformer's view of missions was hampered by the prevailing "territorial" view of Christianity, in which it tended to be assumed that the gospel was to be spread only in areas governed by a Christian ruler; each region was to follow the religion of its ruler ("*cuius regio eius religio*"). Tennent, "William Carey as a Missiologist," 4. On this point see also Bosch, *Transforming Mission*, 246.

45. *Erasmi Opera Omnia*, 7:674, cited in Friesen, *Erasmus, the Anabaptists*, 116. I wish to thank my colleague Timothy Tennent for drawing to my attention this definitive study of the influence of Erasmus's exegesis on the Anabaptist understanding of baptism, theology, and mission.

46. On this, see Littell, "The Anabaptist Theology of Missions," 5–17, containing many citations from Anabaptist writings.

infant baptism against the Anabaptists, to argue that baptism was instituted with John the Baptist rather than after the resurrection, and that the sacraments signify grace, but do not convey grace in and of themselves in some material way.[47] Zwingli's associate and successor in Zurich, Heinrich Bullinger (1504-1575), quoted Matthew 28:19 in order to argue that the right administration of the sacraments of baptism and the Lord's Supper required that they be joined to the sincere preaching of the Word of God.[48]

John Calvin shared the common opinion of his time that the Great Commission had been fulfilled during the time of the apostles. In his comments on 1 Corinthians 12:28, for example, he writes that the apostles were appointed to spread the gospel "throughout the whole world." They differed from pastors of the present day, who do not have a mandate to preach the gospel all the world over, but to look after the churches committed to their charge.[49] In his *Harmony of the Evangelists* his comments on the text "Go out, therefore, and teach all nations" are to the effect that the popes disqualify themselves as true successors of the apostles by their failure to teach the true apostolic doctrine. No missiological point is made.[50] Calvin did not advocate a self-conscious missions program, but believed that the gospel would be extended in ever-widening circles through the normal preaching of the church and by the dispersion of Christians through persecution.[51]

In the seventeenth century the predominant opinion among Protestant theologians seemed to be that the Great Commission was no longer binding on the church.[52] The Lutheran theologian Johann Gerhard (1582-1637) argued that the universal preaching of the gospel was no longer necessary, the apostles having finished the job. Theodore Beza (1519-1605), Calvin's successor in Geneva, was of a similar opinion. Matthew Poole (1624-1679) discusses Matthew 28:18-20 in connection with infant baptism, and believes that the text authorizes pastors in any given place to preach and baptize, but does not obligate them to "go up and down preaching in all nations."[53] There were some exceptions, however. The German nobleman Justinian von Weltz and the Dutchman Adrianus Saravia[54] (1531-1613) argued that the Great

47. Zwingli, "Of Baptism," 160, 161; and "An Exposition of the Faith," 248.

48. Bullinger, "Of the Holy Catholic Church," 300.

49. Calvin, *The Epistles of Paul the Apostle to the Corinthians*, 270-71. For similar comments, see Calvin's expositions of Romans 15:20 and Ephesians 4:11.

50. Calvin, *Commentary on a Harmony of the Evangelists*, 383.

51. Boer, *Pentecost and the Missionary Witness of the Church*, 17.

52. For this period, see R. Davies, "The Great Commission from Calvin to Carey," 45.

53. Poole, *Annotations upon the Holy Bible*, 146. Poole, a London pastor, was ejected from his church in 1662 because of his Puritan and Nonconformist convictions.

54. Saravia, *De Diversis Ministrorum Evangelii Gradibus*.

Commission applied to the church in all ages, but their voices were in the minority. The Protestant churches on the continent felt themselves to be an embattled and threatened minority in the face of the Counterreformation attack, and were more concerned for survival and preserving the purity of doctrine than extending the gospel to foreign lands.[55]

Eighteenth-century interpretation prior to William Carey largely followed the lines that had come to prevail since the fourth century. The Anglican commentator Daniel Whitby, writing in 1703, uses Matthew 28:19 as the occasion to present an elaborate defense of the practice of infant baptism;[56] there is no indication of interest in "world missions" or "marketplace ministries." Cotton Mather, in his *Magnalia Christi Americana* ("Great Works of Christ in America"), written in 1702, directs the reader's attention to the work of Thomas Mayhew, who in the year 1642 settled at Martha's Vineyard and began evangelistic work among the Indians. Mather connects the work of Mayhew with the words of Christ who said, "go teach all nations: lo I am with you," but the missiological significance of the text is not developed.[57]

The influential commentator Matthew Henry, writing during the years 1708–1710, expounds the words "Go ye therefore" as given primarily to the apostles, whose task was to transmit the gospel "from nation to nation." In a secondary sense, however, present-day ministers have a commission to transmit the gospel "from age to age, to the end of the world in time"—i.e., maintaining the gospel witness within the bounds of the existing churches, until the end of the age.[58] Henry does comment that ministers of the gospel have an obligation to teach the commands of Christ by assisting the people "in applying the general commands . . . to particular cases." He notes further, "there is no day, no hour of the day, in which the Lord Jesus is not present with his churches," thus hinting at a "marketplace" application of the text but not fully developing it.[59]

The commentary on the New Testament by the Lutheran scholar J. A. Bengel, *Gnomen of the New Testament* (1742), was widely used in its day, by John Wesley as well as by many others. Bengel's comments on the Great Commission text focus on the confession of the Trinity as seen in the baptismal formula. The words "I will be with you always" signify that the "church

---

55. Kane, *A Concise History of the Christian World Mission*, 73–75.
56. Whitby, *A Commentary on the Gospels and Epistles*, 186–91.
57. Mather, *The Great Works of Christ in Americana*, vol. 2, 429.
58. M. Henry, *A Commentary on the Holy Bible*, vol. 5, 256.
59. Ibid., 257.

of Christ will never die out entirely," but there is no discussion of the ongoing extension of the church in unevangelized lands.[60]

Philip Doddridge (1702-1751) was a friend of Isaac Watts, the Wesleys, and George Whitefield. In his comments on the Great Commission passage in his *Family Expositor* he writes that no arguments to the prejudice of infant baptism can be drawn from the text. Christ's words "I will be with you always, even to the end of the world," cannot be limited to the first generation of the apostles — but Doddridge seems to stop short of drawing clear missiological implications for his own time.[61] The apostles evidently fulfilled the command to "go into all the world," and "We, to this day, in our remote land [England], enjoy the benefit of it."[62]

In his *Explanatory Notes upon the New Testament* (1754), John Wesley follows the then traditional lines of interpretation. Discipling the nations involves baptizing and teaching; in the case of children, baptism will precede the teaching, as was the case in the Jewish era of the divine economy.[63] No missiological implications are drawn from the text.

"Sit down, young man; when God wants to convert the heathen, He'll do it without your help or mine."[64] These now-famous words spoken by John Ryland of Northampton, England in 1785 to William Carey at a ministers' meeting expressed a common sentiment of the day among hyper-Calvinists concerning the heathen overseas. It was necessary to pray for them, but not to use "means" to bring the gospel to them. Seven years later Carey published his famous pamphlet, *An Enquiry into the Obligation of Christians to Use Means for the Conversion of the Heathen* (1792), responding to Ryland and arguing for the present-day validity of the Great Commission. This commission originally given to the apostles is still binding upon the church today, because the command to "make disciples of all nations" is bound up with the commands to *teach* and to *baptize*, both of which are still practiced by the church today; Christ's promise to be with the church till the end of the age is still valid; and unlike the ceremonial laws of the Old Testament, there is no indication in the New Testament that the missionary

---

60. Bengel, *Gnomen of the New Testament*, vol. 1, 312. Bengel's critical text and apparatus of the Greek New Testament (1734) can be seen as pioneering work in this field of study.

61. Doddridge, *The Family Expositor*, vol. 2, 466.

62. Ibid., 468. The miraculous gifts given to the apostles have ceased, but the promise "I will be with you" remains in force, according to Doddridge. His somewhat traditional view of Matthew 28:18-20 notwithstanding, Doddridge was in fact a promoter of evangelical revival in England and of the modern missionary enterprise.

63. Wesley, *Explanatory Notes upon the New Testament*, on Matthew 28:19 (no pagination).

64. Quoted by Ernest Payne in the Introduction to Carey, *An Enquiry*, iii.

mandate of Christ has been repealed. Neither do unfulfilled prophecies in the Old Testament or the existence of unevangelized persons closer to home invalidate the missionary obligation.[65] There is little evidence that Carey's pamphlet was widely read when it first appeared,[66] but this seminal document has been widely seen as marking the birth of the modern Protestant missionary movement and of the modern evangelical understanding of the Great Commission text of Matthew's gospel.

From William Carey to the Present

In the nineteenth and twentieth centuries conservative commentators generally affirm the continuing validity of the Great Commission, while liberal Protestant and Roman Catholic scholars increasingly become preoccupied with source-critical issues.[67] The 1810 commentary of the English Methodist Adam Clarke is, however, an exception to this pattern. Clark's interest in Matthew 28:18–20 is in defending the practice of infant baptism against Baptists and the doctrine of the Trinity against Unitarians and Deists. There is no discussion of foreign missions or marketplace ministries.[68]

Charles Simeon, pastor of Holy Trinity Church in Cambridge, England, writing in 1832, notes that while present-day pastors are not empowered to work miracles, they nonetheless have the same commission "to make known his name to all the different generations from the apostolic age to the present day." Preachers are to instruct their people in "practical religion," and, in a hint of "marketplace" application, are to "inculcate every moral duty, and to enforce every obligation, whether toward God or man."[69]

In their widely-used commentary on the whole Bible, Jamieson, Fausset, and Brown (1864–1870) write that in the Great Commission Jesus addressed all "who, in every age should take up . . . the same work." The Great Commission is the work not only of ministers, but of the whole church; the laity is called to cooperate with, aid, and encourage the ministers in the fulfillment of the task till the end of the age.[70]

65. Ibid., 8–13.
66. According to Ernest Payne, ibid., xv.
67. "Source-critical" in the sense of questions concerning whether the words attributed to Jesus in Matthew 28:18–20 represent the actual words of Jesus or the theology of the early church, whether the triune formula for baptism is original to Jesus or a creation of the early church, etc.
68. Clarke, *Commentary on the Holy Bible*, 835.
69. Simeon, *Horae Homileticae*, vol. 11, 618–19.
70. Jamieson, Fausset, and Brown, *A Commentary Critical, Experimental, and Practical on the Old and New Testaments*, vol. 3, 134–35.

Writing in 1870, George W. Clark does presuppose the present validity of the Great Commission, and hints at "marketplace" ministries when he notes that discipleship "continues in the service of faith in every duty." The predominant amount of space in his commentary on the text is devoted, however, to issues relating to the proper subjects and forms of baptism and to the Trinity.[71] Lyman Abbot, writing in 1876, notes that "Christian missions are the mother of civilization," but devotes more space to the question of baptism.[72] The American Baptist commentator John Broadus, writing in 1886, clearly affirms the Great Commission, stating that "Christianity is essentially a missionary religion . . . . It must be active at the extremities, or it becomes chilled at the heart." The Great Commission involves not simply "teaching them the commandments of Christ, but teaching them to observes his commandments." The Christian teacher falls short in his task unless his students have learned both "what Christ's commandments are, and have learned to observe them."[73] Broadus clearly seeks to affirm the implication of the text for discipleship in everyday life.

In the twentieth century non-evangelical interpreters tend to become preoccupied with source-critical issues in their studies of the Great Commission text. W. C. Allen (1912) devotes a long discussion to the triune formula of Matthew 28 in relation to baptism "in the name of Jesus" in the book of Acts. There is no discussion of world missions or marketplace ministries as such.[74] Alfred Plummer (1915) does note that making disciples obligated the apostles "to make them [the Gentiles] as fully disciples of Christ as they are themselves," and that the light of the world is "to be sent forth to illuminate every branch of the human race," but most of his attention is devoted to a discussion of whether or not the triune baptismal formula is original to Jesus, and whether these words require a definite form of baptism.[75] Floyd Filson (1960) does comment on the world mission of the disciples, but sees this aspect as "Matthew's" reflection rather than the literal words of Jesus, and devotes a significant amount of his commentary on the text to question of the originality of the triune baptismal formula.[76]

W. F. Albright and C. S. Mann (1971) focus a disproportionate amount of attention on baptism and source-critical questions relating to the

---

71. G. Clark, *Notes on the Gospel of Matthew*, 407-9.

72. Abbott, *The New Testament with Notes and Comments*, 327-29.

73. Broadus, *Commentary on the Gospel of Matthew*, 593, 596.

74. Allen, *A Critical and Exegetical Commentary on the Gospel According to S. Matthew*, 305-8.

75. Plummer, *An Exegetical Commentary on the Gospel According to St. Matthew*, 429-31.

76. Filson, *A Commentary on the Gospel According to St. Matthew*, 305-6.

baptismal formula, and devote only two sentences to the phrase "teaching them."[77] David Hill (1972) thinks that the command to disciple all nations came from the early church about fifty years after the death of Jesus; there is no interest in a "marketplace" application of the text.[78] Eduard Schweizer (1975) hints at a marketplace application, noting that the true wise men and teachers are those who "authoritatively interpret Scripture for new situations and problems" and who "follow his [Christ's] teaching and live by his model," but this hint is not fully developed.[79] Francis Beare (1981) notes that the "teaching" is primarily ethical rather than doctrinal in nature, but devotes more space to the issues of baptism and the trinitarian formula.[80] Leopold Sabourin (1983) sees "making disciples" as a reflection of the theology of the early church rather than being the actual words of Jesus.[81] Benedict Viviano (1990) sees the mandate as one to continue the teaching ministry of Jesus, "thus laying the foundations for Christian education, theology, and other intellectual work."[82] M. Eugene Boring (1995) focuses on the redactional history of Matt 28:16-20, and is concerned to argue that resurrection faith "is not identical with affirming the historical factuality of any of the Gospels' resurrection stories" or of the empty tomb.[83] George Wesley Buchanan (1996) focuses on the Old Testament and Jewish backgrounds of the text and is not interested in the marketplace implications of the command to make disciples.[84] W. D. Davies and Dale Allison in their recent magisterial commentary (1997) note that this text, so important to William Carey and the nineteenth-century Protestant missionary movement is, from a literary point of view, "perfect, in that it satisfyingly completes the Gospel," and in fact is a compendium and summary of the theology of the entire book.[85]

In recent evangelical interpretation the missiological significance of the Great Commission is assumed, and there are occasional hints of marketplace applications. In 1968 Robert Culver, noting that the imperative "make disciples" controlled the force of the participles "going," "baptizing," and "teaching," argued that the proper sense of the Commission was "As you

77. Albright and Mann, *The Anchor Bible: Matthew*, 362-63.
78. Hill, *The Gospel of Matthew: New Century Bible*, 361-62.
79. Schweizer, *The Good News According to Matthew*, 180.
80. Beare, *The Gospel According to Matthew*, 545.
81. Sabourin, *The Gospel According to St. Matthew*, vol. 1, 932-39.
82. Viviano, "The Gospel According to Matthew," 674.
83. Boring, *The Gospel of Matthew*, 502-5.
84. Buchanan, *The Gospel of Matthew*, 1029-33.
85. Davies and Allison, *A Critical and Exegetical Commentary on The Gospel According to Saint Matthew*, vol. 3, 687.

go, therefore, and wherever you may be, make disciples . . . in the particular nation among which you dwell."[86] Culver was arguing that the customary interpretations of the text placed too much emphasis on "going," i.e., "foreign" missions, and not enough on making disciples. Peter O'Brien concurred, writing that the central point of the text was ". . . bringing men and women to submit to Jesus as Lord, to become his disciples, wherever they may be."[87] This proposed shift of emphasis has not gained universal consent among conservative interpreters, however. Cleon Rogers agreed that "making disciples" is the main verb in the text, and that such discipleship involves putting the commandments of Jesus into practice in daily life. Nevertheless, this does not reduce the "going" to a non-imperatival sense; "going" remains an integral part of making disciples.[88]

Robert Gundry (1982), notes the Old Testament background of Matthew's phraseology, and observes that "learning includes doing."[89] Robert Mounce (1985) comments that "teaching" in the Great Commission is primarily ethical rather than doctrinal in nature; the converts are to be taught to *obey* all that Jesus has commanded.[90] Leon Morris (1992) states that Jesus is not concerned about "education for education's sake . . . Jesus is concerned with a way of life."[91] Craig Blomberg (1992) argues that the text is to be fulfilled by the whole church. New converts are to be nurtured in the whole counsel of God's revelation; every individual is to develop his or her gifts and strengths for ministry."Jesus calls all Christians to be both witnesses and disciplers."[92]

Commentaries in the popular study Bibles in general reflect the concerns and emphases of the more specialized scholarly literature.[93] Harold

86. Culver, "What Is the Church's Commission?," 252-53.

87. O'Brien, "The Great Commission of Matthew 28:18-20," 78.

88. Rogers, "The Great Commission," 266. For similar conclusions, see also Carson, *Matthew*, 595.

89. Gundry, *Matthew*, 597.

90. Mounce, *Matthew*, 268.

91. Morris, *The Gospel According to Matthew*, 749.

92. Blomberg, *Matthew*, 433.

93. Roman Catholic and mainline Protestants study Bibles tend to focus on "source-critical" questions such as the originality of the triune baptismal formula, and so forth: see, for example, *The New English Bible with the Apocrypha: Oxford Study Edition*, 41; *The New Jerusalem Bible*, 1659 ("This [baptismal] formula is probably a reflection of the liturgical usage established later in the primitive community"); *The Catholic Study Bible*, 65 ("It may have been the baptismal formula of Matthew's church, but primarily it designates the effects of baptism, the union of the one baptized with the Father, Son, and Holy Spirit"); *The Oxford Study Bible*, 1303; *The HarperCollins Study Bible*, 1914 ("This explicit trinitarian formula is rare in the NT and probably derives from early Christian worship").

Lindsell in the *Harper Study Bible* (1964) focuses his comments on baptism and the doctrine of the Trinity.[94] The *Lindsell Study Bible* (1980) likewise focuses on the proper mode and subjects of baptism, and defends the triune formula against modern critics.[95] The *Life Application Bible* (1988) notes that all believers have been given gifts to help fulfill the Great Commission, but no marketplace applications are suggested.[96] The *Serendipity Bible* (1989) is unusual in that in one of the study questions an explicit marketplace connection is made: "In what ways can you fulfill the Great Commission in the context of your family? Work? Community?"[97]

The notes in the *Word in Life Bible* (1993) challenge the reader to ask seriously what it means to accept Jesus' lordship for all nations in a global, cross-cultural context, but, surprisingly, no direct marketplace applications are suggested.[98] The *Quest Study Bible* (1994) comments that all believers are called to share the ministry of disciple-making, but the sphere of this ministry seems to be limited to the traditional evangelistic and missionary contexts.[99] The *Study Bible for Women* (1995) focuses its attention on the appearances of the risen Christ to women.[100] The *New Geneva Study Bible* (1995) notes that this text is the primary reason for missions and evangelism, but more space is devoted to baptism and the sacraments. The editors comment that "teaching" means that "Disciples are not just taught what to believe, but how to obey," though explicit marketplace connections are not drawn.[101]

As noted at the beginning of this chapter, two recent study Bibles are unusual in the history of Christian interpretation in that they make explicit applications of the Great Commission text to the workplace. The editors of the *Christian Growth Study Bible* (1997), associated with the parachurch organization Youth With a Mission, challenge the reader to see this text as having implications for discipleship in all areas of life, e.g., science, education, the arts, medicine, government, and many others. "As believers," they write, "we must not abandon certain professions and places of influence because of the darkness there. Those are the very places where God wants

---

94. Harper Study Bible, 1491.
95. Lindsell Study Bible, 53.
96. Life Application Study Bible, 1721.
97. Serendipity Bible for Groups, 1290.
98. Word in Life Bible, 1482. "Surprisingly" in light of the fact that the editor of this study Bible is a well-known leader in the field of marketplace ministries.
99. Quest Study Bible, 1379.
100. Study Bible for Women, 72.
101. New Geneva Study Bible, 1556–57.

to shine the light of Jesus!"[102] In a similar vein, the editors of the *Promise Keepers Men's Study Bible* (1997), representing the parachurch organization of that name, tell the reader that in the words of the Great Commission Jesus promises to be with his people as they begin "even in the smallest way within our own sphere of influence, to affect positive change in the world." Making disciples can begin by "changing your attitude and being a more positive force at work."[103]

In recent years Dr. Bill Bright, founder of Campus Crusade for Christ International, has given indication that his understanding of the Great Commission has developed beyond the traditional understanding to include equipping the people of God to serve in the workplace. In a letter to Campus Crusade staff workers he stated that he had come to realize that "full-time Christian service" was not limited to pastors, missionaries, or workers in parachurch organizations. Whether Crusade's staff is working with students, mid-career people, or senior executives, "we must give special attention and follow up to those whom God calls to serve Him in the secular world."[104]

Some Concluding Reflections

This survey of some sixteen centuries of Christian interpretation of Matthew's "Great Commission" passage has shown how profoundly the *ecclesiastical* controversies and concerns of the day have dominated the church's understanding of the text. From the fourth century until the time of William Carey the missiological significance of the text was, with few exceptions, essentially lost. Interpreters tended to assume that Christ's mandate was fulfilled by the apostles, and read the text in terms of controversies about the Trinity and the proper subjects of and form of words for baptism. With the publication of Carey's *Enquiry* (1792) the significance of the text for foreign missions was recovered. This "missiological" hermeneutic became the standard for subsequent evangelical Protestant interpreters. With the rise of the historical-critical method of biblical interpretation in Europe in the Enlightenment and post-Enlightenment eras, liberal Protestant and many Roman Catholic interpreters tended to become preoccupied with "source-critical" issues such as the originality of the words of the triune baptismal formula attributed to Jesus. Twentieth-century evangelical interpreters then

102. *The Christian Growth Study Bible*, 1049.
103. *Promise Keepers Men's Study Bible*, 1087.
104. In *Bright Side*. I wish to thank Kelly Madden for drawing my attention to this reference. For a statement of Bright's earlier, more traditional "missiological" and evangelistic understanding of the Great Commission, see Bright, *Revolution Now!*, 167-91.

began to defend traditional views of the text against the liberal, "revisionist" understandings. Both liberal and conservative exegetes gave little or no attention to the implications of the text for ministry in the workplace; interpretation continued to be dominated by the ecclesiastical and academic contexts of the scholarly guild.

In the late 1990s initial signs of a "marketplace hermeneutic" began to appear, with such voices being raised from the contexts of parachurch ministries.[105] This chapter concludes with a call to the community of interpreters and to the church as a whole to move forward to recover the full meaning of the Great Commission. This recovery involves moving beyond the usual "clerocentric" hermeneutic focusing on the concerns of the "full-time Christian professionals" to a "laocentric" hermeneutic focusing on equipping all the people of God to be disciples in every sphere of life, including the workplace. Taking seriously Christ's mandate to make disciples by teaching them "to *observe all* that I have commanded" implies concrete, practical training for all the people of God to be "salt and light" in every sphere of service in the culture. The *horizontal extension* of the kingdom through foreign missions and evangelism must be accompanied by the *vertical penetration* of the kingdom in every dimension of life if the Great Commission is to be truly fulfilled in our or any other generation.

---

105. E.g., in *The Christian Growth Study Bible* (1997) (Youth With a Mission), *The Promise Keepers Men's Study Bible* (1997) (Promise Keepers), and the statement of Bill Bright (1998) as noted above. For historical perspective on the emergence of a "theology of the laity" since the Second World War, see Banks, "Appendix A: Lay Theology and Education Since 1945," in *Redeeming the Routines*, 153–74. Neill and Weber, *The Layman in Christian History*, is a standard reference on the subject indicated by the title. Diehl, *The Monday Connection*, is a fine discussion of the problem of the "disconnect" between much of the church's preaching and teaching and the concerns of the workplace. It could be plausibly argued that the church's less than adequate equipping of the laity to practice Christian discipleship in the workplace has contributed to the secularization of Western culture that has been increasingly evident since the end of World War II.

8

Why Most American Christians Don't Pray Very Much

And Why and How They Could Pray More

Pray without ceasing.

1 THESSALONIANS 5:17

PRAY WITHOUT CEASING: Is it really possible to pray "without ceasing"[1] or "constantly" as modern American Christians in a culture like ours filled with the endless stream of distractions of our digital media, and with the toys and gadgets of our consumer culture? What does this Pauline injunction really mean for us today?

It would seem that few if any American Christians and pastors are approaching what appears to be a very lofty ideal for the practice of prayer. One recent survey of 868 Protestant church pastors found that the average Protestant pastor in the United States prays for thirty-nine minutes a day, although 21 percent reported spending fifteen minutes or fewer each day in prayer.[2] One would assume that most pastors, as "full-time religious pro-

---

1. The Greek *adialeiptos*, "constantly" or "unceasingly," is found four times in the New Testament, only in Paul (Rom 1:9, 1 Thess 1:3, 2:13, 5:17), and in all four instances in relation to prayer: Robertson, *Word Pictures in the New Testament*, 8; Arndt and Gingrich, *A Greek-English Lexicon of the New Testament*, 17.

2. Grey Matter Research and Consulting, "Study Shows Only 16 Percent of Protestant Ministers Are Very Satisfied with their Personal Prayer Lives." Another survey of 1,002 Protestant pastors conducted in 2008 by LifeWay Christian Resources found that 39 percent of *evangelical* pastors reported spending less than four hours a week in personal devotions unrelated to teaching preparation: "Pastors' long work hours can

fessionals," would be praying as much if not more than their parishioners. In most American churches the older custom of holding mid-week prayer meetings has vanished, due to lack of interest, and committee meetings are often conducted with only token prayers being offered at the beginning and end to ask for divine blessing of human plans.[3]

It is certainly worth asking the question as to whether there might be a connection between the virtual disappearance of the mid-week prayer meeting in the post-World War II period and the introduction of television as a primary entertainment medium in America. The average number of television viewing hours per household in America increased steadily from about four and a half hours per day in 1950 to more than seven hours per day at the end of the century.[4] Robert Putnam has noted that while in 1950 barely 10 percent of American homes had televisions, by 1959, 90 percent did, "probably the fastest diffusion of a technological innovation ever recorded."[5] Among equally religious people, Putnam noted, those who reported television watching as their primary form of entertainment attended church substantially less often.[6] With the advent of the Internet revolution, of course, the opportunities for "on-screen" time have only multiplied. Would these figures not suggest that American Christians have been praying less and watching television more in the postwar period?

Korean pastors, on the other hand, typically lead their churches in early morning prayer meetings that begin at 4 or 5 a.m., 365 days a year, often have Friday night prayer meetings that can last all night, and have prayer retreats at "prayer mountains" outside the cities.[7] When Korean

---

come at the expense of people, ministry."

3. As Richard F. Lovelace observed several decades ago, "In much of the church's life in the twentieth century . . . both in Evangelical and non-Evangelical circles, the place of prayer has become limited and almost vestigial. The proportion of horizontal communication that goes on (in planning, arguing, and expounding) is overwhelmingly greater than that which is vertical (in worship, thanksgiving, confession, and intercession) . . . . Why has this come about? Perhaps it stems from the deficient . . . emphasis on God himself throughout the church, and partly from the man-centeredness of much religious activity": *Dynamics of Spiritual Life*: 152; see 151–60, "Dependent Prayer" on the critical role of prayer in the history of spiritual renewal movements.

4. Putnam, *Bowling Alone*, 222.

5. Ibid., 221.

6. Ibid., 234. Neil Postman has observed that Americans have become so habituated to television that it is the omnipresent social universe, barely worth scholarly attention or critical reflection: "Television has become, so to speak, the background radiation of the social and intellectual universe . . . so familiar and so integrated with American culture that we no longer hear its faint hissing in the background or see the flickering gray light": *Amusing Ourselves to Death*, 79.

7. Wagner, *Churches That Pray*, 23–28; Moon, "The Korean Church and Prayer,"

church leaders are asked to explain the remarkable growth of the Christian church in Korea in the twentieth century, the answer is uniformly given in a single word: "Prayer."

It has been reported that leaders of the Chinese house churches typically pray three to four hours a day, and are supported by other "spiritual leaders" whose primary ministry is to support the pastors by prayer and fasting. There are many all-night prayer vigils in the Chinese house churches.[8]

It is surely not without significance that in both the case of the Korean and Chinese churches such extended times of prayer have arisen in the contexts of *persecution* and *poverty*—circumstances that are largely foreign to the experience of Christians in America.[9] These circumstances suggest that the relative lack of prayer in many American churches reflects matters of *felt need* for prayer—or a lack of such felt need. Generally speaking, human behavior is motivated by felt needs: when we feel hungry, we are motivated to find something to eat; when we no longer feel hungry, we generally, if we are healthy, stop eating. When we are thirsty, we are motivated to find something to drink; when we no longer feel thirsty, we stop drinking.

The question arises, then, "Why do American Christians, generally speaking, seem to have little 'hunger' or 'thirst' for prayer?" What circumstances in our American culture and church life, or our understanding and practice of prayer, may be contributing to a diminished sense of the need for prayer?[10] The purpose of raising such questions is not merely to induce

---

especially 5–27, "The Prayer Habits of Korean Christians."

8. Kenaston, "Chinese Christians and Prayer." Though it strains the bounds of credibility in the West, in this interview with Chinese house church leaders it was reported that one such praying "brother" rarely slept more than two hours a night, and at times prayed for twenty-two hours a day. "The brothers and sisters pray always, and there are many all-night prayer vigils. I have been to these prayer meetings. By morning, the floor is slippery because of all the tears that flow during prayer."

9. See Moon, "The Korean Church and Prayer," 7–20, for the historical background of the Korean prayer movement that began in 1907 and continued in subsequent decades the time of Korea's subjugation and occupation by the Japanese invaders; extended and intensive prayer subsequently became a core practice and tradition of the Korean churches down to the present day.

10. To be more accurate, it might be preferable to pose the question as "Why is it that *at present* many American Christians and churches seem to feel little need to pray?," since in previous periods of American history, extended and intensive times of prayer have been practiced and associated with periods of revival and spiritual vitality: see Orr, *The Evangelical Awakening, 1790–1830*; *The Fervent Prayer*; *The Flaming Tongue*, for the connection between prayer and revival in the post-Constitutional period, the frontier revivals in Kentucky and Tennessee, and the prayer revivals of 1858 and 1905 and following that had substantial impact on the churches. On the connection between prayer and revival and renewal in the history of American Christianity, see also Lacy Jr., *Revivals in the Midst of the Years*.

feelings of guilt about our relative lack of prayer, but to raise our awareness of the root causes of the problem, and to point to a possible solution.

The purpose of this article is threefold: 1) to examine the features of contemporary American culture that contribute to a diminished sense of the need for prayer; 2) to reexamine the prayer practices of Jesus with a view to seeing whether or not his practice and "theory" of prayer provides insights that can challenge and correct our current American Christian practices; and 3) to present a method of prayer as "practicing the presence of God" that is 1) consistent with the spirit of the Pauline admonition to "pray without ceasing," 2) that will enhance the spiritual vitality of our churches, and 3) at the same time be a practical, accessible, and sustainable method of prayer for those in secular, non-monastic vocations[11]—effective prayer "for the rest of us."

Why American Christians Don't Pray: American Culture and Romans 12:2

The title of this section, "Why American Christians Don't Pray," is, of course, an overstatement. More fairly, the subtitle could be "Why American Christians Don't Pray as Much as They Really Need To."[12] In this section we will examine some of the features of modern Western culture—especially its confidence in the power of science and technology—that have contributed to a diminished sense of felt need for prayer. It will be suggested that modern Western Christians have in fact allowed the scientific worldview to "colonize" and capture their mind and imagination more than they realize, and need to have their minds and imaginations and prayer practices renewed (Rom 12:2) and transformed by a more biblical understanding of the nature of the kingdom of God, the church, and the forces that oppose them.

---

11. This chapter recognizes and acknowledges with appreciation the long-standing and ancient Orthodox Christian practice of the "prayer of the heart" or the "Jesus Prayer" ("Lord Jesus Christ, Son of God, have mercy on me, a sinner"), constantly repeated, as a way of fulfilling the apostolic admonition to "pray without ceasing." On the history and practices of the Jesus Prayer, see T. Ware, *The Orthodox Church,* 74–75, 312–14; Mathewes-Green, *The Jesus Prayer*; Clendenin, *Eastern Orthodox Christianity,* 67–70. The method of prayer presented in the present article is not understood to be antithetical to such a practice as the Jesus Prayer, but complementary to it—encompassing intercession for the needs of others and the world, in addition to the elements of adoration and confession; and also, seen as adapted to the sensibilities of those in Western traditions of spirituality.

12. A notable exception is the 24-7 Prayer Movement that is gaining traction on many American college campuses, as described in Greig and Roberts, *Red Moon Rising*. I wish to thank Hilary K. Davis for drawing my attention to this reference.

The Russian sociologist P. A. Sorokin characterized the historical period in the West from 1500 AD to the present as a "sensate" or materialistic culture and worldview. In distinction from "ideational" cultures that focus on the spiritual, "sensate" cultures have as their defining principle that true reality is sensory; the material world is the paradigm for defining what is real and the primary source of values.[13] Sensate cultures pursue science and technology, but devote less creative energy to spirituality and religion. The dominant values of a sensate culture are wealth, health, bodily comfort, sensual pleasure, power, and fame. Ethical and legal precepts are considered to be man-made conventions, relative and changeable. Art and entertainment emphasize sensory stimulation, and in the more decadent phases of sensate cultures, there is an increasing emphasis on the new and shocking, the violent and the erotic.[14] As such, sensate cultures focus their minds and energies on this earthly, visible, material world—not a heavenly new creation to come.

The predominant reinforcer in the West and in the United States of such a "sensate" orientation to reality has been the Scientific Revolution of the seventeenth century, inaugurated with the revolutionary work of Galileo and Newton. The Scientific Revolution fundamentally altered modern humankind's understanding of and relationship to the natural world. The historian of science Richard Westfall has summarized the impact of this revolutionary change in worldview in the following four points: 1) Nature was *quantified,* with a shift from a qualitative to a quantitative view of the natural world, and an emphasis on exact measurement and control; 2) Nature was *mechanized*: the image of the "clockwork" universe reflected an emphasis on mechanical explanations in terms of material objects moving in space according to exact mathematical laws; 3) Nature was *disenchanted* and made alien to immediate human experience, with an emphasis on secondary qualities (color, taste, touch, smell) being replaced by the primary qualities (mass, velocity, etc.) of dead, colorless particles in motion; and 4) Nature was *secularized*: God may have acted in the beginning to set the world in motion, but God was no longer actively intervening in the world in the present ("Deism").[15]

The Scientific Revolution that began in seventeenth-century Europe, and which in the space of three hundred years essentially supplanted the

13. This summary of Sorokin's analysis is based on Sorokin, *Social and Cultural Dynamics*; and Uebersax, "Culture in Crisis."

14. Uebersax, "Culture in Crisis."

15. Westfall, "The Scientific Revolution of the Seventeenth Century." On other aspects of the Scientific Revolution, see also Burtt, *The Metaphysical Foundations of Modern Science*; Dijksterhuis, *The Mechanization of the World Picture*; Koyre, *From the Closed World to the Infinite Universe.*

patristic and medieval Christian understandings of man's relation to nature, laid the basis for the Industrial Revolution that changed the face of modern Europe and America. The science and technologies of the Industrial Revolution raised countless people from lives of poverty and gave them standards of material comfort and health that were rare in the premodern world.

In Great Britain, the home of the Industrial Revolution, real wages doubled between 1800 and 1850, and doubled again between 1850 and 1900.[16] Modern science and technology and the Industrial Revolution based on it transformed premodern agriculture into the industrialized agribusiness of today, with tremendous gains in farming productivity. Modern American and European Christians, unlike premodern generations, hardly sense a need to pray "Give us this day our daily bread": the bread is always there to be purchased, and famines and starvation seem like historical curiosities of a premodern past. Modern medicine and public sanitation have dramatically reduced infant mortality and the ravages of infectious diseases; as a result the first instinct of modern Christians is not to pray or "call for the elders of the church" (Jas 5:14) but to call for the doctor when sickness arises. Prayer for sickness is often a means of last resort, a matter of desperation when scientific medicine does not work—rather than a response of first resort.

Anthropologists have observed that Americans, in comparison to other cultures, have a very high reliance upon and confidence in science and technology. Clyde Kluckhohn has observed that in the United States technology "is valued as the very basis of the capitalistic system.... Against the background of all known cultures, American culture would stand out for its *quantitative* and *materialistic* orientations."[17] According to Edward C. Stewart, American culture, viewed in cross-cultural perspective, tends to view problems in economic and technological terms, and places high valuation on material progress and technological and material improvements.[18]

It is beyond dispute that modern science and technology have produced great blessings in the modern period in terms of increased control over the natural order, greater material comfort and prosperity, stable food supplies, and improved health and life expectancies. The point of this essay is not to suggest that modern science and technology are inherently antithetical to the Christian faith, or that their benefits are to be rejected, but rather to again call attention to its dangers and downsides, especially with regard to the spiritual life and to the practice of prayer.

---

16. Novak, *The Spirit of Democratic Capitalism*, 17.
17. Kluckhohn, *Mirror for Man*, 185–86.
18. Stewart, *American Cultural Patterns*, 19, 30.

Scripture clearly warns that increased material prosperity and comfort can lead to forgetfulness of God and a proud and mistaken confidence in human abilities: "When you eat and are satisfied, when you build fine houses and settle down, when ... your silver and gold is multiplied, then your heart will become proud and you will forget the Lord your God" (Deut 8:12-14). The realism of the warnings given by Moses to the generation about to enter the Promised Land has found confirmation in the later history of the Christian church: the wealthy post-Constantinian and late medieval church experienced a "fall" from the spiritual vitality of an earlier persecuted church, and the wealthy Christians of Western Europe and North America tend to lack the vibrant spiritual power of many churches in the impoverished regions of Africa, Asia, and Latin America.[19]

There is a very real danger that the science and technology that give modern man (and modern Christians) almost godlike powers over nature, that have produced unprecedented levels of material wealth, and that enabled Western European powers to colonize and dominate so many of the peoples of Africa, Asia, and Latin America, will displace Christian reliance upon the *supernatural* power of God and the spiritual means of advancing the gospel and building the church. A remarkable expression of such a misplaced confidence in science and technology can be found in the statement of Friedrich Schleiermacher, the so-called "father of modern liberal theology." Schleiermacher is quite aware that in the biblical accounts the Christian church was advanced by apostles with the power of working miracles; but in the present age,

> Even if it cannot be strictly proved that the Church's power of working miracles has died out ... yet in view of *the great advantage in power and civilization that the Christian peoples possess over the non-Christian, almost without exception* [emphasis added] the preachers of today do not need such signs.[20]

Schleiermacher was saying, in effect, that Western Christian pastors and missionaries, with the tremendous power of Western science and technology at their disposal, had little or no need for the supernatural power of God and the Holy Spirit to advance the spread of the Christian religion.

American evangelical Christians would reject, theologically, Schleiermacher's "naturalizing" of the Christian faith with its misplaced reliance on modern science, but *in practice* American Christians can uwittingly rely on the business, marketing, and church-growth tools and the gadgets of digital

---

19. On the vitality of the Christian movement in the poorer regions of the world, see Jenkins, *The New Faces of Christianity*, and also his earlier book, *The Next Christendom*.

20. Schleiermacher, *The Christian Faith*, vol. 2, 450.

technology, rather than primarily upon the supernatural power of God, the Holy Spirit, and prayer.[21] It is precisely such a misplaced reliance on what science and technology can achieve that can undercut reliance on the *power of God* and the prayer that can access such power in our efforts to build the church and to advance the kingdom of God.[22] American Christians, precisely because they live in the context of an enormously rich, powerful, and dominant nation whose "god" is science and technology, need to be especially conscious of the cultural forces that shape their spiritual practices, and need to make conscious efforts to counteract their unintended effects.

The challenges to prayer posed by modern science and technology and the Industrial Revolution spawned by them have only been intensified by the Information Revolution ushered in by computers, the Internet, and digital media. We are now living through what some have rightly characterized as an explosion in the amount of information, data, images, videos, websites, emails, text messages, and advertisements that we are exposed to in a typical day.[23] By the year 2010, 500 billion images were being captured each year by various digital recording devices, and YouTube was streaming more than one billion videos a day.[24] An average adolescent in the United States will be spending seven and a half hours each day, seven days a week, consuming various forms of digital media; when multitasking is taken into account, these young people actually pack about ten hours and forty-five minutes of media consumption into those seven and a half hours. Every type of media use *except* reading has increased in the last ten years.[25]

One recent study found that a typical American office worker checks email or changes windows to other programs nearly thirty-seven times each

---

21. Such a reliance on *human* power and technology could be viewed as a form of "practical Pelagianism" or "practical semi-Pelagianism" in the life of American churches. Historically, Pelagianism refers to the fifth-century teachings of Pelagius, combated by Augustine; the Pelagian system held that man could take the initial steps toward salvation apart from the assistance of divine grace.

22. The question is worth asking: Is it purely coincidental that the apparent decline in the practice of prayer in American churches in the post-World War II period coincides with the period in American history when the United States was at the peak of its military, economic, and political predominance as a global superpower? Not long before his death, James Montgomery Boice had called attention to the virtual disappearance of substantial pastoral prayers as an essential part of many Protestant worship services: cited in Ryken, Thomas, and Duncan, *Give Praise to God*, 18–20.

23. In recent years the amount of data generated by the Internet, computers, research labs, sensors, cameras, and cell phones has been growing at a compound rate of 60 percent annually: "All too much: Monstrous amounts of data," *The Economist*, 5.

24. Gleick, "How Information Became Everything," 60.

25. *Kaiser Family Foundation Study*, "Generation M2: Media in the Lives of 8-to 18-Year-Olds: Key Findings," 1.

hour.[26] Such constant interruptions impose psychic costs; careful studies of multitasking have now shown that such fragmented attention interferes with learning and the long-term retention of information.[27]

Thoughtful observers of the culture have been calling attention to the ways in which the new digital media are reshaping our consciousness and perhaps even "rewiring" the neural pathways of the brain itself.[28] As Christians, we need to be asking ourselves how the new media environment may be undermining our ability to pray, to meditate, and to focus our attention on God. A lifestyle of constantly surfing the net, checking emails, Facebook accounts, and text messages shortens our attention spans, fragments our attention, and makes it more difficult to pray and to give our undivided attention to God. Scripture urges us to still and quiet our soul (Ps 131:2) and to wait upon the Lord (Ps 130:5), but the culture of digital media produces a rushed and restless spirit, constantly pushed to pack more and more tasks into less and less time. The Apostle Paul urges us to focus our attention on the unseen things above, where Christ is enthroned at the right hand of God (Col 3:1–2), and to fix our eyes on the unseen things that are eternal (2 Cor 4:18), but digital media and the entertainment industry focus our minds on the things below and "colonize" our Christian imaginations with the images of entertainers, advertisers, marketers, and corporate capitalism. In order to pray effectively in a culture like ours, we need not only to be aware of the ways in which digital media and the Internet are reshaping our consciousness and imaginations, but also to take intentional steps to separate ourselves—to take the time to "come out and be separate"—from the online world for the purpose of praying and giving our undivided attention to God.[29]

26. Richtel, "Hooked on Gadgets, and Paying a Mental Price."

27. Greenfield, "Technology and Informal Education," 70: "Distracting information exacts a cognitive cost, even from the younger generation who have had more experience with multitasking. A controlled experiment showed that college students recalled significantly fewer facts from four main news stories in CNN's visually complex environment than from the same stories presented in a visually simple format, with the news anchor alone on the screen and the news crawls etc. edited out."

28. Significant recent studies in these areas would include Carr, *The Shallows*; Powers, *Hamlet's Blackberry*; Hipps, *Flickering Pixels*; and Miedema, *Slow Reading*.

29. Several generations ago C. S. Lewis in his spiritual classic, *The Screwtape Letters*, had the devil giving his understudy, Wormwood, shrewd advice about keeping his human targets immersed in the "stream of immediate experience": "Your business is to fix his attention on the stream. Teach him to call it 'real life' and don't let him ask what he means by 'real' . . . . You don't realize how enslaved they are to the pressure of the ordinary": 12. No doubt Wormwood would today welcome the Internet and digital technologies as excellent tools for keeping humans distracted from heavenly things (2 Cor 4:18) and immersed in the streams of immediate experience.

The Prayer Life of Jesus: Practice and "Theory": Why Prayer is Still Essential in a Scientific Age

Having in the foregoing section examined some of the ways in which the Scientific Revolution, the Industrial Revolution, and now the Information Revolution have contributed to a diminished sense of the need for prayer in much of modern American Christianity, we now turn to examine features of the prayer life of Jesus. The purpose here is to examine both Jesus' practice of prayer and the "theory" or worldview that his practices presupposed, with a view to uncovering some insights that can help American Christians understand more clearly *why* prayer is still essential for the work of the kingdom under the conditions of modernity. Prayer will be considered in both its "instrumental" and "intrinsic" forms. By "instrumental" we mean, for example, intercessory prayer—the type of prayer typically offered for "getting things done" or meeting the needs of people in ministry; by "intrinsic" prayer we mean prayers of adoration, praise, and contemplation—enjoying communion with God in worship or private devotion for God's own sake, rather than in relation to tasks and the work of external ministry.

The Gospel accounts make it quite clear that prayer was integral and central in Jesus' own spirituality[30] and practice of ministry. At his baptism at the Jordan River the Holy Spirit descended upon him in the form of a dove *as he was praying* (Luke 3:21). After his baptism, he was led by the Spirit into the desert, where he engaged in fasting and prayer and underwent a time of testing by Satan (Luke 4:1ff.), and then returned to Galilee, in the power of the Spirit (Luke 4:14). He returned to the synagogue in Nazareth, read from the scroll of Isaiah, and announced that "The Spirit of the Lord is upon me" (Isa 61:1), and that this prophecy has been fulfilled in his own person and reading (Luke 4:18-21). He engaged in active ministry, healing the sick, casting out demons, teaching about the kingdom of God with power and authority—and often withdrawing to lonely places to pray (Luke 5:16; see 4:42, "at daybreak Jesus went out to a solitary place").

Before Jesus chooses the twelve to be his apostles, he spends the entire night praying to God (Luke 6:12). This is surely a most remarkable and significant circumstance: Jesus, being the eternal Son of the Father, possessed of a sinless human nature, and living in perfect communion with and obedience to the Father, yet feels the need to spend the whole night in prayer, carefully and prayerfully consulting with God before appointing any one of the twelve to a crucial role in the ministry of the kingdom! Following his

---

30. A fine study of the prayer life of Jesus is found in Spencer and Spencer, *The Prayer Life of Jesus*.

example, should we not feel even more acutely the need for such specific, divine wisdom and guidance in our own "personnel selections" and initiatives for ministry?

Jesus took Peter, James, and John with him to a mountain to pray, and *as he was praying*, his face was transfigured (Luke 9:29). This event of the transfiguration of Jesus on the mountain recalls the radiance on the face of Moses when he came down from Sinai (Exod 34:29–35), and suggests the connection between prayer, being in the divine presence, and the impartation of the glory by the ministry of the Spirit (2 Cor 3:17–18).

Prior to his arrest, trial, and crucifixion Jesus prayed on the Mount of Olives (Luke 22:39–46), seeking strength from God and confirmation and clarification of his understanding of the will of God. He urged his disciples to pray so that they would not fall into temptation (Luke 22:40,46), but they fell asleep while their master prayed fervently and in great anguish.

It is clear from these accounts that Jesus engaged in prayer constantly, and especially at each critical juncture in his earthly ministry. In the Gospel of Luke it is especially evident that Jesus' prayer life is closely associated with his experience of the presence of the Holy Spirit[31] and the confidence to minister in public with power and authority. In John's gospel it is made clear that Jesus never acted independently from the Father, but listened to the Father before he spoke (John 8:26,28) and did not act before he saw what the Father himself was doing (John 5:19).

Through prayer, Jesus was in constant communication with God, following the Father's specific guidance as to persons, priorities, and timing. It was as though Jesus, through prayer and the presence of the Holy Spirit, had his own (heavenly) "Global Positioning System," receiving "turn-by-turn" direction from God concerning the path he was to follow. Through prayer Jesus aligned his will with the will of the Father; prayer was a means by which God's Messiah could not just "work harder" but rather "work smarter" and with lasting fruitfulness and effect.

The example of Jesus' prayer life is clear, then; if the Son of God felt such a need of constant prayer, how much more should we, his sinful, fallible followers likewise feel the need for prayer? It now remains to extend these reflections on the prayer life of Jesus to the next level, and ask, "What *presuppositions*, what worldview and view of reality informed the master's practice?" Here we need to consider: 1) Jesus' understanding of the *power* of God; 2) his understanding of the nature of God's *project*—salvation; the kingdom of God, the church; and 3), his understanding of the nature of the

---

31. Stronstad has observed, "For Luke it is impossible to divorce either the mission of Jesus from the activity of the Spirit, or the mission of the disciples from the activity of the Spirit": *The Charismatic Theology of St. Luke*, 47.

problem—that is, the nature of the opposition and obstacles to the advance of the kingdom. A failure to understand the true nature of the project of God and the forces that oppose it will lead us to adopt faulty and inadequate means as we seek to advance the work of the kingdom.

Jesus' practice of prayer and his teachings about it were based on a firm conviction and vision of the *almighty power* of God. When his disciples were amazed at Jesus' power demonstrated in the withering of the cursed fig tree (Matt 21:18–20), he said to them that if they had faith in God, they could also do what was done to the fig tree, and also say to a mountain, "Be cast into the sea"—and it would be done (Matt 21:21–22). What beliefs are presupposed in this astonishing statement? It is not the disciples' faith as such that can access and unleash such astonishing power over nature; rather, such faith puts the disciples in touch with the will and person of the almighty God who is the "maker of heaven and earth," and whose omnipotent power as Creator is *infinitely greater* than the powers of the laws of nature that he himself has ordained and maintains.

The "Abba Father" to whom Jesus prays is the great "I Am" who spoke to Moses out of the burning bush (Exod 3:14), the eternally self-existent one who calls the universe into existence out of nothing by the word of his infinite power, and who maintains the universe in continuing existence moment by moment. Before him the nations are like a drop in the bucket or as dust on the scales (Isa 40:13).

"The mountains melt like wax before the Lord, before the Lord of all the earth" (Ps 97:5). The psalmist's vivid imagery expresses the biblical truth that the "weight" and intense, concentrated reality of the Creator's infinite being makes the solidity and permanence of the natural world seem like wax by comparison. It is such a vision of God informing the Christian's imagination that we need in our prayers; it was just such a vision that informed Jesus' sayings to his disciples in the passage (Matt 21:21–22) above. Prevailing, believing prayer can "move mountains" because the one who hears the prayers created the mountains, and his power is infinitely greater than any power contained in the visible, natural order of things.

The powers of nature described by a famous formula such a $E=mc^2$, describing the enormous energy that can be released by an atomic bomb, are indeed immense. But the point that can be easily forgotten in our scientific age is that as great and impressive as the powers harnessed and unleashed by modern science and technology may be, the power of *God Almighty* is far greater than anything in creation—greater not just in degree, but in kind—indeed *infinitely* greater. This is why Paul can remind the church that the God who raised Jesus from the dead is able to do "*immeasurably more than all that we can ask or imagine*" (Eph 3:20); this is the God to whom the

Christian prays as "Abba, Father." Like the Sadducees of old, we can have our eyes and imaginations so fixed on the ordinary course of nature in this world that we fail to understand both the Scriptures and the power of God (Matt 22:29), and so lose a vision of the power of the God who raises the dead. As modern American Christians in a culture dominated by science and technology, we can be so impressed and mesmerized by the amazing power of science to control and manipulate the material world that we no longer sense a need to access, by prayer and the Holy Spirit, a divine power that is truly supernatural and transcends all the power of nature.

Not only was Jesus' practice of prayer informed by a firm conviction and clear vision of the almighty *power* of *God*—and the limitations of merely human power—it was informed as well by a clear understanding and vision of the supernatural character of the *project* of God: salvation, the kingdom of God, and the church. Both the plan of salvation and its intended "product"—the kingdom of God and the church that embodies and manifests the reality of the kingdom—require supernatural power from start to finish. The creation of the universe by God the Father, *ex nihilo*, is a supernatural work that God alone could have performed. The redemption of a fallen world through the incarnation, death, and resurrection of Jesus Christ the Son is a supernatural work that God alone can do. The application and perfection of that work in justification, adoption, sanctification, and glorification is likewise a supernatural work that can only be done through the work of the Holy Spirit. Only the Holy Spirit can make a new convert grow into the holy likeness of Christ. Our human efforts can be instrumental to this end, but they can never be efficacious in and of themselves alone, apart from the agency of the Holy Spirit—and that activity of the Holy Spirit in the church is accessed through prayer.

As disciples of Jesus we can be his human agents in ministry, his "hands and feet" on earth, so to speak, but we must always remember that though Paul may have planted the seed and Apollos watered, it was God alone who was causing the growth (1 Cor 3:6). As we work and minister in partnership with the risen Christ and with his Spirit, we must constantly remind ourselves that we are very *junior* partners in this partnership, and that the "production" of the final "product"—holy disciples in a holy church and body of Christ—are beyond the capacities of human power, even human power augmented by the powers of science and all the gadgets of digital technology.

Consider closely the nature of the *church*, the intended "product" of the triune God's eternal plan (Eph 1:4) for the creation, redemption, and perfection of the universe. The church, as the body of Christ, is as to its essential nature and inherent being, both a natural and a supernatural reality. The church can be viewed from an empirical point of view reflective of scientific naturalism, or from a divine, biblical perspective that sees the church as more than just a visible, human organization. Viewed as a group of human beings that meet in a specific place or building for the purpose of engaging in various religious and social activities, the church can be studied by sociologists, anthropologists, psychologists, economists, and historians, who can make wise and helpful observations about the activities and beliefs of those who attend. In a modern culture whose premises are saturated with the assumptions of the modern scientific worldview, it is easy to view the church from the *quantitative* point of view of the scientific method that emphasizes numerical measurements and control. From such a point of the view the "real" church is the one that can be counted and measured—its budget, salaries, membership rolls, and average Sunday attendance, and its programs and activities with their measurable goals and objectives. From this point of view, "church growth" and success is numerical growth. Viewed from a naturalistic perspective, it is quite possible to build a successful "church" by human agency alone, without any divine assistance whatsoever. As it has been observed—seriously or half-seriously—all that is necessary to fill an auditorium for religious purposes is a handsome, dynamic speaker (preferably with a young, attractive wife), a message of health, prosperity, and personal fulfillment, professional quality music and musicians, good child care, and adequate parking space!

In the church of the New Testament, however, the "real" church is not only or even primarily a visible human organization whose "metrics" are primarily quantitative; God's "metrics" are primarily (though not exclusively) *qualitative* in nature—e.g., holiness, agape love, fruit of the Spirit, *koinonia*, communion, and unity. The very being of the church is that of a body of Christ, a unique divine-human, "theanthropic" entity consisting of redeemed human beings bonded in communion to one another and to God by the Holy Spirit (1 Cor 12:13; Eph 4:3–16). The Holy Spirit is an *intrinsic* and *essential* dimension of the reality of the church. The Spirit's action and ministry in the church cannot be controlled and managed or replaced by naturalistic methods and technologies, but only "partnered" with through prayer, obedience, and faith.

The nature of the raw materials and tools for a building project must be appropriate to the nature of the building to be built. For building a sand castle on the beach, sand, a small shovel, and a sand bucket are sufficient. For building a cathedral that will last for centuries or a millennia, sand and a shovel are insufficient. The builders need limestone or granite stones, mortar, and the proper tools for working and laying stones. For building the church of Jesus Christ—as Jesus sees and defines the church—we need the tools and materials ordained by Christ: faith, the Word of God, prayer, and the Holy Spirit. For the building of a natural-supernatural project such at the body of Christ, natural, humanly devised means—youth programs, trained personnel, budgets, church growth principles, demographic studies, professionally trained musicians and state-of-the art sound systems, vision statements and goals and objectives, sales and marketing tools and church business plans—may be helpful and even in some sense necessary. But they can never, in themselves, be *sufficient* means for building the church that God desires. Natural means can produce natural, temporal, and quantifiable results; supernatural results require supernatural methods and materials.

This same point can be made by considering the four classic "attributes" of the church. Christian faith confesses belief in "one, holy, catholic, and apostolic church." These four attributes of the church—unity, holiness, catholicity, and apostolicity—can be viewed and "produced" to some extent from a purely human and empirical perspective, but cannot in the end be reduced to such perspectives. The unity and holiness for which Christ prayed (John 17) can, in the end, only be produced by God himself, through the agency of the Holy Spirit. A catholicity or universality that transcends the natural human desires to associate with "our kind of people" who are like ourselves, is similarly a work of divine grace in the midst of Christian churches all too often characterized by "market niches" of social class, ethnicity, and music preferences.[32] The soundness of orthodox, apostolic doctrine can be preserved to some extent by human creeds and confessions and church courts, but in the last instance, only the Holy Spirit can make that apostolic, biblical Word spiritually fruitful in the lives of God's people. Prayer, throughout church history, has been the essential means for spiritual renewal and vitality in the churches through the Word. All this is to say that unity, holiness, catholicity, and apostolicity—the attributes of the church—are *non-natural* properties of the church; they cannot be produced by natural means alone.

Recognition of prayer as an essential tool in the work of kingdom ministry can be deepened not only by a consideration of the nature of God's *project*—salvation and the church—but also by reflecting on Jesus' understanding of the *problem*: that is, the nature of the opposition to the kingdom of God and the building of the church. The "problem" or the nature of the opposition to the advance of the kingdom of God can be summarized in the classic biblical terminology of "the world, the flesh, and the devil" (1 John 2:15-17). The key point to understand here is that the "world, the flesh, and the devil" are *non-natural* properties and dimensions of human experience

---

32. Niebuhr, *The Social Sources of Denominationalism*, is a classic study of the racial, ethnic, and class divisions that have historically been barriers to the true catholicity or universality of the church.

and the Christian's "warfare" against them cannot be conducted with unaided human powers or naturalistic means alone.

The "ontology of evil" cannot be reduced to scientific, medical, economic, political, educational, or psychological categories. Just as end-stage cancer cannot be cured with a few doses of Tylenol, neither can the "world, the flesh, and the devil" be remedied with naturalistic means alone. There is an irreducibly supernatural or non-natural dimension to evil, though evil manifests and imbeds itself in the natural institutions, laws, and customs of fallen human culture.

The "world" is the biblical term for fallen human culture, unredeemed human culture apart from the grace of God, characterized by "the lust of the flesh, the lust of the eyes, and the pride of life" (1 John 2:16). The "world" takes on different forms in different cultures and historical epochs in its opposition to the cross of Christ and the gospel. In our own time, the "world" can be expressed through the forms of modernity and its science and technology that draw human confidence away from God to confidence in man and human agency.[33] For Jesus, the world is under the power of the Evil One, and Satan's power over the world will only be broken by his atoning death on the cross (John 12:31). The kingdom of Satan will not be overthrown by secular, political means (see Matt 4:8–10, the temptation of political power; John 18:36, "My kingdom is not from this world"). Evil is deeply entrenched in fallen human cultures, and as the early church's conflict with the violent and sensual culture of the Roman empire and Wilberforce's campaign to eradicate slavery from the British empire show, the forces of evil entrenched in the culture will not yield easily or quickly.[34] Christian warfare against such forces requires a deep spirituality rooted in the cross, in faith, and in persevering prayer.

The "flesh" (*sarx*) is the biblical term not only for bodily nature as such, but more specifically, human nature under the power of sin.[35] For Jesus, evil is deeply embedded in the human heart, and is not merely a matter of outward behavior or environmental conditioning: "Out of the *heart* come evil thoughts, murder, adultery, sexual immorality, theft, false testimony, slander" (Matt 15:19). Medical care, education, job training, and psychological

---

33. For an analysis of the "world" under the conditions of modernity, and its impact on the evangelical church, see Wells, *No Place for Truth*. Wells observes that "Technology per se does not assault the gospel, but a technological society will find the gospel irrelevant": ibid., 11; and, we might add, Christians living in a technological society will be tempted to find *prayer* irrelevant.

34. For a perceptive critique of the limited success of evangelicals in recent decades in efforts to "change the world," see Hunter, *To Change the World*, especially 24–31.

35. On the concept of the "flesh" in Pauline theology, see Ridderbos, *Paul*, 93–107.

counseling can mitigate the effects of human sin on human nature, but these naturalistic methods cannot in and of themselves *eradicate* the malignant, metastasized tumor of sin that is embedded in our human "flesh." Evil is a *non-natural* property of human nature. Jesus' solution for a fallen human nature is not just amelioration and mitigation, but repentance and *regeneration*. Even Nicodemus, a devout and observant member of the Sanhedrin, must be born again (John 3:3) in order to enter the kingdom of God, and Nicodemus rightly recognizes this as beyond the power of human agency.

Sanctification, the process of growth in holiness and of experiencing growing freedom from the residual powers of the sinful flesh, does indeed require human effort and agency. But human agency, while necessary, is not sufficient in itself; it requires the non-natural agency of faith, the Word of God, the Spirit, and prayer. Both sanctification and regeneration can only occur through the agency of the Holy Spirit, and God has ordained prayer as the means by which the people of God access the presence and power of the Spirit.

With respect to the third element in the triad of Kingdom opposition—the devil—it is clear that Jesus believed in a personal Satan who unremittingly opposes God and the advance of his kingdom. Satan is the chief of a kingdom of evil, the head of an array of demons and principalities and powers[36] that are under his authority (see Mark 3:22–26). Jesus did not psychologize or medicalize away the reality of demonic possession, but demonstrated the overthrow of Satan's kingdom in his exorcisms as proof of the arriving of the kingdom of God (Matt 12:28: "If I drive out demons by the Spirit of God, then the Kingdom of God has come upon you"). As we have already noted, the decisive blow against the kingdom of Satan was delivered at the cross (John 12:31), which unmasked and disarmed Satan's power (Col 2:15).

In Westernized cultures operating with the naturalistic categories of modern medicine and psychology, the bizarre manifestations of the demonic recorded in the synoptic Gospels tend to be reinterpreted or dismissed as the mistaken beliefs of a pre-scientific age. However, if we admit the possibility that Satan and his operatives can "contextualize" themselves in ways that are more likely to remain "under the radar screens" of modern cultures, then we may be less likely to medicalize or psychologize away the possible

---

36. In the wake of the horrendous evils of the World War II and Nazism and the Holocaust, New Testament scholars began to take more seriously the biblical language of "principalities and powers": see, for example, MacGregor, "Principalities and Powers"; J. S. Stewart, "On a Neglected Emphasis in New Testament Theology"; Reicke, "The Law and This World According to Paul"; R. Yates, "The Powers of Evil in the New Testament."

manifestations of the demonic in our own culture.[37] Scripture reminds us that a demon's activity may not only be the more visible and dramatic act of casting an "epileptic" into the fire (Mark 9:18) or giving superhuman strength to a man in chains (Mark 5:1–5, the Gadarene demoniac), but the more subtle activity of lying and *deception* (1 Tim 4:1; 1 John 4:1, "do not believe every spirit, but test the spirits to see whether they are from God") that undermines the apostolic gospel. Undermining the authority of Scripture in a theological seminary can wreak more havoc in the long run than the more obvious "possession" or oppression of a single individual. Whatever form the manifestation may take, the influence of Satan and the demonic is real, malignant, and *non-natural*, and so, like the "world" and the "flesh," must be combated by the spiritual means of the word of the cross, faith in Christ, the Holy Spirit, and prayer; "This kind can come out only by prayer" (Mark 9:29).

The foregoing discussion has focused on "instrumental" or intercessory prayer, that is, pray for our own needs or the needs of others or for the work of "getting things done" in the kingdom. Before concluding this essay with specific suggestions regarding prayer as "Practicing the Presence of God," a few observations should be offered regarding "intrinsic" prayer, that is, prayers of adoration and contemplation that are focused on communion with God and enjoyment of God for God's own sake.

One of the most fundamental answers to the question, "Why pray?" is, "To enjoy communion with God in the presence of God." As redeemed human beings, we were created for the very purpose of "glorifying God and *enjoying him* forever" (Westminster Shorter Catechism, Q. 1). Aside from any instrumental benefits or the accomplishment of specific tasks, prayer brings us into the presence of the God who is to be enjoyed for God's own sake, whose very being is the embodiment of love, and joy, and beauty.

The psalmist writes, "you will fill me with joy in your presence, with eternal pleasures at your right hand" (Ps 16:11). The redeemed people of God can, in prayerful communion with God, feast on the abundance of God's house and drink from his river of delights (Ps 36:8). In contemplative prayer we participate in the joyous communion of the Son with the Father by the agency of the Holy Spirit (John 17:13; Luke 10:21; 1 John 1:3–4),[38]

---

37. C. S. Lewis made this point concerning the "banality of evil" in modern settings in the 1961 preface to the *Screwtape Letters*: "The greatest evil is not now done in those sordid 'dens of crime' that Dickens loved to paint. It is not even done in concentration camps and labour camps. In those we see its final result. But it is conceived and ordered (moved, seconded, carried, and minuted) in clean, carpeted, warmed and well-lighted offices, by quiet men with white collars and cut fingernails and smooth-shaven cheeks who do not need to raise their voices."

38. For an insightful exposition of worship as the gift of participation through the Holy Spirit in the Son's communion with the Father, see J. Torrance, *Worship*,

and can behold the glory of God in the face of his Son (2 Cor 3:18; John 17:24; Eph 2:6). To enjoy such joyful communion with God in prayer is in itself to begin to experience the eternal life and divine *koinonia* that is not just a temporal extension of ordinary human life, but redeemed human life lifted into a qualitatively higher dimension of the fullness of the inner life of the triune God, Father, Son, and Holy Spirit.

Lack of prayer among modern Christians in affluent, comfortable circumstances may indicate a lack of experiencing such a deeper joy in the divine presence, or a lack of awareness of the obstacles to such communion. Scripture teaches that unconfessed sins can separate us from God (Isa 59:2), as can lack of forgiveness and unreconciled relationships within the church (Matt 6:14–15). Only the pure in heart will be blessed with a vision of the beauty of God (Matt 5:8). Internet pornography, lust, anger, bitterness, envy, greed, sloth and other sins that defile the soul will block our access to God and the enjoyment of being in his presence.

A personal view of a God who is angry or distant[39] can also inhibit joyful communion with God in prayer. The believer's joyful communion with God in prayer needs to be undergirded by a firm conviction that the atoning death of Christ has opened the way of access to the Father (Heb 10:19–22), that this "Abba, Father" is delighted to embrace his forgiven sons and daughters (Luke 15:20; see Zeph 3:17, "He will take great delight in you . . . . He will rejoice over you with singing"), and that by the gift of the Holy Spirit, we too participate in the Father's love for the Son (Gal 4:6) and have the love of God poured into our hearts (Rom 5:5).

From Theory to Practice: Prayer as "Practicing the Presence of God"

This essay will be concluded with some specific suggestions as to how the spirit of the Pauline admonition to "pray constantly" or to "pray without ceasing" can be fulfilled in our modern settings. The essential point of application is the idea that prayer is an intentional act and attitude of *practicing the presence of God* throughout the day. This notion of the continual "practicing the presence of God" recalls the classic devotional work of Brother Lawrence,[40]

Community and the Triune God of Grace.

39. Such personal images of God as distant or angry are common in American religious life: see Froese and Bader, *America's Four Gods*, based on the extensive survey data of the Baylor Religion Survey conducted in 2005 and 2007. At least 40 percent of those surveyed reported an image of God as either distant or judgmental.

40. Lawrence, *Practicing the Presence of God*; see also Payne, *The Healing Presence*,

and, in the present essay, is rooted biblically and theologically on three truths: our union with Christ; our partnership with God in ministry; and a consciousness of the *nearness* of God to the believer and the church.[41]

The believer's prayers are grounded in a continuous, living union with Christ (John 15:5: "I am the vine; you are the branches . . . Apart from me, you can do nothing"). The believer is bonded to Christ by the Holy Spirit (1 Cor 6:17) and subsists in living relationship with Christ. This relationship is a fundamental reality for the believer even when the believer may not be consciously aware of the presence of Christ, just as a husband is still married to his wife even when he is not consciously thinking about the relationship.

The Christian's prayer should also be informed by a notion of partnership with God in all things. Just as Jesus did not first speak without listening to the Father, or act without first seeing what the Father was doing (John 5:19, 8:28), so the believer acts and prays not with a sense of independence or autonomy, but rather of dependence upon and partnership with God, both in action and in prayer.

"Practicing the presence" in prayer is also informed by a conviction and awareness of the *nearness* of God. Jesus ascended physically to heaven and to the right hand of the Father, but he remains near to us by his word, promise, name, and Spirit (Matt 18:20, 28:20; John 14:18, 23; 1 Cor 5:4; Rev 3:20). The risen Christ is with his people and near to them as they make disciples (Matt 28:20)—and as they pray. There is no reason for believers to be "practical Deists" during the church age prior to the Second Advent; Father, Son, and Holy Spirit are near to the believer and to the believing church. By the Spirit we are close to Jesus in the heavenlies (Eph 2:6), and by the same Spirit he is with us and close to us in the church (Matt 18:20; 1 Cor 5:4) and in the heart (John 14:23; 17:26).

Very specifically and practically, then, we can "practice the presence" in prayer throughout our waking moments with the use of such simple sentence prayers as "In your presence, Lord; come, Holy Spirit," and, "In your presence is fullness of joy" (Ps 16:11). These simple prayers can be invoked during corporate worship, before we pray or read our Bibles, before times of extended intercession, or silently in the midst of a conversation with another person. Such a simple prayer renews our own awareness that we are living in the presence of God, and is a way of "inviting" Christ to be present in the

---

23–30, "Practicing the Presence," with reference to the writings of Lawrence, Frank Laubach, C. S. Lewis, and Henri Nouwen.

41. These three concepts are more fully developed in chapter 3, "Practicing Ministry in the Presence of God and in Partnership with God" and in my article, "The Metaphysics of Union with Christ," available by request from the author at jdavis@gordonconwell.edu.

conversation or ministry situation (see Matt 28:20: "make disciples . . . *I will be with you*"). We are reminding ourselves that we are not alone but are in union with Christ, and are praying and ministering in partnership with him, and that indeed, he, not us, is the one who is really the fundamental agent of all ministry. Such prayers of intention are simply ways of "operationalizing" the truth of John 15:5, "apart from me you can do nothing."

In seeking to pray with a constant sense of the presence of God throughout the day, it may be helpful to understand a distinction between "focal" and "subsidiary" states of awareness.[42] When I am sitting at my desk typing this chapter on the keyboard of my laptop, I am *focally* aware of the thoughts that I am trying to express, and only *subsidiarily* aware of the keyboard and my fingers as they type. If I shift my focal attention to my fingers, then I will lose track of the thoughts that I am trying to express. In the most literal sense, I cannot constantly have God as my focal point of attention at all times. When I am driving in heavy, dangerous traffic, I need to be focally aware of the car that is in front of me! During times of worship and private devotion my focal awareness is hopefully fixed on God (though our minds constantly wander), but even in the "secular" moments of the day, I can invoke a "subsidiary" awareness of God, in my spiritual "peripheral vision," so to speak, as I invite Christ to be with me in the conversation that I may be having with a particular individual. Or to use a computer and software analogy, I can have two screens open simultaneously on my laptop—one primary document upon which I am focusing at the moment, and a secondary screen in the background that I may need for reference. The "Jesus screen" can still be open in the background while the "primary screen" is open in the foreground in the conversation I am having with the person before me. I can shift my focal attention back and forth between Christ and the person even as the conversation is in progress, asking the Lord for discernment and wisdom.

Such an understanding of prayer as "practicing the presence of God" is not only applicable to individual prayer and times of intercession, but also to corporate prayer where two or three consciously join to invoke the name and presence of God (Matt 18:20) or pray corporately as a church (see Acts 1:14, "they all joined together constantly in prayer").[43] Such a single-minded, united practice of prayer, focusing on God and the divine presence, is in itself an means of answering Jesus' high priestly prayer for unity among his disciples (John 17:11,21,22,23), a unity that can be the prelude to

---

42. This distinction is drawn from Polanyi, *Personal Knowledge*, 55–57.

43. For suggestions as to how the presence of God could be practiced corporately in the context of a church committee meeting, see chapter 12, "How To Get More Out of Committee Meetings in Your Church."

a powerful, unified reception of the Holy Spirit (Acts 2:4, "*all* were filled") or empowerment for mission (Acts 13:2).

Such are some practical ways, then, that we can practice the presence of God throughout the day, praying with a consciousness of our union with Christ, of the nearness of God, and of our partnership with God in all ministry. Such practices can enhance our own sense of joy in God's presence, lead to more fruitfulness in ministry, break down the barriers between the "sacred" and the "secular" parts of our lives, and help us to fulfill the apostolic admonition to "pray constantly"—even under the very busy, distracting conditions of life in a modern, scientific age.

Pray without ceasing . . . . I will be with you always.
1 THESSALONIANS 5:17; MATTHEW 28:20

9

Is Scripture Memorization *Still* Relevant?

IN A RECENT ARTICLE Dallas Willard asserted that "*Bible memorization is absolutely fundamental to spiritual formation.*" If he were forced to choose only one of all the disciplines of the spiritual life, Willard stated that he "would choose Bible memorization."[1] Bible memorization is a "fundamental way of filling our minds with what they need."[2] The Pentecostal theologian Simon Chan has stated that Scripture memorization "is crucial to the well-being of the modern church, if not its survival."[3] These commendations of the value of Scripture memorization come at a time when this ancient spiritual practice, once common in evangelical circles, has tended, for a variety of reasons to be noted below, to become marginalized, neglected, and seemingly irrelevant as a spiritual discipline.[4]

The purpose of this chapter is to provide an emphatic answer of "Yes" to the question posed above in the title: "Is Scripture Memorization *Still* Relevant?" This positive answer, however, is far from self-evident, given the conditions of modern and postmodern culture. In order to make a case for the retrieval and recovery of the practice of Scripture memorization, this chapter will, first, review the historical evidence for the central place of memorization in ancient cultures and world religions; second, examine the causes for the decline of memorization in modern period since the Enlightenment; third, respond to three major objections to memorization in

---

1. Willard, "Spiritual Formation in Christ Is for the Whole Life and the Whole Person," 48.
2. Ibid.
3. Chan, *Spiritual Theology*, 165. See 163–71, "Meditating on the Word," for valuable insights on Scripture meditation and memorization.
4. As noted, for example, by J. Wilson, "Changing Forever How You Think," 41: "What was common 50 years ago has not entirely disappeared, but neither is it common anymore. . . . We live in a time when memorization is routinely scorned."

general and Scripture memorization in particular; fourth, present a positive case for the value of Scripture memorization based on the biblical data and the broader framework of Christian theology; and fifth and finally, present some practical suggestions and additional resources for personal practice.

I. The Central Role of Memory and Memorization in the Premodern World

In all premodern cultures that have been studied by anthropologists and historians, memorization has played a central role in education and the transmission of the culture's core values to the younger generation.[5] In ancient Greece and Rome memorization and memory skills were an essential element in the study of rhetoric, a core element of classical education.[6] Memory was one of the five divisions of ancient rhetoric, and was considered to be the foundation for all the rest.[7] It was an undisputed assumption among the ancients that the effective public speaker needed to have vast quantities of relevant information available from memory, together with the ability to organize and repeat from memory extended oral discourses.

A schoolboy in ancient Greece was expected to listen to, recite, and finally memorize extensive portions of Greek classical literature, especially from poets and dramatists such as Hesiod, Aeschylus, Sophocles, Euripides, and above all, Homer—whose works were considered to be the "bible" of the Greeks.[8] The historian Xenophon cites a certain Niceratus, who, reflecting on his own childhood education stated, "My father was anxious to see me develop into a good man, and as a means to this end he compelled me to *memorise all of Homer* (emphasis added): and so even now I can repeat the whole *Iliad* and Odyssey by heart."[9]

Such feats of memory seem incomprehensible to the modern mind. It is important to remember, however, that for the Greeks, such accomplishments were not viewed as mere "rote" memorization for its own sake, but rather as a means for internalizing the core values of Greek culture—in

---

5. Hirsch Jr., *Cultural Literacy*, 30, citing the standard anthropological database *Human Relations Area Files,* with examples from Korea, Tibet, Chile, southern Africa, Indonesia, Thailand, and North American Native American tribes.

6. On memorization and rhetoric in ancient Greece and Rome, see Yates, *The Art of Memory,* chapter 1, "The Three Latin Sources for the Classical Arts of Memory," and chapter 2, "The Art of Memory in Greece: Memory and the Soul."

7. Carruthers, *The Book of Memory,* 9.

8. Barclay, *Educational Ideals in the Ancient World,* 117.

9. Ibid., 119.

other words, the inculcation of virtues such as wisdom, justice, courage, and self-control that were celebrated by the Greek poets.

Bible memorization was a basic educational practice in ancient Israel and rabbinic Judaism. A young Hebrew boy would generally begin to attend the *bet sefer* (elementary school) between the ages of five and seven, begin with learning the letters of the alphabet, and then proceed to learn to read the Torah, beginning with the book of Leviticus.[10] The teacher would read a verse out loud and repeat it until the pupils had memorized the pronunciation of every word and were able to read the verse by themselves.[11] According to the rabbis, constant repetition both assured good retention and produced greater clarity of understanding.[12] The verses were taught with a system of musical intonation called "*Pisuk Ta'amim*," so that the texts would be remembered in the form of a rhythmical chant that could be more easily retained.[13]

Students were expected to review the texts memorized so that they would not be forgotten later. Rabbi Elisha b. Abuya said that the accomplishments of twenty years of study could be lost in two years if one failed to review.[14] Other rabbis stated that memorizing Scripture and failing to review was like "a man who sows but does not reap," or like "a woman who bears children and buries them."[15]

These methods enabled the people of ancient Israel to memorize quantities of Scripture and commentary that, by modern standards, seem beyond belief. According to the great bible scholar and translator Jerome (d. 420 AD), the Palestinian Jews of his day knew the Pentateuch and much of the Prophets by heart.[16] Rabbi Natronai b. Habibai, who emigrated to Spain in the eighth century AD, is said to have written a complete copy of the Talmud from memory.[17] These enormous efforts invested in the memorization of religious texts reflected the deep-seated Jewish belief that written texts are dead things if not imprinted on the memory and continuing to function there.[18]

In Islamic cultures the memorization and recitation of the Quran is a core cultural value. Traditionally, from the time he is six or seven the child

---

10. Gerhardsson, *Memory and Manuscript*, 62.
11. Ebner, *Elementary Education in Ancient Israel*, 91.
12. Drazin, *History of Jewish Education from 515 B.C.E. to 220 C.E.*, 112.
13. Ebner, *Elementary Education in Ancient Israel*, 91.
14. Ibid., 92.
15. Ibid., 93.
16. Jerome, *Commentary on Isaiah 58.2*, cited in Gerhardsson, *Memory and Manuscript*, 64n7.
17. Ibid., 115.
18. Ibid., 123.

was expected to memorize sections of the Quran as perfectly as possible, through repetition and imitation of the teacher.[19] These portions of the Quran could then be recited from memory during the five daily prayers.

In many Islamic countries there are national Quran reciting competitions, where skilled reciters chant the holy text in traditional rhythmic and musical forms. The biennial Quranic recitation competition in Indonesia is widely reported in the national press, celebrated with gala processions and dance performances, and attended by the president and other high government officials.[20] The recitation and memorization of the Quran is considered to be a meritorious act of piety, and it is said that even today, under the conditions of modernization, there are in many Islamic countries hundreds if not thousands of individuals who have memorized the entire Quran by heart.[21]

The memorization of the Vedas and other sacred texts was an essential element of traditional Hindu education, especially for members of the Brahmin class. This is still the case in modern times. A professor of Sanskrit in Rajasthan, India reported that his son, an engineer by profession living in England, still recites every morning ten hymns from the Vedas that he had memorized as a child.[22] A conscientious member of the Brahmin class would customarily recite ten memorized hymns each morning, covering in a year all the texts he had learned, and then would begin the cycle again.[23]

Memorization of sacred texts has played an essential role in the Buddhist tradition. For some 400 years after the death of the Buddha, his disciples preserved his teachings through memorization and oral transmission; it was not until the first century before the Christian era that the Buddhist scriptures were committed to writing in Sri Lanka.[24] Ananda, one of the Buddha's closest disciples, was reputed to have had extraordinary powers of memory, said to be able to repeat 60,000 words of the master without omitting a syllable.[25]

Education in ancient China depended heavily on the mastery and memorization of texts from the classic Confucian canon. Study guides and monographs were prepared during the Tang Dynasty (618-906 AD) to help students prepare for the civil service exams based on these texts. These

19. Szyliowicz, "Education: Educational Methods," 416–17.
20. Denny, "Quranic Recitation," 399.
21. "Koran," in *The Concise Encyclopedia of Islam*, 230.
22. Cited in Scharfe, *Education in Ancient India*, 251n56.
23. Ibid., 250.
24. Amore and Ching, "The Buddhist Tradition," 240.
25. Lopez Jr., *The Story of Buddhism*, 105.

civil service exams, based on exact knowledge of the classic texts, were long and physically and mentally demanding. They remained substantially unchanged for over a thousand years down to the modern era, until they were finally abolished in 1905.[26]

Memorization played an important role in the early Christian church. In the first four centuries of the Christian era, candidates for baptism and entrance to communion would be expected to undergo a significant period of catechetical instruction, which included memorizing the Lord's Prayer and the Apostles' Creed.[27] In a monastic context, the members of the community were expected to memorize great quantities of Scripture in order to participate in the daily and weekly liturgies. It is said that in the fourth century, St. Pachomius, a pioneer of Egyptian monasticism, expected those who entered his monastery to memorize—as a *minimum*—the New Testament and the Psalms.[28] Benedictine monks memorized the Psalms so that they could be prayed while working in the fields as well as recited in the monastery.[29]

As a member of the Augustinian monastic order Martin Luther had memorized great quantities of Scripture. One scholar has identified more than 1,600 references to Scripture in Luther's lectures on Romans, and these quotations are given mostly from memory.[30] In his "Tower Experience," when he was given his revolutionary new "Reformational" understanding of the "righteousness of God" as he meditated on Romans 1:17, he stated that "I meditated on those words day and night . . . all at once I had the feeling of being born again . . . . Immediately the whole of Scripture shone in a different light. *I ran through the Scriptures from memory* (emphasis added) and gathered together other terms that had analogous meaning . . . ."[31] It can be said that the key theological insight that sparked the Protestant Reformation arose in the context of Luther's spiritual practice of meditating on

---

26. DiCicco, "The Development of Leaders in Ancient China, Rome, and Persia." The Confucian canon consisted of the "Four Books" (*The Great Learning; Doctrine of the Mean; Confucian Analects;* the works of Mencius) and the "Five Classics" (*Book of Changes; Book of History; Book of Songs; Book of Rites;* and *Spring and Autumn Annals*).

27. Packer and Parrett, *Grounded in the Gospel*, 51-57. On the history of catechetical instruction, see further Dujarier, *A History of the Catechumenate* and Harmless, *Augustine and the Catechumenate*.

28. Van Houtryve, *Benedictine Peace*, 135.

29. Chittister, *The Rule of Benedict*, 122.

30. Kooiman, *Luther and the Bible*, 59.

31. From Luther's Preface of his Bible of 1545, as cited in Isaac, "Monastic Memoria," 130.

Scripture,[32] augmented by his ability to integrate and correlate this seminal insight with other biblical passages that he had stored in his memory.

Memorization has been highly valued in the Reformed and Puritan traditions. In Calvin's Geneva, children and adults were to be thoroughly catechized before being admitted to the Lord's table and full participation in the life of the church.[33] In Scottish Presbyterian homes Sabbath afternoons would often be devoted to the study and recitation of memorized biblical passages and sections of the Westminster Shorter Catechism or Heidelberg Catechism.[34] In colonial New England memorizing the catechism and the New England Primer was the order of the day, and the practice of meditating on Scripture in the early morning hours, before bedtime, and on the Sabbath fixed biblical content on the Puritan heart and mind.[35]

II. Memorization's Decline in the Modern World: Printing Presses, Progressive Education, and Expressive Individualism

For a variety of factors to be noted below, the memorization of texts as a core educational practice—in both church and the general culture—has been in decline since the 1950s. Beginning in the colonial period and for long thereafter, the memorization of biblical texts, poems, and the content of the *New England Primer* (e.g., "A: In Adam's fall, sinned we all . . .") was a basic gateway to the achievement of literacy and a shared culture. The memorization of poems, both at the elementary and high school levels, was a widespread practice in American schools and a basic way of studying English and American literature until the 1960s.[36]

Changes in technology were important factors in the decline of memorization in both church and society. The invention of the printing press

---

32. On Luther's practice of biblical meditation, see the fine article by Kleinig, "The Kindred Heart."

33. Leith, *An Introduction to the Reformed Tradition*, 146. On catechetical instruction in Calvin's Geneva, see "Draft Ecclesiastical Ordinances" in J. K. Reid, ed., *Calvin: Theological Treatises*, 69.

34. W. Reid, *John Calvin*, 318. On the role of catechesis in the Reformed traditions generally, see Janz, "Catechisms."

35. Hambrick-Stowe, *The Practice of Piety*, 157–69; Hall, *The Faithful Shepherd*, 169. On the long and extensive influence of the New England Primer on colonial American education and religion, see Monaghan, *Learning to Read and Write in Colonial America*.

36. The history of poetry memorization and recitation as a core educational practice in American education is documented in Robson, *Heart Beats*; see especially 5–7 and 42–44.

made Bibles and catechisms much more affordable and readily available, but also had the unintended effect of promoting the "rote" memorization of texts rather than the more interactive give-and-take discussions of the topics by catechist and student that characterized the pre-modern periods of Christian catechesis.[37]

With printed Bibles readily available,[38] it was also all too easy to think, "Why memorize? I can always find the text of Scripture when I need it." Now, with Scripture available in a variety of portable electronic devices—smart phones, computers, tablets—the temptation to "outsource" our memory of biblical texts has become even more pronounced.[39]

A powerful influence that contributed to the decline of memorization in general education in society and Scripture memorization in the churches was the rise of the "Progressive" education movement associated with the pragmatic philosopher John Dewey. Beginning in the early part of the twentieth century, in influential books such as *The School and Society* (1907), Dewey argued that the task of educators was to prepare students to be productive members of the new industrial society, and to base their educational methods on the latest scientific thinking. The watchword of the movement was "Teach them how to think, not what to think."[40] The new emphasis in the Progressive movement was on process and "critical thinking skills" rather than on content and fixed bodies of knowledge. Dewey's educational philosophy, focused as it was on the modern social context and a desire for "progress" and "change,"[41] inevitably devalued the historic role of the memorization of classic texts—which implied that normative values were to be found in the culture's tradition, rather than newly discovered in the present by the scientific method.

Yet another powerful cultural influence that works against older values that supported Bible memorization is the modern American outlook that sociologist Robert Bellah has called "expressive individualism." This is

---

37. As noted in Packer and Parrett, *Grounded in the Gospel*, chapter 3, "The Waxing and Waning of Catechesis," 51–73.

38. The printing press made printed Bibles more accessible and affordable; in recent decades, the proliferation of different *versions* and *translations* of the Bible further complicate the task of Bible memorization: which version to memorize? However, it could be said that *any* translation of the Bible that is actually memorized would be more spiritually profitable than a version *not* memorized.

39. See Morgan, "Reviving a Lost Art": "Our world has forgotten how to memorize. Our retrieval devices do it for us . . . [but] there's no substitute for engraving the very words of God into the furrows of our thoughts. The Bible doesn't say, 'Your Word I have clipped to my belt.' It says, 'Your Word I have hidden in my heart' (Psalm 119:11)."

40. Morris, *Philosophy and the American School*, 364.

41. Cremin, *The Transformation of the School*, 136.

an outlook that views the individual's primary task as "finding oneself" in autonomous self-reliance, often independently of family, the larger community, and historic traditions.[42] The autonomous individual in "finding" herself chooses the roles she will play not on the basis of received truths, but according to the criterion of "life-effectiveness as the individual judges it."[43] Such highly psychologized understandings of the self, reflecting as well the influence of the nineteenth-century Romantic movement, would tend to devalue the memorization of texts, inasmuch as one's true identity would be seen to be rooted in the depths of the self and not in the traditions of the past and of one's community of origin.

III. Objections to the Recovery of Scripture Memorization

Before presenting in the subsequent section of this chapter biblical and theological arguments for the retrieval of the practice of Scripture memorization, it might be helpful to anticipate three objections to such a retrieval: that memorization is a) *unnecessary*, in view of the ready accessibility of Scripture, in both print and digital media; b) *undesirable,* in that "rote" memorization represents a lower form of learning, and c) even *unhealthy*, in that it could inhibit the believer's unique individuality and personal creativity.

As to the objection that Scripture memorization is unnecessary in view of ready accessibility of the biblical text in printed and digital media, it can be replied that the *accessibility* of the Word should not be confused with the *assimilation* of the Word in the believer's mind, heart, and life. God's intention is that Holy Scripture be written upon the *heart*—not merely be accessible in a Bible on the shelf or a smart phone in the pocket. Jeremiah looks forward to the days of the New Covenant when God declares that he will "put my law in their minds and write it on their hearts . . . I will be their God, and they will be my people" (Jer 31:33). For the Word of God to be written on the heart, it must first be retained in the brain's short-term memory, then transferred to the *long-term* memory, and then, finally, transferred to the *heart,* where it is connected with other Scripture, and has engaged the will, imagination, and emotions, as well as the mind. Scripture memorization is

---

42. Bellah et al., *Habits of the Heart*, 163. Bellah contrasts "expressive individualism" with the earlier forms of individualism in American history: "biblical," "civic," and "utilitarian": 142ff. Ralph Waldo Emerson and Walt Whitman could be seen as exemplars of "expressive individualism" in American history.

43. Ibid., 47.

a crucial step in transferring the Word from the short-term to the long-term memory—a step that is generally not taken—and then finally to the heart.

A second common objection to memorization reflects the notion, based on current educational theories, that memorization—especially "rote" memorization—is a lower form of learning, and inferior to higher-order forms of learning such as evaluation, analysis, integration, and other "critical" thinking skills.[44] There are several fallacies, however, in such an objection. First of all, it seems to assume that all memorization is "rote" memorization, rather than *reflective* memorization. As we have already seen in the case of Luther's great Reformation discovery and "Tower Experience,"[45] and his new breakthrough understanding of Romans 1:17, his memory recall of a vast quantity of biblical texts enabled him to *integrate* and connect his new insight with a broad range of biblical truths. He was able to reflect in a creative and integrative way on the basis of the Scriptures that had been previously stored in his long-term memory.

And in the second place, the "rote" memorization objection, and modern bias in favor of "critical thinking skills," overlooks the crucial place of *background information* in the actual application of such thinking skills."Higher-order" thinking does not take place in a cultural vacuum, but assumes a body of given information about people, places, concepts and cultural practices that make a written text meaningful to the reader.[46] The memorization of biblical texts, and personal reflection on those texts, provides the invaluable background information for higher-order reflection on biblical truth and its application in life.

A third objection to memorization is that such practices stifle the individual's creativity and discovery of personal uniqueness, and favor tradition and the past over new insights discovered in the present. Such an objection would seem to reflect the modern sentiments of "expressive individualism,"

---

44. See, for example, on the influential "Bloom's Taxonomy" of Cognitive Domains that is widely accepted in modern educational theory: Bloom et al., *Taxonomy of Educational Objectives*. These "cognitive domains" include "Remember"; "Understand"; "Apply"; "Analyze"; "Evaluate"; and "Create."

45. Isaac, "Monastic Memoria."

46. The crucial role of background information in the acquisition of reading skills has been highlighted by Hirsch Jr., *Cultural Literacy*, 28: "Critical thinking and basic skills . . . do not enable children to create out of their own imaginations the essential names and concepts that have arisen by historical accident . . . . Many items of literate culture [e.g. the Rio Grande, the Mason-Dixon line, *Star Wars*, and "The Night Before Christmas," etc.] are arbitrary, but that does not make them dispensable. Facts are essential components of the basic skills that a child entering a culture must have." Hirsch cites the work of Jeanne S. Chall, *Stages of Reading Development*, on the critical role of "world knowledge" in achieving literacy: 216n1.

as noted above. However, some philosophers in recent decades have challenged such assumptions, noting that human thought and discovery do not operate in a vacuum, but in fact arise from bodies of knowledge and practices inherited from a culture's traditions. As Hans-Georg Gadamer has noted in his seminal work, *Truth and Method*, "Long before we understand ourselves through the process of self-examination, we understand ourselves in a self-evident way in the family, society, and state in which we live."[47] In fact, argues Gadamer, "The self-awareness of the individual is only a flickering in the closed circuits of historical life."[48]

The philosopher of science Michael Polanyi has shown how creative scientific work in such disciplines as chemistry, biology, and medicine is based in communities of scientific practice where knowledge and skills are passed down from master practitioners to apprentices; new discoveries are nurtured in tradition and communities, rather than arising *de novo*.[49] Aspiring scientists must learn the tradition before making original contributions themselves.

In the arts, philosophy, and theology, the historian Jaroslav Pelikan has noted how fresh insights have generally arisen not by ignoring the traditions of the past, but rather, by "including the 'dead' in the circle of discourse," the quality and freshness of the conversation is enriched.[50] The observations of Gadamer, Polanyi, Pelikan, and Hirsch, taken together, would indicate that the memorization of traditional (biblical) texts, far from inhibiting creativity, in fact can provide the necessary store of general background information out of which true innovation and creativity can arise.

IV. A Positive Case for Scripture Memorization as a Spiritual Priority

First of all, we can observe that a variety of biblical texts, both in the Old and New Testaments, indicate that the practice of Scripture memorization (and meditation) is both *commended* and *commanded* in a variety of settings, either directly or by implication:

> Deuteronomy 11:18: "*Fix these words of mine in your hearts and minds;* tie them as symbols on your hands and bind them on your foreheads."

47. Gadamer, *Truth and Method*, 245.
48. Ibid.
49. Polanyi, *Personal Knowledge*, 53.
50. Pelikan, *The Vindication of Tradition*, 81.

Deuteronomy 17:19: "It [a copy of the Law] is to be with him [the king], and he is to *read it all the days of his life* so that he may learn to revere the Lord his God and follow carefully all the words of this law and these decrees."

Joshua 1:8: "Do not let this Book of the Law depart from your mouth; *meditate on it day and night*, so that you may be careful to do everything written in it. Then you will be prosperous and successful."

Psalm 1:2-3: "His [the righteous man's] delight is in the law of the Lord, and on his law he *meditates day and night*. He is like a tree planted by streams of water, which yields its fruit in season, and whose leaf does not wither."

Psalm 119:11: "I have *hidden your word in my heart,* that I might not sin against you."

Psalm 119:15: "I meditate on your precepts and consider your ways."

Psalm 119:16: "I delight in your decrees; I will not neglect your word."

Psalm 119:48: "I lift up my hands to your commands . . . and I meditate on your decrees."

Psalm 119:78: "I will meditate on your precepts."

Psalm 119:97: "Oh how I love your law! I *meditate on it all the day long.*"

Psalm 119:99: "I have more insight than all my teachers, for I meditate on your statutes."

Psalm 119:148: "My eyes stay open through the night watches, that I may meditate on your promises."

Jeremiah 31:33: "This is the [New] covenant I will make with the house of Israel after that time, declares the Lord. I will put my law in their minds and *write it on their hearts*. I will be their God, and they will be my people."

Matthew 4:4: "Jesus answered, 'It is written . . . ' " ; 4:7: "Jesus answered him, 'It is written . . . '; 4:10: "Jesus said to him . . . . 'For it is written . . . '" (Jesus quotes Scripture from memory when tempted during the forty days in the wilderness.)

Luke 8:15: "But the seed on good soil stands for those with a noble and good heart, who hear the word *and retain it*, and by persevering produce a good crop."

John 15:7-8: "If you remain in me, *and my words remain in you* [a mark of discipleship], ask whatever you wish, and it will be given to you. This is to my Father's glory, that you bear much fruit, showing yourselves to be my disciples."

The texts above that commend meditating on Scripture "day and night" or continually imply that such texts would, in time, be committed to memory.

Secondly, it is evident that the texts above and others indicate that Scripture memorization can produce a variety of spiritual benefits: spiritual fruitfulness and success in Christian living and ministry (Josh 1:8; Ps 1:3; John 15:5; Luke 8:15); protection in the face of temptation to sin (Ps 119:11; Eph 6:17); renewal of the mind and reinforcement of Christian identity (Rom 12:2: "be transformed by the renewing of your mind"); the experience of the peace of God in stressful circumstances (Phil 4:8-9: "whatever is true . . . think about these things . . . and the peace of God will guard your hearts and minds"); resources for witnessing and sharing the gospel (e.g., the "Roman Way": Rom 3:23; 6:23; 3:25-26; 10:9); wisdom for Christian counseling (Ps 119:99) and intercessory prayer; and, last but not least, the *intrinsic* enjoyment of reflection on God's word (Ps 119:16, 97).

The practice of Scripture memorization can and should be understood within the larger context of Christian theology. The practice is consistent with the fundamental doctrines of *God and the Trinity*, inasmuch as the "Word" (Logos) has been eternally within the life of God (John 1:1, "in the beginning was the Word"), and Father, Son, and Holy Spirit have eternally been in communion with one another by means of the words they speak to one another. Scripture memorization is consistent with the doctrine of *Scripture*, which teaches that while "Heaven and earth will pass away . . . my words will never pass away" (Matt 24:35). The everlasting quality of the Word of God implies that it, unlike many other ephemeral texts, is preeminently worth our time and attention to memorize and retain. It is consistent with our understanding of *salvation* and the New Covenant, in which it is promised that God will write the law of God upon his people's hearts (Jer 31:33; see 2 Cor 3:3). The practice is consistent with the Christian doctrines of *sanctification* and discipleship, in which lasting personal transformation occurs by the concurrent action of Spirit, *Word*, and cooperation of the human will, in union with Christ and the internalization of and obedience to his words (John 15:5, 7). Scripture memorization is consistent with a Christian doctrine of the *church*, in the life of which it is God's will that believers have the Word of God dwelling richly within themselves, so as to be able to "teach and admonish one another with all wisdom" (Col 3:16). And as already noted in the earlier reference above to Matthew 24:35, the practice is consistent with the Christian doctrines of *eschatology*, because the Word of God will never pass away, but will continue to be remembered and celebrated and, finally, perfectly *obeyed*, throughout eternity in the New Creation.

V. Practical Applications and Resources

This chapter will conclude with some practical suggestions on how to begin a personal practice of Scripture memorization, and with some recommendations regarding resources for further study. Where should one begin? It is probably best to begin with Scripture verses or passages that are already familiar, favorite passages, and ones that seem pertinent to one's life circumstances and needs at the time. For example, Psalm 23 is a timeless favorite that can provide a sense of God's protection and guidance; John 15 and its teachings on the vine and the branches and abiding in Christ is foundational for Christian growth and discipleship; Romans 8:28 is a classic text that provides perspective in the midst of trials and suffering; John 3:16, in the estimation of Martin Luther, summarized the very heart of the gospel. The possible starting points are almost endless, and an ancient Chinese proverb said, "First you begin; then you continue."

One could also consider using a variety of "short lists" of important clusters of texts in both the Old and New Testaments. My personal nomination for "Top Three Old Testament Verses" would included Genesis 1:1 ("In the beginning God created the heavens and the earth"), Leviticus 11:44 ("I am the Lord your God; you shall be holy because I the Lord your God am holy"), and Isaiah 6:3 ("Holy, holy, holy is the Lord God Almighty; the whole earth is full of his glory")—texts which are foundational for our understanding of God as the all-holy and almighty Creator of heaven and earth.

The four verses in Romans of the "Roman Way" provide a concise statement of the plan of salvation and a handy way of sharing the gospel: Romans 3:23 ("For all have sinned and fallen short of the glory of God"); Romans 6:23 ("The wages of sin is death, but the gift of God is eternal life in Christ Jesus our Lord"); Romans 3:25 ("God presented him as a sacrifice of atonement, through faith in his blood"); and Romans 10:9 ("If you confess with your mouth that 'Jesus is Lord', and believe in your heart that God raised him from the dead, you will be saved").

If I were asked to nominate a list of "Top Ten New Testament Verses" that are foundational for Christian faith and living, such a list might include: John 1:1 (deity of Christ); John 1:14 (the incarnation); John 3:16 (the love of God and the gospel); Luke 9:23 (discipleship and bearing the cross); Matthew 22:37–39 (the Two Great Commandments); John 15:5 (vine and the branches; abiding in Christ); Ephesians 2:8 (salvation by grace through faith); Ephesians 2:10 (created in Christ for good works); Ephesians 5:18 (be continually filled with the Spirit); Matthew 28:19–20 (the Great Commission to make disciples); and Romans 8:28 (God causes all things to work for good for those who love him).

As to the actual process of memorizing Scripture, two elements are essential: *repetition* and regular *review*. Having selected a text for memorization, and using the version of the Bible that you would customarily read for your personal devotions, the first step would simply be to read the text —either silently or aloud—three or four times, and then to repeat the text from memory, without looking at the Bible. Check yourself and make any necessary corrections, to get the wording exact.

Many people find it helpful to read the passage aloud, since this activates different areas of the brain and encodes the information in a different way. For a truly multi-sensory learning approach, one could first read the passage silently, then read it aloud, and finally, write out the text, either by hand or on a keyboard.[51] Recalling the passage later during the day, and before going to bed at night, can further cement the passage in memory.

At some later time, it is important to *review* the texts that you have memorized earlier, to make sure that the texts have been transferred securely from one's short-term to long-term memory. As the rabbis of ancient Israel stated, one who memorized Scripture but neglected to review was like a man who "sows but does not reap" or like a woman who "bears children and then buries them."

---

51. For those whose preferred learning style is auditory, listening to Scripture on a CD or with a portable electronic device is yet another possibility, although repeatedly "rewinding the tape" could be a bit cumbersome.

For those who would like to do some further reading on the topic of Scripture memorization, articles by John Piper, Rob Morgan, and John Wilson could be recommended.[52] The recent book by Joshua Choonmin Kang, a Korean pastor in Los Angeles, can also be recommended: *Scripture by Heart: Devotional Practices for Memorizing God's Word*. There are useful resources available at the Navigators' website, including the pages on "How to Memorize Scripture" and the "Topical Memory System."[53]

In conclusion, I hope that the reader of this chapter will agree that the answer to the question, "Is Scripture Memorization *Still* Relevant?" should be an emphatic "Yes," and will be motivated to begin or to recover this invaluable biblical and historic Christian practice.

---

52. Piper, "Why Memorize Scripture?"; Morgan, "Reviving a Lost Art"; and J. Wilson, "Changing Forever How You Think."

53. Accessible at www.navpress.com.

10

1 Timothy 2:12, the Ordination of Women, and Pauline Use of Creation Narratives

FIRST TIMOTHY 2:11–15, AND especially verse 12, has long been a focal point in modern discussions of the ordination of women. Traditional reservations about the ordination of women as pastors and elders have generally made two assumptions in the interpretation of this passage: 1) that the meaning of *authentein* in v. 12 is clearly known and should be translated simply as "have authority," and 2) that the appeal to the creation narrative naming Adam and Eve in vv. 13 and 14 implies a universal, "transcultural" principle that prohibits the exercise of ecclesiastical authority by women over men in all (or some) circumstances.

The purpose of this chapter is to argue that both of these assumptions are faulty, and that 1 Timothy 2:11–15, rightly understood lexically and contextually, does not teach any universal prohibition of the ordination of women as pastors or elders. The primary focus of this discussion will be the second assumption, regarding the appeal to the Genesis creation account of Adam and Eve.[1] It will be argued that Paul's *contextual* and *church-specific* appeal to creation texts makes it not only possible but preferable to see the limitation on women's teaching roles in 1 Timothy 2 as a *circumstantial* and not universal prohibition. Before proceeding with this analysis, however, a few observations will be made regarding the meaning of *authentein* in v. 12.

---

1. For the purposes of this paper, the Pauline authorship of the Pastoral Epistles is assumed.

Authentein: "Have Authority" or "Domineer"?

It is well known that *authentein* in v. 12, a *hapax legomenon* in the New Testament, has been the focus of considerable attention among lexicographers and biblical scholars in recent decades. Those who favor "traditional" understandings of male ecclesiastical leadership have tended to translate this word in the neutral sense of "have authority" or "exercise authority," as, for example, Knight in a widely cited article of 1984.[2] In 1988 Wilshire, examining 329 occurrences of this word and its cognate *authentes,* showed that prior to the first century, *authentein* often had negative overtones such as "domineer" or even "murder" or "perpetrate a crime"; only during the later patristic period did the meaning "to exercise authority" come to predominate.[3]

In a 2004 study Belleville[4] carefully examined the five occurrences of *authentein* prior to or contemporary with Paul, and rendered these texts as follows: 1) the *Scholia* (c. 5–1 BC) to Aeschylus's tragedy *Eumenides*: "commit acts of violence"; 2) Aristonicus (c. 1 BC), "the *author*" (of a message); 3) a letter of Tryphon (c. 1 BC), "I *had my way* with him" (*contra* Knight); 4) Philodemus (c. 1 BC), "*powerful* lords"; and 5) the poet Dorotheus (c. 1–2 AD) in an astrological text, "Saturn . . . *dominates* Mercury." It is clear, especially in instances 1, 3, 4, and 5 above that a neutral meaning such as "have authority" is not in view.

Belleville also notes, significantly, that a variety of *pre-modern* versions of the Bible[5] translate this word not simply as "have authority" or "exercise authority," but with some negative sense, e.g., the Old Latin (c. 2–4 AD): "I permit not a woman to teach, neither to *dominate* (*dominari*) a man"; the Vulgate (c. 4–5 AD), "neither to *domineer* over a man"; the Geneva Bible (1560 ed.), "neither to *usurpe* authority over a man"; the Bishops Bible (1589), "neither to *usurpe* authority over a man"; the King James Bible

---

2. Knight, "*Authenteo* in Reference to Women in 1 Timothy 2:12," 145.

3. Wilshire, "The TLG Computer and Further References to *Authenteo* in 1 Tim 2:12." The scholarly literature on this passage is comprehensively surveyed in the article by Blomberg, "Neither Hierarchicalist nor Egalitarian." See also the lexical analysis of Baldwin, "A Difficult Word: *Authenteo* in 1 Tim 2:12." The favoring of a neutral meaning such as "have authority" by Greek church fathers in the fourth and later centuries, could be seen as reflective of the church's changed cultural context subsequent to the legalization of Christianity in 313, permitting Christian worship to move from the private, house-church setting to more public spaces—public spaces in which, in Greek culture, public leadership roles for women were not generally favored. Byzantine social customs favored the veiling and semicloistering of women, and a narrowing of social roles; men and women in general led segregated lives: Bullough, *The Subordinate Sex,* 123, 126; O'Faolin and Martines, eds., *Not in God's Image,* 74.

4. Belleville, "Teaching and Usurping Authority," 214–17.

5. Ibid., 209–10.

(1611), "nor *usurp* authority over a man." In none of these cases can the translators be suspected of having a modern, "feminist" bias in translating *authentein* with a negative sense of "domineer" or "usurp authority." These instances show that the "traditional" translation of *authentein* as "exercise authority" is neither uniform nor self-evident in the history of interpretation; if anything, it could be argued that the burden of proof is on the (now) "traditional" view to justify its translation choice.

It should also be observed that Paul, had he the ordinary exercise of ecclesiastical leadership and authority in mind, had at his disposal a number of words that could have served this sense, notably, *proisteimi*. This latter word, occurring eight times in the New Testament, and used six times *by Paul* in reference to church leaders (1 Tim 3:4, 5, 12; 1 Tim 5:17; 1 Thess 5:12; Rom 12:8), can have the senses of "manage, conduct, rule, direct, be concerned about," and connotes the type of "normal" and "expected" type of leadership that should be exhibited by those selected to lead. The fact that a highly unusual and ambiguous word is chosen in 2:12 would be consistent with an unusual set of circumstances in the context to which the text is addressed. It will be argued below that these circumstances, as indicated by clear references in the Pastoral Epistles themselves, involve women who are being deceived by false teachers, and as such are not suitable for the exercise of teaching or ruling authority in Ephesus.

Pauline Use of the Creation Narratives

The major focus of this chapter is an examination of Paul's appeal to the Genesis creation narratives, with a view to showing that in this (1 Tim 2:11-15) and other passages, the apostle refers to these texts with the local circumstances and the problems of specific churches in view. It is here argued that previous discussions of this passage have not given adequate recognition to the *context-specific* way in which Paul applies the creation texts.

When writing to the church in Ephesus, the apostle states that women are not to teach or have (NIV)/usurp (KJV) authority over men because "Adam was formed first, then Eve; and Adam was not deceived, but the woman was deceived and became a transgressor" (vv.13-14). Paul appeals to the Genesis narratives describing the human situation both prior to the Fall and immediately subsequent to it (Gen 2:18-25; 3:1-7). It has been argued that since v. 13, referring to the chronological priority of Adam over Eve in creation, is both a *creation* narrative and *before the Fall,* the conclusions drawn from it by the apostle are not simply reflective of cultural circumstances or the sinful human condition, but are normative for all times and places, and consequently bar the ordination of women to certain offices in all circumstances. Paul's reasoning appeals to a basic order of creation, and not merely to a limited cultural context or to the practices of particular churches. For those who accept the authority of canonical Scripture and who take Adam and Eve to be historical individuals, such considerations would appear to be weighty and even insuperable objections to the ordination of women as senior pastors or elders. Even if Adam and Eve were considered not to be historical individuals, but rather archetypal representatives of the first human beings, it could still be argued that the implications that Paul draws from these accounts are of transcultural validity precisely because they are drawn from *prelapsarian creation* texts.

The foregoing argument, however, fails to take into account the way in which the Apostle Paul draws implications from creation texts in ways that are specifically related to his pastoral and theological concerns for specific churches and congregations. It should be observed that in other church contexts the apostle derives different applications from these same creation texts. For example, in Paul's writing to the church in Rome, Adam, not Eve, is singled out as the representative figure who brought guilt and death upon the entire human race (Rom 5:12-21); Eve is not so much as mentioned. Adam is singled out as the representative head of the fallen human race, just as Christ is presented as the second Adam, the "one who was to come" (v. 14). The focus on Adam is consistent with Paul's purpose in setting forth his gospel as a gospel for the entire human race, for Jew and Gentile alike. As he had previously stated in 3:9, "*Jews and Gentiles alike* are all under sin"; the righteous standards of the law hold "*the whole world* accountable to God" (3:19). Hence there is a universal need for the gospel. Later in the Epistle to the Romans he deals with matters such as eating meat and observing special days (14:5-23) that are of internal concern to a congregation of both Jewish and Gentile converts, but in the opening chapters (1-3) he is especially concerned with the "global" and universal relevance of the gospel, and consequently reads Genesis 3 in terms of *Adam's* disobedience that led to condemnation for *all* people (5:18).

In writing to the church at Corinth Paul makes different applications of the creation narratives that are specifically related to the problems of this local assembly. In giving directives about the proper conduct of women in public worship (1 Cor 11:2-16), Paul, while pointing to the creational grounding of the headship principle (v. 8, "woman [came] from man"; see Gen 2:21-23), qualifies this in the direction of the mutual dependence of men and women (vv. 11, 12). Evidently the apostle expects that the women in Corinth will continue to pray and prophesy in the assembly (11:5), but should do so in an orderly and respectful way that honors the "headship" principle—however the latter is to be understood.⁶

In his Second Epistle to the Corinthians the apostle addresses the danger of being deceived by false teachers. In 2 Corinthians 11:3 he writes that "I am afraid that just as *Eve* was deceived by the serpent's cunning (Gen 3:1–6), your minds might be lead astray from your sincere and pure devotion to Christ" by the "super apostles" who are preaching a "different Jesus" (vv. 4–5). The point to be noticed is that Paul draws a parallel here between the deception of Eve and the danger of the entire *Corinthian congregation* (or its [male] leaders) being deceived by false teachers.

In this text the figure of Eve is clearly taken to apply to the entire congregation, and not specifically to the women within it, as though they, merely by virtue of their gender, were uniquely susceptible to such deception. This is to be contrasted with the reference to the deception of Eve in 1 Timothy 2:12, when Paul is writing to a church in Ephesus in which he is concerned that some of the younger widows have already "turned away to follow Satan" (1 Tim 5:15), and is aware of "weak-willed women" in Ephesus who are burdened by sins and have not learned the truth, their homes being infiltrated by false teachers (2 Tim 3:6–7).

This comparison of 2 Corinthians 11:3 and 1 Timothy 2:12 shows that Paul does not have a "one size fits all" hermeneutic when reading and applying the Genesis narratives of creation and Fall: "Eve" can be seen as a figure of *women* in Ephesus or as a figure for *an entire church* in Corinth—because the local circumstances differ, though false teaching is a danger in both settings. Applications are drawn from Genesis in a church-specific and contextually sensitive way.

Another example of Paul's contextually sensitive application of creation texts may be seen in the different ways controversies concerning food are addressed when writing to the congregations in Ephesus and Rome. In 1 Timothy 4:1–5, written to Ephesus, Paul's response to false teachers who are forbidding marriage and enjoining abstinence from certain foods is that "Everything created by God is good, and nothing is to be rejected if it is received with thanksgiving" (v. 4). The principle being invoked by the apostle is clearly reflective of the teaching found in Gen 1:31, "God saw all that he had made, and it was very good." The institution of marriage and all types of food—"kosher" or "non-kosher," meat or vegetables, sacrificed to a pagan idol or not—are, intrinsically in and of themselves "clean," reflecting the

---

6. For an extensive review of the recent scholarly literature discussing this difficult passage (1 Cor 11:2–16), see Blomberg, "Neither Hierarchialist Nor Egalitarian," 295–302.

goodness of God's creation itself; Paul strongly asserts this principle as over against the false teachers.

In writing to the Roman congregation, however, on similar issues of permissible foods and observance of special days (Rom 14), Paul makes a somewhat different pastoral approach because of different circumstances. As with the Ephesian congregation, the apostle alludes to the creational principle of the goodness of all food (14:4, "nothing is unclean in itself": see Gen 1:31), but in the Roman church there are other dynamics to be considered: the practices and scruples of Jewish and Gentile converts whose different religious and cultural backgrounds are creating problems of conscience and troubling the unity of the church. While in principle the Gentile believers in Rome could insist on their "creational right" to eat meat, Paul urges them to forbear in Christian love out of regard for the consciences of their Jewish brethren. In this circumstance Paul urges that a central redemptive concern for the unity of the church and respect for Christian conscience in secondary matters take precedence over any individual's "creation right" to eat meat. While Paul is not denying the validity of the creational goodness of meat—as previously noted, in Romans 14:4 he had already stated that "no food is unclean in itself"—this principle is not applied to the life of the Pauline churches without regard to the particular circumstances of the congregation in question. In Ephesus Paul can be more insistent on the "creational right" to eat all foods, because the denial of this right is coming from false teachers who are in danger of abandoning the faith and following deceiving spirits (1 Tim 4:1). Here the issue of food is implicated with the preservation of the faith itself. In Rome, on the other hand, there is no indication in Romans 14 that either party—Jew or Gentile—is in danger of abandoning the faith, being deceived by demons, or drifting in the direction of heretical doctrine.

The foregoing discussion of food controversies in two churches addressed by Paul suggests, further, that just as in one circumstance a creational right to eat (1 Tim 4) does not lead to an unqualified permission to eat in another (Rom 14), so it could also be the case that a creationally endorsed prohibition (1 Tim 2:12-13) of women exercising ecclesiastical authority does not imply prohibition under different circumstances. In both cases, it is here being argued, the Pauline texts show that creation texts are applied in a contextually sensitive manner, and in a way that is concerned to preserve the apostle's core values: sound doctrine and the preservation of the apostolic deposit of faith; the unity of the churches; and harmony and good order in the Christian family.

On this reading of 1 Timothy 2:11-15, Paul is indeed prohibiting women in Ephesus from exercising ecclesiastical authority, and would not support their "ordination"—the reason being that false teachers pose a grave threat in Ephesus, and women are being misled by false teachers and straying after Satan. Paul sees a parallel between the deception of Eve in Genesis 3 and the deception of women in Ephesus—just as he sees a parallel between the deception of Eve in Genesis and the deception of the *congregation* in Corinth. In different circumstances—where women are sound in the faith, and their lives consistent with the apostolic core values of congregational unity and the harmony and good order of the family—the way would be open for their exercise of ecclesiastical leadership. The general, "transcultural" lesson that should be drawn then from the Genesis texts, in light of their contextually differentiated uses in 1 Timothy 2 and 2 Corinthians 11, would be that *whenever* and *wherever* either *women or men* are being misled by false teachers, they should not be ordained as church leaders; soundness in the faith is a necessary (but not sufficient) condition for service as an elder or deacon (1 Tim 3:1–13).

At this point it seems appropriate to consider a possible objection to the foregoing line of argument. Those holding a "traditional" understanding of 1 Timothy 2:11–15 raise the concern that the same logic that would argue that creationally grounded prohibitions concerning women in the church do not necessarily apply in all contexts could be extended to argue that biblical prohibitions against homosexual practices grounded in creation are not necessarily forbidden in all circumstances either. In short, do arguments for women's ordination inevitably lead to justifications for homosexuality? The question is a serious one and deserves a careful answer, for trends in some mainline American churches give plausibility to such concerns.

The response to this concern, however, is to observe that in the course of redemptive history and in the breadth of the biblical canon, there is *uniformity* in the biblical rejection of homosexual practices, while there is *diversity* in the types of public leadership roles played by women in the Old and New Covenant communities.[7] In the case of homosexual practices, there is one consistent position reflected throughout the Scriptures in both testaments; the biblical assessment of homosexuality is uniformly negative.[8] There are no historical or cultural contexts mentioned in Scripture in which homosexuality is portrayed in a positive light. The creational distinctions between

---

7. See the insightful discussions of W. Webb, *Slaves, Women and Homosexuals*, especially 135–84 on the interplay between creation, new creation, and cultural elements as they relate to the biblical statements on women and homosexual practices. Webb's nuanced approach is consistent with the argument of this chapter, but he does not appear to develop my "context-specific use of creation texts" approach in a focused way.

8. For a comprehensive examination of the biblical texts on homosexuality and issues of interpretation, see Gagnon, *The Bible and Homosexual Practice*.

male and female (Gen 1:27) that are foundational for the prohibitions against homosexuality have the same implications for all cultural contexts.

In the case of women's leadership roles, however, there is significant diversity within the canon itself. In 1 Timothy 2, women's roles are restricted, it is here argued, in light of the local problems of women being misled by false teachers and plausibly, teaching men in a *domineering* fashion.[9] Elsewhere one can recall the prominent leadership roles exercised by Deborah the prophetess (Judges 4), Huldah the prophetess (2 Kings 22), Miriam the sister of Moses (Exod 15:20–21), Priscilla (Acts 18:26), the four daughters of Philip who were prophetesses (Acts 21:9), and Phoebe (Rom 16:1) to be reminded of the ways that women have been used by God at different times in biblical history; there is no hint in the canonical texts that the activities of these women was viewed in a negative light. This diversity—the fact that women's authoritative leadership is sometimes prohibited (1 Tim 2) and sometimes permitted (Deborah, Judges 4), indicates that *circumstantial* factors are in play—not merely "transcultural, creational" norms that are applied without regard to local problems.

The case of Deborah is especially relevant to this discussion of Paul's use of creation texts in relation to leadership roles for women in the covenant community. The biblical text states that Deborah was *judging* Israel at that time (Judges 4:4). She "held court" under the palm of Deborah in the hill country of Ephraim and the Israelites "came to her to have their disputes decided" (Judges 4:5); the biblical author clearly understands her to be exercising judicial authority.[10] The verb used to indicate Deborah's activity (*shaphat*) is the same verb used to describe the judicial activity of

---

9. Traditional interpreters of 1 Timothy 2:13 ("Adam was formed first, then Eve") see in this an appeal to the order of creation and the principle of primogeniture or "the first born" who is worthy of greater honor. But it should be noted that Paul can also apply the "primogeniture" principle in context-specific ways. For example, in Romans 3:1–2 and 9:4–5 he reminds his Gentile readers of the spiritual privileges (Law, covenants, temple worship, etc.) of Israel; Israel is God's "first-born" in the order of redemptive history; Gentiles should not boast over the branches, because "you do not support the root, but the root supports you" (11:18); and yet the thrust of the book of Romans as a whole is to argue for the spiritual equality of both Gentiles and Jews before God—through faith in Jesus Christ (Rom 3:28–30; see Gal 3:28). The "Adam was formed first" reference in 1 Timothy 2:13 can plausibly be understood as a context-specific response and corrective to a situation in which women were *not* acting respectfully toward men in the Ephesus congregation, and are being rebuked for their (domineering) behavior.

10. Robert Boling comments on this text: "*Judging.* That is, functioning with reference to a recognized office . . . . *Deborah's Palm.* That she had a tree named after her suggests a setting in which she was responsible for Yahwist oracular inquiry . . . *the judgment.* Heb *ham-mishpat*; here it stands for her decision in response to a particular inquiry": *Judges,* 95.

Moses (Exod 18:13) and Samuel (1 Sam 17:6). The judges that were to be appointed in the various tribes and towns according to the law of Moses (Deut 16:18–20) were to administer justice impartially and were to be respected as serving the "Lord your God" (Deut 17:12) and representing his authority. As Robin Davis has pointed out in a recent study, the parallels between Moses and Deborah are numerous and striking: both Moses and Deborah functioned as judges (Exod 18:13; Judges 4:4); both sat for judgment, and the people came to them (Exod 18:13; Judges 4:5); both proclaimed the word of the Lord (Exod 7:16; Judges 4:6); he was a prophet (Deut 18:15), she was a prophetess (Judges 4:4); both pronounce blessings (Exod 39:43; Judges 5:24); both pronounce curses in the name of the Lord (Deut 27:15; Judges 5:23); both had military generals (Joshua; Barak); both give instructions to the people as to how the Lord would defeat the enemies (Exod 14:14; Judges 4:6); in both cases, the Lord caused the enemy in chariots to panic and flee (Exod 14:24; Judges 4:15); God's victory is told first in prose (Exod 14, Judges 4), then in poetry (Exod 15, Judges 5); Moses (and Miriam) (Exod 15:1), and Deborah (and Barak) (Judges 5:1) led the people in worshiping God after their great deliverance.[11] In Judges, Deborah appears as a "Second Moses" figure whose authority derives from the God of Sinai.

The case of Deborah poses a special dilemma for the "traditional" reading of 1 Timothy 2:12. If it is true that Paul's use of creation texts is intended to prohibit all women in all circumstances from exercising authority over men in the covenant community, then the apostle is *forbidding* what God has in this instance *permitted*—and this would amount to a contradiction within the canon itself.

Various ways of evading this problem are not convincing. Was Deborah usurping authority, rather than exercising it legitimately? There is no indication in the book of Judges, the Old Testament as a whole, or the New Testament that God disapproved of Deborah's activities; on the contrary, Deborah is to be understood in light of the programmatic statement in Judges 2:16 that God, in his mercy, "raised up judges who saved them"; her leadership is a notable example of exactly such divinely empowered activity.

Was Deborah not really "ruling" or "judging" Israel at this time, but merely dealing with people privately when they came to her, as Grudem has suggested?[12] This argument is unconvincing for three reasons: 1) it overlooks the usage of the verb *shaphat*, which is also used to describe the activities of Moses (Exod 18:13) and Samuel (1 Sam 17:6), both of whom engaged

---

11. R. Davis, "Historical and Literary Parallels Between the Moses and Deborah Narratives," 1–7; Davis cites other parallels in addition to those mentioned above.

12. Grudem, *Evangelical Feminism and Biblical Truth*, 133.

in *public* and *authoritative* judging; 2) it overlooks the plain reference to Deborah's place of judgment,[13] the *palm tree of Deborah*—a public location, not a private one, such as a home; and 3) it overlooks the plain statement of the text that Deborah was judging *Israel*—a reference to the nation as a whole, not just various individuals. Deborah's leadership, like that of the other judges, was widely recognized and transcended tribal boundaries.

Was Deborah only God's "second best" because the men of Israel would not lead?[14] This view overlooks the explicit texts such as Judges 5:2 ("When the princes in Israel *take the lead* . . . Praise the Lord!") and 5:9 ("My heart is with Israel's princes, with the *willing* volunteers among the people"), where the leaders of Israel are commended, not rebuked, for answering God's call through Deborah.

Nor is it the case that the Deborah texts can be discounted by suggesting that she exercised only "civil" and not "spiritual" authority; this notion of the separation of civil and religious authority in the life of Israel makes no sense in the theocratic life of Israel at this time. Such a reading imports into the text modern notions of "separation of church and state" that are foreign to it. Deborah issues commands to Barak in the name of the Lord (Judg 5:6, "The Lord, the God of Israel commands you"); the kings of Israel were to rule on the basis of the law of Moses (see Deut 17:18, "he is to write for himself on a scroll a copy of *this law* [law of Moses]"), not some secular or merely "civil" law.[15]

The implication of the foregoing observations is that Deborah should be seen as a positive and not negative example of a woman exercising authority in the covenant community; Deborah may be unusual and somewhat exceptional in biblical history, but she is a positive example notwithstanding. Since God himself raised up Deborah as a judge, and that which God chooses to do cannot be *intrinsically wrong*, it cannot be intrinsically wrong for a woman to exercise authority over a man in ecclesiastical contexts.

---

13. Lindars comments, "Deborah *had her seat* below this tree in the sense that she exercised her function as judge here," *Judges 1–5*, 183; Soggins, *Judges*, 64: "'Used to sit': where she exercised her office as a judge . . . in the forensic sense of this term."

14. Lindars, *Judges 1–5*, 134.

15. With reference to Deborah, Schreiner, "The Valuable Ministries of Women in the Context of Male Leadership," 211, recognizes her prominent leadership role, but then points, correctly, to the distinction in the New Testament between the roles of "prophets" (as in Corinth) and elders: the prophets did not ostensibly have the same type of authority by way of continuing office as did the elders in matters of teaching. This distinction, even if correct, misses the main point with respect to Deborah: she had both "charismatic" authority as a prophetess, and a recognized *office* as a judge. The two aspects were combined in her case—demonstrating that God can approve the exercise of authority under both aspects *by a duly called and gifted woman*.

The case of Deborah, seen as a positive example, is then consistent with a recognition of the *circumstantial* nature of the prohibitions in 1 Timothy 2:12; not all women are prohibited by God from exercising authority over men at all times in the church. The reading here presented then removes the appearance of a "contradiction within the canon," and provides hermeneutical space for the recognition of other "Deborahs" who may be called by God to lead from time to time.[16]

In conclusion, then, the following translation of 1 Timothy 2:12 is proposed: "I do not permit a woman to teach in a way that domineers over men." This rendering of the verse is consistent with the following considerations: 1) the unusual, in fact singular usage of *authentein* in the New Testament, suggestive of unusual circumstances, rather than the more usual Pauline word *proisteimi* for church leadership; 2) the negative connotations for *authentein* found in four of the five uses of the word in texts prior to or contemporary with Paul; 3) the translations of "domineer" or "usurp authority" found in earlier versions of the Bible such as the Old Latin, Vulgate, Geneva, Bishops, and King James; 4) the grammatical and syntactical observation that in the New Testament, pairs of nouns or noun substitutes (e.g., infinitives) connected by a "neither . . . nor" (*de . . . oude*) construction can define a progression of related ideas or define a related purpose or goal;[17] 5) the church-specific way in which Paul cites and applies creation texts, as seen in the comparisons of 1 Timothy 2 and 2 Corinthians 11:3, in matters of deception by false teachers, and 1 Timothy 4:4 and Romans 14 in the matter of permissible foods; and 6) the positive example of Deborah (Judges 4–5) in canonical history as a woman raised up by God to exercise leadership and authority—not just over a local assembly, but over the covenant *nation.*

It is also argued that the proposed reading of 1 Timothy 2:12 is consistent with and supportive of what might be termed Paul's "fundamental concerns for faith and order" in the Pastoral Epistles and his ministry generally: 1) the preservation of sound doctrine and the apostolic faith; 2) the unity and

---

16. Acts 2:17, "In the last days . . . your sons *and daughters* shall prophesy" indicates that in the New Testament age, the age of the outpouring of the Spirit, the church should be expecting more Deborahs, not fewer! What may have been exceptional in the Old Covenant can become usual in the New, fulfilling Moses's hope that at some time in the future "all the Lord's people" would be prophets: Num 11:29.

17. Belleville, "Teaching and Usurping Authority," 218, gives as examples Matthew 6:20, "where thieves neither break in nor steal" [i.e., break in with a view to steal]; and Acts 17:24, God "neither dwells in temples made with human hands nor is served by human hands" [i.e., dwells in human temples with a view to being served by human hands]. The translation proposed here is similar to Belleville's renderings: "I do not permit a woman to teach with a view to dominating a man" or "I do not permit a woman to teach a man in a dominating way": 219.

good order of the churches; 3) the solidarity and harmony of Christian families. It is evident that in the Pastorals the apostle is concerned with problems that are arising on all three fronts. The problem of false teaching is frequently mentioned (1 Tim 1:4-7; 4:1-3,7; 5:15; 6:3-5; 2 Tim 2:16-18, 25-26; 3:8, 9; 4:3, 4; Titus 1:10-11; 3:9-11). There are insubordinate men and empty talkers who are disturbing the church (Titus 1:10). In terms of family life, there are problems with women who are being deceived by false teachers (2 Tim 3:6); some of the younger widows have already strayed after Satan (1 Tim 5:15); some false teachers are even upsetting whole families (Titus 1:11).

In the face of these problems facing the community in Ephesus, Paul stresses the importance of sound doctrine (1 Tim 1:3,10, 4:6,16; 2 Tim 1:14; 4:3; Titus 1:9; 2:1), good order in the church (1 Tim 3:15; see 1 Cor 14:40, "decently and in order"), and good order in the family (1 Tim 3:24, 5:14; Titus 1:6). As Paul contemplates the end of his own life's work and the transition to the second generation of Christian leadership, he is naturally concerned to "tighten up the ship" in its faith and order in order that the churches might weather the storms which are to come in the last days (2 Tim 3:1; see 4:3-4).

In light of these local problems, where women are being misled by false teachers, and where some women may be teaching in a domineering, abrasive, or alienating fashion that creates conflict and division in the assembly and in marriages,[18] the apostle does not permit such women to be placed in positions of leadership in the church. On the other hand, in other circumstances, where gifted women are sound in the faith, and have a way of teaching that is not dividing the assembly or marriage relationships in the church—where the apostle's "fundamental concerns for faith and order" are satisfied, then the way would be clear to recognize the calling of such gifted women and set them apart for leadership in the church.

---

18. Such a circumstance in Ephesus—of "over-liberated" and domineering women—would make understandable the reference in v. 13 to the order of creation, "Adam was formed first, then Eve," reflective of Paul's understanding of male headship in the Christian family, as seen also in 1 Corinthians 11:3 and Ephesians 5:22-24. In terms of contemporary parlance, it could be said that the "in-your-face" demeanor of some women in Ephesus was being rebuked as inconsistent with the respect that should be shown to husbands as the heads of families, in light of the "headship" or "primogeniture" principle read from Genesis. The point of view represented in this paper is not strictly "egalitarian," since it recognizes a "headship" principle in Paul with respect to Christian marriage, and a "traditional" reading of Ephesians 5:22-33, and yet neither is it "traditional" or "hierarchicalist," since it argues for the validity of women in senior leadership positions in the church for all the reasons given above. The position could perhaps be called a "differential" position on matters of gender and role relationships; see the article by Blomberg cited above, "Neither Hierarchicalist Nor Egalitarian."

Arguably, Deborah during the period of the judges could be viewed as an example of such a gifted and called woman, whose ministry was consistent with the "fundamental concerns for faith and order": raised up by the Spirit of God; administering the law of Moses with justice, impartiality, and discernment; recognized and accepted by the community, and with no indications in the biblical text that her ministry created domestic difficulties with her husband Lapidoth. Churches today would be well advised to reconsider the "traditional" readings of 1 Timothy 2:12 that bar women from certain leadership roles in the church. Traditional readings of the text may be in danger, however unintentionally, of quenching the Spirit (1 Thess 5:19), of stifling the service of gifted women, and depriving the churches of able leadership—at a time in redemptive history (Acts 2:17) when the people of God should be expecting more, not fewer "Deborahs."

11

Incarnation, Trinity, and the Ordination of Women to the Priesthood

IN MY EARLIER CHAPTER[1] on 1 Tim 2:12 and the ordination of women I argued that Paul's *contextual* and *church-specific* reading and application of the creation texts indicates that the limitations on women's teaching roles in the church are circumstantial rather than universal prohibitions. In this chapter I wish to address arguments in a specifically Anglican[2] context that were not addressed in the previous one, namely, arguments based on the incarnation and the Father-Son relationship within the Trinity that are thought to bar the ordination of women as priests and bishops. For the purposes of this study I will be focusing on two documents as sources for the main arguments to be considered in this Anglican context: the essay "Priestesses in the Church?" by C. S. Lewis,[3] and "A Report of the Study Concerning the Ordination of Women Undertaken by the Anglican Mission in America," Rev. John H. Rodgers, chairman.[4]

It is not the purpose of this article to discuss three other sets of arguments that are here considered secondary to the primary theological issues being addressed: the canonical irregularity or illegality of the first ordination of women to the priesthood in the Episcopal Church USA (ECUSA) in

---

1. See chapter 10 above. I would like to thank my colleagues in the Division of Christian Thought at Gordon-Conwell Theological Seminary for their comments and suggestions on this present chapter.

2. Similar arguments could be made within Roman Catholic and Orthodox contexts as well.

3. The essay originally appeared under the title "Notes on the Way" in *Time and Tide* 29 (August 14, 1948), when the debate on women's ordination was just getting under way in the Church of England.

4. This report was completed in 2003.

1974 and 1975;[5] issues arising from the feminist movement and the "culture wars"; or the argument against women priests from patristic authority and church tradition. With regard to the "culture wars," cultural conservatives tend to see the ordination of women as symptomatic of a feminist movement that destabilizes the family and society generally;[6] cultural progressives and egalitarians tend to see male-dominant readings of Scripture as increasing the dangers of domestic violence and abuse.[7] Neither side in this "culture wars" discussion is likely to persuade the other, and this line of inquiry will not be considered further.

With respect to patristic authority and church tradition, it is certainly the case that both support the traditional view of a male-only priesthood. Nevertheless, while patristic and ecclesiastical tradition has significant weight in an Anglican context, the tradition is not irreformable, and can be overcome by the Scriptures more rightly and adequately understood. During the Galileo controversy the Vatican could rightly point to a patristic and later church tradition that was solidly on the side of a geocentric understanding of biblical texts such as Psalm 19, Joshua 10:13, and Psalm 93:1, and yet as history shows, the church was later to correct its earlier understanding of these texts in the light of new evidence and better hermeneutical principles.[8] Such may also be the case with regard to traditional understandings of the biblical texts regarding the ordination of women.

Incarnation: The Male Priest as "Icon of Christ"

In his 1948 essay, "Priestesses in the Church?," Lewis recognized that any decision by the Church of England to ordain women as priests would likely be very divisive: dividing the Church of England from other historic churches, and dividing the church internally against itself. In hindsight, Lewis proved to be correct on both counts. But in Lewis's own mind, the central problem

---

5. For background on these ordinations, see Radner and Turner, *The Fate of Communion*, 17–18. The canonically irregular nature of these ordinations notwithstanding, it may still be the case (as here argued) that such ordinations could have been done with proper biblical and theological justification. The actual effect of the ordinations, understandably, was to harden the opposition of conservative clergy within ECUSA to the ordination of women as priests, given the association of its first instances with liberal theology and violation of canon law.

6. See, for example, Ayers, "The Inevitability of Failure."

7. See, for example, Kroeger and Beck, eds., *Women, Abuse, and the Bible*, 16–27.

8. On the role of biblical interpretation during the Galileo controversy, see the excellent scholarly studies by Blackwell, *Galileo, Bellarmine, and the Bible*, and Howell, *God's Two Books*.

was theological in nature, relating to the very nature of the incarnation itself. A priest is a double representative, representing the people to God, and God to the people. Lewis had no problem with a woman representing the people to God, but he did have a problem with a woman representing God to the people.[9] But what is the problem here: "Since God is in fact not a biological being and has no sex, what can it matter whether we say He or She, Father or Mother, Son or Daughter?"[10]

Lewis's answer is that "God himself has taught us how to speak of Him."[11] The masculine language of the Bible is not of merely human origin; it is neither arbitrary nor unessential."A child who has been taught to pray to a Mother in Heaven would have a religious life radically different from that of a Christian child"; "equal" does not mean "interchangeable," and Lewis believed the gender language of the Bible was intended to "symbolize to us the hidden things of God."[12] Jesus Christ was the true High Priest, and the incarnation took place in the form of a male, not a female."Only one wearing the masculine uniform can (provisionally, and until the Parousia) represent the Lord to the Church: for we are all, corporately and individually, feminine to Him."[13]

How compelling is this argument from the incarnation and the male gender of Jesus? There is no question that Jesus was indeed the High Priest of the New Covenant, and that Jesus was of the male gender; however, there are a number of serious problems with this line of argument.

First of all, this line of argument overlooks the fact that the nature of priesthood has fundamentally changed in the transition from the Old to the New Covenant. In the Old Covenant, it was the case that all priests were male; it is also true that Jesus Christ, the great High Priest (Heb 9:11, 10:12–14) of the New Covenant, who completed and fulfilled the meaning of the Old Testament priesthood, was a male. The key change, however, is that in the New Testament church, *all* believers are priests, offering sacrifices of praise and thanksgiving to God (1 Pet 2:5, 9). Both male and female are "priests" in the New Testament usage of the term (see also Rev 5:10, "You have made them to be a Kingdom and priests to our God"). The word *priest* in the New Testament church is not limited to one male who stands before an earthly "altar"; the true altar is in heaven, where Christ, the High Priest, continues to represent us as his people before God (Heb 8:2, 9:24, "to appear

---

9. Lewis, "Priestesses in the Church?," 236.
10. Ibid.
11. Ibid., 237.
12. Ibid.
13. Ibid., 239.

for us in God's presence"; 10:21, "We have a great priest over the house of God"). There is only *one* mediator between man and God, the man Christ Jesus (1 Tim 2:4); believers in the New Testament are no longer dependent on a single human mediator, but have immediate access to the Father, by faith, through Jesus Christ alone (Heb 10:22: "let us draw near to God with a sincere heart *in full assurance* of faith").

In the second place, the (male) priest as "icon of Christ" argument misunderstands and overspecifies the purpose of the incarnation. While it is certainly true that Jesus became incarnate as a male, the fundamental point is that God assumed a full and complete *human nature*—a human nature that represents both male and female. In the prologue of John's gospel, it is famously stated, "And the Word became *flesh* (*sarx*) and dwelt among us . . ." (John 1:14). It does not say, "And the Word became a *male* (*aner*)."

It should also be noticed that in the incarnation, Jesus is not only a male by gender, but more specifically, a *Jewish, unmarried, physically unblemished* male. (No one could be ordained to the Levitical priesthood who was blind, lame, deformed, crippled, or with eye defects: Lev 21:17–21). Would anyone want to argue today, in the New Covenant, that a priest, to be an "icon of Christ," representing God to the people, must necessarily be an unmarried, "unblemished," Jewish male? Certainly not; it is thus apparent that such characteristics are *circumstantial* rather than *essential* characteristics of one who is to assume a full and complete *human* (not merely male) nature for the purpose of redeeming human nature, of both men and women, and bringing them to God.

Both male and female are made in the image of God (Gen 1:27); both genders reflect the character of God. From the fact that God became incarnate as a *Jewish* man it does not follow that Jews can be closer to God than Gentiles, or that Jews are better "icons" of God than Gentiles. Nor does it follow from the fact that God became incarnate as a Jewish *man* that males are inherently better "icons" of God than women. Jesus was in fact a *free* man, but assumed the form of a *slave* (Phil 2:5–11) in the incarnation; both slave and free man can in different ways serve as "icons" of God. The good news is that in the New Covenant, these distinctions are overcome (Gal 3:28: "neither Jew nor Gentile, slave nor free, male nor female, for you are all one in Christ Jesus"); all have equal access to God and to God's grace.

This having been said, it remains the case that Jesus as male Priest/Son of God by fact of the incarnation is reflective of and rooted in the Father-Son language of the Trinity. It is indeed the case that the language of God in Scripture is predominantly though not exclusively male; we can agree that the male language of God in the Bible is neither "arbitrary nor nonessential."

It is not to be construed simply as a culturally conditioned expression of the patriarchal Jewish culture of the biblical writers.

What then is the fundamental significance of the fact the God is revealed in Scripture as "Father, Son, and Holy Spirit," and not, say, as "Father, Mother, Child"? The question is, does the "Father-Son" language "valorize" the male imagery over the female? If so, is it really the case that "God is more like a man than a woman? That men are intrinsically closer to the nature and essence of God than women? That male gender is intrinsically more fitting to reflect the nature of God than the female?" These are crucial questions, and entire social orders have been built on the answers!

The position here argued, however, is a "No" to the above questions; that maleness is not in fact more similar to the divine essence than femaleness; and that the male language of the Trinity is a *circumstantial* (though not arbitrary) and not *essential* characteristic of the trinitarian revelation of Scripture.

First of all, following Aquinas and the mainstream of historic orthodox theology generally, it is to be recognized that all biblical and human language about God is *analogical* and not strictly *literal* in nature. As Aquinas stated, "things are said of God and creatures analogically and not in a purely equivocal nor in a purely univocal sense . . . . These names are said of God and creatures in an analogous sense, that is, according to proportion."[14] The word "Father" is predicated of a human father and of God as Father in an analogical sense, according to proportion. God is really like a human father in some respects, but being infinite and perfect, not *just* like or *only* like a human father, but infinitely greater than any human father.

God is a spirit by nature (John 4:24), and so is not literally a gendered being, though revealed (analogically) through gendered human language. If the nature of God was in fact "male" in some metaphysically ultimate sense, then one might have expected a revelation of the triune name in *exclusively* male imagery, such as "Father, Son, and Elder Brother," or something of the like. The language of "Father, Son, Holy Spirit," while seemingly predominantly (two-thirds?) male, is "neuter" on the Spirit (*pneuma*). And "Ruach" (Spirit) in the Hebrew is feminine, while *ho paraklatos* ("the Comforter") is masculine in the Greek—which is an indication that the Holy Spirit transcends literal human gender categories. Since the Holy Spirit is a coequal, coeternal person of the Holy Trinity, possessing the same "power, substance, and glory," the *lack* of a specific gender for the Spirit can be no less truly revelatory of the nature of God than the "male" gender language of Son and Father.

---

14. Aquinas, *Summa Theologica* Pt. I, Q. 13, art. 5, "Whether What Is Said of God and of Creatures Is Univocally Predicated of Them?"

It can also be noted that God is also described in Scripture even in terms that are *impersonal:* God is a "Rock" (Isa 17:1: "You have forgotten God your Savior; you have not remembered the Rock, your fortress); "Fire" (Deut 4:24: "the Lord your God is a consuming fire"); "Light" (1 John 1:5, "God is Light, and in him there is no darkness at all"). These impersonal, analogical descriptors reflect the strength, solidity, holiness, moral purity, and truthfulness of God's nature, while balancing overly *anthropomorphic* conceptions of God (as, for example, in the gods and goddesses of the Greek pantheon).

The fundamental core assertion of the triune name of God as Father, Son, and Holy Spirit is the *personal* nature of God: *ultimate reality is a communion of coequal, coeternal divine persons in holy, loving relationships.* The triune community is the ontological basis of all human community and communion. It is here argued that the fundamental significance of the "male" language of the Trinity is an analogical revelation of the *strength and power of God to create and redeem:* God is the "Almighty" maker of heaven and earth, the "Divine Warrior" (e.g., Exod 15:3, "the Lord is a warrior") who is strong to redeem his people from their enemies.[15] The male language of God is *power* language that signifies that God is powerful to create and to save—that God is indeed the true God; there is no other.

At the same time, the feminine images of God in Scripture—less prominent, but not insignificant—"Mother" (Isa 42:14); woman (Luke 15:8–10); hen (Matt 23:37), and so forth—signify that God *nurtures and protects* as well as creates and redeems. Both the "power" language and the "nurturing" language speak truly of God; both are reflective of God's character, just as male and female made in God's image can both reflect the true character of God.

The revelation of the personal, triune God as "Father, Son, Holy Spirit" and not as, say, "Father, Mother, Child" distinguishes the true God from the sexually active gods and goddesses of ancient Near Eastern polytheism: from Baal and Asherah and other gods and goddesses of the ancient world.[16] *Yahweh has no consort:* the God of Abraham, Isaac, and Jacob, later more fully revealed as the God and Father of Jesus Christ, as Father, Son, and Holy Spirit, is no *fertility god* tied to the cycles of nature. In the Bible,

---

15. Bloesch also relates the masculine imagery of God in Scripture to the power, initiative, and mighty acts of God (*Is the Bible Sexist?*, 72), but also makes the questionable claim that "masculine images predominate for all three persons of the Trinity": 69. This latter claim seems rather dubious in light of the scriptural images of the Spirit: wind, fire, oil, water, dove—all of which are *impersonal* and not masculine.

16. On the development of the Yahwistic religion of Israel against the background of the gods and goddesses of Canaanite religion, see Day, *Yahweh and the Gods and Goddesses of Canaan*.

"father gods" and "mother goddesses" do not sexually procreate "baby gods and goddesses." The true God is the creator of human sexuality and genders, yet is not literally a gendered being, but eternally an infinite, personal spirit. The Father-Son relationship of the Bible is a personal and covenantal but not a *sexual* relationship.

At the same time, it is not the case that the biblical language of God as Father is merely arbitrary or only a reflection of cultural conditioning. The Father-Son language of the biblical and trinitarian tradition is rooted in the prayer language of Jesus, who taught his disciples to address God as "Father." Jesus took a designation of God that was relatively infrequent in the Old Testament, and reflective of God's fatherhood of the *nation* of Israel, and made it *central* to the Christian understanding of God, and intensely *personal* as well, foundational to the disciples' personal relationship to God.

The Father-Son language of the Scriptures, and especially the nature of Jesus' relation to the Father in the New Testament, is a revelation of a true Father-Son relationship, and a model of how human fathers and sons should relate in the community of faith. The father-son relationship is a crucial human relationship in all cultures, and the biblical revelation of Father and Son teaches a healthy balance of strength and love, of authority and intimacy,[17] that makes for healthy families, healthy churches, and a healthy social order generally.

The Rodgers-Grudem Argument: Eternal Subordination in the Trinity?

The second major type of argument against the ordination of women as priests (and bishops) is based on a claim that in the life of the Trinity, the Son is eternally subordinate to the Father, and that this, by way of analogy, provides justification for the subordination of women to men in the ordained ministry of the church. Examples of this type of argument may be found in the writings of John Rodgers[18] and Wayne Grudem.[19]

According to Rodgers, "God's ordering of the relations of male and female in the family ultimately reflects and rests upon God's own triune nature.... An eternal headship and submission are lived out in the divine

---

17. One evangelical pastor made the observation that in his pastoral counseling experience, many men in the church were either *abusive* or, on the other hand, too *passive*: it was the exception rather than the rule in his experience to find a healthy balance of strength and love, of authority and intimacy in these Christian marriages.

18. Rodgers Jr., "A Report."

19. Grudem, *Countering the Claims of Evangelical Feminism*, 230–56. See also his *Systematic Theology*, 248–54, and *Evangelical Feminism and Biblical Truth*, 45–48.

life of love. God the Father . . . is eternally the Father of the Son . . . . Loving headship and submission are eternal in the life of God."[20] "The headship of the man reflects God's Fatherhood in the life of the Trinity . . . . The nuclear family is the 'little church in the Church' and the Church is the family of the families of God."[21] The submission by women to male authority in the church presumably is a reflection of the Son's eternal submission to the Father in the Trinity.[22]

Grudem makes the striking claim that the "subjection of the Son to the Father for all eternity, a subjection that never began but always existed, and a subjection that will continually in the future, does not nullify the deity of the Son."[23] Grudem wants to preserve the historic Nicene orthodoxy which insists that in the divine essence the Son is fully equal to the Father (*homoousios*), but insist that in *role and status* the Son is eternally subordinate to the Father. (As we shall see, this claim cannot be sustained.) He cites texts that speak of the Father "giving" and "sending" the Son to argue for a "unique headship, a unique authority for the Father *before* the Son came to earth,"[24] and appeals to texts such as Ephesians 1:4, John 1:3 ("all things were made *through* him"), and 1 Corinthians 15:28 to argue that the "Son is eternally submissive to the Father."[25] Grudem concludes that the alleged "eternal subordination of the Son to the Father" shows how "equality in being, in value and in honor can exist together with differences in roles between husband and wife as well,"[26] and by implication, in the subordination of women to men in the church as well.

These arguments of Grudem show, unfortunately, how a particular social and cultural agenda—arguing for male "headship" over women—can lead to serious distortions in the reading of Scripture and of the historic doctrine of the Trinity. The thesis of the "eternal subordination of the Son to the Father" is, as we shall see, a serious doctrinal deviation from the historic understanding of the doctrine of the Trinity. The fact that this point of view appears to be gaining some ground in evangelical circles is to be viewed with alarm.[27] This way of arguing on (mistaken) trinitarian grounds for the

---

20. Rodgers Jr., "A Report," 23.

21. Ibid., 25.

22. Rodgers does not seem to consider the question, "If the Son is eternally subordinate to the Father, does this mean that women should be *eternally* subordinate to men—even in heaven?"

23. Grudem, *Countering the Claims of Evangelical Feminism*, 244.

24. Ibid., 231.

25. Ibid., 246.

26. Ibid.

27. See, for example, Ware, *Father, Son, and Holy Spirit*, 76–102; and Kostenberger,

subordination of women to men in the ordained ministries of the church has serious logical, historical, and biblical-theological problems, as we shall see below.

In the first place, it is simply a *non sequitur* to conclude from the premise "The Son is eternally subordinate to the Father" that "Women are subordinate to men in the church." (Let it be noted clearly: the truth of this first premise is *not* being granted in this chapter; it is in fact believed to be false.) The argument seems to be of the following structure: "Suppose that it is the case that the Son is eternally subordinate to the Father; this shows that subordination in role or function is compatible with equality of essence or nature; therefore, this supports our conclusion that women should be subordinate to men in the ordained offices of the church, since women can have equality with men by nature but be subordinate to men in roles and authority in the church."

This is an attempted argument by analogy, and arguments from analogy are only persuasive, and rarely demonstrative, since argument by analogy depends on the degrees of likeness or dissimilarity between the items being compared. In this case the analogy is more *dissimilar* than similar. Consider the comparison in question: "Father is to Son (in the eternal Trinity) as man should be to woman (in the ordained ministries of the church)." The problem here is that the comparison is between, *eternal, infinite, divine, discarnate persons* in the eternal Trinity, of the "same gender," and *temporal, finite, enfleshed, human persons* of different genders in the historical church: the differences are much greater than the similarities. This stretches the analogy to the breaking point and evacuates the plausibility of the comparison. Furthermore, even if it could be argued that "subordination in role is consistent with equality of dignity or nature," it does not follow that this *must* be the case in male-female role relationships in ministry; this must be argued on other (exegetical) grounds.

This type of argument also seems to be guilty of the fallacy of reading a certain understanding of the human father-son relationship in time back into the eternal life of the Trinity. Human father-son relationships change over time. From birth through adolescence and until full adulthood is achieved, the son is dependent upon and subordinate to the father's

---

Encountering John, 160, 170. For earlier criticism of this trend, see Giles, *The Trinity and Subordinationism* and *Jesus and the Father*. See also Letham, *Holy Trinity*, 479-96, for Letham's responses to the (egalitarian) positions of Gilbert Bilezikian and Kevin Giles. Letham correctly notes that the historic orthodox recognition of an order (*taxis*) within the Trinity—Father first, Son second, Spirit third—does not imply any subordination of rank, status, or hierarchy within the Trinity: "I repeatedly assert that this order is compatible with the full equality of the three persons in the undivided Trinity": 481.

authority. Over time, however, the relationship changes; the adult son can relate to his father as a friend, according to the father continuing respect, but not owing unquestioning obedience. At the end of the life cycle, it can be the father who is "subordinate" to the son financially and otherwise, and dependent upon a younger and healthier son. The so-called complementarian argument in this matter seems to be guilty of selecting one aspect of a changing relationship (when son is dependent on the father) and importing *that* temporally conditioned aspect back into the eternal Father-Son relationship within the Trinity. When George W. Bush was president, he still owed his father George H. W. Bush respect, but while the son was in the White House, the older Bush was subordinate to the younger Bush in authority and prestige.

Historic Trinitarian Orthodoxy: Eternal Equality of the Father and Son

The historic, orthodox understanding of the Christian doctrine of the Trinity is that in eternity, in the "immanent" Trinity (the *theologia*), the Son is in all things equal to the Father. In time, during his incarnate, earthly ministry (the *oikonomia*, or "economic" Trinity), the Son was *voluntarily* subordinate (in function, not essence) to the Father. The historic creeds and the church fathers were insistent that this distinction between the *theologia* and the *oikonomia* was crucial for right interpretations of the Scriptural texts regarding Christ, and for avoiding the various forms of subordinationism that had arisen in the church from the time of Origen to that of Arius. The basic error of the "New Evangelical Subordinationists"[28] is their failure to maintain this proper distinction between the *theologia* and the *oikonomia*.

The Constantinopolitan Creed, generally known as the Nicene Creed, has, since the time of the Council of Chalcedon (451), been associated with the second ecumenical Council of Constantinople (381), and has been used in the liturgy of the Eucharist from the sixth century onward. Since the time of Chalcedon, it has become the most universally accepted of all the Christian creeds, acknowledged as a standard of orthodoxy by East and West alike.[29] Formulated to refute the Arian subordinationism of the Son to the Father, the creed emphatically asserts the essential equality of the Son and the Father:

---

28. On this terminology, see note 34 below.
29. Leith, *Creeds of the Churches*, 31–32.

> We believe ... in one Lord Jesus Christ, the only-begotten Son of God, begotten from the Father before all time, Light from Light, true God from true God, begotten not created, of the same essence as the Father (*homoousion to patri*), through Whom all things came into being ... .[30]

An important commentary on this expression of Nicene orthodoxy is contained in a synodical letter of the bishops who had gathered in Constantinople, issued shortly afterward in 382. Some of these bishops had suffered violent persecution from the Arians for defending the Nicene faith: "It was barely yesterday ... that some [of the orthodox bishops] were freed from the bonds of exile and returned to their own churches through a thousand tribulations .... Even after their return from exile some experienced a ferment of hatred from the heretics .... Others were torn to shreds by various tortures and still carry around on their bodies the marks of Christ's wounds and bruises."[31] For these orthodox bishops, the full deity and equality of the Son to the Father was no small matter, but a truth worth dying for!

The synodical letter makes it clear that the bishops affirmed the eternal equality of nature and dignity of the Father and the Son. The Nicene Creed, stated the bishops,

> tells us how to believe in the name of the Father, the Son and of the Holy Spirit: believing also, of course, that the Father, the Son and the Holy Spirit have a single Godhead and power and substance, *a dignity deserving the same honour and a co-eternal sovereignty* [emphasis added] in three most perfect hypostases, or three perfect Persons .... To sum up, we know that he was before the ages fully God the Word, and that in the last days he became fully man for the sake of our salvation.[32]

The last sentence above reflects the distinction that was to become classic in orthodox Christology and trinitarian doctrine, namely, that in eternity, in the *theologia*, the Son is in all things equal to the Father as to deity, while in the *oikonomia*, he became voluntarily subordinate to the Father with respect to his human nature.

The critical phrase in the synodical letter above is "a dignity deserving the same honour and a co-eternal sovereignty" (*homotimou te axias kai sunaidiou tes basileias*).[33] Having just stated that the Father, Son, and Holy

---

30. Ibid., 33.
31. Tanner, ed., *Decrees of the Ecumenical Councils*, 25.
32. Ibid., 28.
33. Ibid.

Spirit have a "single Godhead (*theoteitos*) and power and substance (*ousias*), the bishops make it clear that they believe that the Father and the Son have a "coeternal sovereignty" (*basileias*). There is simply no way that "coeternal sovereignty" can be squared with an eternal *subordination* of the Son to the Father. Equal sovereignty means equal *authority, power, and honor*—not less.

The "New Evangelical Subordinationists"[34] have simply misread the tradition on this crucial point.

This reading of the Nicene Creed is further supported by the statements of Gregory of Nazianzus, one of the Cappadocian fathers who was greatly influential in the formation of historic trinitarian orthodoxy. In his *Fifth Theological Oration*, in a series of influential lectures given in the Church of the Anastasis in Constantinople prior to the Council of 381, Gregory ("the Theologian") clearly articulated his understanding of the eternal equality of the Father and the Son:

> We believe in three Persons. For one is not more and another less God; nor is one before and another after; nor are they divided in will or parted in power . . . . When we look at the Godhead . . . at the Persons in whom the Godhead dwells, and at those who *timelessly and with equal glory* [emphasis added] . . . there are three whom we worship. Each of these Persons possesses unity . . . by reason of the identity of essence and power . . . I hope it may always be my position . . . to worship God the Father, God the Son, God the Holy Ghost, three Persons, one Godhead, *undivided in honor and glory and substance and kingdom* . . . .[emphasis added][35]

For Gregory, one of the founders of Nicene, trinitarian orthodoxy, the Father and the Son were eternally equal not only in *substance*, but also in *honor* and *glory* and *kingdom*. A coequal and coeternal "kingdom" implies coequal *authority* of the Son with the Father, and flies in the face of the misunderstandings of the "New Evangelical Subordinationists."

---

34. The "New Evangelical Subordinationists" are those who, like Grudem, Ware, and Kostenberger, are trying to argue for the eternal subordination of the Son to the Father in the interests of arguing for the subordination of women to men in the family and in the ordained ministries of the church.

35. Nazianzus, *Fifth Theological Oration*, 14, 28. On Gregory's trinitarian thought, see Fulford, "'One Commixture of Light.'" Fulford points out that Gregory does speak of the Father as the "source" and "cause" of the Son, but these statements are to be read in the context of Gregory's equally clear statements about the equality of the Father and the Son.

In a synod at Rome in 382, Pope Damasus issued the so-called "Tome of Pope Damasus," clearly affirming the deity and equality of the Son and Spirit with the Father:

> 1. We anathematize those who do not wholly freely proclaim that he (the Holy Spirit) is one power and substance with the Father and the Son. . . . 12. Anyone who does not say that the Son of God is true God, as the Father is true God, that he can do all things, and knows all things, and is equal to the Father, is heretical . . . . 20. Anyone who does not say that there is only one godhead, one might, one majesty, one power, one glory, one lordship, one kingdom, one will and one truth of the Father and of the Son and of the Holy Spirit is heretical.[36]

This declaration of 382 clearly asserts the equality of the Son to the Father not only in "substance" or essence, but also in *might, majesty, power, glory, lordship, kingdom*, and *will*. Denial of the equality of the Son with the Father in "might, majesty, power, glory, lordship, kingdom, and will" is considered heretical.

These latter statements leave no room for an eternal subordination of the Son to the Father in "role" or "status" before the incarnation. This statement representative of the Latin church is consistent with the earlier statements noted above (the synodical letter of 382 of the bishops meeting in Constantinople, and the *Fifth Theological Oration* of Gregory Nazianzus) from the leaders of the Greek churches, and shows the East-West consensus of trinitarian orthodoxy that was emerging at the close of the fourth century.

The so-called "Athanasian" Creed was likely written sometime between 381 and 428, and first appears in its currently accepted form toward the close of the eighth or the beginning of the ninth century.[37] It has long been considered a standard of trinitarian orthodoxy in the West. The Athanasian Creed is an able summary of the christological and trinitarian doctrines of the first four ecumenical councils, and emphatically and repeatedly asserts the equality of the Son with the Father, not any eternal *subordination* of the Son to the Father:

> 6. But the Godhead of the Father, of the Son, and of the Holy Ghost, is all one; the Glory equal, the majesty coeternal (*aequalis Gloria, coaeterna majestas*) . . . . 13. So likewise the Father is Almighty: the Son Almighty (*omnipotens*): and the Holy Ghost Almighty . . . . 17. So likewise the Father is Lord: the Son Lord

---

36. Quoted in Rahner, ed., *The Teaching of the Catholic Church*, 90–91.

37. Cross, "Athanasian Creed," *The Oxford Dictionary of the Christian Church*, 98–99; Schaff, *The Creeds of Christendom*, vol. 2, 31–36.

> (*dominus*): and the Holy Ghost Lord . . . . 19. For like as we are compelled by the Christian verity: to acknowledge every Person by himself to be God and Lord (*Deum ac Dominum*) . . . . 25. And in this Trinity none is before, or after another: none is greater, or less than another (*nihil majus, aut minus*) . . . . 26. But the whole three Persons are coeternal, and coequal (*coaequales*) . . . . 33. Equal to the Father, as touching his Godhead: and inferior to the Father as touching his Manhood (*minor Patre secundum humanitem*).[38]

It is abundantly evident that the explicit terminology of the Athanasian Creeds excludes any notion of "eternal subordination" of the Son to the Father: "the Glory equal, the Majesty coeternal . . . the Son Almighty . . . the Son Lord . . . every Person *by himself* [emphasis added] God and Lord . . . in this Trinity . . . None is greater, or less than another . . . But the whole three Persons are coeternal, and *coequal* [emphasis added]." There is no eternal subordination of rank or status of the Son to the Father; the Son is only "inferior to the Father as touching his *Manhood*" [emphasis added], that is, after the incarnation, and with respect to the economy (*oikonomia*), not the eternal, pretemporal *theologia* or immanent Trinity. Schaff has correctly noted that in the Athanasian Creed, in the Trinity "there is no priority or posteriority of time, no superiority or inferiority of rank, but the three persons are coeternal and coequal."[39]

In 675 a local council at Toledo formulated a creed expressing clear formulations regarding the doctrines of the Trinity and the incarnation:

> In all things the Son is equal to God the Father, for his being born had no beginning and no end . . . . It must also be confessed and believed that each single Person is wholly God in himself and that all three Persons together are one God. They have one, or undivided, equal godhead, majesty or power, which is not diminished in the individuals nor augmented in the three.[40]

This creed, reflecting the teachings of the Athanasian Creed and doctors of the church such as Augustine should, in the estimation of the noted Roman Catholic theologian Karl Rahner, "be numbered among the most important doctrinal declarations of the Church."[41] It clearly gives no support to ideas of an "eternal subordination" of the Son to the Father.

---

38. Schaff, *The Creeds of Christendom*, vol. 2, 66-69.
39. Ibid., 38.
40. Rahner, ed., *The Teaching of the Catholic Church*, 92, 95.
41. Ibid., 92.

In 680 the sixth ecumenical council, meeting in Constantinople, issued a dogmatic decree against the Monothelites, who held that there was only one will in Christ. The council's definition stated that Jesus Christ had two distinct but inseparable wills—a human will and a divine will—both acting in harmony, with the human will always acting in subordination to the divine will; will being regarded as an attribute of the nature rather than the person:[42]

> And we preach, according to the doctrine of the holy Fathers, *two natural wills* and two natural active principles inseparably, immovably, undividedly, and unconfusedly in him (Christ). And two natural wills, *not opposing each other,* as heretics assert, but his human will following without resistance or reluctance, but rather subject to his divine and omnipotent will . . . The human will had to be moved to submit to the divine will . . . as he (Christ) himself says: 'Because I came down from heaven, not to do my own will, but the will of him who sent me (John 6:38), calling his own will the will of the flesh. For the flesh, too, was his own.[43]

In this important dogmatic definition regarding the person of Christ there are significant implications for the present discussion of the nature of the Father-Son relationship in the Trinity. The orthodox teaching is that the "subordination" of the Son to the Father is the willing subordination of the *human* will of the incarnate Christ, in the *oikonomia,* to the *one* undivided *divine* will common to Father, Son, and Holy Spirit.

There are not three separate wills in the Trinity, but one undivided will common to all three, as stated earlier in the tradition. Recall the statement of Pope Damasus (382) noted earlier: "Anyone who does not say that there is only one godhead, one might, one majesty, one power, one glory, one lordship, one kingdom, *one will* and one truth of the Father and of the Son and of the Holy Spirit is heretical."[44] The letter of Pope Agatho and the Roman synod of 125 bishops sent to instruct the legates of the Council of Constantinople in 680 states that in the Holy Trinity "one is the godhead, one the eternity, one the power, one the kingdom, one the glory, one the adoration, *one the essential will and operation* [emphasis added] of the same Holy and inseparable Trinity."[45]

---

42. Schaff, *The Creeds of Christendom,* vol. 2, 72.
43. Rahner, ed., *The Teaching of the Catholic Church,* 169.
44. Ibid., 90–91.
45. Quoted in Percival, *The Seven Ecumenical Councils of the Undivided Church,* 340.

If there were *three* wills in the godhead, it could make sense to posit an "eternal subordination" of the will of the Son to the will of the Father, but there is one will common to the three persons, not three. Historic orthodoxy teaches one nature and three persons but not three wills in the Trinity. The "New Evangelical Subordinationists" seem to be guilty of projecting the economic subordination of the human will of the incarnate Son back into the eternal life of the Trinity, and so erase the historic trinitarian distinction of the *theologia* and the *oikonomia*—the patristic hermeneutical principle for interpreting the New Testament Christological texts and guarding against the heresies of Arianism and semi-Arianism.

The historic Reformation and post-Reformation creeds continue the earlier traditions of trinitarian orthodoxy. The Belgic Confession of 1561 states that all three persons of the Trinity are "co-eternal and co-essential. *There is neither first nor last* [emphasis added]; for they are all three one, in truth, *in power*, in goodness, and mercy."[46]

Chapter three of the Second Helvetic Confession of 1566 states that in the Trinity there are not "three gods, but three persons, consubstantial, coeternal, and coequal. . . . We also condemn all heresies and heretics who teach . . . that there is something created and subservient, or subordinate to another in the Trinity (*item creatum ac serviens aut alteri officiale in trinitate*) and that there is something unequal in it, a greater or a less (*inaequale, majus aut minus*) . . . something different with respect to character or will (*voluntate*) . . . as the Monarchians . . . and such like, have thought."[47] If the Father and the Son do not differ according to *will*, there can clearly be no eternal subordination of the will of the Son to the Father; the Father and the Son are indeed coeternal, coequal, nothing "unequal" or a "greater or a less." The creed excludes all forms of subordinationism in very specific and explicit language.

Question nine of the Westminster Larger Catechism (1646) asks, "How many persons are there in the Godhead?" The answer is, "There be three persons in the Godhead, the Father, the Son, and the Holy Ghost, and these three are one true, eternal God, the same in substance, equal in power and glory; although distinguished by their personal properties."[48] This language of the Father, Son, and Holy Spirit being "equal in power and glory" reflects the historic trinitarian orthodoxy of the Athanasian creed.

Grudem appeals to biblical statements that the Son was "sent" by the Father (John 17:3 and 18, 4:34, 5:24, 8:16, 9:4, 16:5, 20:21), that all things

---

46. Schaff, *The Creeds of Christendom,* vol. 3, 390.
47. Ibid., 241.
48. *The Confession of Faith and Catechisms,* 160.

were made *through* [not "by"] him (John 1:3), and 1 Corinthians 15:28 ("The Son himself shall be subject to Him that put all things under him") to argue for "eternal differences in relationship within the Trinity."⁴⁹ These texts, however, and the orthodox trinitarian tradition do not support such an interpretation.

In his reply to the Macedonians, who denied the full equality and deity of the Holy Spirit, together with the Father and the Son, Basil ("the Great") of Caesarea, one of the Cappadocian fathers who laid the foundations of historic trinitarian orthodoxy, vigorously defended the equality of rank and glory of the Son with the Father:

> 13. The Son, according to them [Macedonians] is not together with the Father, but after the Father ... inasmuch as "with him" expresses equality of dignity, while "through him" denotes subordination. They further assert that the Spirit is not to be ranked along with the Father and the Son, but under the Son and the Father.... 14. Let us first ask them this question: In what sense do they say that the Son is "after the Father"; later in time, or in *order, or in dignity?* [emphasis added] .... 15. If they really conceive of a kind of degradation of the Son in relation to the Father, *as though he were in a lower place* [emphasis added], so that the Father sits above, and the Son is thrust off to the next seat below, let them confess what they mean .... What excuse can be found for their attack upon Scripture, shameless as their antagonism is, in the passages "Sit thou on my right hand," and "Sat down on the right hand of the majesty of God"? The expression "right hand of God" does not, as they [and Grudem: *Countering the Claims of Evangelical Feminism*, 235] contend, indicate the lower place, but *equality of relation* [emphasis added].... What just defence shall we have in the day of the aweful universal judgment of all creation, if ... we attempt to degrade him who shares the honor and the throne, from his condition of equality, to a lower state?⁵⁰

Basil clearly asserts the equality of dignity, honor, and rank of the Son with the Father, and would likely have seen the interpretations of the "New

---

49. Grudem, *Countering the Claims of Evangelical Feminism*, 246.

50. Basil the Great, *On the Holy Spirit*, vi. 13–15. The Macedonian heretics argued that biblical texts that said that the Spirit was "sent" by the Father and the Son implied that the Spirit was inferior to the Father and the Son; that the "Gift" was not on an equality with the Giver: Hanson, *The Search for the Christian Doctrine of God*, 768. The "New Evangelical Subordinationists" seem to apply something of a "Macedonian" hermeneutic and logic to their reading of biblical texts in the interest of finding an "eternal subordination of the Son to the Father."

Evangelical Subordinationists" as having some significant similarities with the Macedonian heresies that he attempted to combat.

In his great treatise on the Trinity, a foundational text for orthodox Western trinitarian theology, Augustine addresses the question of why it is said that the Son was "sent" by the Father:

> 27. But if the Son is said to be sent by the Father . . . this does not in any manner hinder us from believing the Son to be equal, and consubstantial, and coeternal with the Father . . . . Not because the one is greater, the other less; but because the one is Father, the other Son . . . . The Son . . . is said to have been sent because the "Word was made flesh" . . . that he might perform through his bodily presence those things which were written . . . . He was not sent in respect to any inequality of power or substance, *or anything that in Him was not equal to the Father* [emphasis added] . . . .[51]

For Augustine, the biblical language of the Father sending the Son implies not any eternal subordination of the Son to the Father, but rather the personal *distinction* between the Father and the Son, and the obedience of the incarnate Son in the *economy*.

Grudem appeals to 1 Corinthians 15:28, a text that was also a favorite text of the Arians in support of their subordinationist Christology. This text is understood by Aquinas in a way consistent with the historic orthodox tradition. In considering the question, "Whether the Son is equal to the Father in greatness," Aquinas argues that such a text, and others such as John 14:28 ("the Father is greater than I"), are to be understood "of Christ's human nature, wherein He is less than the Father, and subject to him; but in his divine nature He is equal to the Father. This is expressed by Athanasius, 'Equal to the Father in His Godhead; less than the Father in humanity.'"[52] "The Son is necessarily equal to the Father in power . . . . The command of the Father [John 14:31, "As the Father gave me commandment so do I"] . . . may be referred to Christ in His human nature."[53] Texts such as 1 Corinthians 15:28 may be properly understood to refer to Christ in the *economy*, with respect to his final act as the mediator and accomplisher of redemption in time, reporting "mission accomplished" to the Father, rather than to any eternal subordination of the Son to the Father.[54]

---

51. Augustine, *On the Trinity*, bk. IV, chs. 20, 27.
52. Aquinas, *Summa Theologica* I, Q. 42, art.4.
53. Ibid. I, Q. 42, art.6, "Whether the Son Is Equal to the Father in Power?"
54. In the same way, 1 Corinthians 11:3, "the head of Christ is God" refers to Christ in his human nature, in the economy, not to the eternal state.

This reading of 1 Corinthians 15:28 is confirmed by John's heavenly vision in the Apocalypse, where he sees the exalted Lamb in the *center* of God's throne (Rev 5:6), not in some lower position, and the Lamb receiving *coequal honor and praise* from every creature in the universe: "To him who sits upon the throne, *and* to the Lamb be praise and honor and glory and power, forever and ever!" (Rev 5:13). John's vision of the heavenly throne pictures the Son's coequal reign with the Father subsequent to his exaltation and the mediatorial actions presupposed in 1 Corinthians 15:28.

Grudem mistakenly argues that Jesus' being exalted to God's "right hand" (Ps 110:1) can still imply that Jesus was "subject to the Father's authority," and occupied a place of secondary authority.[55] As Richard Bauckham has correctly noted, while some rabbis read Psalm 110:1 to mean that the Messiah was only given a position of honor as a favored subject beside the throne, the early Christians read the text quite differently: Jesus is seated on the divine throne itself, "exercising God's own rule over all things."[56] The position of the exalted Messiah is not one of subordination, but one of equality and sovereign, universal lordship.

Since the central focus of the New Testament is the mighty acts of Jesus Christ in history for the redemption of his people, it is not surprising that most of the biblical revelation concerning Christ relates to the historical *economy* rather than to the pre-temporal *theologia*. Nevertheless, there is substantial witness in the New Testament to the full equality of the Son with the Father from eternity. The classic text with which John opens his gospel, John 1:1 ("In the beginning was the Word, and the Word was with God, and the Word *was God: kai theos hen ho logos*), clearly asserts the equality of the Son with the Father. As Murray J. Harris has noted, commenting on this text, "John seems intent to begin his work as he will end it (20:28), with an unqualified assertion of the supreme status of Jesus Christ, in both his preincarnate (1:1) and resurrection (20:28) states.... He, equally with the Father, is the legitimate object of human worship."[57] Harris suggests that

---

55. Grudem, *Countering the Claims of Evangelical Feminism*, 234–35.

56. Bauckham, *God Crucified*, 30. In Bauckham's groundbreaking new approach to New Testament Christology, focusing on a "Christology of Divine Identity" rather than on the older categories of "functional vs. ontological" Christologies, it can be recognized that "the unique sovereignty of God was not a mere 'function' which God could delegate to someone else. It was one of the key identifying characteristics of the unique divine identity.... When extended to include Jesus in the creative activity of God, and therefore in the eternal transcendence of God, it becomes unequivocally a matter of regarding Jesus as *intrinsic* to the unique identity of God.... The Christology of the divine identity common to the whole of the New Testament is the highest Christology of all": 41–42.

57. M. Harris, *Jesus as God*, 65. A text such as Ephesians 1:4 ("chosen [by the Father]

part of John's purpose in (1:1c, "was God") may have been to avoid any erroneous inference that might have been drawn from (1:1b, "with God") "and that since the Word was said to be 'with' the Father—not the Father 'with' the Word—he was in some way inferior or subordinate to God."[58]

Elsewhere in the New Testament Jesus Christ is called "our great God and savior" (Titus 2:13; see 2 Pet 1:1), *tou megalou theou kai soteros*, not, "our (lesser or subordinate) God and savior." The writer of Hebrews ascribes deity to Christ: "But of the Son he says, 'Your throne, O God, will last forever and ever" (Heb 1:8; Ps 45:6). The Son sits on Yahweh's throne, and there is no hint here whatsoever that the Son's throne is of a second or subordinate rank. The Son is the radiance of God's glory, and the "exact representation of his being, sustaining all things by his powerful word" (Heb 1:3). There is no hint of subordination here.

Perhaps the most explicit witness in the New Testament to the Son's eternal, pretemporal equality with the Father is found in the famous "kenosis" passage of Philippians 2:5–11:

> Your attitude should be the same as that of Christ Jesus: Who, being in very nature God (*en morphe theou huparkon*), did not consider equality with God (*to einai isa theo*) something to be grasped, but made himself nothing, taking the very nature of a servant, being made in human likeness. And being found in human appearance as a man, he humbled himself and became obedient unto death—even death on a cross!

The crucial point to be seen here is that prior to his incarnation, the Son existed in the very nature of God, and *equality* (*isa*) with God was his by right."He had divine equality as his own prerogative," as Ralph P. Martin has noted in his extensive commentary, "but gave it up when he exchanged the mode of existence in heaven for the mode of existence as Man upon earth."[59] There is *equality* of the Son with the Father before the incarnation; voluntary subordination of the Son to the Father only at the point of the incarnation—not before. This passage clearly supports the historic distinction

---

in him [Christ] before the foundation of the universe") does not imply an eternal subordination of the Son to the Father, since the eternal, pretemporal decree of election is not an act of the Father alone, but a decision of the one undivided will common to Father, Son, and Spirit—of all three persons acting in cooperation and mutual consultation, in *perichoresis*, so to speak (the Father "in" the Son, and the Son "in" the Father, eternally).

58. Ibid.

59. R. Martin, *A Hymn of Christ*, 150. See the translation of this passage by Moises Silva: "Though he existed in the form of God, Christ took no advantage of his equality with God. Instead, he made himself nothing by his assuming the form of a servant, that is, by becoming incarnate": Silva, *Philippians*, 112.

from the time of Athanasius[60] to the present between the *theologia* and the *economy*—that the Son is in all things equal to the Father as to his divinity, and only subordinate to the Father as to his humanity.

This review of Scripture and of the history of orthodox trinitarian theology has shown that the notion of the "eternal subordination of the Son to the Father" is a serious misunderstanding of both Scripture and tradition. It seems that the "New Evangelical Subordinationists" have revived the subordinationist elements in christological and trinitarian thought that were introduced into early Christian theology by Origen and that have lingered as a troublesome and confusing presence ever since.[61] It also seems that in an earlier generation, even conservative theological stalwarts such as Charles Hodge and A. H. Strong did not entirely escape from these subordinationist misunderstandings.[62]

In the tradition of Eastern theology there has been a significant tendency to ground the unity of the Trinity in the person of the Father as the "source" (*arche*) or "cause" (*aitia*) of the Son and the Spirit as to their

---

60. Athanasius, *Against the Arians*, 1.4.41.

61. On the subordinationist elements in Origen, see his *Commentary on John* 2.20 (henceforth abbreviated *Comm. John*), the Father is the source of divinity; the Son is the source of reason; *Comm. John* 2.73, "the Holy Spirit too was made through the Word, since the Word is older than he." See also McGuckin, *The Westminster Handbook to Origen*, "Trinitarianism," 207-9; and Rowe, *Origen's Doctrine of Subordinationism*. J. N. D. Kelly notes that in the East the intellectual climate was "impregnated with Neoplatonic ideas about the hierarchy of being," ideas that were favorable to subordinationist understandings: *Early Christian Doctrines*, 136.

62. Hodge spoke of a "subordination" of the Son and the Spirit to the Father with respect to "mode of subsistence and operation," *Systematic Theology*, vol. 1, 462. Strong spoke of a subordination of the Son to the Father "of order, office, and operation": *Systematic Theology*, 342 (yet on 343, Strong wrote that each of the three persons "is the proper and *equal* [emphasis added] object of Christian worship"). This language of "subordination" is an unfortunate confusion. The distinct modes of subsistence, for example—generation, procession—are the basis not of *subordination* of one person to another, but rather of the eternal *distinctions* of the persons, Father, Son, and Holy Spirit. The "order" (*taksis*) of the persons—Father first, Son second, Spirit third—in the New Testament texts reflects the historical order in which the three persons were revealed in the economy of redemption (God the Father as Creator, God the Son as Redeemer, and God the Holy Spirit as Sanctifier and Perfecter), and not any intrinsic and eternal subordination of one person to another. The "order" of the Father as "first" and of the Son as "second"—different "roles" within the triune life—does not imply unequal *authority*, as the orthodox tradition's insistence on the coeternal, coequal "majesty, glory, lordship, and *kingdom*" makes clear. In their comments on the history of trinitarian thought, both Hodge and Strong appear to be too dependent on secondary sources such as Pearson, Hooker, and Gieseler, rather than upon the primary sources of the patristic tradition.

modes of subsistence, but this Eastern view has always posed the danger of subordinationism, as noted above.[63] This subordinationist tendency, growing out of the notion of the Father as the "source" or "cause" of the Son, was itself rooted in the notion of the Father (eternally) "begetting" the Son and its anthropomorphic and causal connotations.[64] It is now rather widely recognized that the crucial word *monogenes* (e.g., John 3:16) is properly translated as "unique" or "one and only," rather than by "only begotten" as in the patristic and later tradition.[65] Jesus is the *unique* or *one and only* Son of the Father, rather than the Only "begotten" Son of the Father, properly speaking. Since the language of "begetting" became embedded in the Nicene Creed ("begotten, not made") and the later theological tradition, it can scarcely be removed, but such language should be read and understood as a way of affirming the *homoousios* or consubstantiality of the Father and the Son, rather than as implying the subordination of a son to a father who "begat" him. The Father is Father eternally, and the Son is Son eternally; no anthropomorphic notions of human "begetting" need to be read back into the eternal life of the Trinity.[66]

63. See Cary, "The Logic of Trinitarian Doctrine," 8, and also T. Torrance, *The Christian Doctrine of God*, 178.

64. On the notion of "eternal generation" of the Son in Origen and its background, see Wiles, "Eternal Generation."

65. See the important article by Moody, "God's Only Son," on the meaning and usage of *monogenes*. Karl Barth in his trinitarian theology continued to use the traditional concept of the Father as "origin," and argued that "In His mode of being as the Son He fulfills the divine subordination, just at the Father in His mode of being fulfills the divine superiority": *Church Dogmatics* IV.1, 209; see the section "The Way of the Son of God into the Far Country," 192–210. Barth properly wants to emphasize with this (problematic) language of an (eternal) subordination/obedience of the Son that the incarnate Jesus Christ was indeed a true and not apparent revelation of the true essence of God, but in so doing runs the risk, in the judgment of this writer, of blurring the distinctions between the *theologia* and the *economy*, between time and eternity, and between the *inherent* freedom of the Son of God (to become incarnate and obedient) and the *actualization* of that freedom in the history of redemption. Philippians 2:5–11 maintains this critical distinction: in eternity, before the incarnation, the Son existed in equality with God; only as a result of the incarnation did he freely give up this equality and become *obedient* to the point of death on a cross.

66. Similarly, with all due respect to the Greek Fathers, the notion of "cause" within the eternal life of the Trinity, i.e., the Father "causing" the hypostasis or person of the Son and the Spirit, needs to be questioned, if not jettisoned entirely. The category of causation applies properly to God as Creator or First Cause of all that exists or occurs within creation, or to cause and effects *within* creation, but not with respect to one person of the Trinity "causing" another — for God per se is *uncaused* as First Cause; only things that *begin to exist* need causes, and all three persons are God per se and equally coeternal and uncaused. This notion of "causation" within the eternal Trinity has been a root of subordinationist tendencies that have plagued trinitarian theology from the

This subordinationist danger was largely avoided in the trinitarian teaching of Gregory of Nazianzus, for whom the divine "Monarchy" (*monarchia*) was not limited to one person, the Father, but was common to the three.[67] The unity of the three divine persons is found in their eternal *perichoretic* relations—the Father, the Son, and the Spirit—being eternally and equally "in" one another, in an unending unity and communion of power, authority, glory, and mutual love.[68]

In conclusion, then, it can be stated that the attempt to argue against the ordination of women to the priesthood on the basis of some supposed "eternal subordination of the Son to the Father" must be judged to be a failed and misguided project. One wonders if the proponents of this point of view are willing to extend the logic of their arguments beyond time into eternity: If the subordination of the Son to the Father in *time* supposedly justifies the subordination of women to men in the earthly church, does the supposed subordination of the Son to the Father in eternity justify the *eternal subordination* of women to men in the heavenly church of the new creation? Are women to be *eternally* second-class citizens in the kingdom of God? Such specious arguments and misunderstandings of Scripture and tradition condemn women to positions of unending subordination, and worse still, *rob God the Son* of his coeternal and coequal glory, majesty, and lordship.

We can recall the words of Basil of Caesarea cited earlier: "What just defence shall we have in the day of the aweful universal judgment of all creation if . . . we attempt to degrade him who shares the honor and the throne, from his condition of equality, to a lower state?" This is surely too high a price to pay, and the "New Evangelical Subordinationists" would do well to reconsider their positions and look elsewhere for arguments to exclude women from the priesthood.

---

time of Origen to the present.

67. Gregory of Nazianzus, *Third Theological Oration*, ii, "On the Son": "It is, however, a Monarchy that is not limited to one Person . . . but one which is made of an equality of nature and a union of mind, and an identity of motion, and a convergence of its elements to unity."

68. This "perichoretic" understanding of the basis of the inner-trinitarian equality and unity is developed by T. Torrance, *The Christian Doctrine of God*, 176-79, and by Boff, *Trinity and Society*, 4, 5, 70, 83, 140-47.

12

How to Get More Out of Committee Meetings in Your Church

Can you relate to the following scenario? Two friends meet one evening in the church parking lot and one says, "I have just come out of a mind-numbing budget committee meeting at the church. I can only stare at lines of numbers on spreadsheets for so long before my eyes glaze over."

Most of us can remember committee meetings in our churches that, if not exactly "mind-numbing," have left us tired and frustrated, with the feeling that all the talk and discussion and debate had not accomplished as much as we would have hoped. Perhaps we find it difficult to rest well that night, our minds still running with the unresolved issues and tensions of the meeting. Many of us spend a lot of time in our churches or other Christian organizations going to meetings. Does Scripture give us any hints as to how committee meetings in the church can be more satisfying and productive? The good news is that the answer is a definite "Yes!" Let's consider briefly a number of key passages that can take our meetings to a whole new level of satisfaction and fruitfulness.

Before looking at the first passage—Exodus 4:2—we can stop to observe that typically, church committee meetings follow a pattern like this: 1) open with a sincere (but somewhat token) prayer for God's guidance; 2) individuals on the committee share their ideas and have discussion and debate; 3) a plan of action is adopted; 4) the meeting is closed in prayer, asking God to bless the plans that we have made. As we shall see, a more biblical pattern would look something like this: 1) united prayer, seeking a common mind; 2) corporately listening for the voice and plan of God in the midst of the discussion; 3) being energized by the Spirit of God to execute God's ideas (see Acts 13:1-2, the church at Antioch, energized and united for mission).

Principle One: Relinquishing Our Agendas to God: "What Is That In Your Hand?"

In the call of Moses God meets Moses at the burning bush, and later in the conversation asks Moses the question, "What is that in your hand?" (Exod 4:2). Moses answers, "a staff." God tells Moses to throw the staff on the ground, and it becomes a serpent. God commands Moses to pick it up again, and it becomes a staff—which later God uses, in the hands of Moses, to part the Red Sea waters. The "staff" can be a symbol for those things that we bring to the meeting: our ideas, our agendas, our knowledge, expertise, training, and hopes for the church. God asks us to throw our staffs on the ground—to relinquish and surrender our ideas and agendas to him, so that he can return them in a form that has been transformed and energized by God's own power. This conscious and intentional act of each committee member being willing to relinquish control and surrender his or her "staff" to God is the first step for having God's empowerment for the committee's work.

Principle Two: Seeking a Common Mind: The Principle of Spiritual Alignment

Another beautiful picture of extraordinarily fruitful "committee work" in the church is found in Acts 1:14: "They all joined together constantly in prayer" (Acts 1:14). Jesus had commanded the disciples to wait in Jerusalem until the Father sent the gift of the Holy Spirit to energize them for mission (Acts 1:4, 8). In 1:14 Luke uses the relatively infrequent word in New Testament Greek, *homothumadon,* which means "of one mind" or "of one purpose." Luke also uses the same word to describe the unity of the early Jerusalem church in worship and fellowship (Acts 2:46) and in the praise of God (Acts 4:24). This significant word *homothumadon* signifies that the disciples in Acts 1 were "on the same page"—not only being in the same place physically and geographically (in the upper room), but in the "same place" mentally and consciously, with shared understanding and purpose. This could be called the principle of spiritual alignment: when the disciples were united, with their minds aligned with the purpose and plan of God, the Spirit powerfully energized their mission (Acts 2), and the church expanded in effective mission (Acts 3–28). The key here is to see the critical order of the process: 1) achieving unity of mind; 2) being empowered by the Spirit; 3) engaging in fruitful mission. All too often, "conventional" work in the church tries to accomplish step 3 without first achieving steps 1 and 2. The powerful transition from Acts 1 ("common mind"; "alignment") to Acts 2 (empowerment by the Spirit) is reflective of the fact that the "Acts 1" unity is an answer to Jesus' John 17 prayer for Christian unity—and of the fact that Jesus blesses richly those who obediently align themselves as answers to his prayer!

This crucial principle of *alignment* can be illustrated as follows: an ordinary bar of iron has countless iron molecules, each of which is a tiny magnet ("dipole"), but the bar of iron as a whole has no magnetic force, because the individual iron molecules are oriented in random directions, and the little individual molecular magnets cancel one another out. If you take a powerful magnet and stroke the iron bar repeatedly, the molecules in the bar become aligned, the little magnets are working in the same direction, and an ordinary bar itself has become a powerful magnet that can do some "heavy lifting."

Or consider the advice given to his players by the coach of the legendary hockey team—Team USA—that upset the Russians in the 1980 Winter Olympics: "Forget the name on the back of your jersey—your name—the only name that matters is the name on the front of the jersey: Team USA." The being-of-one-mind alignment of Team USA lifted a talented collection of individual hockey players to an extraordinary level of team effectiveness.

Principle Three: Lectio Divina *Committee Listening: Listening as Body of Christ*

A third principle of effective committee meetings in the church could be called "*lectio divina* committee listening." Most of us are familiar with the lectio divina method of scriptural prayer and meditation: a quiet, unhurried, contemplative, and meditative listening to a passage of Scripture read, perhaps several times, with a view to hearing the voice of God speaking to us through the biblical word. The same posture and attitude can inform how we listen to one another during the meeting. All too often, in the typical meeting, after the opening prayer we revert to our individualistic mode of relating, not really acting as though we really believed that we were connected as body of Christ; not listening to one another intently and empathically, but being preoccupied with preparing our own statements so that we can voice our own ideas when we "get the microphone." In the *lectio divina* model of committee listening, the committee members bring an awareness that as they meet, they are an expression of the body of Christ, not autonomous individuals. They patiently try to hear what God might be wanting to say through the other members of the body.

This lectio divina style of committee listening can in itself be a small answer to Jesus' High Priestly prayer for Christian unity (John 17:21) that the disciples would be one as he was one with the Father. Christian unity is not just about the "macro" issues of interdenominational relations—but can start at the "micro" level of a church committee meeting.

This type of listening was modeled by Jesus himself: "I do nothing on my own but speak just what the Father has taught me ... What I have heard from him I tell to the world" (John 8:28,26). These principles of having a "common mind" and "listening" are so powerful because they reflect the very inner life of the triune God, manifested in the life and ministry of Jesus, and in Jesus' relation to the Father: Jesus first *listens* to the Father; then *aligns* his mind with the Father's mind; *relinquishes* his will to the Father's will; and is then *empowered* by the Spirit for effective and fruitful ministry (see Luke 3:21, at the baptism: "as he was praying"; 4:1–13: listening to God/testing in the desert; 4:14: "Jesus returned to Galilee in the power of the Spirit").

In the plan of salvation, the Father, the Son, and the Holy Spirit always work as a team—not as independent individuals. A church committee that patterns its methods of work on the model of the Trinity and on Jesus' relationship to the Father will discover that God will bless the work in extraordinary ways.

A Concluding Summary: Some Suggestions on "How To"

To conclude, how could these principles be applied in practice? Here are some suggestions: First, the leader of the meeting could recount the story of Moses ("What is that in your hand?"), and invite the members to "throw their staffs on the ground" at the outset of the meeting. Second, the committee spends some time in quiet prayer, asking for Christ to bring about a common mind, and asking the Holy Spirit to be present, and to help in attentive listening for hearing and discerning the Father's ideas as the members speak with one another. Third, the committee then engages in its discussions and agenda items, but with a consciousness that "We are 'body of Christ' as we meet as a committee—not separate and autonomous individuals."

Fourth, and finally, before the close of the meeting, the committee again spends some time in quiet, silent reflection, asking God to "push forward" the ideas and action items that he wants to go forward. At the close of the time of silent reflection, the leader attempts to articulate any consensus that seems to have emerged, or items about which consensus has not been achieved.

It's not rocket science; it is really quite simple. Try it in your next church committee meeting, and see if God turns what could be just another meeting into a surprisingly fruitful event in the life of the parish. Believe me—it really worked for Jesus—and it can work for us as well!

For Further Reading:

Roy Oswald and Robert E. Friedrich Jr. *Discerning Your Congregation's Future.* Herndon, VA: Alban Institute, 1996. Especially 5 and 145–46, on "Centering Prayer."

Charles M. Olsen. *Transforming Church Boards into Communities of Spiritual Leaders.* Herndon, VA: Alban Institute, 1995.

13

"Would John Calvin Stay in the Episcopal Church?"

[This article was written in May of 2009, when many of the members of Christ Church of Hamilton and Wenham, Massachusetts were wrestling at that time with the questions, "What is our proper response to the theological issues and disagreements within the Episcopal Church and the worldwide Anglican Communion? Should we stay, or separate and join the new Anglican Church in North America?" The chapter argues that Calvin, the mainstream Reformers, and the historic Anglican tradition are "catholic" and not "separatist" in their ecclesiology, and that Christian witness and conscience should value *both* fidelity to apostolic doctrine *and* commitment to the visible unity of the church. Similar issues face other mainline denominations.]

READERS OF THIS CHAPTER in the Episcopal Church may rightly ask, "Why should we care about what John Calvin would think about the current problems in the Episcopal Church and the worldwide Anglican communion? He lived in the sixteenth century, and we live in the twenty-first; and he was a Presbyterian anyway, not an Anglican." The reason why the question posed in the title is of interest to Episcopalians asking themselves, in the midst of the current debates over human sexuality and biblical theology, "Should we go, or should we stay?," is that John Calvin, the founder of the Presbyterian tradition, and Thomas Cranmer and the English Reformers, founders of the historic Anglican tradition, both shared a common view of the church: they were "catholic" and not "separatist" in their ecclesiology. They saw themselves as attempting to bring into being a *reformed catholic church*—not as starting a new "denomination."

The answer to the question posed in the title above, is, in short, "Yes, Calvin would encourage evangelicals in the Episcopal Church (and the PCUSA, the mainline Presbyterian church) to stay, to maintain an evangelical voice, and to work for the renewal and unity of the broader church." The reasons in support of this conclusion can be seen by examining Calvin's discussion of the unity of the visible church in the *Institutes of the Christian Religion*, Bk. IV, ch. 1.9–21, "Means of Grace: Holy Catholic Church."

Calvin cites the example of Old Testament prophets, who at times understood themselves to be a lonely minority in the midst of a theologically and morally compromised Jewish nation."Religion was in part despised, in part besmirched. In morals one frequently notes theft, robbery, treachery, slaughter, and like evil deeds. Still the prophets did not because of this establish new churches for themselves, or erect new altars on which to perform separate sacrifices."[1]

The Genevan Reformer also cites the example of Christ and the apostles, who worshiped in the Jerusalem temple, despite their disagreements with the religious leaders of their day: "Even then the desperate impiety of the Pharisees and the dissolute life which commonly prevailed could not prevent them from practicing the same rites along with the people, and from assembling in one temple with the rest for public exercises of religion. How did this happen," asks Calvin, "except that those who participated in these same rites with a clean conscience knew that they were not at all contaminated by association with the wicked?"[2]

Jesus cleansed the temple of money changers (Matt 21:12–17), but did not tell his disciples to abandon its worship or liturgy. Jesus commends the poor widow who makes her financial contribution to the temple treasury (Luke 21:1–4); Jesus does not consider her expression of faith in God to be contaminated by the personal shortcomings of the religious leaders who controlled the temple. Jesus instructed Peter to find a coin in the fish's mouth to pay the annual tax required of every Jewish male over the age of twenty, used for the upkeep of the temple (Matt 17:24–27; Exod 30:13). Jesus expected his disciples to pay taxes to Caesar (Matt 22:21), knowing full well that the personal lives and policies of the Roman emperors were not fully in keeping with the standards of God's law; nevertheless, the disciples would not be "defiled" by paying the tax.

Jesus was not a "separatist" in relation to the Jewish church of his day. Someone might say, "Jesus had no choice: there were no other 'denominations' from which to choose at the time." This in fact is not quite the case;

---

1. Calvin, *Institutes of the Christian Religion*, IV.1.18.
2. Ibid., IV.1.19.

the community of the Dead Sea scrolls at Qumran considered themselves to be the "true Israel" in a "new Covenant" with God. They felt they alone interpreted the Holy Scriptures correctly; they were the "final remnant." They considered the temple leadership to be compromised and hopelessly corrupt.[3] Jesus did not go out into the Judean desert to join the Qumran sectarians, but stayed among the people to bring spiritual renewal by preaching repentance and faith in God. Jesus did not "come out" and separate himself, but became known as the friend of "publicans and sinners."[4]

Strikingly, the apostles and the early Jerusalem church continued to go up to the Jewish temple to pray (Acts 3:1)—to a temple controlled by the party of the Sadducees, who denied the resurrection and the reality of angels and spirits (Acts 23:8). Evidently Peter and John and Paul did not understand the admonition to "come out from them and be separate" (2 Cor 6:17) to require that they separate themselves from the Jewish "national church," so to speak.[5] The temple, despite its problematic leadership—Sadducees and priests who had conspired to have Jesus condemned—was still a divinely ordained institution, dedicated to the worship of Yahweh, not Baal; the temple liturgy, based on the Scriptures of the Old Testament, was still a liturgy that the early Christians could pray without compromising their Christian convictions. The early Jewish Christians continued to attend the Jewish synagogues well into the second century, until changes in the synagogue liturgy—prayers anathematizing the Christians—made it impossible to attend.[6]

In commenting on the Apostle Paul's relationship to the troubled Corinthian church, Calvin notes that among the Corinthians "no slight number had gone astray; in fact, almost the whole body was infected. There was not one kind of sin only, but very many; and they were no light errors but

---

3. Vermes, *The Dead Sea Scrolls in English*, 37-8: "The Religious Ideas of the Community."

4. The sectarian and separatist impulse in Christianity tends to focus on "truth" at the expense of unity and love; theological liberals tend to focus on love and unity, but at the expense of historic truth. Scripture indicates (e.g., John 17: Jesus' "High Priestly Prayer") that all three values—truth, love, unity—are essential for a healthy and vibrant church.

5. In the context of pastoral issues in Corinth, the plausible context of this statement to "come out and be separate" is the apostles' earlier admonition (1 Cor 10:14-22) for the Corinthian believers to "flee from idolatry"—to avoid active participation in the sacrifices of pagan temples dedicated to Apollo, Asclepius, Demeter, Aphrodite, and the other gods and goddesses of the Greek pantheon. They were not morally contaminated by *indirect* contact with idolatrous practices, e.g., meat sacrificed to idols (1 Cor 8:1-13); but they would be contaminated by *direct* participation in the temple rituals of the pagan gods (1 Cor 10:14-22).

6. For background on the so-called "Benediction against the Heretics" (*Birkath ha-Minim*), see J. Martin, *History and Theology in the Fourth Gospel*, 56ff.

frightful misdeeds; there was corruption not only of morals but of doctrine. What does the holy apostle . . . do about this? Does he seek to separate himself from such? Does he cast them out of Christ's kingdom? . . . He not only does nothing of the sort; he even recognizes and proclaims them to be the church of Christ and the communion of saints [1 Cor 1:2]! . . . The church abides among them because the ministry of Word and sacraments remains unrepudiated there."[7]

Calvin, like Thomas Cranmer, John Jewel,[8] and the other English Reformers, had a high regard for patristic authority,[9] and, like the fathers, had a "catholic" and not "separatist" or "sectarian" view of the church. Their "catholic" ecclesiology is drawn largely from Augustine and Cyprian. Calvin cites Augustine's admonition that zeal for the purity of the church should be tempered with charity and mercy: "The godly manner and measure of church discipline ought at all times to be concerned with 'the unity of the Spirit in the bond of peace' [Eph 4:3] . . . Holy Scripture bids us correct our brother's vices with more moderate care, while preserving sincerity of love and unity of peace." The godly, says Augustine, are to "correct what they can; bear patiently and lovingly to bewail and mourn what they cannot; until God either amends or corrects or in the harvest uproots the tares and winnows the chaff" (Matt 13:40; 3:12; Luke 3:17).[10] For Augustine, the visible church was a "mixed bag"; only at the end would the Lord of the harvest be able to unerringly separate the wheat from the chaff.

He also cites Cyprian, the North African church father who had a very high view of the unity of the church: "Even though there seem to be tares or unclean vessels in the church, there is no reason why we ourselves should withdraw from the church; rather, we must toil to become wheat; we must strive as much as we can to be vessels of gold and silver."[11] Having cited Cyprian, Calvin adds further: "First, he who voluntarily deserts the outward communion of the church (where the Word of God is preached and the sacraments are administered) is without excuse. Secondly, neither the vices of

---

7. Calvin, *Institutes*, IV.1.14.

8. In his celebrated *Apology for the Church of England* (1562) Bishop John Jewel distinguished the Church of England both from the Roman Catholic Church and from sectarians such as the Anabaptists; the Church of England was continuous with the primitive catholic church of Christ, the apostles, and the holy fathers: *The Works of John Jewel*, vol. 3, 67, 77.

9. On the high regard for patristic authority by the Anglican divines, see Middleton, *Fathers and Anglicans*.

10. Augustine, *Against the Letter of Parmenianus* III.i.1; III.ii.15; cited by Calvin in *Institutes*, IV.1.16.

11. Cyprian, *Letters* liv.3, cited by Calvin, *Institutes*, IV.1.19.

the few nor the vices of the many in any way prevent us from duly professing our faith there in ceremonies ordained by God. For a godly conscience is not wounded by the unworthiness of another, whether pastor or layman; nor are the sacraments less pure and salutary for a holy and upright man because they are handled by unclean persons."[12]

Cyprian's views on the visible unity of the church were worked out against the backdrop of the third century Novatianist schism,[13] and Augustine's in the context of the Donatist schism of the fourth century.[14] The followers of the North African bishop Donatus considered themselves the "one true church," in distinction from the compromising catholics; they refused to accept as valid the sacramental ministry of bishops who had been ordained by *traditores*—catholic bishops, who during the Decian persecution had yielded to the pressure of the Roman authorities and handed over copies of the Holy Scriptures. In the context of this controversy Augustine articulated the crucial "catholic" view of the church, in which the validity of the sacrament does not depend on the personal holiness of the minister, but on the words of Christ, who is in fact the true minister of the sacrament.

This Cyprianic-Augustinian view of the church is the historic Anglican view, enshrined in article twenty-six of the Thirty-Nine Articles, "Of the Unworthiness of Ministers, which Hindereth not the Effect of the Sacraments":

> Although in the visible church the evil be ever mixed with the good,[15] and sometimes the evil have chief authority in the Ministration of the Word and Sacraments, yet forasmuch as they do not the same in their own name, but in Christ's, and do minister by his commission and authority, we may use their Ministry, both in hearing the Word of God, and in receiving the Sacraments. Neither is the effect of Christ's ordinance taken away by their wickedness, nor the grace of God's gifts diminished from

---

12. *Institutes,* IV.1.19.

13. See the article on "Novatianism," *Oxford Dictionary of the Christian Church,* 968.

14. See the article on "Donatists," *Catholic Encyclopedia.*

15. See the similar statement in the Westminster Confession of Faith (1647), chapter 25.5, "Of the Church": "The purest churches under heaven are subject both to mixture and error." Similarly, the Augsburg Confession (1530), ch.8, "The Church," states: "Again, although the Christian church, properly speaking, is nothing else than the assembly of all believers and saints, yet because in this life many false Christians, hypocrites, and even open sinners remain among the godly, the sacraments are efficacious even if the priests who administer them are wicked men, for as Christ himself indicated, 'The Pharisees sit on Moses' seat' (Matt 23:2). Accordingly, the Donatists and all who hold contrary views are condemned."

such as by faith, and rightly do receive the Sacraments ministered unto them; which be effectual, because of Christ's institution and promise, although they be ministered by evil men. Nevertheless, it appertaineth to the discipline of the Church, that inquiry be made of evil ministers, and that they be accused by those that have knowledge of their offences; and finally, being found guilty, by just judgment be deposed.

In his response to the Donatists Augustine also observed that one split from the church usually leads to another: the followers of Donatus began feuding among themselves, separating into further factions: the Urbanists, the Claudianists, the Rogatists, and the Maximianists. The Donatist schism was to persist for over a hundred years, troubling the peace of the church. This pattern has been repeated in church history: those who "come out" of the parent body then conclude that the new church is not pure enough, and come out of the new church to form a church purer still.

In the sixteenth century Anabaptists,[16] Baptists, and various independent sects separated from the Church of England and from the Lutheran and Reformed churches on the continent because they judged that the magisterial Reformers had not gone far enough in purifying the church. In modern American church history, J. Gresham Machen and his followers left the mainline Presbyterian Church in the midst of the Modernist-Fundamentalist controversy, to found in 1936 the Presbyterian Church of America (later renamed the Orthodox Presbyterian Church). Machen and his follower Carl McIntire then had disagreements over biblical interpretation and abstinence from alcohol, and McIntire decided in 1937 to found his own denomination, the Bible Presbyterian Church.[17]

---

16. On the sectarian impulse in the Anabaptist tradition, with its search for the "pure New Testament church," see Littell, *The Origins of Sectarian Protestantism*. The English Reformers rejected this sectarian view of the church: see article twenty-six of the Thirty-Nine Articles above. Ironically, new Anglican groups in the United States are closer in some aspects of their ecclesiology to the Anabaptist-separatist tradition than to historic Anglicanism.

17. For historical background on these Presbyterian controversies and church splits, see Loetscher, *The Broadening Church*; and Longfield, *The Presbyterian Controversy*. For a separatist perspective on these controversies, see G. Cohen, "The Bible Presbyterian Position on Ecclesiastical Separation." In the context of current controversies in the Presbyterian Church USA over sexual ethics and biblical authority, Richard J. Mouw, former president of Fuller Theological Seminary, urged evangelicals to stay in the denomination: "I worry much about what would happen to Presbyterian evangelicals if we were to leave the PCUSA. When we evangelical types don't have more liberal people to argue with, we tend to start arguing with each other . . . . The cause of Reformed orthodoxy was diminished when . . . conservatives . . . left the mainline denomination. They quickly began to argue among themselves, and it was not long before new splits

Recent Anglicanism[18] in America has also seen its share of church splits. In 1977 the "Anglican Catholic Church" was formed in response to the Episcopal Church's revisions to the Book of Common Prayer and the ordination of women to the priesthood.[19] In 1991 about one-third of the churches in the Anglican Catholic Church left to join the Anglican Church in America.[20] In 1988 the small Anglican denomination of the "Holy Catholic Church Anglican Rite" was formed, but it now appears that the unity of this small body is threatened by disagreements over questions of Marian devotion, "the place and importance of the Mother of God."[21]

As the new Anglican Church in North America emerges and organizes itself, time will tell if the various subgroups within the new denomination can maintain unity with one another without the "common enemy" of theological liberalism in the Episcopal Church, or whether historic tensions over the ordination of women, and cleavages between evangelicals and Anglo-Catholics will once again rear their ugly heads. Will there be historic replays of earlier nineteenth- and twentieth-century battles between evangelicals and Anglo-Catholics in the new denomination over baptismal regeneration, the place of the Thirty-Nine Articles, the reservation and adoration of the Blessed Sacrament, the invocation of angels and the saints, Marian devotion, reunion with Rome, and so forth?[22] Will the new denomination

---

occurred in their ranks. The result was that conservative Calvinism itself became a fractured movement": "Why Conservatives Need Liberals," 22–25.

18. In nineteenth-century America, evangelicals in the Episcopal Church separated from the parent body to form the Reformed Episcopal Church. Prichard, *A History of the Episcopal Church*, 148: "Frustrated by their church's inability to root out Oxford theology, a small number of evangelicals led by Bishop George David Cummins of Kentucky and priest Charles E. Cheney formed a separate Reformed Episcopal Church (1873)." The denomination remains a rather small splinter group, currently numbering some 141 congregations with an aggregate membership of 13,600. The Reformed Episcopal Church is expected to affiliate with the North American province of the emerging Anglican Church in North America.

19. On the "Anglican Catholic Church," see online article at http://en.wikipedia.org/wiki/Anglican_Catholic_Church; the denomination remains a relatively small group of 135 churches with a membership of some 10,000.

20. For information on this small Anglican denomination, see their website at http://acahomeorg0.web701.discountasp.net/. The denomination is said to have some 100 congregations and approximately 5,200 members.

21. See the denomination's website and discussion of the Marian issues, "The Challenge to the Holy Catholic Church Anglican Rite," at http://holycatholicanglican.org/resources/challenge.php.

22. For various accounts of these evangelical/Anglo-Catholic tensions, see: Chapman, *Anglicanism*, 57–93; DeMille, *The Catholic Movement in the American Episcopal Church*, esp. chapter 3, "The Impact of the Tracts," chapter 4, "The Beginnings of Ritualism", chapter 5, "The Fifties—The Storm Subsides," chapter 6, "The Second Ritualistic

have clear answers to such questions as, "By what principle or principles do we decide what Roman Catholic doctrines and practices are acceptable in this denomination? What Roman Catholic beliefs and practices, if any, are excluded?" The ACNA provisional constitution art. I.7 states that "We receive the Thirty-Nine Articles . . . as expressing fundamental principles [not, "doctrines"] of authentic Anglican belief"—but what exactly are these "fundamental principles," and where are they specified? Without clear answers to such questions, the Protestant/Anglo-Catholic/Roman Catholic elements that influence the ACNA's basic identity remain ambiguous, and a potential source of future intramural conflict.

Some Concluding Thoughts

So when all is said and done, what final thoughts might John Calvin have for conservative Episcopalians who are asking themselves, "Should we leave, or should we stay?" I could imagine Calvin saying something like this: "The bottom line is, *stay with the parent body—for the sake of the unity of the church visible—as long as you have the freedom the practice your faith according to conscience, and the Prayer Book and liturgy express the historic Nicene faith*. Distinguish carefully between the beliefs and practices of an individual member of the church: an individual priest; a particular parish; a particular bishop or group of bishops, and the denomination as a whole; distinguish between confessional repudiation of *doctrine* and ecclesiastical failure of *discipline*. The Augustinian, 'catholic' and historic Anglican view of the church would be that the church as a whole, considered as a denomination, remains a viable church of Christ as long as the 'Word is preached and the sacraments duly administered,' which in your Episcopal context means, 'As long as the creeds have not been repudiated, and the Prayer Book expresses in the liturgy the historic orthodox faith.' You would have cause to leave if the creeds are repudiated or essentials of the faith removed from the Prayer Book; or: you are either *forbidden* to preach the gospel in your parish, or *required* to do that which you believed violated Scripture and your conscience; until such point, stay and maintain your orthodox witness, and work for renewal."

Calvin's ecclesiological advice might, to some, sound unrealistic and hopelessly idealistic, especially in our modern American context of individual freedom, "consumer choice," and a "free market" in religion; it is

---

War"; Reed, *Glorious Battle*—see especially chapter 3, "Ritualism Rampant"; Pickering, *Anglo-Catholicism;* and Penhale, *The Anglican Church Today*. On the marginalized place of the Thirty-Nine Articles in the life of the Church of England today, see Packer and Beckwith, *The Thirty-Nine Articles*.

certainly easier to simply leave a troubled church and shop around for or start another.

At the end of the day, some conservative Episcopalians will choose to stay, and others will choose to leave—both for reasons which seem to them to be compelling and sound. Even with such an outcome, the spirit of Christ's prayer for unity could in some measure be answered not in terms of institutional or denominational unity, but at the level of *attitude* and mutual perception. Could both groups in charity recognize one another as fellow Christians? Could both groups perceive each other as acting out of conscience and good faith? Could the "leavers" refrain from seeing the "stayers" as "compromisers," and the "stayers" refrain from seeing the "leavers" as "schismatics"? Much depends on attitude and mutual perceptions. Could both groups in a parish caught in the current conflict continue to cooperate with one another in some occasions of local ministry and mission? One might hope so; and upon such a less than ideal outcome, one suspects that John Calvin—and more importantly, Jesus Christ—could look with some measure of approbation.

14

Thoughts on Hell and Everlasting Punishment

THE FIRST OBSERVATION THAT I would like to make on these difficult topics is that on the eternal state, I am an optimist: I believe that the number of the redeemed will be far greater than the number of the lost. The location of the finally lost is pictured as a *lake;* the final abode of the redeemed is pictured as a *vast city* (Rev 21:16) 1,400 miles wide, long, and high; the finally redeemed will be a "great multitude that no one can count" (Rev 7:9). God is a God of great mercy; a "mustard seed of faith" can save; a simple "look" toward Jesus at the end of life can open the doors of Paradise (Luke 23:43).

The second observation would be that, in my view, the position known as "conditional immortality" would be a "second-tier" option in terms of biblical plausibility—with not as much biblical warrant, in my opinion, as the "traditional" view, but much more than universalism. Imagery such as the chaff that is burned up (Matt 3:12) does seem to suggest an end to existence after a process of judgment; this view would seem to offer, from the point of view of biblical and systematic theology, a way of dealing with the justice and the mercy of God, both of which are biblical nonnegotiables. (On a somewhat more speculative note, I could conceive of how the language of "unending destruction" [2 Thess 1:9] might suggest an "asymptotic" process where a continuing process of "destruction" diminishes the existence of the one suffering this condition, approaching the "limit" of non-existence without reaching the limit, but getting ever closer to it: a mathematical analogy; in the "limit," evil remains—barely—as a very tiny "black hole" in a vast universe of light. But, as I say, this is to speculate.)

Six Problems for Universalism

Having stated my optimistic hope for the results of God's saving purposes, let me indicate briefly why I believe there are at least six insuperable problems for universalism; each one of these six can be expanded, and calls for further discussion to consider the evidence in detail:

1. *Universalism explains away (unconvincingly) the many clear teachings of Jesus (as they have been understood by the great majority of the church fathers, saints, martyrs, and godly, learned, and orthodox Bible scholars over the course of church history):*

   According to universalism, the blasphemy against the Holy Spirit (Mark 3:29) *will* be forgiven; the unending fire of gehenna does in fact go out (Mark 9:44); the worm that does not die, according to Jesus (Mark 9:48), does in fact die; those to whom Jesus says "depart into eternal fire" (Matt 25:46) actually return, and the fire is not eternal. Jesus says "Unless you repent, you too will perish" (Luke 13:5); universalism says, "Even if you do not repent in this life, you will not finally perish"; note that the first great deception and lie of Satan recorded in Scripture was the lie, "You will not surely die"—if you disbelieve God's Word (Gen 3:4); this is the "gospel" of universalism to the wicked: "You will not die." Jesus teaches, "enter by the *narrow* gate . . . many will try to enter, and *will not be able*"; Universalism teaches, "The 'gate' is wide, and *no one* will ever not be able to enter"; Jesus says, "*Away from me, all you evildoers . . .*"; universalism says, "Eventually all you evildoers will come back . . . ." Jesus teaches that the weeds are burned in the fire at the end of the age (Matt 13:40); universalism teaches that all the weeds that are burned in fact come out of the fire and are turned into wheat. Jesus teaches that at the end of the age the bad fish will be thrown away (Matt 13:48); universalism teaches that the bad fish become good fish. Jesus teaches that there is an unbridgeable chasm between the saved and the lost (Luke 16:26); universalism teaches that the chasm is only temporary. Jesus teaches that if Scripture does not convince the wicked, even great miracles will not convince them (Luke 16:31); universalism teaches that all the wicked will finally repent in hell. Jesus teaches that it would have been better for Judas not to have been born (Matt 26:24); universalism teaches that Judas will be saved and enjoy eternal bliss.

   It is not enough to dismiss these teachings of Jesus by a general appeal to "Jewish hyperbole"; you need to show that each and every such saying is merely "hyperbole." Why should we believe, for example, that it is just "hyperbole" to speak of a *narrow* door; could it in fact be the case that the "door" really is narrow? If Jesus in fact had intended to teach unending punishment of the wicked, how would he have said it? How could he have made it clear? It was clear enough to his contemporaries and to the great majority of the early church.

It is important to understand the words of Jesus in terms of the meaning of words in their historical, grammatical, and cultural context, in order to avoid *eisegesis*—our reading meanings into the text that reflect our own desires, wishes, cultural biases, or our ideas of what a just and loving God should or should not do. And here one must recognize the fact that Jesus' teachings as recorded in the Gospels are consistent with the Judaism of his day and intertestamental Judaism. On this subject Jesus agreed with the position of the strict Pharisees that the punishment of the wicked was unending; only the Sadducees in the first century denied such final punishment (they also rejected the resurrection). Jesus taught *publicly* on this issue, and he was not criticized by the Pharisees for his teaching—and they were "out to get him," and would have "nailed" him for teachings that were considered heterodox. There is *no evidence* from intertestamental Judaism or first-century Judaism that any Jewish teacher believed in universalism.

2. *Universalism fails to explain away the meaning of* aionios *("eternal, everlasting") in the New Testament:*

It will not do to say that this word only means "age-lasting"; this works for some instances in the Old Testament that refer to things of *this age* or the Mosaic dispensation that did in fact pass away, being superseded and fulfilled by the things of the New Covenant (e.g., the ritual of the ashes of the red heifer for cleansing—Num 19:10,21, "a statute forever"), or the temple of Solomon or the Levitical priesthood, etc.; but examine carefully the seventy or so uses of the word in the New Testament that refer to the *Age to Come,* and in no instance does this refer to a period of time that is limited.

The flaw in the universalist appeal to the "age-lasting" rendering of this term is that it overlooks the fundamental fact that in the New Testament, the *Age to Come* is everlasting or eternal or unending—the Age to Come lasts forever! Precisely the same word is used to describe in the Age to Come the glory of God, redemption, salvation, the Holy Spirit, the kingdom of God, the life of the redeemed—and the punishment of the wicked.

3. *Universalism lacks a clear biblical basis for the notion of "post-mortem evangelism" or "second chance" theology:*

In the light of Jesus' teachings on the finality of the state of the dead (Luke 16; see also Heb 9:27: after death comes judgment—the writer says nothing of a "second chance"; this has to be read into the text on the basis of conclusions reached on other grounds), universalists need compelling biblical warrant for post-mortem evangelism; otherwise, universalism simply doesn't work.

The biblical passage most often quoted in this regard—1 Peter 3:19 ("he went and preached to the spirits in prison") does not support post-mortem evangelism; this passage is in fact describing the proclamation of Christ's victory over the rebellious spirits and angels (see v. 22) after his resurrection (v. 18b) and during his ascension to the right hand of the Father (v. 22); it is not about a "descent into hell."[1]

The "post-mortem" evangelism reading of this text (e.g., by Clement of Alexandria and Origen) is based on a misunderstanding of the words "made alive in the spirit" (v. 18), reading a Platonic dichotomy of soul and body into the text where it is not intended; being "made alive in the spirit" refers to the *bodily* resurrection of Jesus, not any going down into hell by his soul during the three days in the tomb.

The post-mortem evangelism misreading of this text commits the hermeneutical fallacy of setting aside the meaning of clearer texts on the state of the dead by appealing to a disputed and highly debatable reading of an obscure text.

4. *Universalism fails to demonstrate that all instances of punishment or "destruction" in the Old and New Testaments are intended to be "remedial":*

Are we really to believe that John the Baptist thought that the unquenchable fire that burned up the chaff (Matt 3:12) was only remedial and temporary? What Jewish texts can one point to that would support such an understanding? Do we really believe that the writer of Revelation believed that the lake of fire was intended to "remediate" the Devil, the beast, and the false prophet? Is this based on a careful word study of all the instances of words such as "punish" (*kolasin*) and "destruction" (*olethros* and other words: see concordance), and found that *all* are remedial? Read Isaiah 13 and 14 carefully; do we really

---

1. On this see J. N. D. Kelly, *The Epistles of Peter and of Jude*, 150-64, and the massive scholarly study on this topic by Dalton, *Christ's Proclamation to the Spirits*, with detailed exegesis, historical background, and study of the long and complex history of interpretation of the passage.

believe that Isaiah thought the punishment of Babylon was "remedial" and temporary? See also the destruction of Babylon in chapter 51 of Jeremiah; do we suppose that Jeremiah thought this destruction was temporary? That when God says that "Babylon will sink to rise no more" (v. 64) this really means that a renovated Babylon will rise in the Age to Come? Are we to believe that the destruction of Gog and Magog in Ezekiel 38 and 39 are only temporary and not final? That the bodies of the wicked that are eaten by the wild animals and the vultures (38:17–20) will be disgorged and reconstituted in the Age to Come? It is also to be noted that the stated purpose of these divine judgments on the violent enemies of the people of God are not stated as for the benefit of Gog and Magog, but for the vindication of God's glory (Ezek 39:21). Retributive justice is for *God's benefit*, not just man's benefit (see Rom 3:25); the standpoint from which Ezekiel 38 and 39 are written is *God-centered*, not man-centered.

5. *Universalism is based on an optimism about the wicked repenting in hell not shared by Jesus and the biblical writers:*

Universalists are optimistic that even the most hardened sinners will finally repent in hell, when faced with the awesome reality of God and his holiness, love, and mercy. Can those who reject Christ have a valid excuse: "God, it's really *your* fault that I did not believe; you did not make it clear enough what the conditions of salvation were; you did not give me enough evidence"?

But where is it stated *in Scripture* that the wicked repent in hell? Where is there one clear instance or description of such a thing taking place? Of Satan being evangelized in the lake of fire? Of the lost receiving great light in the outer darkness? Of the wicked being *in the presence* of the glorious Christ rather than being *sent far away*? Of having unlimited time for remediation in hell rather than experiencing "eternal destruction"? Jesus taught that the chasm was unbridgeable and that even great miracles would not convince the hardened unbelievers (Luke 16); the prophet Daniel, who thought that the wicked would arise to "everlasting contempt" believed that "the wicked would *continue* to be wicked" (Dan 12:10); the writer of Revelation states that the wicked being judged "still did not repent of the works of their hands" (Rev 9:20–21); in Revelation 16:11 it is stated that the wicked "cursed the God of heaven . . . and *refused to repent* of what they had done."

The theory of the "wicked repenting in hell" is evidently based on an unrealistic view of human nature: that sin cannot finally and irreversibly harden anyone, even the Devil, beyond remedy; that the sinner and his actions are based on *rationality* rather than being fundamentally irrational and self-destructive in nature. It is also connected with the fallacious assumption that *all* punishment *must* be remedial in nature—but this is reading into the biblical text a meaning not found in it (some, not all punishment is remedial in nature).

6. *Universalism is based on quoting certain statements of Paul (Rom 5; 1 Cor 15; Col 1) out of their total context in the writings of Paul:*

Romans 5:18 ("one act of righteousness . . . that brings life for *all men*"), if taken alone, and out of context, could sound as though Paul were teaching universalism. However, this does not follow, for a number of reasons: in 5:19, the "all" language of v. 18 is paralleled by the "many" language of v. 19; in Romans, it is abundantly clear that Paul understands salvation to be tied to *faith* in Jesus Christ (3:25–28; 4:24, "God will credit righteousness for us who *believe in him* who raised our Lord Jesus from the dead"; 10:9, "if you *confess* with your mouth and *believe* in your heart that God raised him from the dead, you will be saved." Universalism has to transfer this "faith requirement" into the "post-mortem/second-chance" scenario, but this does not work, for the reasons discussed in 3 and 5 above. The appeal to Romans 5:18 also overlooks Paul's references to the wrath of God (1:18), and to the *distinction* that the apostle makes between those who by seeking good will have eternal life (2:7) and those who reject the truth (2:8) and who will experience wrath and anger; all who sin apart from the law will perish apart from the law (2:12).

First Corinthians 15:22 ("as in Adam all die, so in Christ all will be made alive") sounds like universalism, when taken alone; but see v. 23: "those who belong to him," by which Paul means the Christians, those who have believed him and are in him through faith. Likewise, Colossians 1:20 sounds like a good text for universalism ("reconcile to himself all things") when taken alone; but note the "universal-" sounding language elsewhere in the epistle: "all over the world [China? North America?] the gospel is bearing fruit and growing" (1:6); the gospel has been preached *to every creature under heaven* (1:23): does Paul intend for this to be understood in its most strict literal sense? Or is the point that the gospel is of universal significance and value, that is it meant for all types and conditions of people, for Gentiles as well as Jews, etc.? In Colossians 2:15 Paul teaches that the rebellious spiritual powers have been disarmed and defeated at the cross, and have been taken captive like defeated enemy soldiers being paraded through the streets of Rome by the victorious general; the imagery is that of the military conquest of the enemy—not the peaceful persuasion of evangelism; see also 1 Corinthians 15:24 ("then the end will come . . . after he has *destroyed* all dominion, authority, and power") where Paul looks forward to the final *destruction* of the rebellious powers, not their repentance!

Universalists can also misunderstand language such as that of Philippians 2:11 ("every tongue confess") in terms of universal salvation, because this language is not understood in light of the proper Old Testament background, e.g., Isaiah 66:22–24: here, Isaiah foresees the new heaven and the new earth (v. 22; background for Rev 21–22); "all mankind will come and *bow down* before me" (v. 23). This is *after* the wicked have been destroyed by Yahweh as the Divine Warrior on the Day of the Lord (v. 14, "his fury will be shown to his foes; v. 16, "many will be those slain by the Lord"; the "dead bodies of those who rebelled," v. 24, are still visible in the new earth).

This critical passage—Isaiah 66:22–24—is core background for the understanding of Jesus' teachings on the "worm that does not die and the fire that is not quenched"—and shows that in the mind of the biblical writers, the road to final peace and the new creation is by God's destruction of the wicked, not by the rehabilitation of Sodom and Gomorrah and Babylon.

7. *The testimony of church history:*

Though not as compelling as the six issues above, it should give pause that the great majority of learned and godly readers of Scripture have not found universalism to be taught in the Bible. Early witnesses such as Clement of Alexandria, Origen, and Gregory of Nyssa (especially the first two) were writing at a time in the development of Christian doctrine when the canon of Scripture, liturgy, church order, and the formulation of doctrine were still at earlier stages. Origen had peculiar and unbiblical views on such matters as the pre-existence of human souls and their sinning before becoming incarnate in human bodies. The majority view has been held by such godly Christians as Ignatius, Polycarp, Justin Martyr, the early Christian martyrs, Irenaeus, Cyprian, Jerome, Augustine, John of Damascus (a "gold standard" for the theology of the Eastern Orthodox churches), Aquinas, Calvin, Luther, the Augsburg and Westminster Confessions, Jonathan Edwards, Wesley, Hodge, Spurgeon, J. I. Packer, and many, many others. Universalists, on the other hand, are traveling in the same company with Friedrich Schleiermacher ("the father of modern Liberal Protestant theology"), Theodore Parker, the modern Unitarian-Universalist denomination, the heritage of the Harvard Divinity School, Buddhists, Hindus, "New Agers," and many others that have departed from cardinal doctrines of the faith. Denominations that have adopted the universalist teaching have given up on evangelism and missions as the church has historically understood them.

15

Will There Be *New* Work in the New Creation?

THE SHINY GLASS AND steel buildings seem to spring up like mushrooms in Bangalore, India, and the corporate signs of Epson, Microsoft, IBM, Texas Instruments, and the home-grown Infosys Technologies herald the presence of a new Asian "Silicon Valley." The newly globalized economies of Bangalore, Jakarta, Beijing, Hong Kong, and other booming metropolises around the Pacific basin, based on software, brainpower, knowledge workers, and the outsourcing of service and information technologies, have been vividly described in Thomas Friedman's *The World Is Flat*.[1]

The question arises: will any of these activities of the new global economy be present in the new creation? Will the redeemed people of God have any work to do in the world come, or will worship be their exclusive preoccupation? Many Christians have traditionally expected that all work will cease in the life to come, and that life in this world is greatly discontinuous with human activity in the world to come—implicitly denying the intrinsic value of our "secular" work in the present.

Many Christians seem to struggle with a sense that their "secular" work has no eternal or intrinsic value, but at best, is only a platform for evangelism or a source of income to contribute to the church and foreign missions. Theologians have, of course, developed various theologies of work to undergird Christian witness in the workplace,[2] but little attention has been given

---

1. Friedman, *The World Is Flat*, 115; 181–83; 318–20.

2. See, for example, Banks, *God the Worker* and *Redeeming the Routines*; Cosden, *A Theology of Work*; Hardy, *The Fabric of This World*; Novak, *Business as a Calling*; Richardson, *The Biblical Doctrine of Work*; Ryken, *Redeeming the Time*; Stevens, *The Other Six Days*; and Sherman and Hendricks, *Your Work Matters to God*.

to the biblical theme of the *new creation*[3] and what implications it might have for our understanding of the value of work. This chapter will argue that there will be *new work* for the redeemed people of God to do in the new creation, and that worship will be central but not the exclusive activity in the world to come. Biblical and theological arguments for this thesis will be presented, the nature of this work explored, and various objections considered. Along the way, notice will be given to the changing nature of work in our rapidly changing, globalized economies, and to contemporary scientific cosmologies, insofar as these might shape our images of work in the world to come. Expanded visions of the cosmos in a post-Hubble age give vastly enlarged dimensions to the "new heavens" and make the entire cosmos a potential "workplace" for a redeemed humanity journeying to the stars.

This proposition that there will be new work to do in the new creation, if correct, would be a further basis for investing human work in both Western and non-Western contexts with lasting meaning and significance. Admittedly, all attempts to foresee specific conditions in the world to come are somewhat speculative, and this must be recognized at the outset. Nevertheless, such exercises in speculative theology can have significant value insofar as they raise fresh questions and re-energize the Christian imagination with respect to both the meaning of work and the realities of the new creation.

A Very Brief History of Heaven

Before examining the biblical and theological arguments for the proposition that there will be new work in the new creation, it will be helpful to note, if only briefly, some highlights from the history of Christian understandings of heaven and the world to come, to provide perspective for what is to follow. In their valuable scholarly survey, *Heaven: A History*, Colleen McDannell and Bernhard Lang argue that Christian understandings of the future life have tended to fall into one of two broad categories: the "theocentric" and "anthropocentric."[4] "Theocentric" conceptions focus on the fulfillment of the believer's relationship to God and see worship and praise as the primary if not exclusive activities of heaven."Anthropocentric" conceptions, while not excluding worship, tend to emphasize reunion with family and friends, social relationships, and activities of service and work. McDannell and Lang see the "theocentric" model exemplified in the New Testament,

---

3. Notable exceptions are Cosden, *A Theology of Work*, and Volf, *Work in the Spirit*.

4. McDannell and Lang, *Heaven*. Their general conclusions are summarized on 353-58, "Paradise Found: Themes and Variations." Less comprehensive but also helpful is McGrath, *A Brief History of Heaven*.

the earlier Augustine, medieval scholasticism, the Protestant Reformers, the Puritans, and much of contemporary theology, both Roman Catholic and Protestant.[5] "Anthropocentric" conceptions can be found in Irenaeus, the later Augustine, the Renaissance, and in various eighteenth- and nineteenth-century authors.[6]

McDannell and Lang show how differing social and historical conditions have affected conceptions of the future state. Authors whose social locations have reflected more optimistic worldly conditions and less alienation from the social order have tended to favor more anthropocentric conceptions. Since World War I, both liberal and conservative Protestants have tended toward some form of "theocentric minimalism," but for very different reasons. Theological conservatives note that the biblical texts give very little specific detail about heaven, and theological liberals, perhaps influenced by the scientific naturalism of the age, seem prone to believe that concrete knowledge of any future life is essentially unknowable.[7] Unlike the doctrines of Christology, the Trinity, or justification, the doctrines of heaven and the new creation have not been the focus of major confessional attention in the history of the church, and as a result has remained somewhat undeveloped in matters of detail.[8]

The point of view advanced in this chapter could be characterized as a "theocentric maximalism." Praise and worship in the unclouded presence of God is understood to be the central but not exclusive activity of the world to come. If "theocentric" orientations have tended to reflect the first

---

5. McDannell and Lang, *Heaven*, 353-54. At times this has taken the form of a "theocentric minimalism" in which there is little envisioned except the believer in the presence of God, apart from the created order. Augustine, for example, speaks of the happiness of heaven as a condition in which God will be all in all, and where "there will be no weariness to call for rest, no need to call for toil, no place for any energy but praise": *City of God,* Bk. xxii, ch. 30. Chapter xxxiii of the Westminster Confession of Faith (1646), in speaking of the Last Judgment and the world to come, states that "then the righteous shall go into everlasting life, and receive that fullness of joy and refreshing which shall come from the presence of the Lord," but gives no further details of the nature of the heavenly state.

6. McDannell and Lang, *Heaven*, 355-56. More activistic conceptions of heaven can be found in authors as theologically diverse as Ralph Waldo Emerson and Charles Haddon Spurgeon.

7. Ibid., 350. In the brief concluding section on "The Eternal Abode of the Righteous," L. Berkhof states that "the joy of each individual will be perfect and full," and that there will be "social intercourse on an elevated plane," but adds little specific detail: *Systematic Theology,* 737. The somewhat more detailed descriptions of the future state offered by Erickson and Grudem will be noted below.

8. This point has been made by Walls, *Heaven,* 9. Pages 3-9 in this work present a helpful overview of historical and contemporary trends in beliefs about heaven.

Great Commandment (love of God), and "anthropocentric" orientations have tended to emphasize the second (love of neighbor), then "theocentric maximalism" would argue that love of God, love of neighbor, and *care for creation* (and culture) must be envisioned together as redeemed activities in the new creation.

It seems that a major defect of historic "theocentric" views of the world to come has been that *creation* as such tends to disappear or become marginalized in Christian eschatologies—there is not, as it were, enough "creation" in the new *creation*! A more robust theology of the new creation should inform Christian visions of the future.

A biblical view of the consummation of God's redemptive work involves a universe in which humans are rightly related to God, to other humans, and to creation—the latter broadly understood to include both the biosphere and, by extension, the world of culture. Stated in a different way, it could be said that "theocentric maximalism" envisions a future state in which both the great commandments *and* the cultural mandate (Gen 1:28) will be fulfilled—and continue to be fulfilled in the new creation in obedient and joyful acts of worship, service, and work.[9]

Biblical and Theological Arguments for Work in the New Creation

In this section arguments for the validity and existence of new human work in the new creation will be presented on the basis of the biblical doctrines of God, work, the history of the Flood, Old and New Testament images of the new creation, and the doctrine of man as *Imago Dei*. Several possible objections to this conclusion will also be considered.

The biblical doctrine of God teaches that all three persons of the Trinity are involved in the works of creation, providence, and redemption. While the work of redemption was completed in principle at the cross and will be finally consummated at the end of history, it can be argued that God's works of creation and providence can be expected to continue into the new creation and even beyond. With respect to the work of providence, God works to sustain the present creation by the word of his power (Heb 1:3; Col 1:17; Acts 17:28). The creation as such, whether in its original or fallen state, is not self sufficient or self-sustaining; every creature is maintained in being by the omnipotence and sovereign will of God. The new creation will still

---

9. The cultural mandate, instituted before the Fall, and renewed after the Flood (Gen 9:1), is here understood to have continuing validity into the new creation (procreation excepted: Matt 22:30).

be a *creation*, that is, a creaturely reality that will continue to be sustained by God. It will still be true in the new creation that a redeemed human being will need to confess that "in him we live and move and have our being" (Acts 17:28). God will continue his work of sustaining and maintaining creatures in the new creation.

With respect to the divine work of creation, it can be argued that God the Creator is essentially creative in his being. God's original act of creation was a free act, an act of divine love and freedom, not one necessitated by any lack or need on God's part. In the words of Karl Barth, God, "under no other inward constraint than that of the freedom of His love, has in an act of the overflowing of His inward glory, posited such a reality which is distinct from Himself."[10] Or as Colin Gunton has observed, "Like a work of art, creation is a project, something God wills for its own sake and not because he has need of it."[11] God's essential nature as a free, creative, and omnipotent being will never change throughout eternity; God the Creator will still be *creative* in the new creation. God will be free to create new things in the new creation, and even to create new worlds beyond the existing one, should he so desire.

Since man, as the image of God, was created to mirror the nature and works of God, it follows that if God continues to work in acts of creation and providence, redeemed humans in the new creation will continue to reflect the Creator by caring for fellow creatures and by engaging in new, creative acts of art, invention, culture, and worship.

But is it not the case that in some sense the creative work of God is finished, not continuing, and that God's people have entered a "Sabbath rest" (Heb 4:3–4, 9)? It is certainly the case that the biblical texts speak of God resting subsequent to the originating acts of creation (Gen 2:2); however, biblical texts also speak of God continuing to create in a continuing sense in the present (Ps 104:30, animals created by the Spirit of God). Jesus says that the Father "is always at work to the present day" in works of mercy and providence. Jesus' healing on the Sabbath reflects God's acts of mercy and care for his creatures throughout history. The work of redemption was finished at the cross, and God's people can enter into that spiritual rest now by faith, but God's works of providence, mercy, and creation continue.

In Genesis 2:15 it is said that the "Lord God took the man and put him in the Garden of Eden to work it and take care of it." The word translated as "take care of" (*shamar*) has the sense of "watchful care and preservation."[12]

---

10. Barth, *Church Dogmatics*, III, 1, *The Doctrine of Creation*, 15.
11. Gunton, "The Doctrine of Creation," 142.
12. Dyrness, "Stewardship of the Earth in the Old Testament," 54.

The narrative continues by saying that God also brought the animals to the man "to see what he would name them" (Gen 2:19–20). The man is not only given the task of preserving the garden, but also functions as a "naturalist" and "knowledge worker" who classifies and assigns nomenclature to God's creatures, in keeping with the mandate to exercise dominion (Gen 1:28). The naming of the animals is an expression of the human ability to use symbols and to make a "cultural" world from the raw materials of a "natural" world; the animals become part of man's cultural world by the very act of naming. A "cow" is no longer just a "natural" object, but a part of a human domestic economy. The power of naming constitutes a "second act of creation" that completes, as it were, God's originative act of creation, unlocking and developing the potentials inherent in the creature.

The first man is assigned the task of tending the garden *before the Fall*. In biblical theology, work predates the Fall, and is not a consequence of sin. The burdensome and painful aspects of work that are the consequences of sin (Gen 3:17) are not inherent in the nature of work itself. Work was assigned in an unfallen world as an activity reflective of man's nature as the image of God, who is himself a "worker." Just as it was "not good" for the man to be alone (Gen 2:18)—man being by nature a social being—so, by implication, it was *good* that man should work and care for God's creation. Viewed in this perspective, work is not inherently burdensome, much less a punishment, but rather a privilege and opportunity to reflect the character, activity, and creativity of the Creator. Consequently, if this is true of the nature of work in the first or original creation, and if the new creation is the fulfillment of God's original intention, then it would follow that *new* work would be a feature of the new world to come.

In the narrative of the Genesis Flood the post-deluge world can be seen as a type of the new creation. Noah and his family emerge from the ark subsequent to God's judgment on the old sinful order and enter not into a period of perpetual rest, but resume the work of the cultural mandate and development of God's creation. Human culture advances from agriculture in general to viticulture (grape cultivation; wine-making) in particular. The mandate to work is not revoked, but continued into the "new creation" after the Flood. This analogy from redemptive history would again suggest that work will characterize redeemed human life in the world to come.

Some of the imagery of the new creation in the Old Testament prophets points in a similar direction. In Isaiah's vision of a new heavens and earth the prophet foresees a new world in which the redeemed will "*build houses and live in them*" (Isa 65:21). The obvious question, of course, is to what extent such imagery is to be taken in a literal or physical sense, or whether only a metaphorical sense of "secure relationships" or the like is intended.

The interpretation favored here is that both senses could be understood: the people of God will indeed enjoy eternally secure relationships with God and one another, but as *embodied*, physical beings will still live not in caves or in the open fields, but in structures that they themselves have shaped. Building houses—and countless other constructive activities—can be envisioned as enjoyable experiences in the new creation.

The expectation that redeemed humans will have new work to do in the world to come is also implied by man's essential nature as *Imago Dei*. Human beings will continue to exist as image-bearers of God in the new creation. Man was created to reflect, in a finite and analogical sense, the character of God, and his works of creation, providence, and redemption. Just as Jesus the Son reflected the Father's work (John 5:17, 19), so the redeemed daughters and sons of God can be expected to reflect God's work in the life to come.

Humankind creates, of course, not in the absolute, *ex nihilo* sense of God's creation, but through "adding value" to creation, by transforming that which already exists, through invention, discovery, innovation, and by the production of new artistic, musical, and literary works.

Humans reflect the providential work of God when they serve their fellow creatures, care for the biosphere, and maintain the existing physical and cultural orders. Humans imitate the redemptive work of God when they act in such a way as to mitigate the effects of sin, e.g., a doctor serving her patients, or a reformer working to remove social injustices. While in the new creation the need for *redemptive* actions would be unnecessary, works of creativity and providence would still obtain. The damage done to the divine image in man having been fully restored (see Col 3:10), the creativity and energy entailed in that image would be fully expressed in the new creation.

Works of providence or provision will also still apply, since humans, animals, and plants, though redeemed and transformed, still remain *creatures*. Creatures, by definition, have needs that are met by others.[13] God alone has the attribute of aseity or metaphysical independence; all creatures depend on God and, secondarily, on other creatures for their existence, life, and health. When houses are built in the world to come (Isa 65:21), they will presumably be built not by owners struggling alone, but by a team of

---

13. Even though God could meet the needs of creatures *immediately*, i.e., without any mediaries, he chooses in his providence to meet these needs *mediately* through others. God could give us our daily bread immediately by miraculous action, but normally chooses to give us this bread through the activities of wheat farmers, bakers, distributors, and grocery store employees. This mediate provision of human needs is consistent with our finite and social human nature and reminds us of our dependence on others. This mediated provision for creaturely needs will plausibly continue in the world to come.

willing helpers. Even the fruit yielded every month by the tree of life planted by the river of life in the New Jerusalem, as envisioned by John (Rev 22:2), would plausibly not be "self-harvesting," magically falling off the tree and rolling to a final destination, but would be joyfully harvested by the people of God who "tend the Garden" (see Gen 2:15) in the New Eden. Works of service would continue throughout eternity, as the people of God care for one another and for God's redeemed creation.[14]

The presence of the image of God in man and the cultural mandate (Gen 1:26-28) imply that human beings are inherently shapers and creators of culture. The concept of culture, so crucial as a mediating category between man's inner and outer worlds, can be further developed here with insights from the disciplines of modern cultural anthropology and paleoanthropology.[15]

Traditional theological discussions often speak of "humanity" and "creation" without recognizing *culture* as an essential intervening variable. As already noted, human beings rarely if ever relate to "nature" as such apart from the mediation of culturally defined symbols and artifacts. Even backpackers on a hike in a remote virgin wilderness in Alaska are carrying backpacks, stoves, food supplies, maps, sleeping bags, and other artifacts that are products of human culture; the very categories of "wilderness" and "backpacking" are themselves culturally defined and historically situated.

One contemporary anthropologist, Amos Rapoport, defines culture as "a system of symbols and meanings transmitted [from one generation to another] through enculturation."[16] It is through such culturally defined frameworks that human societies give meaning to particulars, and organize the domains of space, time, meaning, and communication.[17] Roads, maps, boundary lines, houses, office buildings, "Keep Out" signs, calendars, clocks, anniversaries, laws, stop signs, musical notation, mathematical sym-

---

14. My colleague Scott Hafemann has pointed out that since faith, together with hope and love, are eternal (1 Cor 13:13), and so characterize the world to come, and since faith expresses itself in love for the neighbor (Gal 5:6), this aspect of Pauline theology provides yet another reason to expect the continuation of such works in the future life.

15. Paleoanthropology is the discipline that studies the ancient hominid species, now extinct, such as the Australopithicenes, *Homo habilis, Homo erectus, Homo Neanderthalis,* and so forth, together with the remains of *Homo sapiens* from the prehistoric Paleolithic periods. See Reader, *Missing Links,* for a helpful historical overview.

16. Rapoport, "Spatial Organization and the Built Environment," 474. Enculturation can involve any process that transmits learned, symbolic meanings from one generation to another: myths, stories, rituals, holidays, formal education, training, apprenticeship, mentoring, and so forth.

17. Ibid., 465.

bols, hymns, prayers, clothing styles, conventional greetings, and language itself are just a few examples of the many ways that humans build their own cultural environments through the use of symbols. In modern information-driven economies, most "work" involves the manipulation of symbols. A chimpanzee or a beaver[18] can relate to the world in a "natural" environment, but *Homo sapiens* relates to nature and works through the mediation of "built" or culturally created environments.

Another anthropologist, Tim Ingold, has noted that a human being is by nature "a designer, imposing symbolic schemes of his own devising upon the world of inanimate objects."[19] The aesthetic aspect of human cultural and symbolic activity, expressed in art and music, seems so deeply embedded in human nature that humans will spend hours honing their skills and practicing, not primarily for some external reward, but for the intrinsic satisfaction of mastering the skill involved.[20]

This connection of the "human" and the "cultural" is so strong and so integral that Clifford Geertz has asserted that "Most bluntly . . . there is no such thing as a human nature independent of culture." Human beings without culture would not be so much like the clever young savages in William Golding's *Lord of the Flies,* but more like "unworkable monstrosities" with few useable instincts, few recognizable human emotions and sentiments, and little intellect as we know it.[21]

It is precisely this uniquely human ability to form culture through symbolic activity that paleoanthropologists have used to identify the emergence of modern *Homo sapiens* in the history of the hominid fossil record. The remarkable Cro-Magnon cave paintings at Lascaux and other sites in the Pyrennes region of southwestern France and northern Spain are among the earliest examples of human art. Such examples of art, music, and symbolic activity have been dated to at least 30,000 years before the present. The

---

18. While it is true that a beaver in building a dam is "building" an environment, such behavior is instinctive or "hard-wired," rather than "cultural" in the sense used here. Human culture and processes of enculturation are not merely "hard-wired" or instinctive, but have a history and change dynamically over time, incorporating new learned behaviors and meanings in response to changing circumstances and individual creativity.

19. Ingold, ed., *Companion Encyclopedia of Anthropology*, 26.

20. Premack and Premack, "Why Animals Have Neither Culture nor History," 359. Such artistic and musical propensities distinguish humans from the lower animals.

21. Geertz, *The Interpretation of Cultures*, "The Impact of the Concept of Culture on the Concept of Man," 49. Geertz goes on to say that we "are in sum incomplete or unfinished animals who complete or finish ourselves through culture—and not through culture in general but through highly particular forms of it . . . Javanese, Hopi, Italian, upper class and lower class, academic and commercial": ibid.

Cro-Magnons, who were biologically and anatomically modern *Homo sapiens*, left other evidences of symbolically and culturally defined behaviors such as burial of the dead with ritual and ceremony, body decoration and ornamentation as signs of social status, and the use of eyed boned needles for the production of carefully tailored clothing.[22]

One leading paleoanthropologist, Ian Tattersall, has stated that such symbolic activity "lies at the very heart of what it means to be human." The ability to generate complex symbols and to transform them, to use symbols to "create a world in the mind and to re-create it in the real world" outside the mind is at the very foundation of the uniquely human powers of imagination and creativity.[23]

Earlier hominid species show little or no evidence of complex symbolic behaviors. *Homo erectus* used standardized stone tools and may have harnessed the use of fire as early as 700,000 years before the present, but left no evidence of art or musical instruments.[24] Neanderthal man, while having a cranial capacity larger on the average than modern *Homo sapiens*, left no clear evidence of art or other symbolic activity.[25]

Both the hominid fossil record and the biblical accounts of human origins and early human history (Gen 1, 2, 4) portray those whom we would recognize as "like ourselves" as culture-forming, symbol-manipulating beings. The first man of Genesis is portrayed in the cultural terms of a Neolithic farmer (see Gen 2:15), and cultural activities such as music, metalworking, and animal domestication are mentioned soon thereafter (Gen 4). The implication of these considerations is that if man, historically, in the "first" creation is essentially a culture maker, then man in the second or new creation will be a shaper of culture as well. In both the first and new creations, humans bearing the image of God relate to God, to other humans, and to the natural environment not immediately, but mediately through symbols that they themselves have shaped and transmitted. Redeemed human beings in a new creation, then, can be expected to produce *new* cultural artifacts as they do new work in the world to come.

---

22. Tattersall, *The Human Odyssey*, chapter 12, "The Human Spirit," 153–71, is a succinct description of the evidence, with illustrations of art and other material artifacts.

23. Tattersall, *Becoming Human*, 177.

24. Leakey and Lewin, *Origins Reconsidered*, 47.

25. Stringer and Gamble, *In Search of the Neanderthals*, 160.

Images of Work in the New Creation

This final section of the chapter will attempt to explore what types of work and activity might characterize life in the new creation. Can we expect that there will be new works of art, music, and scientific discovery? What about business and finance? Will there be an "economy" in the world to come? Eating and drinking? Manufacturing or maintenance activities? Farming or wildlife conservation? Will the fundamental laws of physics be entirely different in the world to come? Such questions may seem speculative and even bizarre, but are posed not so much with a view to developing definitive answers, but somewhat provisionally, in the hope of providing new perspectives and questions for further reflection in the areas of eschatology and Christian understandings of work.[26]

These questions will be explored from the standpoint of a "theocentric maximalism" that attempts to take the notion of new *creation* seriously. Such a standpoint is contrasted with various forms of "theocentric minimalism." A more extreme form of theocentric minimalism would be represented by various Gnostic eschatologies in which the future life involves only disembodied spirits in the presence of God, apart from all matter and the lower creation. A less extreme form of theocentric minimalism is found in Aquinas, who anticipated the renewal of the earth and the heavenly bodies, but believed that animals and plants would have no place in the eternal state, because of their corruptible nature.[27]

In the theocentric maximalism presupposed here, the new creation is envisioned as a state of affairs in which redeemed humans are rightly related to God, to other humans, to the world of culture, to the biosphere, and to the cosmos as a whole. This reference to the *cosmos* is a recognition of the fact that in a post-Hubble world the Christian eschatological imagination must encompass not only a new earth, but a new *cosmos* as well. The new *heavens* have been vastly expanded since the discoveries of Galileo, Einstein, and Hubble; the "playing field" of redemption, so to speak, has been vastly enlarged for the Christian in this era of human history.

---

26. Just as the "other worlds" of C. S. Lewis's *Chronicles of Narnia* and the *Space Trilogy* and the works of J. R. R. Tolkien have enriched the Christian imagination and Christian living in the present, so, hopefully, might explorations of the issue of new work in the new creation.

27. Aquinas, *Summa Theologica* Supplement, Q. 91, Art. 5, "Whether the Plants and Animals Will Remain in This Renewal?" Aquinas's conclusion—that plants and animals will have no place in the world to come—seems inconsistent will the *intrinsic value* of the biosphere in Genesis 1, and with God's preservation of animals on the ark during the Flood.

The questions noted above will be explored from an interpretative perspective that could be called "hermeneutical maximalism," i.e., a hermeneutical perspective that posits elements of both continuity and discontinuity between the old and new creations; that presupposes the fundamentally *analogical* nature of religious language;[28] and that posits "inclusionary maximalism." This last term is shorthand for the following working supposition: All things and human activities from the old creation are expected to be found in the new creation except those clearly excluded, e.g., a) things logically impossible; b) things clearly sinful;[29] c) things explicitly excluded by New Testament revelation. The principle of maximal inclusiveness would seem to be consistent with the intrinsic goodness of the original creation and the divine preservation of representatives of the biosphere through the Genesis Flood.

In the new creation it will be just as impossible for it to be true that $2+2=5$ as it is in the present creation. Clearly sinful activities such as murder, rape, theft, envy, idolatry, or blasphemy could have no place in the world to come.

The statement of Christ in Matthew 22:30 that in the resurrection there will be no marrying or giving in marriage would seem to exclude sexual activity and procreation in the life to come. Admittedly, such a prospect might not seem desirable to many in modern cultures saturated with sexual images and expectations! However, it is not the case that the cessation of sexual activity would imply a diminishing of pleasure per se in the world to come. On the contrary, the new creation can be expected to entail a state of affairs in which right pleasures—physical, emotional, relational, intellectual, aesthetic, and spiritual—would be intensified, not diminished, in a context in which redeemed human beings are in right relationships with God, other humans, and the entire cosmic environment.[30]

The cessation of sexual and procreative activity would not imply the cessation of gender distinctions; redeemed humans would still be recognizably male or female in the new creation. The transcendence of sexual

---

28. An analogical understanding of religious language holds that such language, while not in a given case necessarily being strictly *literal*, is not, at the same time *equivocal*; rather, it is supposed that language used in normal human contexts has some points of similarity and correspondence to actual states of affairs when used of things in the world to come.

29. Citing 1 Corinthians 3:12–15, Volf refers to a final judgment on human works, expecting that those works done not in cooperation with God, but "in cooperation with the demonic powers that scheme to ruin God's good creation" (*Work in the Spirit*, 120) will be burned up at the end and not enter the new creation.

30. Erickson suggests the term "suprasexual" in reference to the surpassing pleasures of the world to come: *Christian Theology*, 1240.

activity would, however, have a specific benefit for women: with the cessation of pregnancy, labor, childbirth, and childcare responsibilities, women would be freed to pursue the full range of artistic, scientific, and cultural activities that have historically been dominated by men.

A key assumption made in this discussion is that there will be some measure of continuity (as well as discontinuity) in the ways in which the basic laws of physics and biology operate now and in the new world to come. For example, it can be supposed that space will still have three dimensions, not one or two. A complex world of human and animal life could not be possible in a world of only one or two dimensions. If the law of gravity or the fundamental subatomic forces were substantially different, carbon-based life as we know it would not be possible.[31] Redeemed human bodies will still be transformed *physical* bodies that are subject to a form of gravity, rather than floating freely through space. The new creation is a transformed *creation*, an ordered and law-governed world, not a world of magic and mythical fantasy, free from all creaturely constraints.

Biblical images found in texts such as Revelation 22:2 ("tree of life . . . yielding fruit *every month*") and Isaiah 65:21 ("plant vineyards . . . eat their fruit") would seem to apply a state of affairs in the new creation in which biological and metabolic processes—including eating—are still occurring. This last inference concerning *eating food* seems consistent with the Gospel accounts of Christ, with a resurrection body, preparing a meal for the disciples (John 21:13). To demonstrate the material reality of his resurrection body, Christ takes a piece of broiled fish and eats it in the presence of the disciples (Luke 24:42-43). The Pauline statement that the kingdom of God is not a matter of eating and drinking (Rom 14:17) does not prove that eating and drinking are inconsistent with existence in the new creation—for eating and drinking can be done to the glory of God (1 Cor 10:31)—but rather, that disputes about clean and unclean foods (Rom 14:13-16) should not disrupt the unity of the Christian fellowship.

With these general hermeneutical considerations in mind, we can now proceed to explore more specifically the question, "What types of work might be expected in the new creation?" As a point of departure, the divine work-triad of creation, providence, and redemption can be used as a heuristic model. The works of the triune God in time are constituted by acts of creation, providence, and redemption; man, as the image of God, reflects the activities of "God the Worker" imperfectly in the first creation, and more adequately in the Age to Come.

---

31. Recent scientific discoveries have shown how the fundamental constants of nature are "fine-tuned" for life: see, for example, Barrow, and Tipler, *The Anthropic Cosmological Principle*; P. Davies, *The Mind of God*; and Denton, *Nature's Destiny*.

It is not hard to imagine that *creative* human activities such as art, music, literature, drama, and scientific discovery would flourish in a renewed creation. Such activities are pursued for the intrinsic values and enjoyment[32] they produce, and as humans move from a "kingdom of necessity" to a "kingdom of freedom," it seems plausible to suppose that such activities would be even more widely practiced and enjoyed.

The aesthetic values constituted by art, music, and literature, for example, and produced by humans as image-bearers of God, can be said to reflect in a finite way the nature of God, whose "glory" epitomizes all true beauty. God is a *beautiful* and glorious being; the new creation is a glorious and beautiful creation, and redeemed humans in the world to come will enjoy activities that add new (aesthetic) values to the world and conserve values that already exist.

Aesthetic values can be thought of in terms of the variables of complexity, variety, harmony, and intensity.[33] Other things being equal, a musical composition, for example, characterized by greater complexity, variety, harmony, and intensity would have greater aesthetic value than one characterized by less complexity, variety, harmony, and intensity. The tune "Twinkle, Twinkle Little Star" has some degree of musical value, but far less than the "Ode to Joy" in Beethoven's Ninth Symphony. Insofar as the new creation, suffused with the beauty and glory of God, is a preeminently *beautiful* creation, then it is to be expected that the human environment in the world to come would be characterized by increasingly greater degrees of complexity, variety, harmony, and intensity. The movements toward greater complexity and variety, for example, would be consistent with the overall biblical metanarrative that moves from the "Garden" to the glorified "City," and with the "complexification" of human civilizations moving from agricultural to industrial to information-based economies from the Neolithic eras to the present.

These variables of complexity, variety, harmony, and intensity, while originating in a context of aesthetic values, could be further generalized to apply to redeemed human relationships with God, fellow humans, and the biosphere. New and varied ways of praising God, experiencing human

32. Insofar as sports and athletics are intrinsically enjoyable, there would seem to be no reason to suppose that such activities, freed from egoism and violence, would be absent from the new creation. Sporting events at their best display human enjoyment of the pursuit of excellence, and are characterized by variety and *unpredictability* that humans also find enjoyable.

33. This schema is from Cobb Jr. and Griffin, *Process Theology*, 64–65. Cobb and Griffin have developed the process metaphysics of Alfred North Whitehead. The usefulness of the schema in question (complexity, variety, harmony, intensity) would not, however, necessarily imply agreement with process theology or metaphysics.

friendship, doing work, and enjoying the lower creation would flourish in the world to come, and continue to unfold without foreseeable limit.

It does not seem that "redemptive" work—activities such as medicine and nursing, for example, that repair the effects of sin and the curse—would have any place in a fully redeemed world where sin and the effects of sin are no longer present. However, it might be suggested that acts of Christian *service* that "memorialize" the acts of the Son of Man who came "not to be served but to serve" and give his life as a ransom for many (Mark 10:45), are, in that extended sense, redemptive acts. Redeemed humans will continue to help and serve one another in the world to come, as inherently social beings who can then more fully enjoy the satisfaction of free, altruistic action.

The continuation of redemptive work in the world to come would obtain more directly under a more radically speculative scenario: the existence of other worlds or universes. Should other universes exist, and should there be fallen and redeemable sentient beings in such universes, then it is hypothetically possible that God would enlist redeemed humans in this world to announce the message of a cosmically valid redemption (see Col 1:19) to such beings.[34] "Cross-cultural missions" becomes "cross-galactic missions"; the Great Commission is extended to all possible universes. In such an admittedly bizarre scenario, God uses redeemed human, not angels, as "missionaries" bearing the redemptive message to creatures in other worlds.

What about "maintenance" work in the new creation? Would redeemed humans still be engaged in farming, forestry, wildlife conservation, recycling, and the manufacturing of replacement goods in the world to come? In the prophet Isaiah's vision of the new earth (Isa 65:21), he envisions a state of affairs in which "they will plant vineyards and eat of their fruit." This text clearly presupposes a continuation of eating, drinking, the growth of grapes, harvesting, and the biological processes involved. If redeemed humans are still eating and drinking in the new creation, this would seem to imply the continuation of cooking, food processing, restaurants, and entire industries associated with the culture of food.

Does it make any sense to think of "consumer goods" in the world to come? For example, are we to think that shoes and clothing will last forever, never wear out, and never need replacement? Or will they still be subject to wear and tear, and so need to be replaced with similar manufactured items?[35]

---

34. On the implications of Colossians 1:19 for the cosmic scope of the cross, see J. J. Davis, "The Search for Extraterrestrial Intelligence and the Christian Doctrine of Redemption," in *Frontiers of Science and Faith* 141–57. For a history of the discussion of the existence of other worlds, see Dick, *Plurality of Worlds*.

35. The discussion of this questions assumes, of course, that clothing will be worn

Some writers have supposed that the Second Law of Thermodynamics, which states that disorder has a tendency to increase, and that available energy in a machine or living being inevitably dissipates over time, is a consequence of sin, and would not have applied before the Fall.[36] It might be thought that Romans 8:21, where the apostle Paul speaks of the creation itself being liberated "from its bondage to decay" in the world to come, supports such a notion.

There are, however, good reasons to believe that the Second Law is not a product of sin and is in fact a normal and essential feature of creation as God originally intended it. The Second Law implies that all living beings need to eat and have energy replenished from external sources, because heat and other forms of energy naturally tend to dissipate and move from warmer to cooler areas. From the beginning God provided plants as food for animals and humans (Gen 1:29–30), having created them as beings that needed to eat. This implies, as Alan Hayward has noted, that "they were subject to the Second Law from the moment of their creation."[37]

Viewed in this light, it could then be understood that the naturally dissipative and disordering tendencies implied by the Second Law, that applied from the time of creation, were then directed by God for the particular judicial punishment of human sin, e.g., death (Rom 6:23). The removal of the curse envisioned in Romans 8:21 implies not a revocation of the Second Law, but rather, the ending of human death and all forms of alienation of God's creation from the Creator.

Scripture provides other examples of "natural" processes being redirected by God for a specific redemptive or judicial purpose. Rainbows presumably existed from the time that rain showers and sunshine existed, but were invested with new meaning after the Flood as a sign of the covenant with creation (Gen 9:13). The law of gravity that caused the millstone to drop on Abimilech's head and crack his skull was both present from creation, and used of God in judgment of Abimilech's wicked deeds (Judges 9:53, 56). In Thomas Aquinas's view, thorns and thistles grew on earth before the Fall, but afterward were used of God for the punishment of human sin.[38]

The upshot of this discussion is that some form of the Second Law could be expected to apply in the new creation. Energy will still dissipate,

---

in the world to come—not as a sign of shame (see Gen 2:25), but as signs of gender distinctions, cultural diversity, personal adornment and self-expression, and for purely utilitarian considerations of maintaining bodily comfort.

36. See, for example, Morris, *The Twilight of Evolution*, 56–57, cited by Hayward, *Creation and Evolution*, 183.

37. Hayward, *Creation and Evolution*, 184.

38. Aquinas, *Summa Theologica* Pt. 1, Q. 69, art. 2.

living creatures will still eat, and shoes and clothing will experience wear and tear and eventually need replacement. Redeemed humans could still be expected, in the world to come, to be involved in the manufacturing and repair of such consumable items as are necessary for the maintenance of human life and culture. Such "maintenance work" would be a reflection of the activity of "Christ the Maintenance Worker," who even now is "upholding the universe by the word of his power" (Heb 1:3; Col 1:17).[39]

Finally, consider the question, "Will there be *business* and *economic* activities in the new creation?" Jesus' Parable of the Ten Minas[40] (Luke 19:11–27) would seem to indicate a positive answer to this question. The servant who managed the master's resources well is rewarded by being given charge of ten cities (Luke 19:17). As with the case of Joseph in the Genesis narrative (Gen 39–50), wise administration of worldly responsibilities is rewarded by God with greater responsibility, and is seen as a way of serving God's purposes and God's people. The parable presupposes that business and financial activities that are done in accordance with God's commands are consistent with the overall plan and purposes of God; the very fact that Jesus chooses such an illustration to illustrate kingdom life undercuts any false dichotomy between business and "spiritual" activities. The reference to management of *ten cities* would imply not only business activities, but also the administrative, governmental, legal, financial, banking, and information-technology services as well that are associated with modern information-based economies."We" could still freely choose to enjoy serving others by networking computer systems in a new creation, and would not need to enroll in some heavenly seminary to retool and be involved in meaningful work.

Now it might seem counter-intuitive that *money* and *economics* could be thought to have a continuing place in heaven or the new creation. Is it not the case that economics only reflects a situation where *scarce resources* have to be allocated among competing uses and users?[41] The point here is that in the new creation material resources, though presumably abundant, will still

---

39. Christ would presumably continue to maintain the new creation in being, since the new creation is still a *creation*, and as such lacks the property of aseity or metaphysical self-sufficiency that is true of God alone.

40. In the currency of the day, ten minas was an amount equivalent to approximately two or three years' average wages; one mina was about three months' wages.

41. According to the economists James Gwartney and Richard Stroup, the basic ingredients of economic theory are scarcity and choice: "Since scarcity of productive resources, time, and income limit the alternatives available to us, we must make choices. Choice is the act of selecting among restricted alternatives. A great deal of economics is about how people choose when the alternatives open to them are restricted": Gwartney and Stroup, *Economics*, 4–5.

not be *infinite*, and choices will still need to be made. Presumably the building of a new home (Isa 65:21) would not be attended by the delays, conflicts, injuries, or even fraud that sometimes characterizes construction projects in the present age; however, desirable lakefront property for building a home at a given lake is still limited, and choices would need to be made.

In the new creation, it is postulated that human beings will still need to eat, to grow food, to harvest and process it, and to replace consumables because of normal wear and tear. A given plot of farmland could be planted with apples or pears or cherries, and the actual choice could reflect the aggregate preferences of the users and producers. Human beings in the world to come will still be *creatures*—not gods—and will have choices to make, having only so many hours in the day, and not having the ability to be everywhere at once or to do all things simultaneously.

Providing food would still require human effort and the exertion of energy; the grapes in the vineyards in Isaiah's new earth (Isa 65:21b) would not harvest themselves, but would still need to be picked from the vine. Choosing to raise apples rather than cherries, choosing to practice soccer rather than write a book, choosing to bid for a prime lot by the lake rather than a beautiful new painting, are all economic choices, in that such choices allocate individual and societal resources through a continuing "auction" that reflects the varying preferences and valuations of the parties to the auction. The diversity of preferences is not necessarily a result of sin, but can reflect the created diversity of human personality, temperaments, and interests.

This discussion presupposes that private property and economic competition are not inherently sinful or inconsistent with a redeemed state of human affairs. The prophet Micah looks forward to the messianic age when swords will be beaten into plowshares and each man will sit under "his own vine and under his own fig tree" (Mic 4:3–4). Micah envisions the conditions of the Age to Come not in images of a vast collective farm, but smaller farms individually held. The reference to "plowshares" is an indication that Micah, like Isaiah, expected agriculture to be feature of the world to come. People in the new creation will still need to eat.

In the present world competition is often notably characterized by sinful greed and pride. However, competition per se need not be inherently sinful. The Apostle Paul can use the athletic imagery of running a race (1 Cor 9:24) as a positive illustration for the Christian life. Lawful, rule-based, and nonviolent competition can be expressive of an intrinsic human enjoyment of "play" and the sense of satisfaction derived from the achievement of excellence in the use of a human ability or skill.

It could be postulated that the economic inequalities that now result from the impersonal operations of market economies would, in the world to come, be mitigated both by a "cosmic Jubilee" principle (see Lev 25:8–55), which would, as needed, correct any disproportionate distributions of property and wealth, as well as by Spirit-prompted acts of generosity that freely share with those with less (see Acts 2:44–45).

If it seems strange or even bizarre to contemplate an "economy of heaven," consider some possible alternatives: Would all finite goods be distributed randomly by some heavenly lottery? Or would all economic decisions be made by divine fiat, with no human involvement whatsoever? Neither of these alternatives would seem to be consistent with either the general way that God has providentially delegated most such decisions throughout the course of human history, or with God's purpose of fostering human responsibility, rightly exercised. In the new creation we can expect more responsible human choices and decisions, not fewer.[42]

As this chapter is drawn to a close, it also needs to be stated that the scenario envisioned here involves not just new work in the new creation, but a *new Sabbath* as well. The regular rhythm of work alternating with rest, celebration, and worship that characterized the divine creation week in the first creation would also apply in some way in the world to come. The redeemed people of God would not be involved in ceaseless work, but the worship of the triune God would forever be the highest and most pleasurable of all experiences, as they delight in their glorious redeeming God, and right relationships with other humans and the entire created cosmos. Such a vision of the new creation, it is here suggested, energizes and valorizes all forms of human work in the present that are done for the glory of God, until that time when the kingdoms of this world have become "the Kingdom of our Lord and of his Christ."

---

42. This latter conclusion seems consistent with the Parable of the Ten Minas: the faithful manager is rewarded with greater responsibility, not less, or with a life of ease and inactivity.

Bibliography

Abbott, Lyman. *The New Testament with Notes and Comments.* New York: A. S. Barnes and Co., 1876.
Abbot, Walter, ed. *The Documents of Vatican II.* New York: Corpus, 1966.
The Acts of the Holy Apostle Thomas. http://www.newadvent.org/fathers/0823.htm.
Adams, Jay. *Competent to Counsel.* Grand Rapids: Baker, 1970.
Albright, William, and C. S. Mann. *The Anchor Bible: Matthew.* Garden City, NY: Doubleday, 1971.
Alexander, Eben. *Proof of Heaven: A Neurosurgeon's Journey into the Afterlife.* New York: Simon and Schuster, 2012.
"All too much: Monstrous amounts of data." *The Economist,* February 25 (2010) 5.
Alleine, Joseph. *Alarm to the Unconverted.* London: Banner of Truth, 1964.
Allen, Willoughby. *A Critical and Exegetical Commentary on the Gospel According to S. Matthew.* 3rd ed. Edinburgh: T & T Clark, 1912.
Amore, Roy, and Julia Ching. "The Buddhist Tradition." In *A Concise Introduction to World Religions,* edited by Willard G. Oxtoby, 376–439. New York: Oxford University Press, 1996.
Anderson, Ray S., ed. *Theological Foundations for Ministry: Selected Readings for a Theology of the Church in Ministry.* Edinburgh: T & T Clark, 1979.
———. *The Shape of Practical Theology: Empowering Ministry with Theological Praxis.* Downers Grove, IL: InterVarsity, 2001.
Aquinas, Thomas. *Summa Theologica.* 3 vols. Translated by the Fathers of the English Dominican Province. New York: Benzinger Brothers, 1920.
Aristotle. *Physics.* Vol. 1, Books 1–4. Translated by P. H. Wicksteed and F. M. Cornford. Loeb Classical Library 228. Cambridge, MA: Harvard University Press, 1957.
———. *Posterior Analytics. Topica.* Translated by Hugh Tredennick and E. S. Forster. Loeb Classical Library 391. Cambridge, MA: Harvard University Press, 1960.
Arjakovsky, Antoine. *The Way: Religious Thinkers of the Russian Emigration in Paris and Their Journals, 1925-1940.* Notre Dame, IN: University of Notre Dame Press, 2013.
Arnold, Clinton. *Ephesians: Exegetical Commentary on the New Testament.* Grand Rapids: Zondervan, 2010.
Ashton, John. *The Religion of Paul the Apostle.* New Haven, CT: Yale University Press, 2000.
Athanasius. *Ad Serapion.* http://www.newadvent.org/fathers/2806028.htm.
———. *Against the Arians.* http://www.newadvent.org/fathers/2816.htm.
Augustine. *The City of God.* Translated by William Babcock. Hyde Park, NY: New City, 2013.
———. *On the Trinity.* http://newadvent.org/fathers/130104.htm.

Ayers, David. "The Inevitability of Failure: The Assumptions and Implementations of Modern Feminism." In *Recovering Biblical Manhood and Womanhood: A Response to Evangelical Feminism*, edited by John Piper and Wayne Grudem, 212–331. Wheaton, IL: Crossway, 1991.

Bagchi, David, and David C. Steinmetz, eds. *The Cambridge Companion to Reformation Theology*. Cambridge: Cambridge University Press, 2004.

Bainton, Roland. *Here I Stand: A Life of Martin Luther*. Nashville: Abingdon, 1950.

Baker, L. D. G. "The Shadow of the Christian Symbol." In *The Mission of the Church and the Propagation of the Faith*, edited by G. J. Cuming, 17–28. Cambridge: Cambridge University Press, 1970.

Baldwin, Scott. "A Difficult Word: *Authenteo* in 1 Tim. 2:12." In *Women in the Church: A Fresh Analysis*, edited by Andreas Kostenberger, Thomas Schreiner, and Scott Baldwin, 65–80. Grand Rapids: Baker, 1995.

Balmer, Randall. *Blessed Assurance: A History of Evangelicalism in America*. Boston: Beacon, 1999.

Banks, Robert. "Appendix A: Lay Theology and Education Since 1945." In *Redeeming the Routines: Bringing Theology to Life*, edited by Robert Banks, 153–74. Wheaton, IL: Victor, 1993.

———. *God the Worker*. Valley Forge, PA: Judson, 1994.

———. *Paul's Idea of Community: The Early Church House Churches in Their Historical Setting*. Grand Rapids: Eerdmans, 1980.

———. *Redeeming the Routines: Bringing Theology to Life*. Wheaton, IL: Victor, 1993.

Barclay, William. *Christ in You: A Study in Paul's Theology and Ethics*. Lanham, MD: University Press of America, 1999.

———. *Educational Ideals in the Ancient World*. Grand Rapids: Baker, 1974.

Barna Research Group. "Year-in-Review Perspective (2009)." www.barna.org/barna-update/article/12-faithspirituality/.

Barron, Bruce. *The Health and Wealth Gospel*. Downers Grove, IL: InterVarsity, 1987.

Barrow, John D., and Frank J. Tipler. *The Anthropic Cosmological Principle*. Oxford: Clarendon, 1986.

Barth, Karl. *Church Dogmatics III.1: The Doctrine of Creation*. Edinburgh: T & T Clark, 1958.

———. *Church Dogmatics IV.1: The Doctrine of Reconciliation*. Edinburgh: T & T Clark, 1956.

———. *Church Dogmatics IV.3.ii: The Doctrine of Reconciliation*. Edinburgh: T & T Clark, 1962.

———. *The Humanity of God*. Louisville: Westminster John Knox, 1968.

Basil the Great. *On the Holy Spirit*. http://www.newadvent.org/fathers/3203.htm.

Bauckham, Richard. *God Crucified: Monotheism and Christology in the New Testament*. Grand Rapids: Eerdmans, 1998.

Baumstark, Anton. *Comparative Liturgy*. Westminster, MD: Newman, 1958.

Baxter, Richard. *Call to the Unconverted*. Grand Rapids: Sovereign Grace, 1971.

———. *The Reformed Pastor*. Carlisle, PA: Banner of Truth Trust, 1974.

Beare, Francis Wright. *The Gospel According to Matthew*. San Francisco: Harper and Row, 1981.

Beasley-Murray, G. R. *Jesus and the Kingdom of God*. Grand Rapids: Eerdmans, 1986.

Beaver, Pierce R. *Church, State, and the American Indians*. St. Louis: Concordia, 1966.

Bebbington, David. "Evangelical Conversion, c. 1740-1850." *North Atlantic Missiology Project*. Cambridge: University of Cambridge, 1996.

———. "How Moody Changed Revivalism," *Christian History* 25 (9, 1) 22–25.

Becker, U. "Gospel." In *Dictionary of New Testament Theology*, edited by Colin Brown, vol. 2, 107–15. Grand Rapids: Zondervan, 1976.

Beckwith, Roger T. *The Thirty-Nine Articles: Their Place and Use Today*. Oxford: Latimer House, 1984.

Bell, Rob. *Love Wins: A Book About Heaven, Hell, and the Fate of Every Person Who Ever Lived*. New York: HarperCollins, 2011.

Bellah, Robert N, et al. *Habits of the Heart: Individualism and Commitment in American Life*. New York: Harper and Row, 1985.

Bello, David. "What are dark matter and dark energy and how are they affecting the universe?" *Scientific American*, August 28, 2008. http://www.scientificamerian.com/article.cfm?id=what-are-dark-matter-and.

Belleville, Linda. "Teaching and Usurping Authority: 1 Timothy 2:11–15." In *Discovering Biblical Equality*, edited by Ronald Pierce and Rebecca Groothius, 205–23. Downers Grove, IL: InterVarsity, 2004.

Bengel, John Albert. *Gnomen of the New Testament*. Vol. 1. Philadelphia: Perkinpine & Higgins, 1864.

Berger, Peter. *Religious America, Secular Europe?* Burlington, VT: Ashgate, 2008.

———. *The Sacred Canopy: Elements of a Sociological Theory of Religion*. New York: Doubleday, 1967.

Berkhof, Hendrikus. *Christian Faith: An Introduction to the Study of the Faith*. Rev. ed. Grand Rapids: Eerdmans, 1986.

Berkhof, Louis. *Systematic Theology*. 4th ed. Grand Rapids: Zondervan, 1941.

Berkley, James, ed. *Leadership Handbook of Management and Administration*. Grand Rapids: Baker, 2007.

Berkouwer, G. C. *Man: The Image of God*. Grand Rapids: Eerdmans, 1962.

Best, Ernest. *One Body in Christ*. London: SPCK, 1955.

Bethune, Brian. "The Heaven Boom: Why So Many People—Including Scientists—Suddenly Believe in an Afterlife." *Maclean's* (May 12, 2013) 44–48.

Bielfeldt, Dennis. "Deification as a Motif in Luther's *Dictata super psalterium*." *Sixteenth Century Journal* 28 (1997) 401–20.

Bietenhard, H. "Name." In *The New International Dictionary of New Testament Theology and Exegesis*, edited by Moisés Silva, 2:648–56. Grand Rapids: Zondervan, 2014.

Billings, J. Todd. *Calvin, Participation, and the Gift*. Oxford: Oxford University Press, 2007.

———. "United to God through Christ: Assessing Calvin on the Question of Deification." *Harvard Theological Review* 98:3 (2005) 315–34.

Blackwell, Richard. *Galileo, Bellarmine, and the Bible*. Notre Dame, IN: University of Notre Dame Press, 1991.

Bloesch, Donald. *Is the Bible Sexist? Beyond Feminism and Patriarchalism*. Westchester, IL: Crossway, 1982.

Blomberg, Craig. *Matthew: The New American Commentary*, vol. 22. Nashville: Broadman, 1992.

———. "Neither Hierarchicalist nor Egalitarian." In *Paul and His Theology*, edited by Stanley Porter, 212–324. Leiden: Brill, 2006.

Bloom, B. S. *Taxonomy of Educational Objectives: The Classification of Educational Goals*. New York: Longmans, Green, 1956.
Boer, Harry. *Pentecost and the Missionary Witness of the Church*. PhD diss., Free University of Amsterdam, 1955.
Boff, Leonardo. *Trinity and Society*. Eugene, OR: Wipf & Stock, 2005.
Boling, Robert. *Judges: Introduction, Translation, and Commentary*. Anchor Bible. Garden City, NY: Doubleday, 1975.
Bonaventure. *The Mind's Journey into God*. In *The Essential Writings of Christian Mysticism*, edited by Bernard McGinn, 162–71. New York: Modern Library, 2006.
Bonner, Gerald. "Augustine's Conception of Deification." *Journal of Theological Studies* n. s. 37:2 (1986) 369–86.
Borgmann, Albert. *Crossing the Postmodern Divide*. Chicago: University of Chicago Press, 1992.
———. *Technology and the Character of Contemporary Life*. Chicago: University of Chicago Press, 1987.
Boring, Eugene. *The Gospel of Matthew: The New Interpreter's Bible*, vol. 8. Nashville: Abingdon, 1955.
Bosch, David J. "The Structure of Mission: An Exposition of Matthew 28:16–20." In *Exploring Church Growth*, edited by Wilbert R. Shenk, 218–48. Grand Rapids: Eerdmans, 1983.
———. *Transforming Mission: Paradigm Shifts in the Theology of Mission*. Maryknoll, NY: Orbis, 1991.
Bostrom, Nick. "A History of Transhumanist Thought." *Journal of Evolution and Technology* 14:1 (2005) 1–25.
Bowman, Robert, Jr. *The Word-Faith Controversy: Understanding the Health and Wealth Gospel*. Grand Rapids: Baker, 2001.
Braaten, Carl, and Robert W. Jenson, eds. *Christian Dogmatics*. Vol. 1. Philadelphia: Fortress, 1984.
———. *Union with Christ: The New Finnish Interpretation of Luther*. Grand Rapids: Eerdmans, 1998.
Bradford, Gamaliel. *D. L. Moody: A Worker in Souls*. New York: George H. Doran, 1927.
Brauer, Jerald C. "Conversion: From Puritanism to Revivalism." *Journal of Religion* 58:3 (1978) 227–43.
Bright, Bill. *Bright Side* 31:3 (1998).
———. *Revolution Now!* San Bernadino, CA: Campus Crusade for Christ, 1969.
Broadus, John. *Commentary on the Gospel of Matthew*. Philadelphia: American Baptist Publication Society, 1886.
Bromiley, G. W. *Christian Ministry*. Grand Rapids: Eerdmans, 1959.
Brown, Elijah P. *The Real Billy Sunday*. New York: Fleming H. Revell, 1914.
Bruce, F. F. *The Pauline Circle*. Grand Rapids: Eerdmans, 1985.
Bucer, Martin. *Concerning the True Care of Souls*. Translated by Peter Beale. Carlisle, PA: Banner of Truth Trust, 2009.
Buchanan, George Wesley. *The Gospel of Matthew*. The Mellen Biblical Commentary New Testament Series. Vol. 1, bk. 2. Lewiston, ME: Mellen Biblical, 1996.
Bullinger, Heinrich. "Of the Holy Catholic Church." In In *The Library of Christian Classics*, vol. 24, *Zwingli and Bullinger*, translated by G. W. Bromiley, 288–325. Philadelphia: Westminster, 1953.

Bullough, Vern. *The Subordinate Sex: A History of Attitude Toward Women*. Urbana, IL: University of Illinois Press, 1973.
Bunting, Ian. *A History of Pastoral Care*. London: Cassell, 2000.
Burke, Trevor J. *Adopted into God's Family: Exploring a Pauline Metaphor*. Downers Grove, IL: InterVarsity, 2006.
Burtt, Edwin A. *The Metaphysical Foundations of Modern Science*. Garden City, NY: Doubleday Anchor, 1954.
Butin, Philip. "Preaching as a Trinitarian Event." In *Trinitarian Theology for the Church*, edited by Daniel Treier and David Lauber, 204–24. Downers Grove, IL: IVP Academic, 2009.
Cairns, David. *The Image of God in Man*. London: Collins, 1972.
Caldwell, Patricia. *The Puritan Conversion Narrative of Puritan Religious Experience*. New York: Oxford University Press, 1986.
Calvin, John. *Commentary on a Harmony of the Evangelists*. Translated by William Pringle. Grand Rapids: Eerdmans, 1949.
———. "Draft Ecclesiastical Ordinances." In *Calvin: Theological Treatises*. Library of Christian Classics XXII. Translated by J. K. S. Reid. Philadelphia: Westminster, 1954.
———. *The Epistles of Paul the Apostle to the Corinthians*. Translated by John W. Fraser. Grand Rapids: Eerdmans, 1960.
———. *Institutes of the Christian Religion*. 2 vols. Edited by John T. McNeill. Translated by Ford Lewis Battles. Philadelphia: Westminster, 1960.
Candlish, R. S. *The Fatherhood of God*. Edinburgh: Adam and Charles Black, 1865.
Carey, William. *An Enquiry into the Obligation of Christians to Use Means for the Conversion of the Heathen*. London: Carey Kingsgate, 1961.
Carman, John B. *The Theology of Ramanuja: An Essay in Interreligious Understanding*. New Haven, CT: Yale University Press, 1974.
Carr, Nicholas. *The Shallows: What the Internet Is Doing to Our Brains*. New York: W. W. Norton, 2010.
Carroll, Jackson, and Wade Clark Roof. *Bridging Divided Worlds: Generational Cultures in Congregations*. San Francisco: Jossey-Bass, 2002.
Carroll, Robert P. *Jeremiah: A Commentary*. Philadelphia: Westminster, 1986.
Carruthers, Mary. *The Book of Memory: A Study of Memory in Medieval Culture*. Cambridge: Cambridge University Press, 1982.
Carter, Stephen. *The Culture of Disbelief*. New York: Basic, 1993.
Carson, D. A. *Becoming Conversant with the Emerging Church: Understanding a Movement and Its Implications*. Grand Rapids: Zondervan, 2005.
———. *Matthew: The Expositor's Bible Commentary*, vol. 8. Grand Rapids: Zondervan, 1984.
Carson, D. A., Peter T. O'Brien, and Mark Seifrid, eds. *Justification and Variegated Nomism*. 2 vols. Grand Rapids: Baker Academic, 2001.
Cary, Phillip. "The Logic of Trinitarian Doctrine." *Religious and Theological Studies Fellowship Bulletin*, no. 8 (September–October 1995) 2–9.
Catechism of the Catholic Church. Liguori, MO: Liguori, 1994.
The Catholic Study Bible: The New American Bible. Edited by Donald Senior, John J. Collins, and Mary Ann Getty-Sullivan. Oxford: Oxford University Press, 2011.
Cerfaux, L. *The Church in the Theology of St. Paul*. New York: Herder and Herder, 1959.
Chadwick, Owen. *The Reformation*. Baltimore: Penguin, 1964.

Chafer, Lewis Sperry. *Systematic Theology*. Dallas: Dallas Seminary, 1949.
Chall, Jeanne. *Stages of Reading Development*. New York: McGraw-Hill, 1983.
Chan, Simon. *Spiritual Theology: A Systematic Study of the Christian Life*. Downers Grove, IL: IVP Academic, 1998.
Chandler, Paul. *God's Global Mosaic: What We Can Learn from Christians Around the World*. Downers Grove, IL: InterVarsity, 2000.
Chapman, Mark. *Anglicanism: A Very Short Introduction*. Oxford: Oxford University Press, 2006.
Chaves, Mark. *American Religion: Contemporary Trends*. Princeton, NJ: Princeton University Press, 2011.
Chittister, Joan. *The Rule of Benedict: A Spirituality for the 21st Century*. New York: Crossroad, 1992.
Choonmin, Joshua. *Scripture by Heart: Devotional Practices for Memorizing God's Word*. Downers Grove, IL: InterVarsity, 2010.
Christensen, Michael J. "Theosis and Sanctification: John Wesley's Reformation of a Patristic Doctrine." *Wesleyan Theological Journal* 31 (1996) 71–92.
Christensen, Michael J., and Jeffery A. Wittung, eds. *Partakers of Divine Nature: The History and Development of Deification in the Christian Tradition*. Grand Rapids: Baker Academic, 2007.
Christensen, Torben, and William R. Hutchinson, eds. *Missionary Ideologies in the Imperialist Era: 1880-1920*. Aarhus, Denmark: Aros, 1982.
The Christian Growth Study Bible: New International Version. Edited by Zondervan Publishing House. Grand Rapids: Zondervan, 1997.
The Church of Jesus Christ of the Latter-Day Saints Newsroom. "A Christ-Centered Faith." http://www.mormonnewsroom.org/article/christ-centered-faith.
Clark, Andy, and David J. Chalmers. "The Extended Mind." *Analysis* 58 (1998). http://consc.net/papers/entended.html.
Clark, George W. *Notes on the Gospel of Matthew*. New York: Sheldon and Co., 1870.
Clarke, Adam. *Commentary on the Holy Bible*. Abridged from the original by Ralph Earle. Grand Rapids: Baker, 1966.
Clendenin, Daniel B. *Eastern Orthodox Christianity: A Western Perspective*. Grand Rapids: Baker, 1994.
Cobb, John B., Jr., and David Ray Griffin. *Process Theology: An Introductory Exposition*. Philadelphia: Westminster, 1976.
Cohen, Charles Lloyd. *God's Caress: The Psychology of Puritan Religious Experience*. New York: Oxford University Press, 1986.
Cohen, Gary. "The Bible Presbyterian Position on Ecclesiastical Separation." *Western Reformed Seminary Journal* 11:2 (August 2004) 5–12.
Coleman, Simon. *The Globalisation of Charismatic Christianity*. New York: Cambridge University Press, 2000.
Cole-Turner, Ronald, ed. *Transhumanism and Transcendence: Christian Hope in an Age of Technological Advancement*. Washington, DC: Georgetown University Press, 2011.
The Confession of Faith and Catechisms. Willow Grove, PA: Committee on Christian Education, 2005.
Conyers, A. J. *The Loss of Transcendence and Its Effect on Modern Life*. South Bend, IN: St. Augustine's, 1999.

Cosden, Darrell. *A Theology of Work: Work and the New Creation.* Carlisle, Cumbria, UK: Paternoster, 2004.
Cremin, Lawrence. *The Transformation of the School: Progressivism in American Education, 1876-1957.* New York: Alfred A. Knopf, 1962.
Cross, F. L. "The Athanasian Creed." In *The Oxford Dictionary of the Christian Church*, edited by F. L. Cross, 98–99. London: Oxford University Press, 1958.
Cross, William R. *The Burned-Over District: The Social and Intellectual History of Enthusiastic Religion in Western New York, 1800-1850.* Ithaca, NY: Cornell University Press, 1950.
Culver, Robert. "What Is The Church's Commission? Some Exegetical Issues in Matthew 28:16–20." *Bibliotheca Sacra* 125 (1968) 239–53.
Cuneo, Bernard Henry. *The Lord's Command to Baptize: An Historical-Critical Investigation with Special Reference to the Works of Eusebius of Caesarea.* Washington, DC: Catholic University of America, 1923.
Cushman, Philip. *Constructing the Self, Constructing America: A Cultural History of Psychotherapy.* Boston: Addison-Wesley, 1995.
Dalton, William J. *Christ's Proclamation to the Spirits: 1 Peter 3:18—4:6.* Rome: Gregorian University Press, 1989.
Danielou, Jean. *From Glory to Glory: Texts from Gregory of Nyssa's Mystical Writings.* New York: Charles Scribner's Sons, 1961.
Davies, J. G. "The Disintegration of the Christian Initiation Rite." *Theology* 50 (1947) 407–12.
Davies, Paul. *The Mind of God: Science and the Search for Ultimate Meaning.* London: Simon and Schuster, 1992.
Davies, Ronald E. "The Great Commission from Calvin to Carey." *Evangel* (Summer 1996) 44–49.
Davies, William D., and Dale C. Allison. *A Critical and Exegetical Commentary on the Gospel According to Saint Matthew.* Vol. 3. Edinburgh: T & T Clark, 1997.
Davis, John Jefferson. "Buddha, the Apostle Paul, and John Hick: The Challenge of Inter-Religious Epistemologies." *Philosophia Christi* 14:1 (2012) 95–114.
———. *Foundations of Evangelical Theology.* Grand Rapids: Baker, 1984.
———. *Frontiers of Science and Faith: Examining Questions from the Big Bang to the End of the Universe.* Downers Grove, IL: InterVarsity, 2002.
———. "How Personal Agents Are Located in Space: Implications for Worship, Eucharist, and Union with Christ." *Philosophia Christi* 13:2 (2011) 449–55.
———. *Reality in Meditation: Communion with God in an Age of Distraction.* Downers Grove, IL: IVP Academic, 2012.
———. "Teaching Them to Observe All That I Have Commanded You: The History of the Interpretation of the 'Great Commission' and Implications for Marketplace Ministries." *Evangelical Review of Theology* 25:1 (2001) 65–80.
———. "Very Brief Perspectives on the New Perspectives". Unpublished paper, 2009.
———. *Worship and the Reality of God: An Evangelical Theology of Real Presence.* Downers Grove, IL: IVP Academic, 2010.
Davis, Robin E. "Historical and Literary Parallels Between the Moses and Deborah Narratives." Unpublished paper, January, 2006.
Dawkins, Richard. *The Blind Watchmaker.* New York: Penguin, 1988.
Day, John. *Yahweh and the Gods and Goddesses of Canaan.* Sheffield, UK: Sheffield Academic, 2000.

Dean, Kenda Creasy. *Almost Christian: What the Faith of Our Teenagers Is Telling the American Church.* New York: Oxford University Press, 2010.

Demarest, Bruce A. *General Revelation: Historical Views and Contemporary Issues.* Grand Rapids: Zondervan, 1982.

DeMille, George. *The Catholic Movement in the American Episcopal Church.* Philadelphia: Church Historical Society, 1950.

Denton, Michael J. *Nature's Destiny: How the Laws of Biology Reveal Purpose in the Universe.* New York: Free Press, 1998.

Denny, Frederick. "Quranic Recitation." In the *Oxford Encyclopedia of the Modern Islamic World,* vol. 3, edited by John L. Esposito, 397–400. New York: Oxford University Press, 1995.

Dick, Steven J. *Plurality of Worlds: The Origins of the Extraterrestrial Life Debate from Democritus to Kant.* Cambridge: Cambridge University Press, 1982.

Dickens, A. G. *The English Reformation.* 2nd ed. London: B. T. Batsfor, 1964.

DiCicco, Joel. "The Development of Leaders in Ancient China, Rome, and Persia." *Public Administration Quarterly* 27:1 (Spring 2003) 6–40.

Diehl, William. *The Monday Connection: On Being An Authentic Christian in a Weekday World.* San Francisco: HarperSanFrancisco, 1993.

Dijksterhuis, E. J. *The Mechanization of the World Picture.* London: Oxford University Press, 1961.

Dillenberger, John, ed. *Martin Luther: Selections from His Writings.* Garden City, NY: Anchor Books: 1992.

Dillenberger, John, and Claude Welch. *Protestant Christianity: Interpreted Through Its Development.* New York: Charles Scribner's Sons, 1954.

Dodd, C. H. *The Apostolic Preaching and Its Development.* New York: Harper and Brothers, 1962.

Doddridge, Philip. *The Family Expositor.* Vol. 2. London: C. and J. Rivington, 1828.

Dodds, E. R. *Pagan and Christian in an Age of Anxiety.* Cambridge: Cambridge University Press, 1965.

"Donatists." *Catholic Encyclopedia.* http://www.newadvent.org/cathen/05121.htm.

Dorsett, Lyle W. *A Passion for Souls: The Life of D. L. Moody.* Chicago: Moody, 1997.

———. *Billy Sunday and the Redemption of Urban America.* Grand Rapids: Eerdmans, 1991.

Drazin, Nathan. *History of Jewish Education from 515 B.C.E. to 220 C.E.* Baltimore: John Hopkins Press, 1940.

Dujarier, Michael. *A History of the Catechumenate.* New York: Sadlier, 1979.

Dunn, James. *Jesus and the Spirit: A Study of Religious and Charismatic Experience of Jesus and the First Christians as Reflected in the New Testament.* Philadelphia: Westminster, 1975.

Dupre, Louis. "The Christian Experience of Mystical Union." *Journal of Religion* 69 (1989) 1–13.

Dyrness, William. "Stewardship of the Earth in the Old Testament." In *Tending the Garden: Essays on the Gospel and the Earth,* edited by Wesley Granberg-Michaelson, 54. Grand Rapids: Eerdmans, 1987.

Dyson, Freeman J. "Time Without End: Physics and Biology in an Open Universe." *Reviews of Modern Physics* 51:3 (1979) 447–60.

Ebner, Eliezer. *Elementary Education in Ancient Israel: During the Tannaitic Period (10–220 C.E).* New York: Bloch, 1956.

Eck, Diana L. *A New Religious America: How a "Christian Country" Has Become the World's Most Religiously Diverse Nation*. New York: HarperCollins, 2001.

Edwards, Jonathan. *The Great Awakening*. Vol. 4 of The Works of Jonathan Edwards. Edited by C. G. Goen. New Haven, CT: Yale University Press, 1972.

Edwards, Wendy J. Deichmann. *Forging an Ideology for American Missions: Josiah Strong and Manifest Destiny*. Cambridge: North Atlantic Missiology Project, 1998.

Elliot, Mark Adam. *The Survivors of Israel: A Reconsideration of the Theology of Pre-Christian Judaism*. Grand Rapids: Eerdmans, 2000.

Ellis, E. *Prophecy and Hermeneutic in Early Christianity*. Grand Rapids: Eerdmans, 1980.

Ellul, Jacques. *The Technological Society*. New York: Vintage, 1964.

Epperly, Bruce G., and Katherine Epperly. *Tending to the Holy: The Practice of the Presence of God in Ministry*. Herndon, VA: Alban Institute, 2009.

Erdmann, Carl. *The Origin of the Idea of Crusade*. Princeton, NJ: Princeton University Press.

Erickson, Millard. *Christian Theology*. 2nd ed. Grand Rapids: Baker, 1987.

Escobar, Samuel. *The New Global Mission: The Gospel from Everywhere to Everywhere*. Downers Grove, IL: InterVarsity, 2003.

Eusebius. *The History of the Church from Christ to Constantine*. Edited by Andrew Louth. Translated by G. Williamson. New York: Penguin, 1989.

Evans, G. R., ed. *A History of Pastoral Care*. London: Cassell, 2000.

Ezdenci, Slavko. *Deification and Union with Christ: A Reformed Perspective on Salvation in Orthodoxy*. Latimer Studies 74. London: The Latimer Trust, 2011.

Fairbairn, Donald. *Eastern Orthodoxy through Western Eyes*. Louisville: Westminster John Knox, 2002.

———. *Grace and Christology in the Early Church*. Oxford: Oxford University Press, 2003.

———. *Life in the Trinity: An Introduction to Theology with the Help of the Church Fathers*. Downers Grove, IL: IVP Academic, 2009.

———. "Patristic Soteriology: Three Trajectories." *Journal of the Evangelical Theological Society* 50:2 (June 2007) 289–310.

Fairbairn, Patrick. *Pastoral Theology: A Treatise on the Offices and Duties of the Christian Pastor*. Edinburgh: T & T Clark, 1875.

Farley, Edward. *Theologia: The Fragmentation and Unity of Theological Education*. Philadelphia: Fortress, 1983.

Fee, Gordon. "Christology and Pneumatology in Romans 8:9–11: Reflections on Paul as a Trinitarian." In *Jesus of Nazareth: Lord and Christ*, edited by Joel Green and Max Turner, 312–31. Grand Rapids: Eerdmans, 1994.

———. *The Disease of the Health and Wealth Gospels*. Beverly, MA: Frontline, 1985.

Filson, Floyd. *A Commentary on the Gospel According to St. Matthew*. New York: Harper and Row, 1960.

Findlay, James F., Jr. *Dwight Moody: American Evangelist 1837-1899*. Chicago: University of Chicago, 1969.

Findlay, James F., Jr., and Samuel W. Dike. "A Study of New England Revivals." *American Journal of Sociology* 15 (1909) 361–78.

Finn, Thomas. *Early Christian Baptism and the Catechumenate*. 2 vols. Collegeville, MN: Liturgical, 1992.

Finney, Charles. *Lectures on Revivals of Religion*. Edited by W. G. McLoughlin. Cambridge, MA: Harvard University Press, 1960.

Fisher, J. D. C. *Christian Initiation: Baptism in the Medieval West: A Study in the Disintegration of the Primitive Rite of Initiation*. London: SPCK, 1965.

Fitzmyer, Joseph A. *To Advance the Gospel: New Testament Studies*. 2nd ed. Grand Rapids: Eerdmans, 1998.

Friedman, Thomas L. *The World Is Flat: A Brief History of the Twenty-First Century*. New York: Farrar, Straus, and Giroux, 2005.

Friedrich, Gerhard. "Euanggelion." *Theological Dictionary of the New Testament*, edited by G. Kittel, 2:721–36. Grand Rapids: Eerdmans, 1964.

Friesen, Abraham. *Erasmus, the Anabaptists, and the Great Commission*. Grand Rapids: Eerdmans, 1998.

Froese, Paul, and Christopher Bader. *America's Four Gods: What We Say About God and What That Says About Us*. New York: Oxford University Press, 2010.

Fukuyama, Francis. *Our Posthuman Future: Consequences of the Biotechnology Revolution*. New York: Farrar, Straus, and Giroux, 2002.

Fulford, Ben. "One Commixture of Light: Rethinking Some Modern Uses and Critiques of Gregory of Nazianzus on the Unity and Equality of the Divine Persons." *International Journal of Systematic Theology* 11:2 (April 2009) 172–89.

Gadamer, Hans-Georg. *Truth and Method*. New York: Seabury, 1975.

Gaffin, B., Jr. "Union with Christ: Some Biblical and Theological Reflections." In *Always Reforming: Explorations in Systematic Theology*, edited by A. T. B. McGowan, 271–81. Downers Grove, IL: IVP Academic, 2006.

Gagnon, Robert. *The Bible and Homosexual Practice*. Nashville: Abingdon, 2001.

Garrett, James Leo, Jr. *Systematic Theology: Biblical, Historical, and Evangelical*. Vol. 1. Grand Rapids: Eerdmans, 1990.

Gathercole, Simon. *Where is Boasting? Early Jewish Soteriology and Paul's Response in Romans 1–5*. Grand Rapids: Eerdmans, 2002.

Geertz, Clifford. *The Interpretation of Cultures*. New York: Basic, 1973.

George, Archimandrite. *The Deification as the Purpose of Man's Life*. Mt. Athos: Holy Monastery of St. Gregorios, 1997.

Gergen, Kenneth J. *The Saturated Self: The Dilemma of Identity in a Contemporary Life*. New York: Basic, 1991.

Gerhardsson, Birger. *Memory and Manuscript: Oral Tradition and Written Transmission in Rabbinic Judaism and Early Christianity*. Lund: C. W. K. Gleerup, 1961.

Gibbs, Eddie, and Ryan K. Bolger. *Emerging Churches: Creating Christian Community in Postmodern Cultures*. Grand Rapids: Baker Academic, 2005.

Giddens, Anthony. *Modernity and Self-Identity: Self and Society in the Late Modern Age*. Stanford, CA: Stanford University Press, 1991.

Giles, Kevin. *Jesus and the Father: Modern Evangelicals Reinvent the Doctrine of the Trinity*. Grand Rapids: Zondervan, 2006.

———. *The Trinity and Subordinationism: The Doctrine of God and the Contemporary Gender Debate*. Downers Grove, IL: InterVarsity, 2002.

Gill, David. *The Opening of the Christian Mind: Taking Every Thought Captive*. Downers Grove, IL: InterVarsity, 1989.

Gladden, Washington. *The Christian Pastor and the Working Church*. New York: Charles Scribner's Sons, 1898.

Gleick, James. "How Information Became Everything." *Discover* (July/August 2011) 58–60.
Glover, T. R. *Paul of Tarsus*. London: Student Christian Movement, 1925.
Goldberg, Philip. *American Veda: How Indian Spirituality Changed the West*. New York: Harmony, 2010.
Gomes, Alan. "Evangelicals and the Annihilation of Hell." *Christian Research Journal* (Spring 1991) 15–19.
Gould, Stephen Jay. *Wonderful Life: The Burgess Shale and the Nature of History*. New York: W. W. Norton, 1989.
Graham, Billy. *Just As I Am: The Autobiography of Billy Graham*. San Francisco: HarperSanFrancisco, 1997.
Greenfield, Patricia. "Technology and Informal Education: What Is Taught, What Is Learned." *Science* 23 (January 2, 2009) 69–71.
Greenslade, S. L. *Church and State from Constantine to Theodosius*. London: SCM, 1954.
Greig, Peter, and David Roberts. *Red Moon Rising: How 24-7 Prayer is Awakening a Generation*. Lake Mary, FL: Relevant, 2003.
Grenz, Stanley. "The Social God and the Relational Self." In *Personal Identity in Theological Perspective*, edited by Richard Lints, Michael Horton, and Mark R. Talbot, 70–92. Grand Rapids: Eerdmans, 2006.
Grey Matter Research and Consulting. "Study Shows Only 16 Percent of Protestant Ministers Are Very Satisfied with Their Personal Prayer Lives." http://greymatterresearch.com/index_files/Prayer.htm.
Griffiths, Paul J. "Purgatory." In *The Oxford Handbook of Eschatology*, edited by Jerry L. Walls, 427–45. New York: Oxford University Press, 2008.
Grudem, Wayne. *Countering the Claims of Evangelical Feminism*. Colorado Springs, CO: Multnomah, 2006.
———. *Evangelical Feminism and Biblical Truth*. Colorado Springs, CO: Multnomah, 2004.
———. *Systematic Theology: An Introduction to Biblical Doctrine*. Grand Rapids: Zondervan, 1994.
Gruenler, Royce Gordon. *The Trinity in the Gospel of John: A Thematic Commentary on the Fourth Gospel*. Grand Rapids: Baker, 1986.
Gundry, Robert. *Matthew: A Commentary on His Literary and Theological Art*. Grand Rapids: Eerdmans, 1982.
Gunton, Colin. "The Doctrine of Creation." In *The Cambridge Companion to Christian Doctrine*, edited by Colin Gunton, 141–57. Cambridge: Cambridge University Press, 1997.
Gwartney, James. D., and Richard Stroup. *Economics: Private and Public Choice*. 3rd ed. New York: Academic, 1982.
Hall, David. *The Faithful Shepherd: A History of the New England Ministry in the Seventeenth Century*. Chapel Hill, NC: University of North Carolina, 1972.
Hambrick-Stowe, Charles E. *Charles Finney and the Spirit of American Evangelicalism*. Grand Rapids: Eerdmans, 1996.
———. *The Practice of Piety: Puritan Devotional Disciplines in Seventeenth-Century New England*. Chapel Hill, NC: University of North Carolina Press, 1982.
Hansen, Collin. "Why Johnny Can't Read the Bible." *Christianity Today*, July 28, 2010. www.christianitytoday.com/ct/article_print.html?id=87842.

Hansen, David. *The Art of Pastoring: Ministry Without All the Answers*. Downers Grove, IL: InterVarsity, 1994.
Hanson, R. P. C. *The Search for the Christian Doctrine of God: The Arian Controversy 318-381*. Grand Rapids: Baker Academic, 2006.
Hardy, Lee. *The Fabric of This World: Inquiries into Calling, Career Choice and the Design of Human Work*. Grand Rapids: Eerdmans, 1990.
Harper Study Bible: Revised Standard Version. Edited by Harold Lindsell. Grand Rapids: Zondervan, 1988.
The HarperCollins Study Bible: New Revised Standard Version, Including the Apocryphal/Deuterocanonical Books. Edited by Harold W. Attridge, Wayne A. Meeks, and Jouette M. Bassler. San Francisco: HarperSanFrancisco, 2006.
Harris, Ian. "Attitudes to Nature." In *Buddhism*, edited by Peter Harvey, 235-56. New York: Continuum, 2001.
Harris, Murray. *Jesus as God: The New Testament Use of Theos in Reference to Jesus*. Grand Rapids: Baker, 1992.
Harmless, William. *Augustine and the Catechumenate*. Collegeville, MN: Liturgical, 1995.
Hatch, W. H. P. "The Primitive Christian Message." *Journal of Biblical Literature* 58 (1939) 1-13.
Hawkins, Greg, and Cally Parkinson. *Reveal: Where Are You?* Barrington, IL: Willow Creek Resources, 2007.
Hayward, Alan. *Creation and Evolution: Rethinking the Evidence from Science and the Bible*. Minneapolis: Bethany House, 1985.
Heath, Chip, and Dan Heath. *Made to Stick: Why Some Ideas Survive and Others Die*. New York: Random House, 2007.
Heim, Mark. *Salvations: Truth and Difference in Religion*. Maryknoll, NY: Orbis, 1995.
Henderson, D. Michael. *John Wesley's Class Meeting: A Model for Making Disciples*. Nappanee, IN: Evangel, 1997.
Henry, Carl F. H. *Evangelicals in Search of Identity*. Waco, TX: Word, 1976.
Henry, Matthew. *A Commentary on the Holy Bible*, vol. 5. London: Ward, Lock, and Co., n.d.
Herberg, Will. *Protestant, Catholic, Jew: An Essay in Religious Sociology*. Garden City, NY: Anchor, 1960.
Hidi, Suzanne. "Interest and Its Contribution as a Mental Resource for Learning." *Review of Educational Research* 60:4: 549-71.
Hill, David. *The Gospel of Matthew: New Century Bible*. London: Oliphants, 1972.
Hillgarth, J. N., ed. *Christianity and Paganism 350-370*. Philadelphia: University of Pennsylvania Press, 1986.
Hiltner, Seward. *Preface to Pastoral Theology*. Nashville: Abingdon, 1958.
Himmelfarb, Gertrude. *One Nation, Two Cultures*. New York: Alfred A. Knopf, 1999.
Hipps, Shane. *Flickering Pixels: How Technology Shapes Your Faith*. Grand Rapids: Zondervan, 2009.
Hirsch, E. D., Jr. *Cultural Literacy: What Every American Needs to Know*. Boston: Houghton Mifflin, 1987.
Hocken, P. D. "Charismatic Movement." In *Dictionary of Pentecostal and Charismatic Movements*, edited by Stanley Burgess and Gary McGee, 130-60. Grand Rapids: Zondervan, 1988.
Hodge, Charles. *Systematic Theology*, vol. 1 Grand Rapids: Eerdmans, 1878.

Hodges, Zane. *The Gospel Under Siege*. Dallas, TX: Redencion Viva, 1981.
Holifield, E. Brooks. *A History of Pastoral Care in America: From Salvation to Self-Realization*. Nashville: Abingdon, 1983.
Hollenweger, Walter. *Pentecostalism: Origins and Developments Worldwide*. Peabody, MA: Hendrickson, 1997.
Hollinger, Dennis. "Enjoying God Forever: An Historical/Sociological Profile of the Health and Wealth Gospel." *Trinity Journal* 9 NS (1988) 131–49.
———. *Individualism and Social Ethics: An Evangelical Syncretism*. Lanham, MD: University Press of America, 1983.
Hoppin, James. *Pastoral Theology*. 5th ed. New York: Funk & Wagnalls, 1901.
Horton, Michael. *The Christian Faith: A Systematic Theology for Pilgrims on the Way*. Grand Rapids: Zondervan, 2011.
———. *Covenant and Salvation: Union with Christ*. Louisville: Westminster John Knox, 2007.
Howell, Kenneth. *God's Two Books: Copernican Cosmology and Biblical Interpretative in Early Modern Science*. Notre Dame, IN: University of Notre Dame Press, 2002.
Huey, F. B. *Jeremiah, Lamentations*. The New American Commentary 16. Nashville: Broadman, 1993.
Hughes, Philip Edgcumbe. *The True Image: The Origin and Destiny of Man in Christ*. Grand Rapids: Eerdmans, 1989.
Hunter, James Davison. *American Evangelicalism: Conservative Religion and the Quandary of Modernity*. New Brunswick, NJ: Rutgers University Press, 1982.
———. *To Change the World: The Irony, Tragedy, and Possibility of Christianity in the Late Modern World*. New York: Oxford University Press, 2010.
Husbands, Mark, and Daniel J. Treier, eds. *Justification: What's at Stake in the Current Debates*. Downers Grove, IL: InterVarsity, 2004.
Huston, Sterling W. *The Billy Graham Crusade Handbook*. Minneapolis: World Wide Publications, 1983.
Hvalvik, Reidar. "In Word and Deed: The Expansion of the Church in the Pre-Constantinian Era." In *The Mission of the Early Church to Jews and Gentiles*, edited by Jostein Adna and Hans Kvalbein, 265–87. Tübingen: Mohr Siebeck, 2000.
Hybels, Bill, and Mark Mittelberg. *Becoming a Contagious Christian*. Grand Rapids: Zondervan, 1994.
Inglehart, Ronald, and Daphna Oyserman. "Individualism, Autonomy, Self-Expression." In *Comparing Cultures: Dimension of Culture in a Comparative Perspective*, edited by Hek Vinken and Joseph Soeters, 74–96. Leiden: E. J. Brill, 2004.
Ingold, Tim, ed. *Companion Encyclopedia of Anthropology*. New York: Routledge, 1994.
Inwagen, Peter Van. *Metaphysics*. Boulder, CO: Westview, 1993.
Irenaeus, *Against Heresies*. In *The Faith of the Early Fathers*, translated by W. A. Jurgens, 3, 17, 1. 3 vol. Collegeville, MN: Liturgical, 1979.
Isaac, Gordon. "The Finnish School of Luther Interpretation: Responses and Trajectories." *Concordia Theological Quarterly* 76 (2012) 251–68.
———. *Left Behind or Left Befuddled: The Subtle Dangers of Popularizing the End Times*. Collegeville, MN: Liturgical, 2008.
———. "Monastic Memoria." *Luther Digest* 20 (2012) 127–40.
Jamieson, Robert, A. R. Fausset, and David Brown. *A Commentary, Critical, Experimental, and Practical, on the Old and New Testaments*. 3 vols. Grand Rapids: Eerdmans, 1948.

Janz, Denis. "Catechisms." In *The Oxford Encyclopedia of the Reformation*, vol. 1, edited by Hans J. Hillebrand, 275–80. New York: Oxford University Press, 1996.

Jenkins, Philip. *The New Faces of Christianity: Believing the Bible in the Global South*. New York: Oxford University Press, 2006.

———. *The Next Christendom: The Coming of Global Christianity*. New York: Oxford University Press, 2002.

Jennings, J. Nelson. *God the Real Superpower: Rethinking Our Role in Missions*. Phillipsburg, NJ: Presbyterian and Reformed, 2007.

Jewel, John. *The Works of John Jewel*. 4 vols. Edited by John Ayre. Cambridge: Cambridge University Press, 1845–1850.

Jewett, Robert. *Paul's Anthropological Terms*. Leiden: E. J. Brill, 1971.

John Paul II, Pope. *Ut Unum Sint: On Commitment to Ecumenism*. Philadelphia: Pauline, 2005.

Johnson, Charles A. *The Frontier Camp Meeting: Religion's Harvest Time*. Dallas: Southern Methodist University Press, 1955.

Johnson, Ronald. *How Will They Hear If We Don't Listen?* Nashville: Broadman & Holman, 1994.

Johnson, Terry. "Our Collapsing Ecclesiology." *New Horizons* 32:3 (March 2011) 6–8.

Johnson, Todd, and Kenneth M. Ross, eds. *Atlas of Global Christianity: 1910-2010*. Edinburgh: Edinburgh University Press, 2009.

Johnson, Todd, and Sun Young Chung, "Christianity's Center of Gravity, AD 33-2100." In *Atlas of Global Christianity*, edited by Todd Johnson and Kenneth M. Ross, 50–51. Edinburgh: Edinburgh University Press, 2009.

Jonas, Hans. *The Gnostic Religion: The Message of the Alien God and the Beginnings of Christianity*. Boston: Beacon, 1963.

Jones, David W., and Russell S. Woodbridge. *Health, Wealth, and Happiness: Has the Prosperity Gospel Overshadowed the Gospel of Christ?* Grand Rapids: Kregel, 2010.

Jones, Tony. *The New Christians: Dispatches from the Emergent Frontier*. San Francisco: Jossey-Bass, 2008.

Jungmann, Joseph. "Catechumenate." In *New Catholic Encyclopedia*, 3:238–40. New York: McGraw-Hill, 1967.

———. *Pastoral Liturgy*. New York: Herder and Herder, 1962.

Jurgens, William A. *The Faith of the Early Fathers*. 3 vols. Collegeville, MN: Liturgical, 1979.

Kaiser Family Foundation Study. "Generation M2: Media in the Lives of 8-to-18-Year-Olds: Key Findings." (January 2010) 1.

Kane, J. Herbert. *A Concise History of the Christian World Mission*. Grand Rapids: Baker, 1982.

Kealy, Sean. *Matthew's Gospel and the History of Biblical Interpretation*. 2 vols. Lewiston, ME: Mellen Biblical, 1997.

Kelley, Bennet. *Saint Joseph Baltimore Catechism: The Truths of Our Catholic Faith Clearly Explained and Illustrated with Bible Readings, Study Helps and Mass Prayers*. New York: Catholic Book Publishing Company, 1969.

Kelly, Dean. *Why Conservative Churches Are Growing: A Study in the Sociology of Religion*. New York: Harper and Row, 1972.

Kelly, J. N. D. *The Epistles of Peter and Jude*. London: A & C Black, 1969.

———. *Early Christian Doctrines*. 2nd ed. New York: Harper & Row, 1960.

Kim, Seyoon. *The Origin of Paul's Gospel*. 2nd ed. Tübingen: J. C. B. Mohr, 1984.

———. *Paul and The New Perspective: Second Thoughts on the Origins of Paul's Gospel.* Grand Rapids: Eerdmans, 2002.
King, N. Q. *The Emperor Theodosius and the Establishment of Christianity.* Philadelphia: Westminster, 1960.
Kinnaman, David, and Gabe Lyons. *UnChristian: What a New Generation Really Thinks About Christianity.* Grand Rapids: Baker, 2007.
Kittleson, James M. *Luther the Reformer.* Minneapolis: Augsburg, 1986.
Klapp, Orrin. *Overload and Boredom: Essays on the Quality of Life in the Information Society.* New York: Greenwood, 1986.
Klauser, Theodor. *A Short History of the Western Liturgy: An Account and Some Reflections.* Oxford: Oxford University Press, 1979.
Kleinig, John W. "The Kindred Heart: Luther on Meditation." *Luther Theological Journal* 20 (1986) 142–54.
Klostermaier, Klaus. *A Survey of Hinduism.* 2nd ed. Albany, NY: State University of New York Press, 1994.
———. *Hinduism: A Short History.* Oxford: One World, 2000.
Kluckhohn, Clyde. *Mirror for Man.* Greenwich, CT: Fawcett, 1949.
Knight, George W. "*Authenteo* in Reference to Women in 1 Timothy 2:12." *New Testament Studies* 32 (1984) 145.
Knitter, Paul F. *Without Buddha I Could Not Be a Christian.* Oxford: One World, 2009.
Kooiman, Willem Jan. *Luther and the Bible.* Philadelphia: Muhlenberg, 1961.
Kostenberger, Andreas. *Encountering John.* Grand Rapids: Baker, 1999.
Koyre, Alexandre. *From the Closed World to the Infinite Universe.* Baltimore: John Hopkins, 1957.
Kreider, Alan. *The Change of Conversion and the Origin of Christendom.* Eugene, OR: Wipf & Stock, 1999.
———. "Prayer, Evangelization, and Spiritual Formation." http://www.billygrahamcetner.com/ise/RTpapers/Papers01/Peace.PDF.
Kroeger, Catherine, and James Beck, eds. *Women, Abuse, and the Bible: How Scripture Can Be Used to Hurt or Heal.* Grand Rapids: Baker, 1996.
Kurzweil, Raymond. *The Age of Spiritual Machines.* New York: Viking, 1999.
———. *The Singularity Is Near: When Humans Transcend Biology.* New York: Viking, 2005.
LaCugna, Catherine. *God For Us: The Trinity and the Christian Life.* San Francisco: HarperSanFrancisco, 1973.
Lacy, Benjamin Rice, Jr. *Revivals in the Midst of the Years.* Hopewell, VA: Royal Press, 1968.
Laing, Mark. "Donald McGavran's Missiology: An Examination of the Origins and Validity of Key Aspects of the Church Growth Movement." *Indian Church History Review* 36:1 (2002) 30–52.
Lasch, Christopher. *The Culture of Narcissism: American Life in an Age of Diminishing Expectations.* New York: Warner, 1979.
Latourette, Kenneth Scott. *A History of the Expansion of Christianity. Vol. 2: The Thousand Years of Uncertainty A.D. 500–A.D. 1500.* New York: Harper & Bros., 1938.
Lawrence. *Practicing the Presence of God.* Edited by David Winter. Christian Classics in Modern English. Wheaton, IL: H. Shaw, 1991.

Leakey, Richard, and Roger Lewin. *Origins Reconsidered: In Search of What Makes Us Human*. New York: Doubleday, 1992.

Le Goff, Jacques. *The Birth of Purgatory*. Chicago: University of Chicago Press, 1984.

Leith, John, ed. *An Introduction to the Reformed Tradition*. Atlanta: John Knox, 1977.

———. *Creeds of the Churches*. Rev. ed. Richmond, VA: John Knox, 1973.

Leithart, Peter J. *Defending Constantine: The Twilight of an Empire and the Dawn of Christendom*. Downers Grove, IL: IVP Academic, 2010.

Leonard, Bill J. "Evangelism and Contemporary American Life." In *The Study of Evangelism: Exploring a Missional Practice of the Church*, edited by Paul W. Chilcote and Laceye C. Warner, 101–16. Grand Rapids: Eerdmans, 2008.

Letham, Robert. *Holy Trinity: In Scripture, History, Theology, and Worship*. Phillipsburg, NJ: Presbyterian and Reformed, 2004.

Lewis, C. S. *Mere Christianity*. New York: Macmillan, 1952.

———. "Priestesses in the Church?" In *God in the Dock: Essays on Theology and Ethics*, edited by Walter Hooper, 234–39. Grand Rapids: Eerdmans, 1970.

———. *The Screwtape Letters*. New York: Macmillan, 1944.

Libanius. *Selected Works*. Vol. 2. Translated by A. F. Norman. Loeb Classical Library. Cambridge, MA: Harvard University Press, 1977.

Life Application Study Bible. Grand Rapids: Zondervan; Carol Stream, IL: Tyndale House, 2011.

LifeWay Christian Resources. "Pastors' long work hours can come at expense of people, ministry." http://www.lifeway.com/lwc/rd_article_content/.

Lindars, Barnabas. *Judges 1–5: A New Translation and Commentary*. Edinburgh: T & T Clark, 1995.

Linder, Eileen W., ed. *Yearbook of American and Canadian Churches*. Nashville: Abingdon, 2012.

Lindsell Study Bible: The Living Bible Paraphrased. Edited by Harold Lindsell. Wheaton, IL: Tyndale House, 1980.

Lints, Richard. "Theological Anthropology in Context." In *Personal Identity in Theological Perspective*, edited by Richard Lints, Michael Horton, and Mark R. Talbot, 1–10. Grand Rapids: Eerdmans, 2006.

Littell, Franklin. "The Anabaptist Theology of Missions." *Mennonite Quarterly Review* 21 (1947) 5–17.

———. *The Origins of Sectarian Protestantism: A Study of the Anabaptist View of the Church*. New York: MacMillan, 1964.

Lodders, A. *Pocket Catechism: St. Joseph Edition: Essential Catholic Teachings*. Totowa, NJ: Catholic Book Publishing Company, 1973.

Loetscher, Lefferts. *The Broadening Church: A Study of Theological Issues in the Presbyterian Church Since 1869*. Philadelphia: University of Pennsylvania Press, 1954.

———. "Presbyterianism and Revivalism in Philadelphia since 1875." *Pennsylvania Magazine of History and Biography* 68 (January 1944) 56–84.

Longfield, Bradley. *The Presbyterian Controversy: Fundamentalism, Modernists, and Moderates*. Oxford: Oxford University Press, 1991.

Lopez, Donald, Jr. *The Story of Buddhism: A Concise Guide to Its History and Teachings*. San Francisco: HarperSanFrancisco, 2001.

Lossky, Vladimir. *The Mystical Theology of the Eastern Church*. Crestwood, NY: St. Vladimir's Seminary Press, 1976.

Lovelace, Richard F. *Dynamics of Spiritual Life: An Evangelical Theology of Renewal*. Downers Grove, IL: InterVarsity, 1979.
Luther, Martin. *Luther's Works*. 55 vols. Edited by Jaroslav Pelikan et al. St. Louis: Concordia; Philadelphia: Muhlenberg, 1900–1986.
———. "Selected Psalms III." In *Luther's Works*, vol. 14. Edited by Jaroslav Pelikan. St. Louis: Concordia, 1958.
MacArthur, John. *The Gospel According to Jesus*. Grand Rapids: Zondervan, 1989.
MacDonald, Gregory. *The Evangelical Universalist*. Eugene, OR: Wipf & Stock, 2006.
MacGregor, G. H. C. "Principalities and Powers: The Cosmic Background of Paul's Thought." New Testament Studies 1:1 (1954) 17–28.
MacMullen, Ramsay. *Christianizing the Roman Empire: A.D. 100-400*. New Haven, CT: Yale University Press, 1984.
Malina, Bruce J. *The New Testament World: Insights from Cultural Anthropology*. Atlanta: John Knox, 1981.
Mantzaridis, Georgios I. *The Deification of Man: St. Gregory Palamas and the Orthodox Tradition*. Crestwood, NY: St. Vladimir's Seminary Press, 1984.
———. "Spiritual Life in Palamism." In *Christian Spirituality: High Middle Ages and Reformation*, edited by Jill Raitt, 208–22. New York: Crossroad, 1987.
Maritain, Jacques. *Distinguish to Unite: The Degrees of Knowledge*. London: Geoffrey Bles, 1959.
Markus, Robert A. "From Rome to the Barbarian Kingdoms (330-700)." In *The Oxford History of Christianity*, edited by John McManners, 70–100. New York: Oxford University Press, 1993.
Marsden, George M. *Evangelicalism and Modern America*. Grand Rapids: Eerdmans, 1984.
———. *The Soul of the American University: From Protestant Establishment to Established Nonbelief*. New York: Oxford University Press, 1994.
Martin, James Louis. *History and Theology in the Fourth Gospel*. Philadelphia: Westminster John Knox, 2003.
Martin, Mary. "Hell Disappeared. No One Noticed. A Civic Argument." Harvard Theological Review 78:3-4 (1985) 381–98.
Martin, Ralph. *A Hymn of Christ: Philippians 2:5-11 in Recent Interpretations*. 3rd ed. Downers Grove, IL: InterVarsity, 1997.
Martin, Robert F. *Hero of the Heartland: Billy Sunday and the Transformation of American Society, 1862-1935*. Bloomington, IN: Indiana University Press, 2002.
Martin, William. *A Prophet with Honor: The Billy Graham Story*. New York: William Morrow, 1991.
Martos, Joseph. *Doors to the Sacred: A Historical Introduction to Sacraments in the Catholic Church*. Garden City, NY: Doubleday & Co., 1981.
Mascall, E. L. *Christ, the Christian and the Church*. London: Longmans and Green, 1946.
Mather, Cotton. *The Great Works of Christ in Americana*, v. 2. Edinburgh: Banner of Truth Trust, 1979.
Mathewes-Green, Frederica. *The Jesus Prayer: The Ancient Desert Prayer that Tunes the Heart to God*. Brewster, MA: Paraclete, 2009.
Matarrese, Sabino, Monica Colpi, Vittorio Gorini, and Ugo Moschella, eds. *Dark Matter and Dark Energy*. Dordrecht, the Netherlands: Springer, 2011.

Mayr-Harting, Henry. "The West: The Age of Conversion (700–1050)." In *The Oxford History of Christian*, edited by John McManners, 101–29. New York: Oxford University Press, 1993.

McClintock, Wayne. "Sociological Critique of the Homogenous Unit Principle." *International Review of Missions* 77:305 (1988) 107–16.

McConnell, D. R. *A Different Gospel: A Historical and Biblical Analysis of the Modern Faith Movement*. Peabody, MA: Hendrickson, 1988.

McCormick, K. Steve. "Theosis in Chrysostom and Wesley: An Eastern Paradigm of Faith and Love." *Wesleyan Theological Journal* 26:1 (1991) 38–103.

McDannell, Collen, and Bernhard Lang. *Heaven: A History*. New Haven: Yale University Press, 1988.

McDonnell, Killian, and George T. Montague. *Christian Initiation and Baptism in the Holy Spirit: Evidence from the First Eight Centuries*. Collegeville, MN: Liturgical, 1991.

McGavran, Donald. *The Bridges of God: A Study in the Strategy of Missions*. New York: Friendship, 1955.

———. *How Churches Grow: The New Frontiers of Missions*. London: World Dominion, 1959.

McGavran, Donald, and C. Peter Wagner. *Understanding Church Growth*. 3rd ed. Grand Rapids: Eerdmans, 1990; 1970.

McGrath, Alister E. *A Brief History of Heaven*. Oxford: Blackwell, 2003.

———. *Christian Theology: An Introduction*. Malden, MA: Blackwell Publishing, 1993.

———. *Iustitia Dei: A History of the Doctrine of Justification*. 3rd ed. Cambridge: Cambridge University Press, 2005.

McGuckin, Anthony. *The Westminster Handbook to Origen*. Louisville: Westminster John Knox, 2004.

McIntosh, Gary L. *Church That Works: Your One Stop Resource for Effective Ministry*. Grand Rapids: Baker, 2004.

McKnight, Scot, et al. *Church in the Present Tense*. Grand Rapids: Brazos, 2011.

McLaren, Brian. *A Generous Orthodoxy*. Grand Rapids: Zondervan, 2004.

———. *A New Kind of Christian*. San Francisco: Jossey-Bass, 2001.

McLoughlin, William G., Jr. *Billy Graham: Revivalist in a Secular Age*. New York: Ronald, 1960.

———. *Billy Sunday Was His Real Name*. Chicago: University of Chicago Press, 1955.

———. *Modern Revivalism: Charles Grandison Finney to Billy Graham*. New York: Ronald, 1959.

———. *Modern Revivals, Awakenings, and Reform*. Chicago: University of Chicago Press, 1978.

McManners, John, ed. *The Oxford History of Christianity*. New York: Oxford University Press, 1993.

McNally, Robert. *The Unreformed Church*. New York: Sheed and Ward, 1965.

Mead, Daniel L., and Darrell J. Allen. *Ministry By Objectives*. Wheaton, IL: Evangelical Teacher Training Association, 1978.

Medley, Mark S. "Participation in God: The Appropriation of Theosis by Contemporary Baptist Theologians." In *Theosis: Deification in Christian Theology*, edited by Vladimir Kharlamov, 205–46. Eugene, OR: Pickwick, 2006.

Meyendorff, John. *Byzantine Theology: Historical Trends and Doctrinal Themes*. New York: Fordham University Press, 1979.

———. *St. Gregory Palamas and Orthodox Spirituality.* Crestwood, NY: St. Vladimir's Seminary Press, 1974.
Meyendorff, John, and Robert Tobias, eds. *Salvation in Christian: A Lutheran- Orthodox Dialogue.* Minneapolis: Augsburg-Fortress, 1992.
Micklethwait, John, and Adrian Wooldridge. *God Is Back: How the Global Revival of Faith Is Changing the World.* New York: Penguin, 2009.
Middleton, Arthur. *Fathers and Anglicans: The Limits of Orthodoxy.* Leominster, UK: Gracewing, 2001.
Miedema, John. *Slow Reading.* Duluth, MN: Litwin, 2009.
Minear, Paul. *Images of the Church in the New Testament.* Philadelphia: Westminster, 1960.
Mohler, Albert, Jr. "Modern Theology: The Disappearance of Hell." In *Hell Under Fire*, edited by Christopher Morgan and Robert Person, 15–41. Grand Rapids: Zondervan, 2004.
Moltmann, Jürgen. *The Trinity and the Kingdom.* Minneapolis: Fortress, 1993.
Monaghan, Jennifer. *Learning to Read and Write in Colonial America.* Amherst, MA: University of Massachusetts Press, 2005.
Montgomery, John. "Luther and Missions." *Evangelical Missions Quarterly* 3:4 (1967) 193–202.
Moody, Dale. "God's Only Son: The Translation of John 3:16 in the Revised Standard Version." *Journal of Biblical Literature* 72 (1953) 213–19.
Moore, David. *The Battle for Hell: A Survey and Evaluation of Evangelicals' Growing Attraction to the Doctrine of Annihilationism.* Lanham, MD: University Press of America, 1995.
———. *The Nature of Hell: A Report by the Evangelical Alliance's Commission on Unity and Truth Among Evangelicals.* London: Paternoster, 2000.
Morgan, Edmund S. *Visible Saints: The History of a Puritan Idea.* New York: New York University Press, 1963.
Morgan, Rob. "Reviving a Lost Art: Memorizing Scripture." *Decision Magazine* (January 2012) 28–29.
Moroney, Stephen. *God of Love and God of Judgment.* Eugene, OR: Wipf and Stock, 2009.
———. *The Noetic Effects of Sin: A Historical and Contemporary Exploration of How Sin Affects Our Thinking.* Lanham, MD: Lexington, 1999.
Morris, Henry. *The Twilight of Evolution.* Philadelphia: Presbyterian and Reformed, 1963.
Morris, Leon. *The Gospel According to Matthew.* Grand Rapids: Eerdmans, 1992.
Morris, Van Cleve. *Philosophy and the American School.* Boston: Houghton Mifflin, 1961.
Mosser, Carl. "The Greatest Possible Blessing: Calvin and Deification." *Scottish Journal of Theology* 55:1 (2002) 36–57.
Mounce, Robert. *Matthew: New International Biblical Commentary.* Peabody, MA: Hendrickson, 1985.
Mouw, Richard. "Why Conservatives Need Liberals." *Christian Century* (January 2004) 22–25.
Muller, Richard A. *Calvin and the Reformed Tradition: On Work of Christ and the Order of Salvation.* Grand Rapids: Baker Academic, 2012.

Murphy Center for Liturgical Research. *Made, Not Born: New Perspectives on Christian Initiation and the Catechumenate*. Notre Dame, IN: University of Notre Dame Press, 1976.

Murray, John. *Redemption: Accomplished and Applied*. Grand Rapids: Eerdmans, 1955.

Naam, Ramez. *More than Human: Embracing the Promise of Biological Enhancement*. New York: Broadway, 2005.

Nakamura, Hajime. *Ways of Thinking of Eastern Peoples*. Honolulu: University of Hawaii Press, 1971.

Naugle, David K. *Worldview: The History of a Concept*. Grand Rapids: Eerdmans, 2002.

Nazianzus, Gregory. *Third Theological Oration*. http://www.newadvent.org/fathers/310229.htm.

———. *Fifth Theological Oration*. http://www.newadvent.org/fathers/310231.htm.

Neill, Stephen. *A History of Christian Missions*. New York: Penguin, 1964.

Neill, Stephen, and Hans-Reudi Weber. *The Layman in Christian History*. Philadelphia: Westminster, 1963.

Neuhaus, Richard. *The Naked Public Square*. Grand Rapids: Eerdmans, 1984.

The New English Bible with the Apocrypha: Oxford Study Edition. New York: Oxford University Press, 1976.

New Geneva Study Bible: Bringing the Light of the Reformation to Scripture. Edited by Luder G. Whitlock, R. C. Sproul, and Moisés Silva. Nashville: Thomas Nelson, 1995.

The New Jerusalem Bible. Garden City, NY: Doubleday, 1985.

Newbigin, Lesslie. *The Gospel in a Pluralist Society*. Grand Rapids: Eerdmans, 1989.

Niebuhr, H. Richard. *The Social Sources of Denominationalism*. New York: Meridian, 1957.

Niehaus, Jeffrey. *Ancient Near Eastern Themes in Biblical Theology*. Grand Rapids: Kregel, 2008.

Noll, Mark A. *American Evangelical Christianity: An Introduction*. Malden, MA: Blackwell, 2001.

———. *The New Shape of World Christianity*. Downers Grove, IL: IVP Academic, 2009.

Noll, Mark A., and Carolyn Nystrom. *Is The Reformation Over? An Evangelical Assessment of Contemporary Roman Catholicism*. Grand Rapids: Baker, 2005.

Novak, Michael. *Business as a Calling*. New York: Free Press, 1996.

———. *The Spirit of Democratic Capitalism*. New York: Simon & Schuster, 1982.

"Novatianism." In *Oxford Dictionary of the Christian Church*, edited by F. L. Cross, 968. London: Oxford University Press, 1958.

Oates, Wayne. *Pastoral Counseling*. Philadelphia: Westminster, 1974.

Oberman, Heiko A. *Luther: Man Between God and the Devil*. New York: Image, 1992.

O'Brien, P. T. "The Great Commission of Matthew 28:18-20." *Reformed Theological Review* 35 (1976) 66–78.

Oden, Thomas. *Pastoral Theology: Essentials of Ministry*. San Francisco: HarperSanFrancisco, 1982.

O'Faolin, Julia, and Lauro Martines, eds. *Not in God's Image*. New York: Harper Torchbooks, 1973.

O'Meara, Thomas. *Theology of Ministry*. New York: Paulist, 1983.

Origen. *Commentary on John*. http://www.newadvent.org/fathers/1015.htm.

Orr, J. Edwin. *The Evangelical Awakening, 1790-1830*. Chicago: Moody, 1975.

---. *The Fervent Prayer: The Worldwide Impact of the Great Awakening of 1858*. Chicago: Moody, 1974.

---. *The Flaming Tongue: Evangelical Awakenings, 1900-*. Chicago: Moody Press, 1973.

"Our New Name: Cru." http://www.cru.org/about-is/donor-relations/our-new-name.

The Oxford Study Bible: Revised English Bible with the Apocrypha. Edited by James R. Mueller, Katharine Doob Sakenfeld, and M. Jack Suggs. New York: Oxford University Press, 1992.

Packer, J. I. *Knowing God*. Downers Grove, IL: InterVarsity, 1973.

---. *A Quest for Godliness: The Puritan Vision of the Christian Life*. Wheaton, IL: Crossway, 1990.

Packer, J. I., and R. T. Beckwith. *The Thirty-Nine Articles*. Vancouver: Regent College, 2007.

Packer, J. I., and Gary A. Parrett. *Grounded in the Gospel: Building Believers the Old-Fashioned Way*. Grand Rapids: Baker, 2010.

Padilla, Rene C. "The Unity of the Church and the Homogeneous Unit Principle." *International Bulletin of Missionary Research* 6:1 (1982) 23-30.

Pannenberg, Wolfhart. "Excursus: The Place of Ecclesiology in the Structure of Dogmatics." In *Systematic Theology*, vol. 3, 21-27. Edinburgh: T & T Clark, 1998.

---. *Systematic Theology*. Vol. 3. Grand Rapids: Eerdmans, 1993.

Papantonopoulos, Lefteris. *The Invisible Universe: Dark Matter and Dark Energy*. Berlin: Springer, 2007.

Parrett, Gary A., and S. Steve Kang. *Teaching the Faith, Forming the Faithful*. Downers Grove, IL: IVP Academic, 2009.

Parshall, Phil. *Bridges to Islam: a Christian Perspective on Folk Islam*. Grand Rapids: Baker, 1983.

Payne, Leanne. *The Healing Presence*. Westchester, IL: Crossway, 1989.

Peace, Richard. "Prayer, Evangelization, and Spiritual Formation." http://www.billygrahamcenter.com/ise/RTpapers/Papers01/Peace.PDF.

Pelikan, Jaroslav. *The Emergence of the Catholic Tradition (100-600)*. Chicago: University of Chicago Press, 1971.

---. *The Vindication of Tradition*. New Haven: Yale University Press, 1984.

Penhale, Francis. *The Anglican Church Today: Catholics in Crisis*. London: Mowbray, 1986.

Percival, Henry. *The Seven Ecumenical Councils of the Undivided Church: Their Canons and Dogmatic Decrees*. New York: Charles Scribner's Sons, 1901.

Perriman, Andrew, ed. *Faith: Health and Prosperity*. Carlisle, UK: Paternoster, 2003.

Peters, Ted. *Playing God? Genetic Determinism and Human Freedom*. New York: Routledge, 1997.

Peterson, Robert A. "Toward a Systematic Theology of Adoption." *Presbyterion* 27:2 (Fall 2001) 120-31.

Pettit, Norman. *The Heart Prepared: Grace and Conversion in Puritan Spiritual Life*. New Haven, CT: Yale University Press, 1966.

Peura, Simo. "Christ Praesentissimus: The Issue of Luther's Thought in the Lutheran-Orthodox Dialogue." *Pro Ecclesia* 2 (Summer 1993) 364-71.

Pew Forum. "'Nones' on the Rise: One-in-Five Adults Have No Religious Affiliation." http://www.pewforum.org/files/2012/10/NonesOnTheRise-full.pdf.

The Pew Forum on Religion and Public Life. "U.S. Religious Landscape Survey (2010)." http://religions.pewforum.org/reports.

Phillips, J. B. *Your God Is Too Small*. London: Epworth, 1952.

Pickering, W. S. F. *Anglo-Catholicism: A Study in Religious Ambiguity*. London: Routledge, 1989.

Pinnock, Clark, and Robert Brow. *Unbounded Love: A Good News Theology for the 21st Century*. Downers Grove, IL: InterVarsity, 1994.

Piper, John. *The Future of Justification: A Response to N. T. Wright*. Wheaton, IL: Crossway, 2007.

———. *The Pleasures of God: Meditations on God's Delight in Being God*. Sisters, OR: Multnomah, 2000.

———. "Why Memorize Scripture?" www.desiringgod.org/articles/why-memorize-scripture.

Plummer, Alfred. *An Exegetical Commentary on the Gospel According to St. Matthew*. Grand Rapids: Baker, 1982.

Polanyi, Michael. *Personal Knowledge: Towards a Post-Critical Philosophy*. New York: Harper Torchbooks, 1962.

Pollock, John. *Billy Graham, Evangelist to the World: An Authorized Biography of the Decisive Years*. San Francisco: Harper and Row, 1979.

Poole, Matthew. *Annotations upon The Holy Bible*. New York: Robert Carter and Bros., 1852.

Pope, Robert. *The Half-Way Covenant*. Princeton, NJ: Princeton University Press, 1969.

Postman, Neil. *Amusing Ourselves to Death: Public Discourse in an Age of Show Business*. New York: Penguin, 1985.

Powers, William. *Hamlet's Blackberry: A Practical Philosophy for Building a Good Life in the Digital Age*. San Francisco: HarperCollins, 2010.

Premack, David, and Ann James Premack. "Why Animals Have Neither Culture nor History." In *Companion Encyclopedia of Anthropology*, edited by Tim Ingold, 350–65. New York: Routledge, 2002.

Prichard, Robert. *A History of the Episcopal Church*. Harrisburg, PA: Morehouse, 1999.

Pritchard, G. A. *Willow Creek Seeker Services: Evaluating a New Way of Doing Church*. Grand Rapids: Baker, 1996.

The Promise Keepers Men's Study Bible: New International Version. Edited by Sid Buzzell. Grand Rapids: Zondervan, 1997.

Puera, Simon. "Christus Praesentissimus: The Issue of Luther's Thought in the Lutheran-Orthodox Dialogue." *Pro Ecclesia* 2:3 (1993) 364–71.

"Purgatory." *Catholic Encyclopedia*. http://www.newadvent.org/cathen/12575a.htm.

Purves, Andrew. *The Crucifixion of Ministry: Surrendering Our Ambitions to the Service of Christ*. Downers Grove, IL: InterVarsity, 2007.

———. *Pastoral Theology in the Classical Tradition*. Louisville: Westminster John Knox, 2001.

———. *Reconstructing Pastoral Theology: A Christological Foundation*. Louisville: Westminster John Knox, 2004.

Putnam, Robert D. *Bowling Alone: The Collapse and Revival of American Community*. New York: Simon & Schuster, 2000.

Quest Study Bible: New International Version. Grand Rapids: Zondervan, 1998.

Rack, Henry. "John Wesley and Early Methodist Conversion." *North Atlantic Missiology Project*. Cambridge, UK: University of Cambridge, 1997.

Radner, Ephraim, and Philip Turner. *The Fate of Communion: The Agony of Anglicanism and the Future of a Global Church*. Grand Rapids: Eerdmans, 2006.

Rahner, Karl, ed. *The Teaching of the Catholic Church As Contained In Her Documents*. Staten Island, NJ: Alba House, 1967.

Rahula, Walpola. *What the Buddha Taught*. 2nd ed. New York: Grove, 1974.

Rakestraw, Robert V. "Becoming Like God: An Evangelical Doctrine of Theosis." *Journal of the Evangelical Theological Society* 40:2 (June 1997) 257–69.

Ramm, Bernard. *Then He Glorified: A Systematic Study of the Doctrine of Glorification*. Grand Rapids: Eerdmans, 1963.

Rapoport, Amos. "Spatial Organization and the Built Environment." In *Companion Encyclopedia of Anthropology*, edited by Tim Ingold, 460–502. New York: Routledge, 1994.

Reader, John. *Missing Links: The Hunt for Earliest Man*. New York: Penguin, 1988.

Reed, John Shelton. *Glorious Battle: The Cultural Politics of Victorian Anglo-Catholicism*. Nashville: Vanderbilt University Press, 1996.

Reicke, Bo. "The Law and This World According to Paul." *Journal of Biblical Literature* 70 (1951) 259–76.

Reid, J. K., ed. *Calvin: Theological Treatises*. Philadelphia: Westminster, 1954.

Reid, W. Standford, ed. *John Calvin: His Influence in the Western World*. Grand Rapids: Zondervan, 1982.

Richard, Lucien J. *The Spirituality of John Calvin*. Atlanta: John Knox, 1974.

Richards, Lawrence, and Gib Martin. *A Theology of Personal Ministry*. Grand Rapids: Zondervan, 1981.

Richardson, Alan. *The Biblical Doctrine of Work*. London: SCM, 1963.

Richtel, Matt. "Hooked on Gadgets, and Paying a Mental Price." *New York Times*, June 7, 2010. www.nytimes.com/2010/06/07/technology/07brain.html.

Ridderbos, Herman. *Paul: An Outline of His Theology*. Grand Rapids: Eerdmans, 1975.

Rieff, Philip. *The Triumph of the Therapeutic: Use of Faith After Freud*. New York: Harper and Row, 1968.

Riesman, David. *Individualism Reconsidered, and Other Essays*. New York: Free Press, 1966.

Rivera, Luis N. *A Violent Evangelism: The Political and Religious Conquest of the Americas*. Louisville: Westminster John Knox, 1992.

Robinson, John A. T. *The Body: A Study in Pauline Theology*. Philadelphia: Westminster, 1977.

Robson, Catherine. *Heart Beats: Everyday Life and the Memorized Poem*. Princeton, NJ: Princeton University Press, 2012.

Rodgers, John H., Jr. "A Report on the Study Concerning the Ordination of Women Undertaken by the Anglican Mission in America." www.theamia.org/assets/AMia-Womens/Ordination/Study-Aug-03.

Rogers, Cleon. "The Great Commission." *Bibliotheca Sacra* 130 (1973) 258–67.

Roof, Wade. *A Generation of Seekers: The Spiritual Journeys of the Baby Boom Generation*. San Francisco: HarperSanFrancisco, 1993.

Rosenkranz, Gerhard. *Die Christliche Mission: Geschichte und Theologie*. Munich: Chr. Kaiser Verlag, 1977.

Rosell, Garth, ed. *Commending the Faith: The Preaching of D. L. Moody*. Peabody, MA: Hendrickson, 1999.

———. *The Surprising Work of God: Harold John Ockenga, Billy Graham, and the Rebirth of Evangelicalism*. Grand Rapids: Baker Academic, 2008.

Rosell, Garth, and Richard A. G. Dupuis, eds. *The Memoirs of Charles G. Finney*. Grand Rapids: Zondervan, 1989.

Rowe, J. Nigel. *Origen's Doctrine of Subordinationism: A Study of Origen's Christology*. Berne: Peter Lang, 1987.

Rudnick, Milton L. *Speaking the Gospel Through the Ages: A History of Evangelism*. St. Louis: Concordia, 1984.

Russell, James. *The Germanization of Early Medieval Christianity*. New York: Oxford University Press, 1994.

Russell, Norman. *The Doctrine of Deification in the Greek Patristic Tradition*. Oxford: Oxford University Press, 2004.

Ryken, Leland. *Redeeming the Time: A Christian Approach to Work and Leisure*. Grand Rapids: Baker, 1995.

Ryken, Philip, Derek Thomas, and J. Ligon Duncan. *Give Praise to God: A Vision for Reforming Worship*. Phillipsburg, NJ: Presbyterian and Reformed, 2003.

Ryrie, Charles C. *Balancing the Christian Life*. Chicago: Moody, 1969.

Saarinen, Risto. "The Presence of God in Luther's Theology." *Lutheran Quarterly* 8 (1994) 3–13.

Sabourin, Leopold. *The Gospel According to St. Matthew*. Vol. 1. Bombay: St. Paul, 1983.

Sacirbey, Omar. "Pew Study Charts Growth in Muslim Population." *The Christian Century*, January 27, 2011. http://www.christiancentury.org/2011-01/us-muslim-population-double-20-years.

Sanders, E. P. *Paul and Palestinian Judaism: A Comparison of Patterns of Religion*. London: SCM, 1977.

Sanders, Fred. "The Trinity." In *The Oxford Handbook of Systematic Theology*, edited by John Webster, Kathyrn Tanner, and Ian Torrance, 35–53. Oxford: Oxford University Press, 2007.

Saravia, Adrianus. *De Diversis Ministrorum Evangelii Grandibus*. London: George Bishop, 1590. Microfiche: Inter Documentation Company AG, Postrasse 14 Zug Switzerland.

Scazzero, Peter. *Emotionally Healthy Spirituality*. Nashville: Thomas Nelson, 2006.

Schaff, Philip, ed. *The Creeds of Christendom*. 3 vols. New York: Harper and Bros, 1877.

———. *The Seven Ecumenical Councils*. Nicene and Post-Nicene Fathers vol. 14. Grand Rapids: Eerdmans, 1979.

Scharfe, Hartmut. *Education in Ancient India*. Leiden: Brill, 2002.

Schleiermacher, Friedrich. *Brief Outline Of The Study of Theology*. Translated by Terrence N. Tice. Richmond, VA: John Knox, 1966.

———. *The Christian Faith*. Vol. 2. Edited by H. R. Mackintosh and J. S. Stewart. New York: Harper Torchbooks, 1963.

Schnackenburg, Rudolf. *The Church in the New Testament*. New York: Herder and Herder, 1965.

Schneemelcher, Wilhelm, and R. McL. Wilson, eds. *New Testament Apocryphia, Vol. 2: Writings Relating to the Apostles; Apocalypses and Related Subjects*. London: James Clarke & Co., 1992.

Schutz, Samuel. "The Truncated Gospel in Modern Evangelicalism: A Critique and Beginning Reconstruction." *Evangelical Review of Theology* 33:4 (2009) 292–305.

Schreiner, Thomas. "The Valuable Ministries of Women in the Context of Male Leadership." In *Recovering Biblical Manhood and Womanhood*, edited by John Piper and Wayne Grudem, 209–24. Wheaton, IL: Crossway, 2006.
Schweizer, Eduard. *The Good News According to Matthew*. London: SPCK, 1975.
Sen, K. M. *Hinduism*. New York: Penguin, 1961.
Serendipity Bible for Groups. Grand Rapids: Zondervan; Littleton, CO: Serendipity House, 1998.
Shaw, John Mackintosh. *The Christian Gospel of the Fatherhood of God*. London: Hoddler and Stoughton, 1925.
Shawchuck, Norman, and Roger Heuser. *Managing the Congregation: Building Effective Systems to Serve People*. Nashville: Abingdon, 1996.
Shedd, William. *Homiletics and Pastoral Theology*. New York: Scribner, Armstrong & Co., 1873.
Shelley, Bruce. *Evangelicalism in America*. Grand Rapids: Eerdmans, 1967.
Sherman, Doug, and William Hendricks. *Your Work Matters to God*. Colorado Springs, CO: NavPress, 1987.
Shinners, John R. *Medieval Popular Religion, 1000–1500: A Reader*. 3rd ed. Readings in Medieval Civilizations and Cultures. Toronto: University of Toronto Press, 2006.
Sider, Ronald. *The Scandal of the Evangelical Conscience: Why Are Christians Living Just Like the Rest of the World?* Grand Rapids: Baker, 2005.
Silva, Moises. *Philippians: Wycliffe Exegetical Commentary*. Chicago: Moody, 1988.
Simeon, Charles. *Horae Homileticae*. Vol. 11. London: Holdsworth and Ball, 1832.
Simpson, George G. *The Meaning of Evolution*. Rev. ed. New Haven, CT: Yale University Press, 1967.
Small, Joseph. "A Company of Pastors." In *Calvin and the Company of Pastors*, edited by David Foxgrover, 9–15. Grand Rapids: Calvin Studies Society, 2004.
Smedes, Lewis B. *All Things Made New: A Theology of Man's Union with Christ*. Grand Rapids: Eerdmans, 1970.
Smith, Christian. *American Evangelicalism: Embattled and Thriving*. Chicago: University of Chicago Press, 1998.
———. "On 'Moralistic Therapeutic Deism' as U.S. Teenagers' Actual, Tacit, De Facto Religious Faith." In *Religion and Youth*, edited by Sylvia Collins-Mayo and Pink Dandelion, 41–46. Burlington, VT: Ashgate, 2010.
———. *Souls in Transition: The Religious and Spiritual Lives of Emerging Adults*. New York: Oxford University Press, 2009.
Smith, Christian, and Melinda Denton. *Soul Searching: The Religious and Spiritual Lives of American Teenagers*. New York: Oxford University Press, 2005.
Smith, David. *Mission After Christendom*. London: Darton, Longman and Todd, 2003.
Smith, Joseph. "Chapter 17: The Great Plan of Salvation." In *Teachings of Presidents of the Church: Joseph Smith*, 206–16. Salt Lake City: The Church of Jesus Christ of the Latter-Day Saints, 2011.
Soggins, J. Alberto. *Judges: A Commentary*. Philadelphia: Westminster, 1981.
Sorokin, P. A. *Social and Cultural Dynamics*. Vols. 1 and 2. New York: Bedminster, 1962.
Spencer, William David, and Aida Besancon Spencer. *The Prayer Life of Jesus: Shout of Agony, Revelation of Love, a Commentary*. Lanham, MD: University Press of America, 1990.
Stanford Encyclopedia of Philosophy. "Logic and Ontology." http://plato.stanford.edu/contents.html.

Stark, Rodney. *The Rise of Christianity: How the Obscure, Marginal Jesus Movement Became the Dominant Religious Force in the Western World in a Few Centuries*. San Francisco: HarperSanFrancisco, 1997.

Stedman, Ray C. *Body Life*. Glendale, CA: Regal, 1972.

Stevens, Paul. *The Other Six Days: Vocation, Work, and Ministry in Biblical Perspective*. Grand Rapids: Eerdmans, 1999.

Stewart, Edward. *American Cultural Patterns: A Cross-Cultural Perspective*. Yarmouth, ME: Intercultural Press, 1972.

Stewart, J. S. "On a Neglected Emphasis in New Testament Theology." *Scottish Journal of Theology* 4 (1951) 292–301.

Stott, John, and David Edwards. *Essentials: A Liberal-Evangelical Debate*. Downers Grove, IL: InterVarsity, 1988.

Stout, Harry. *The Divine Dramatist: George Whitefield and the Rise of Modern Evangelicalism*. Grand Rapids: Eerdmans, 1991.

Strachan, R. H. "The Gospel in the New Testament." In *The Interpreter's Bible*, edited by G. A. Buttrick, 7:3–31. Nashville: Abingdon, 1979.

Stringer, Christopher, and Clive Gamble. *In Search of the Neanderthals: Solving the Puzzle of Human Origins*. New York: Thames and Hudson, 1993.

Strong, A. H. *Systematic Theology*. Valley Forge, PA: Judson, 1907.

Stronstad, Roger. *The Charismatic Theology of St. Luke*. Peabody, MA: Hendrickson, 1984.

The Study Bible for Women: Holman Christian Standard Bible. Edited by Rhonda Kelley and Dorothy Kelley Patterson. Nashville: Holman, 2014.

Sullivan, Richard. "Carolingian Missionary Methods." *Catholic Historical Review* 42:3 (1956) 273–95.

———. "Early Medieval Missionary Activity: A Comparative Study of Eastern and Western Methods." *Church History* 23:1 (1954) 17–35.

Swanson, R. N. "The Burdens of Purgatory." In *A People's History of Christianity: Vol. 4, Medieval Christianity*, edited by Daniel E. Bornstein, 353–80. Minneapolis: Fortress, 2009.

Sweeney, Douglas. *The American Evangelical Story: A History of the Movement*. Grand Rapids: Baker Academic, 2005.

Swift, Louis. *The Early Fathers on War and Military Service*. Wilmington, DE: Michael Glazier, 1983.

Szyliowicz, Joseph. "Education: Educational Methods." In the *Oxford Encyclopedia of the Modern Islamic World*, vol. 3, edited by John L. Esposito, 416–20. New York: Oxford University Press, 1995.

Tannehill, Robert C. *Dying and Rising with Christ: A Study in Pauline Theology*. Berlin: Topelmann, 1967.

Tanner, Norman, ed. *Decrees of the Ecumenical Councils*. Washington, DC: Georgetown University Press, 1990.

Tattersall, Ian. *The Human Odyssey: Four Million Years of Human Evolution*. New York: Prentice Hall, 1993.

———. *Becoming Human: Evolution and Human Uniqueness*. New York: Harcourt Brace, 1998.

Taylor, Charles. *Sources of the Self: The Making of Modern Identity*. Cambridge, MA: Harvard University Press, 1989.

Tennent, Timothy. "The Gospel in Historical Reception." *Evangelical Review of Theology* 33:1 (2009) 77–92.

———. "William Carey as a Missiologist: An Assessment." *American Baptist Evangelical Journal* 7:1 (March 1999) 3–10.

Thiselton, Anthony C. *The First Epistle to the Corinthians: A Commentary on the Greek Text*. Grand Rapids: Eerdmans, 2000.

Thornton, Martin. *Pastoral Theology: A Reorientation*. London: SPCK, 1958.

Thurneysen, Eduard. *A Theology of Pastoral Care*. Translated by Jack A. Worthington and Thomas Wieser. Richmond, VA: John Knox, 1962.

Tinker, George E. *Missionary Conquest: The Gospel and Native American Cultural Genocide*. Minneapolis: Fortress, 1993.

Todorov, Tzvetan. *The Conquest of America*. New York: Harper and Row, 1982.

Torrance, James B. *Worship, Community and the Triune God of Grace*. Downers Grove, IL: InterVarsity, 1996.

Torrance, Thomas. *The Christian Doctrine of God: One Being Three Persons*. Edinburgh: T & T Clark, 1996.

———. *The School of Faith: The Catechisms of the Reformed Church*. Eugene, OR: Wipf and Stock, 1996.

Trumper, Tim J. R. "The Theological History of Adoption." *Scottish Journal of Evangelical Theology* 20:1, 2 (2002) 4–28, 177–202.

Turkle, Sherry. *Alone Together: Why We Expect More From Technology and Less From Each Other*. New York: Basic, 2011.

Turrentin, Francis. *Institutes of Elenctic Theology* (1679-1685). Vol. 3. Phillipsburg, NJ: Presbyterian and Reformed, 1997.

Uebersax, John. "Culture in Crisis." http://satyagraha.wordpress.com/2010/08/19.

Vallicella, Bill. "Michael Sudduth Converts to Vaishnava Vedanta!" http://maverickphilosopher.typepad.com/maverick_philosopher/2012/01/michael-sudduth-converts-to-vaishnava-vedanta.html.

Van Houtryve, Dom Idesbald. *Benedictine Peace*. Westminster, MD: Newman, 1950.

Vermes, G. *The Dead Sea Scrolls in English*. New York: Penguin, 1987.

Vickers, Brian. *Jesus' Blood and Righteousness: Paul's Theology of Imputation*. Wheaton, IL: Crossway, 2006.

Vinet, A. *Pastoral Theology: The Theory of the Pastoral Ministry*. Translated by Thomas Skinner. New York: Ivison and Phinney, 1854.

Vitz, Paul. *Psychology as Religion: The Cult of Self-Worship*. Grand Rapids: Eerdmans, 1977.

Viviano, Benedict. "The Gospel According to Matthew." In *The New Jerome Biblical Commentary*, edited by Raymond E. Brown, Joseph A. Fitzmyer, and Roland Murphy, 630–74. Englewood Cliffs, NJ: Prentice-Hall, 1990.

Volf, Miroslav. *Work in the Spirit: Toward a Theology of Work*. New York: Oxford University Press, 1991.

Wagner, C. Peter. *Churches That Pray*. Ventura, CA: Regal, 1993.

Walls, Andrew F. *The Missionary Movement in Christian History*. Maryknoll, NY: Orbis, 1996.

Walls, Jerry L. *Heaven: The Logic of Eternal Joy*. New York: Oxford University Press, 2002.

Ward, Keith. *More than Matter?* Grand Rapids: Eerdmans, 2010.

Ware, Bruce. *Father, Son, and Holy Spirit: Relationships, Roles, and Relevance*. Wheaton, IL: Crossway, 2005.

Ware, Timothy. *The Orthodox Church*. Baltimore: Penguin, 1963.

Warfield, Benjamin. *Calvin and Augustine*. Philadelphia: Presbyterian and Reformed, 1974.

Waters, Guy. *Justification and the New Perspectives on Paul*. Philipsburg, NJ: Presbyterian and Reformed, 2004.

Webb, Robert A. *The Reformed Doctrine of Adoption*. Grand Rapids: Eerdmans, 1947.

Webb, William. *Slaves, Women and Homosexuals: Exploring the Hermeneutics of Cultural Analysis*. Downers Grove, IL: InterVarsity, 2001.

Webber, Robert, ed. *Listening to the Beliefs of Emerging Churches*. Grand Rapids: Zondervan, 2007.

Weinberg, Steven. *The First Three Minutes*. New York: Basic, 1977.

Weisberger, Bernard. *They Gathered at the River: The Story of the Great Revivalists and Their Impact upon Religion in America*. Boston: Little Brown, and Co., 1958.

Wells, David. *Above All Earthly Powers*. Grand Rapids: Eerdmans, 2005.

———. *The Courage to Be Protestant: Truth-Lovers, Marketers, and Emergents in the Postmodern World*. Grand Rapids: Eerdmans, 2008.

———. *God in the Wasteland*. Grand Rapids: Eerdmans, 1994.

———. *Losing Our Virtue: Why the Church Must Recover Its Moral Vision*. Grand Rapids: Eerdmans, 1998.

———. *No Place for Truth: Or Whatever Happened to Evangelical Theology?* Grand Rapids: Eerdmans, 1993.

———. *Turning to God: Biblical Conversion in the Modern World*. Grand Rapids: Baker, 1989.

Wells, David, and John D. Woodbridge, eds. *The Evangelicals: Who They Are, Where They Are Changing*. Nashville: Abingdon, 1975.

Wesley, John. *Explanatory Notes Upon The New Testament*. London: Wesleyan-Methodist Book Room, 1800.

Westerhoff, John, and O. C. Edwards Jr. *A Faithful Church: Issues in the History of Catechesis*. Eugene, OR: Wipf & Stock, 2003.

Westfall, Richard S. "The Scientific Revolution of the Seventeenth Century: The Construction of a New World View." In *The Concept of Nature*, edited by John Torrance, 63–93. Oxford: Clarendon, 1992.

Whitby, Daniel. *A Commentary on the Gospels and the Epistles of the New Testament*. London: William Tegg and Co., 1853.

White, James. *A Brief History of Christian Worship*. Nashville: Abingdon, 1993.

———. *Introduction to Christian Worship*. 3rd ed. Nashville, Abingdon, 2000.

Wikenhauser, Alfred. *Pauline Mysticism: Christ in the Mystical Teaching of St. Paul*. Edinburgh/London: Nelson, 1960.

Wiles, Maurice. "Eternal Generation." *Journal of Theological Studies* n.s. 12:2 (1961) 284–91.

Wilken, Robert Louis. "The Link Interview." *Christian History* 57 (1998) 44.

Willard, Dallas. "Spiritual Formation in Christ Is for the Whole Life and the Whole Person." In *For All the Saints: Evangelical Theology and Christian Spirituality*, edited by Timothy George and Alister McGrath, 39–53. Louisville: Westminster John Knox, 2003.

Williams, Charles, ed. *The Letters of Evelyn Underhill*. London: Longmans, Green and Co., 1943.
Williams, Paul. *Mahayana Buddhism: The Doctrinal Foundations*. London: Routledge, 1989.
Williams, Stephen, and Gerald Friell. *Theodosius: The Empire at Bay*. New Haven, CT: Yale University Press, 1994.
Wilshire, Leland. "The TLG Computer and Further References to *Authenteo* in 1 Tim. 2:12." *New Testament Studies* 32 (1988) 120–34.
Wilson, Douglas. "The Sacred Script in the Theater of God." Desiring God National Conference, 2009. http://www.passionforpreaching.net/?tag-spurgeon.
Wilson, John. "Changing Forever How You Think: Recovering the Lost Art of Scripture Memorization." *Christianity Today* 55:1 (January 2011) 41–42.
Winter, David. *Christian Classics in Modern English*. Wheaton, IL: H. Shaw, 1991.
Woodward, James, and Stephen Pattison. "An Introduction to Pastoral and Practical Theology." In *The Blackwell Reader in Pastoral and Practical Theology*, edited by James Woodward and Stephen Pattison, 1–22. Malden, MA: Blackwell, 2000.
Word in Life Bible: Contemporary English Version. Nashville: Thomas Nelson, 1998.
Wright, N. T. *Jesus and the Victory of God*. Minneapolis: Fortress, 1996.
———. *Justification: God's Plan and Paul's Vision*. Downers Grove, IL: IVP Academic, 2009.
———. *The Resurrection of the Son of God*. Minneapolis: Fortress, 2003.
———. *Surprised by Hope: Rethinking Heaven, Resurrection, and the Mission of the Church*. New York: HarperCollins, 2008.
———. *What Saint Paul Really Said*. Grand Rapids: Eerdmans, 1997.
Wuthnow, Robert. *After Heaven: Spirituality in America Since the 1950s*. Berkeley, CA: University of California Press, 1998.
———. *America and the Challenges of Religious Diversity*. Princeton, NJ: Princeton University Press, 2005.
———. *The Struggle for America's Soul: Evangelicals, Liberals, and Secularism*. Grand Rapids: Eerdmans, 1989.
Wynne, Morgan. *Holy Spirit and Religious Experience in Christian Literature ca. AD 90–200*. Milton Keynes, UK: Paternoster, 2006.
Yandell, Keith, and Harold Netland. *Buddhism: A Christian Exploration and Appraisal*. Downers Grove, IL: IVP Academic, 2009.
Yannaris, Christos. "Orthodoxy and the West." In *Orthodoxy, Life, and Freedom: Essays in Honor of Archbishop Iakovos*, edited by A. J. Phillopou, 130–147. Oxford: Studion, 1973.
Yao, Kevin. "At the Turn of the Century: A Study of the China Centenary Missionary Conference of 1907." *International Bulletin of Missionary Research* 32:2 (2008) 65–68.
Yates, Frances. *The Art of Memory*. London: Pimlico, 1992.
Yates, Roy. "The Powers of Evil in the New Testament." *Evangelical Quarterly* 52 (April-June 1980) 97–111.
Zengotita, Thomas de. *Mediated: How the Media Shapes Your World and the Way You Live in It*. New York: Bloomsbury, 2005.
Zizioulas, John D. *Being as Communion*. Crestwood, NY: St. Vladimir Seminary Press, 1993.
———. *Communion and Otherness*. London: T & T Clark, 2007.

Zwingli, Ulrich. "An Exposition of the Faith." In *The Library of Christian Classics*, vol. 24, *Zwingli and Bullinger*, translated by G. W. Bromiley, 119–75. Philadelphia: Westminster, 1953.

———. "Of Baptism." In *The Library of Christian Classics*, vol. 24, *Zwingli and Bullinger*, translated by G. W. Bromiley, 245–79. Translated by G. W. Bromiley. Philadelphia: Westminster, 1953.